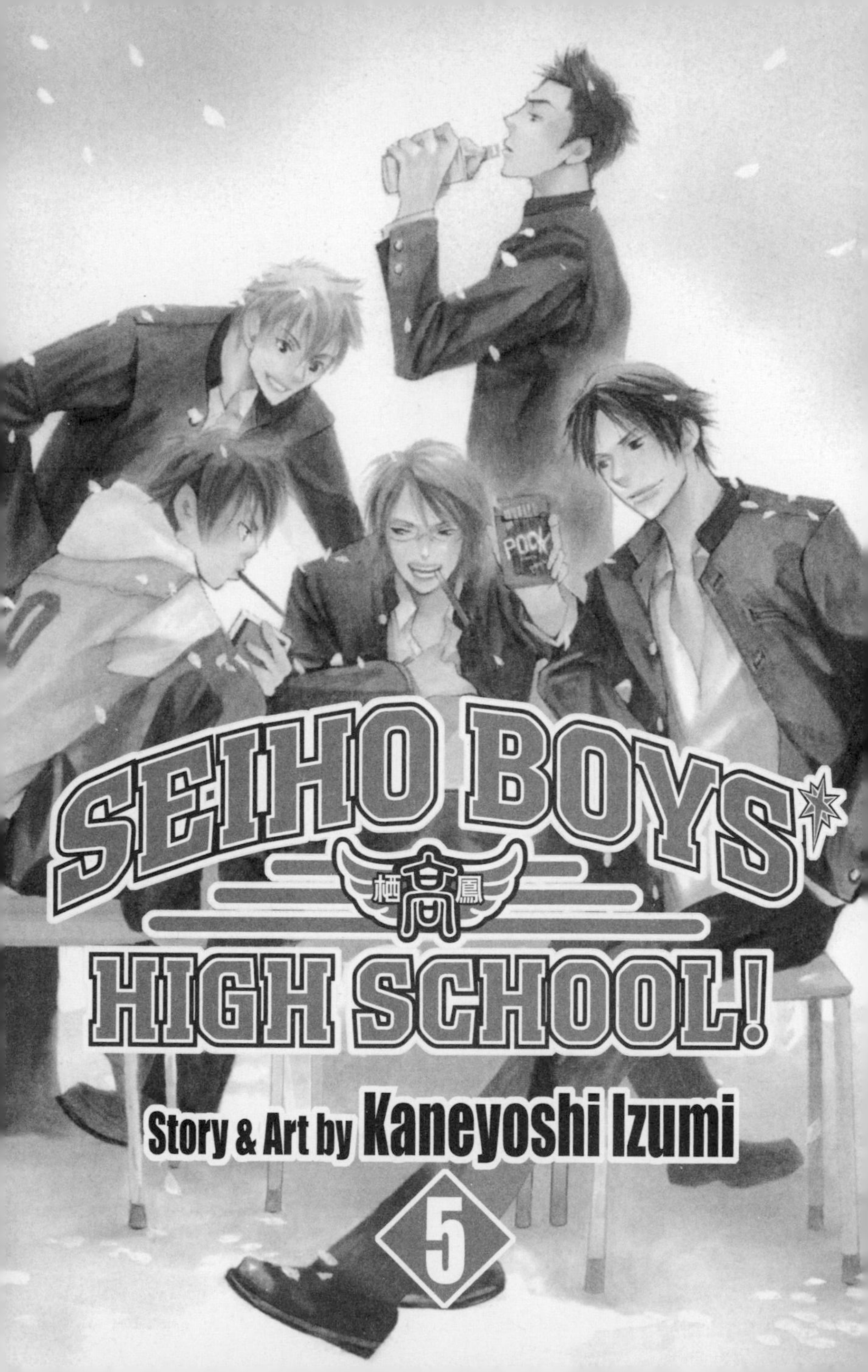
SEIHO BOYS
HIGH SCHOOL!
Story & Art by Kaneyoshi Izumi
5

# SEIHO BOYS' HIGH SCHOOL!

## 5

## CONTENTS

# ♠♠♠STORY SO FAR♠♠♠

Nestled in the distant countryside you'll find Seiho High, a private boys' school surrounded by the mountains and sea. For its students, overflowing with youthful energy and desires, the daily grind of being unable to meet any girls makes their isolated school feel like Alcatraz!

Despite his questionable ideas about courtship, Nogami manages to sweep Miss Fukuhara off her feet. Maki, who's been getting over his junior high crush who died in an accident, finds himself a new girlfriend. As for Kamiki, he's currently being pursued by the naive Fuyuka Miyaji.

# ♠CHARACTERS♠

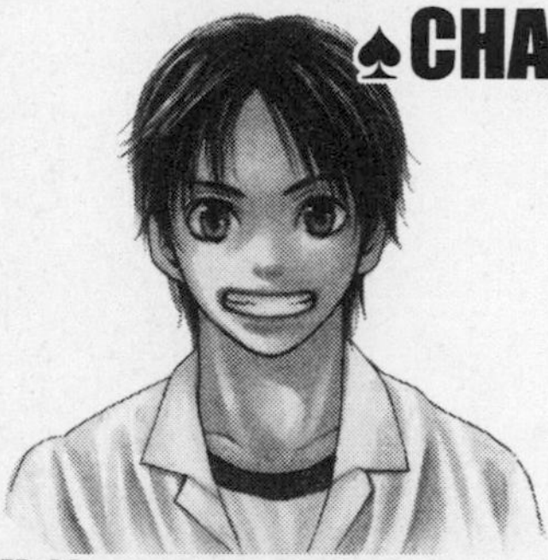

■**Maki**■ Adored by men and women of all ages, Maki is a cute guy and a peacemaker, but he has an unexpected violent streak.

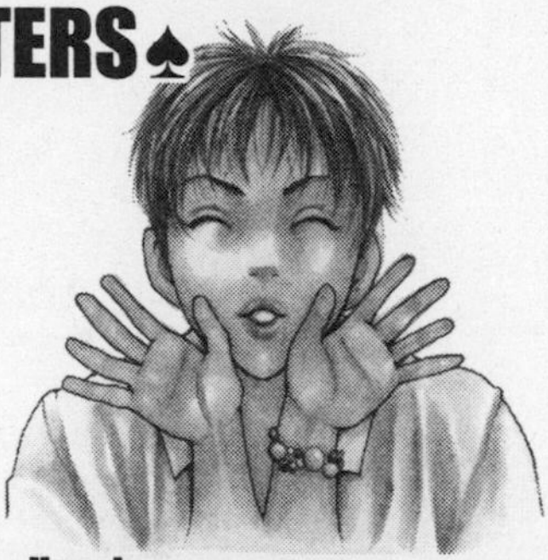

■**Hanai**■ A girl trapped in a boy's body, to put it bluntly. He loves cute accessories. He had a girlfriend until recently, but he had to break up with her.

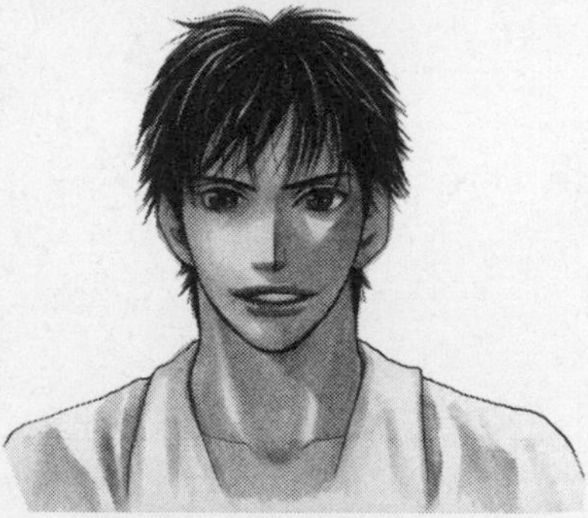

■**Kamiki**■ The hottest boy at school. He's got everything it takes to make girls fall for him, but he's surprisingly tactless.

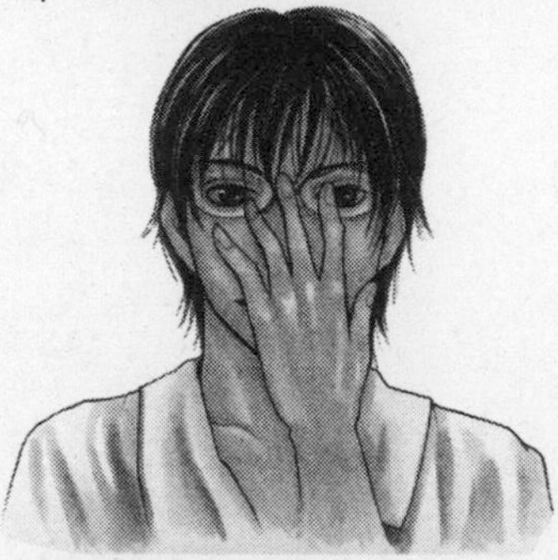

■**Nogami**■ Sees himself as far superior to the other students. He likes the school nurse, Miss Fukuhara.

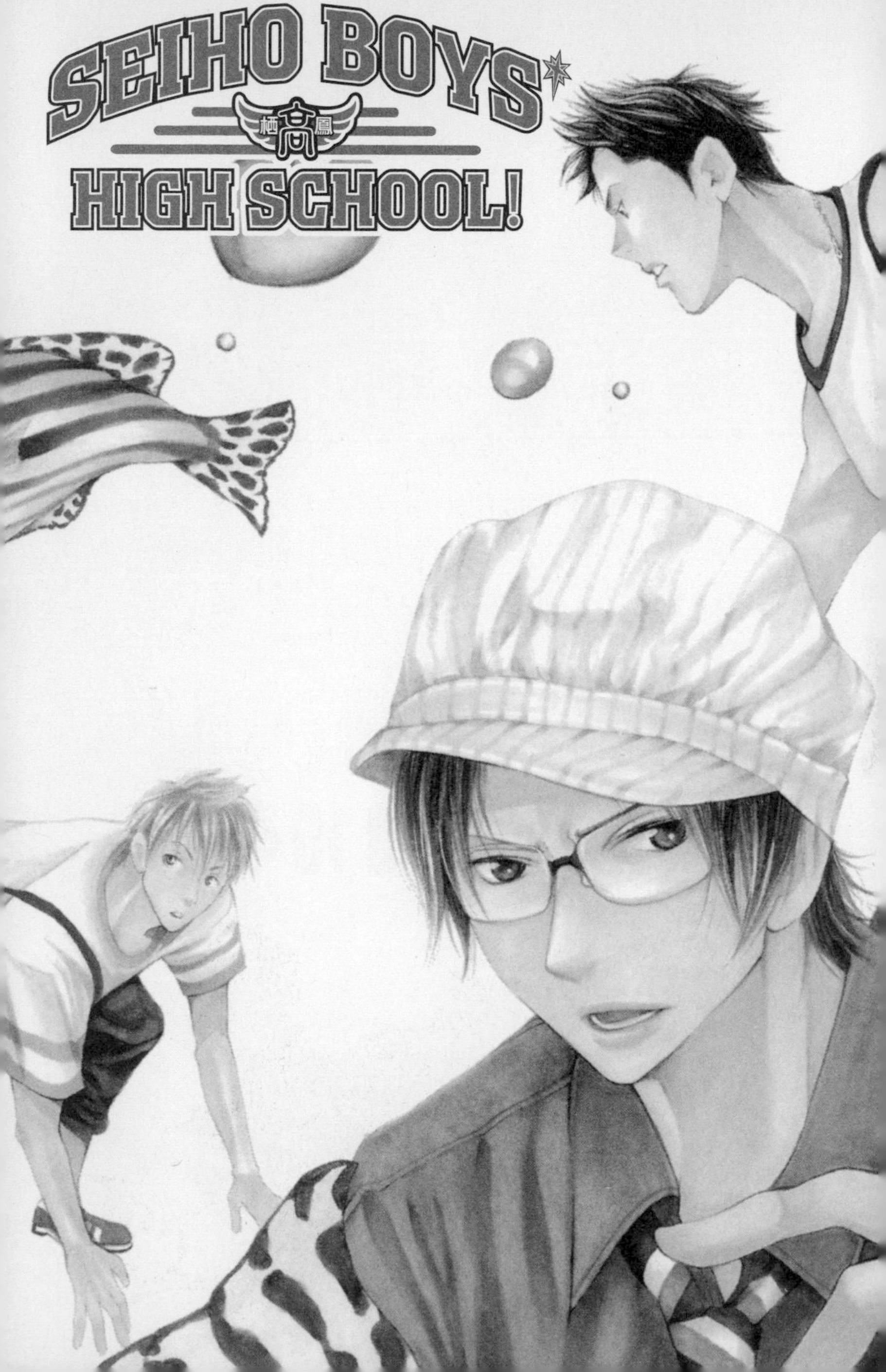
SEIHO BOYS
栖高鳳
HIGH SCHOOL!

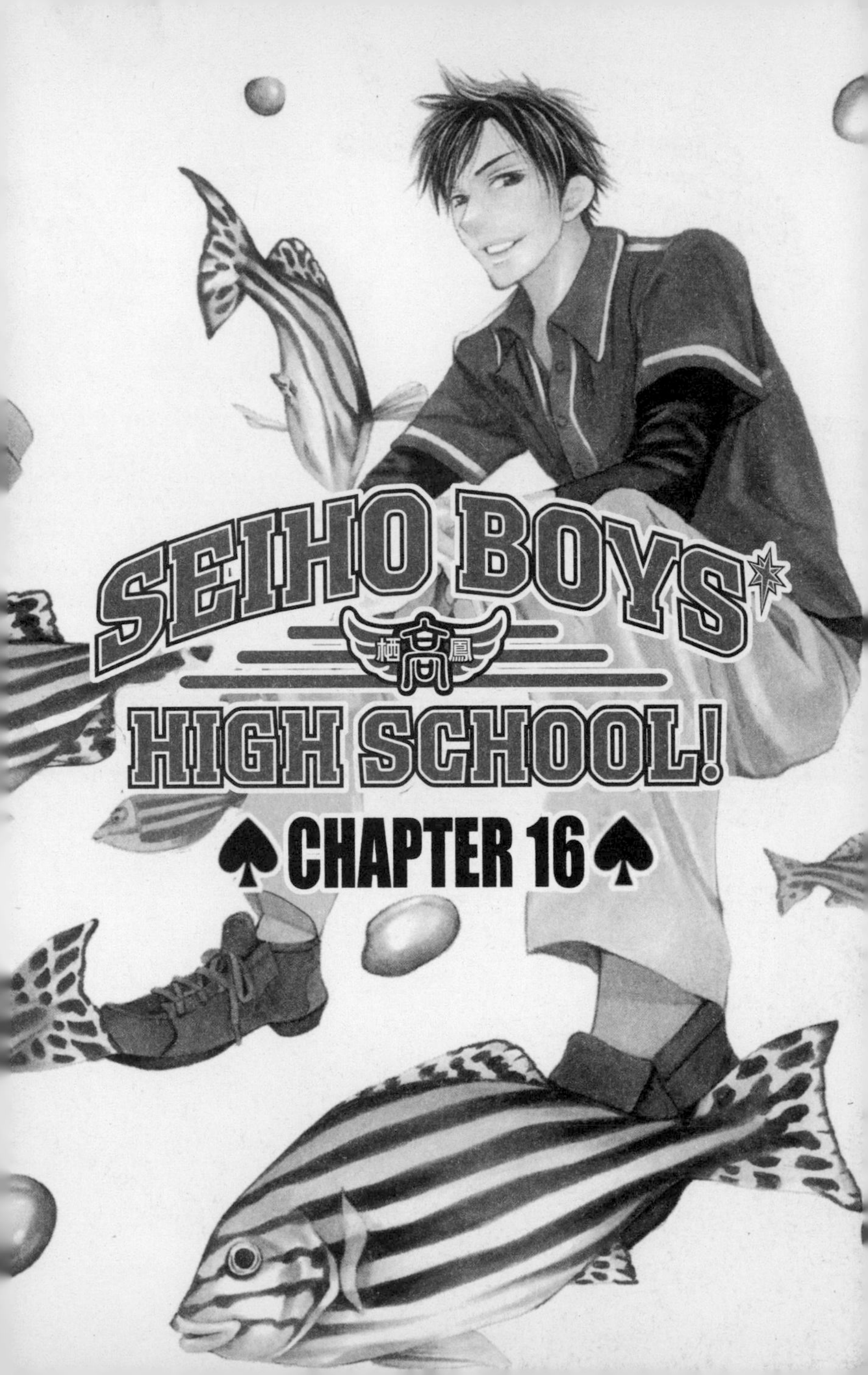
SEIHO BOYS HIGH SCHOOL!
CHAPTER 16

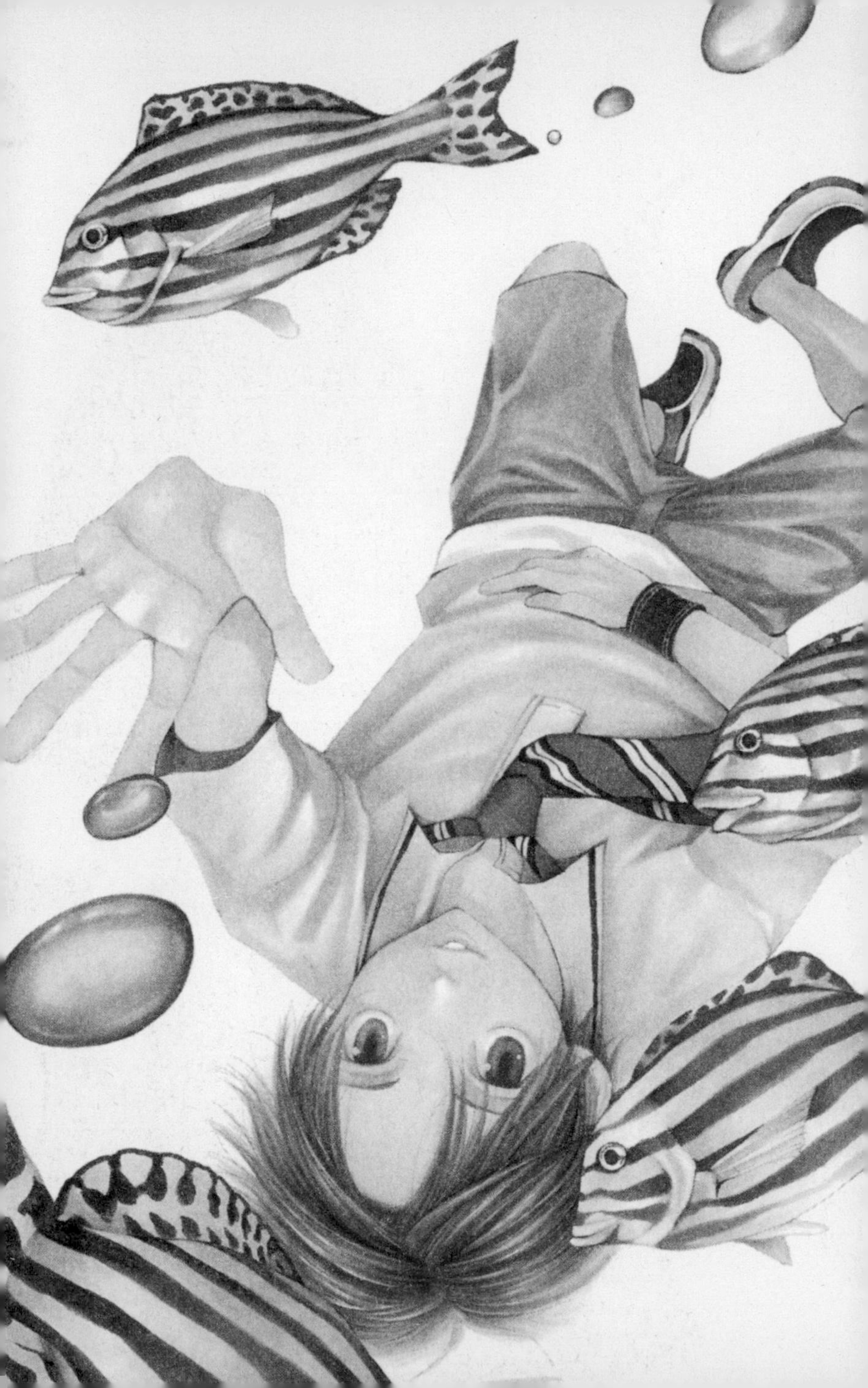

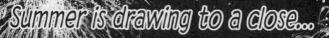

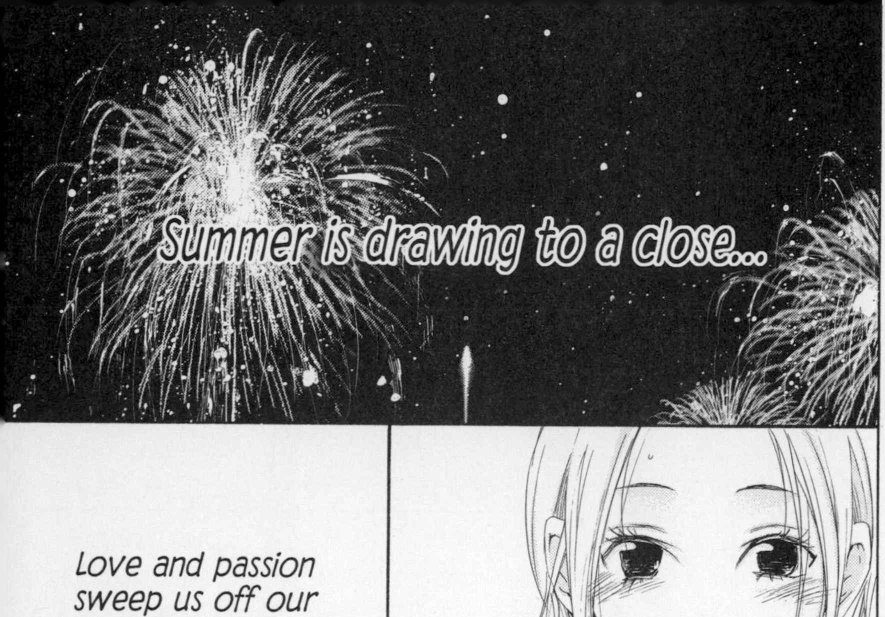

Summer is drawing to a close...
The girl I met at the beach is smiling at me...
Love and passion sweep us off our feet and make us act like fools...

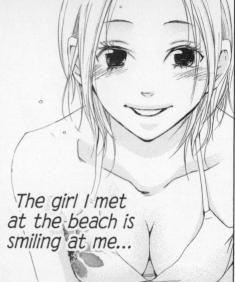

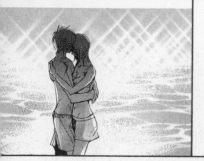

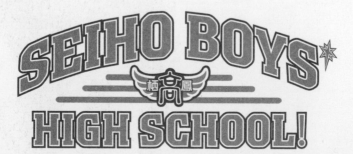

# SEIHO BOYS HIGH SCHOOL!

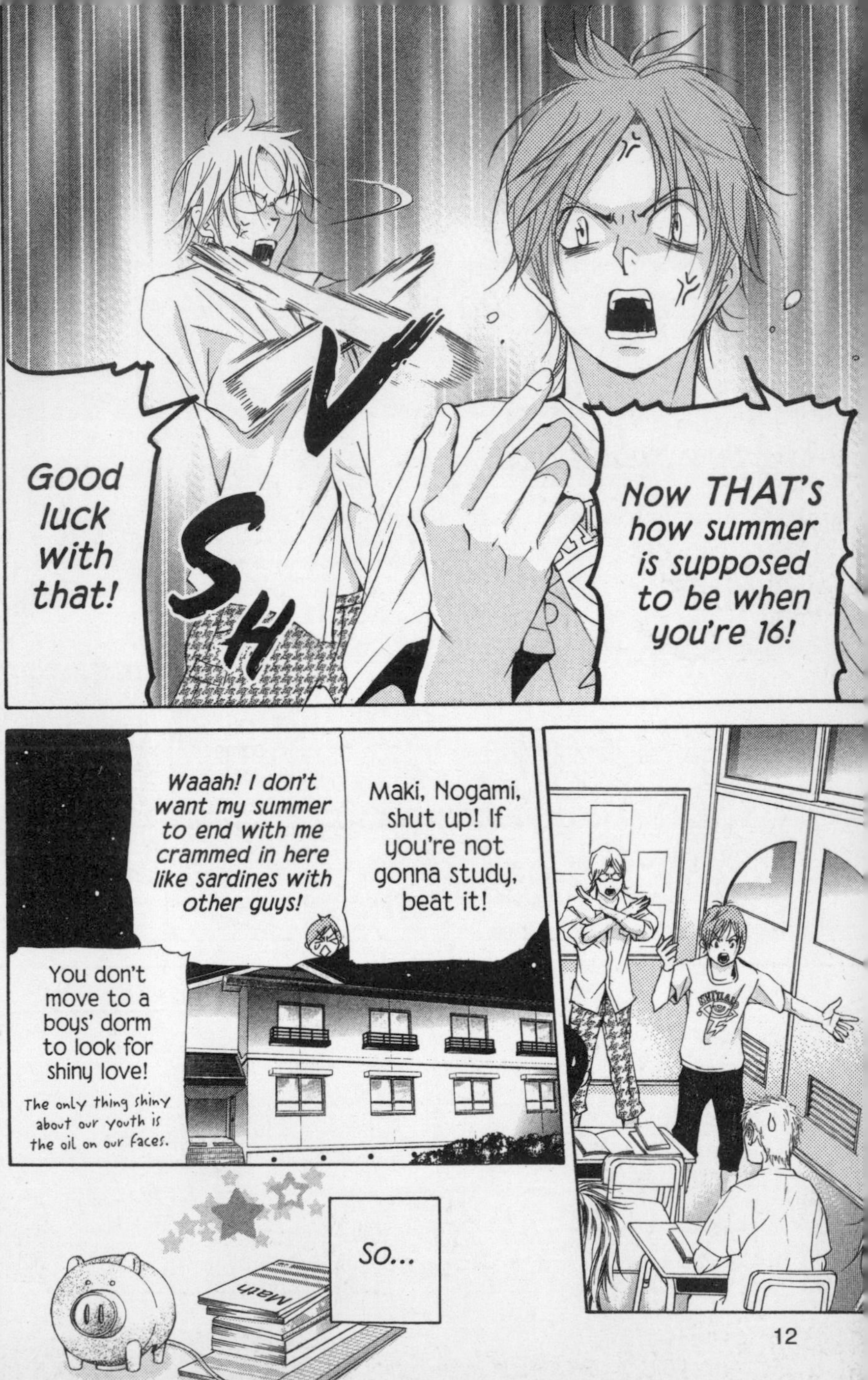

Now THAT's how summer is supposed to be when you're 16!
Good luck with that!
Maki, Nogami, shut up! If you're not gonna study, beat it!
Waaah! I don't want my summer to end with me crammed in here like sardines with other guys!
You don't move to a boys' dorm to look for shiny love!
The only thing shiny about our youth is the oil on our faces.
So...
Math

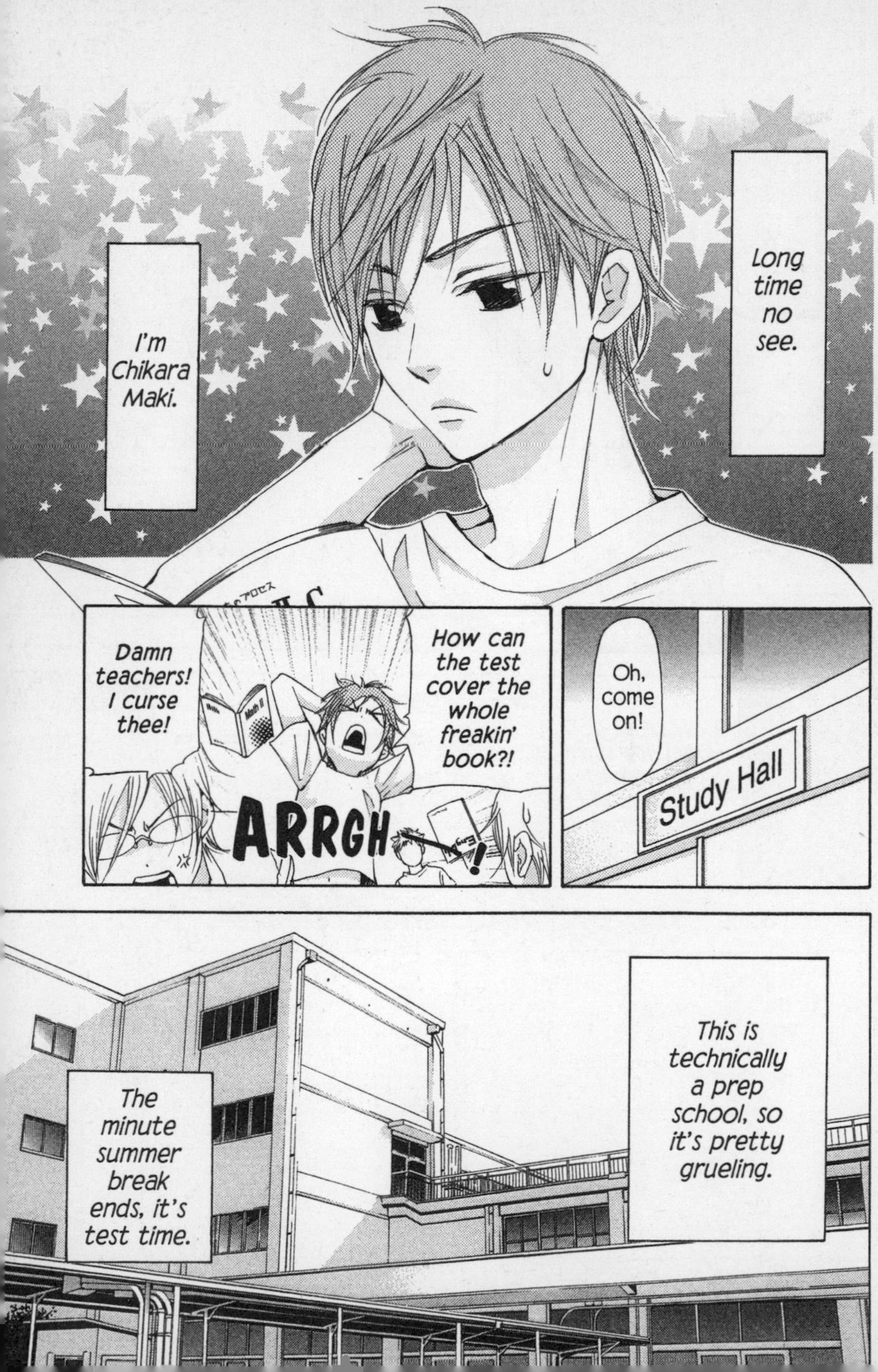
Long time no see.
I'm Chikara Maki.
Oh, come on!
Study Hall
How can the test cover the whole freakin' book?!
Damn teachers! I curse thee!
ARRGH
This is technically a prep school, so it's pretty grueling.
The minute summer break ends, it's test time.

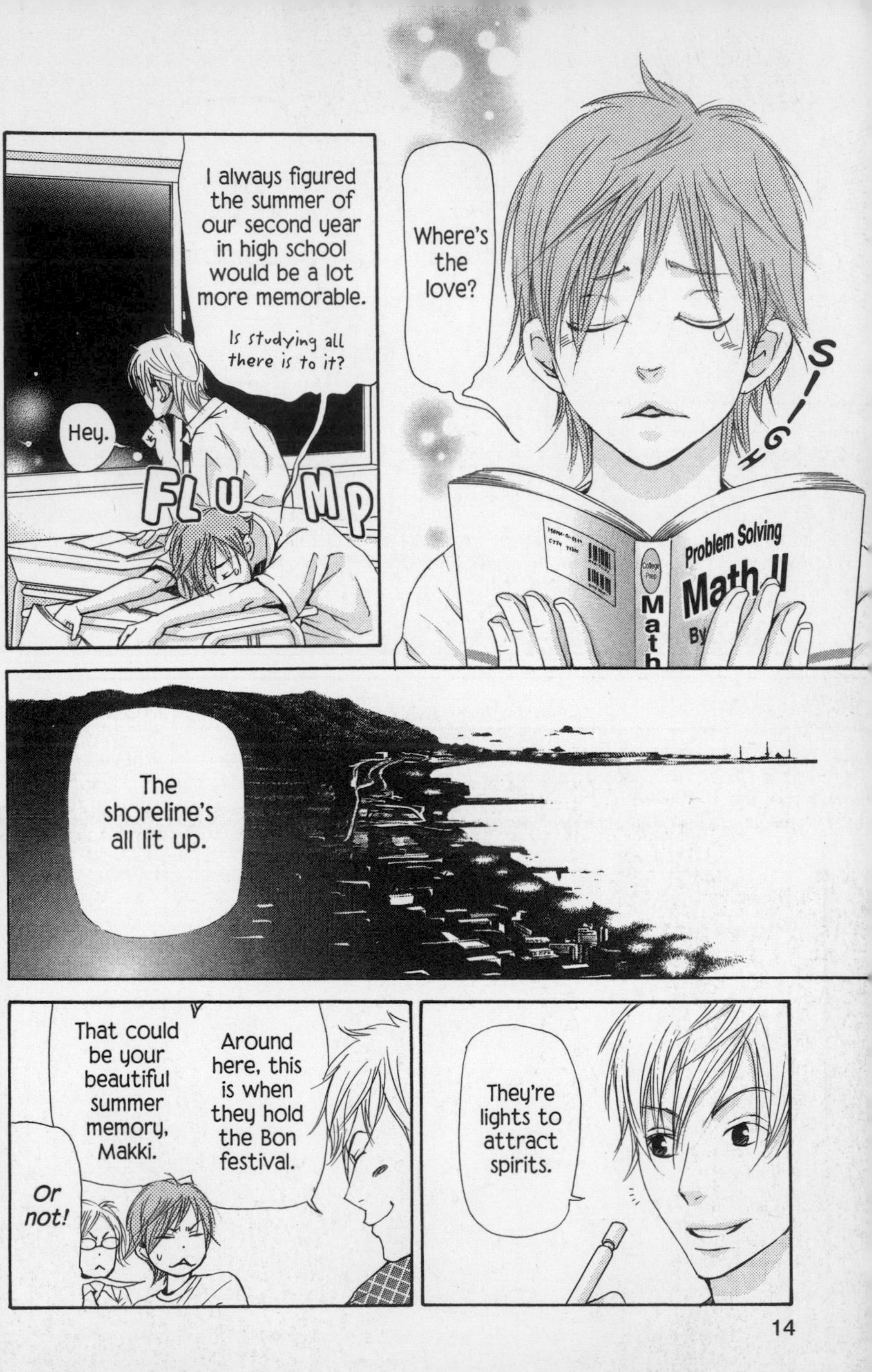
Where's the love?
SIGH
College Prep
Math
Problem Solving
Math II
By
I always figured the summer of our second year in high school would be a lot more memorable.
Is studying all there is to it?
Hey.
FLUMP
The shoreline's all lit up.
They're lights to attract spirits.
Around here, this is when they hold the Bon festival.
That could be your beautiful summer memory, Makki.
Or not!

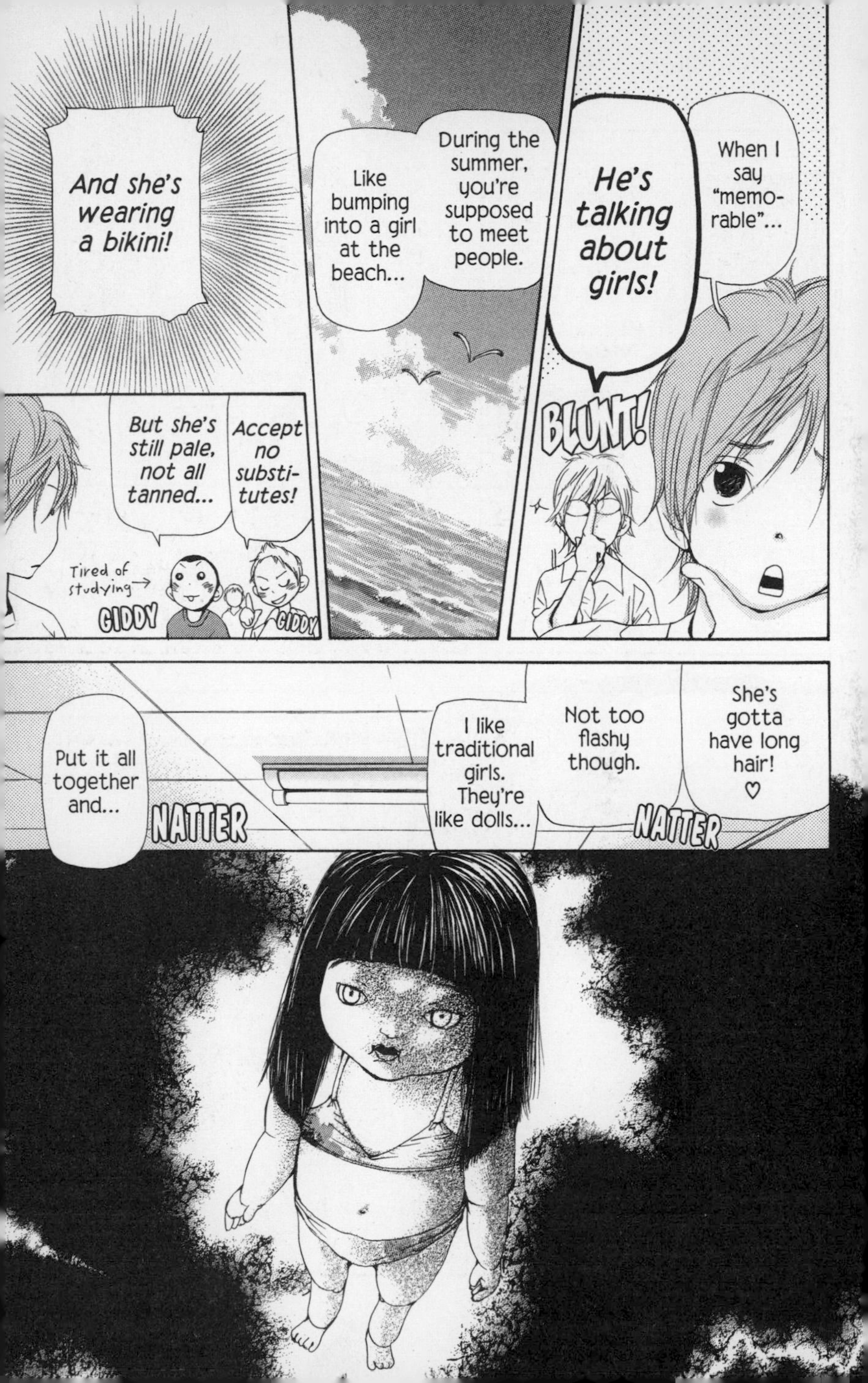
When I say "memorable"...
He's talking about girls!
BLUNT!
During the summer, you're supposed to meet people.
Like bumping into a girl at the beach...
And she's wearing a bikini!
Accept no substitutes!
But she's still pale, not all tanned...
Tired of studying→
GIDDY
GIDDY
She's gotta have long hair! ♡
Not too flashy though.
NATTER
I like traditional girls. They're like dolls...
NATTER
Put it all together and...

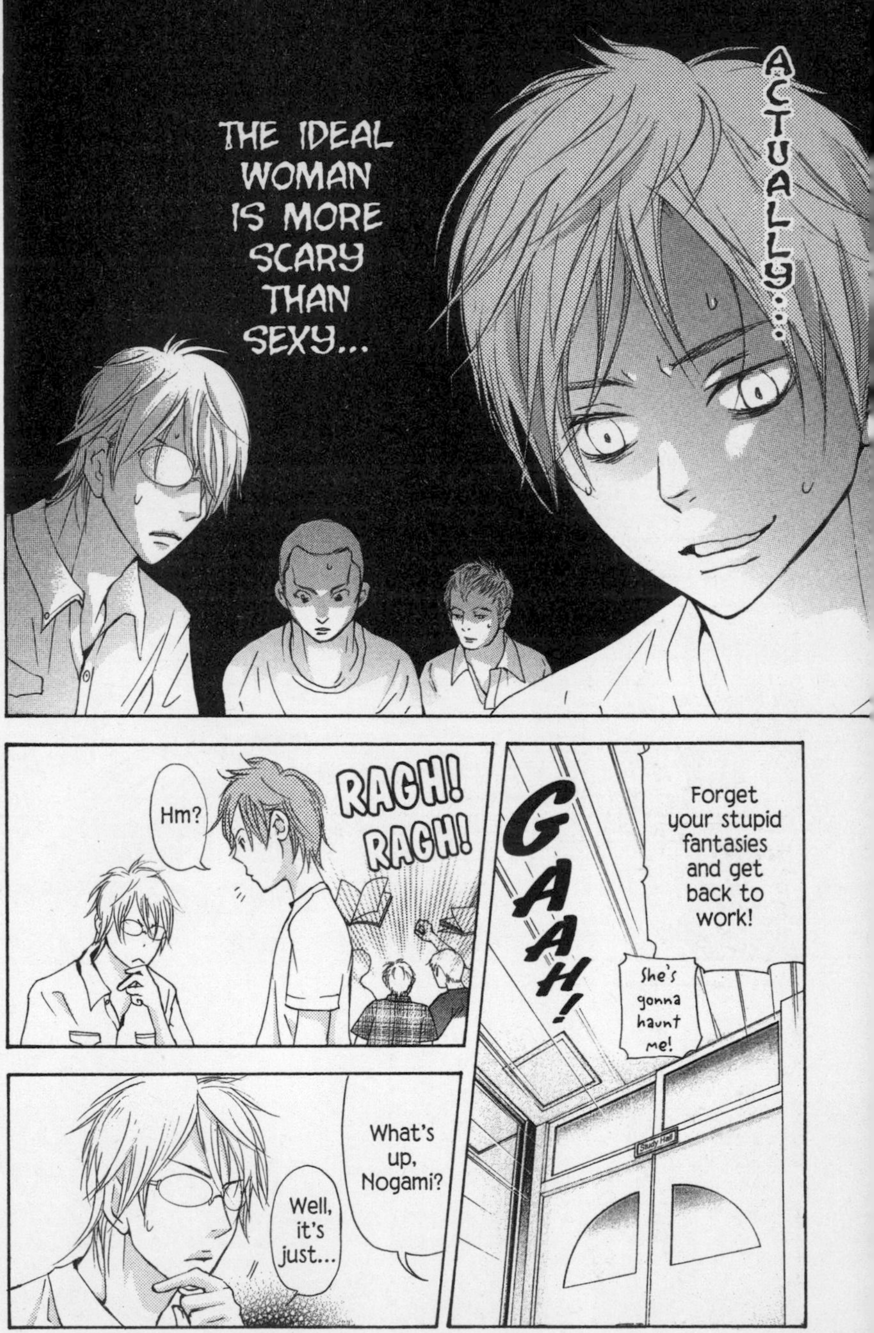
ACTUALLY...
THE IDEAL WOMAN IS MORE SCARY THAN SEXY...
Forget your stupid fantasies and get back to work!
GAAAH!
She's gonna haunt me!
Study Hall
RAGH! RAGH!
Hm?
What's up, Nogami?
Well, it's just...

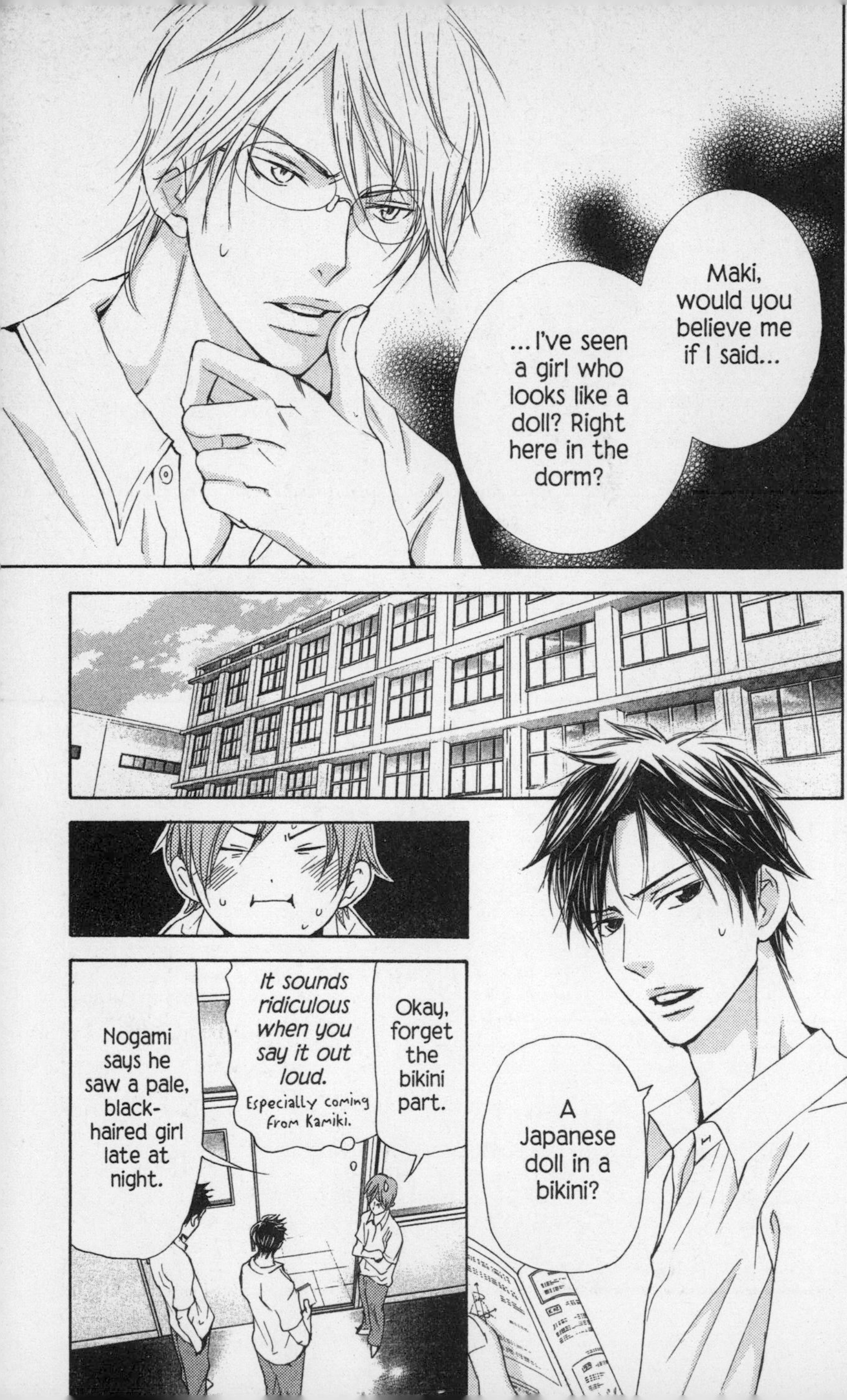
Maki, would you believe me if I said...
...I've seen a girl who looks like a doll? Right here in the dorm?
A Japanese doll in a bikini?
Okay, forget the bikini part.
It sounds ridiculous when you say it out loud.
Especially coming from Kamiki.
Nogami says he saw a pale, black-haired girl late at night.

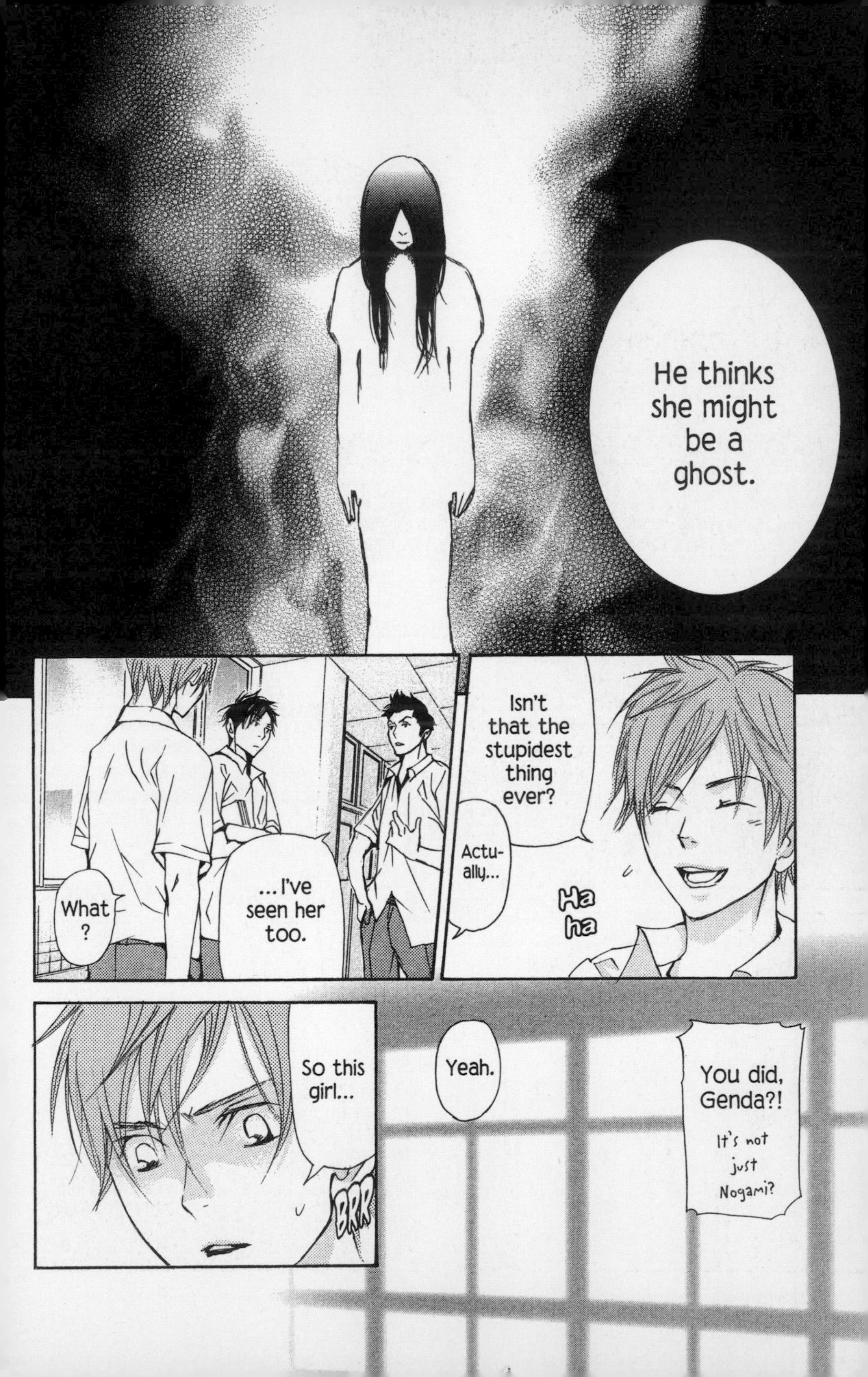
He thinks she might be a ghost.
Isn't that the stupidest thing ever?
Ha ha
Actu-ally...
...I've seen her too.
What?
You did, Genda?!
It's not just Nogami?
Yeah.
So this girl...
BRR

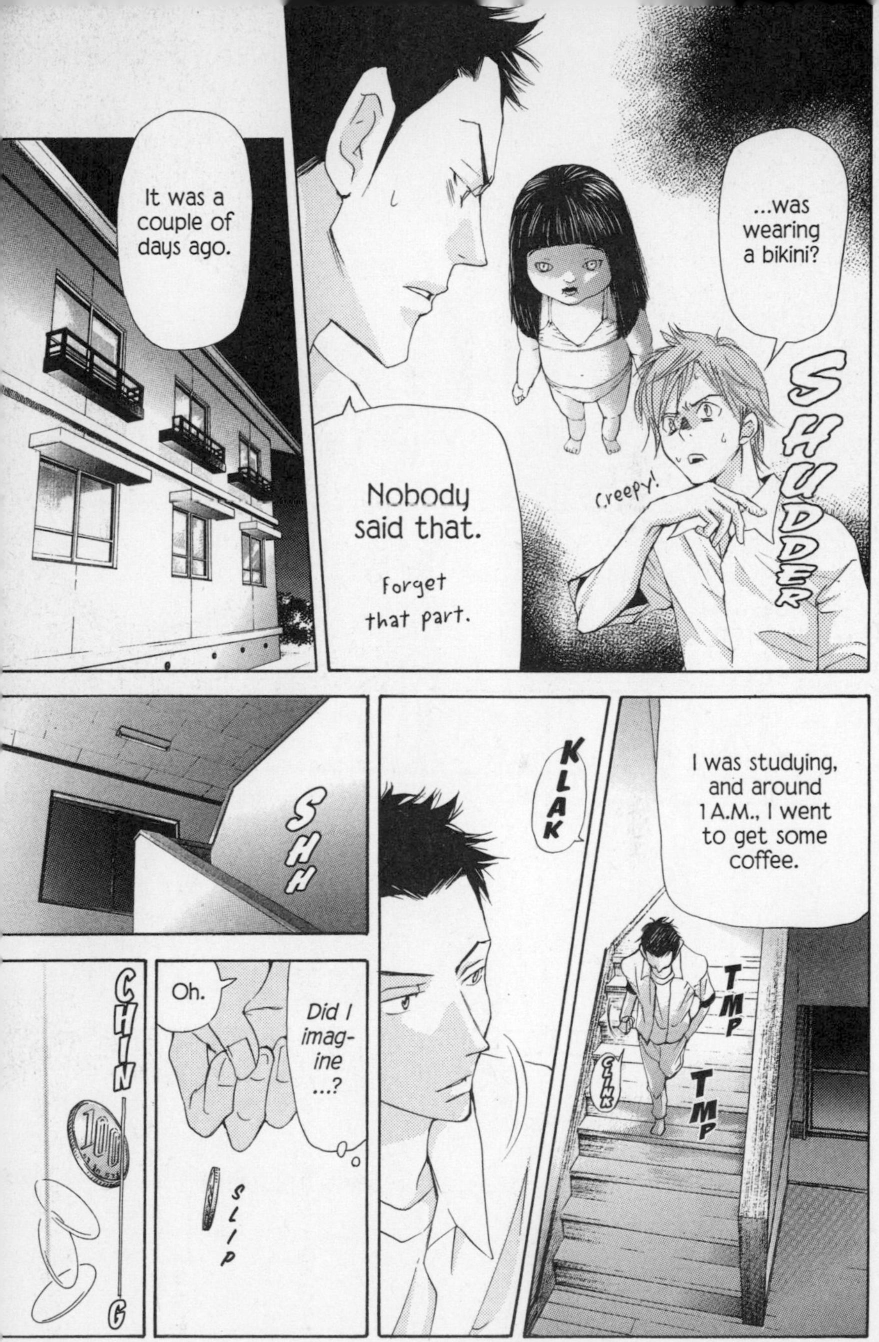

...was wearing a bikini?
SHUDDER
Creepy!
Nobody said that.
Forget that part.
It was a couple of days ago.
I was studying, and around 1 A.M., I went to get some coffee.
TMP
TMP
CLINK
KLAK
SHH
Oh.
Did I imagine...?
SLIP
CHIN-G

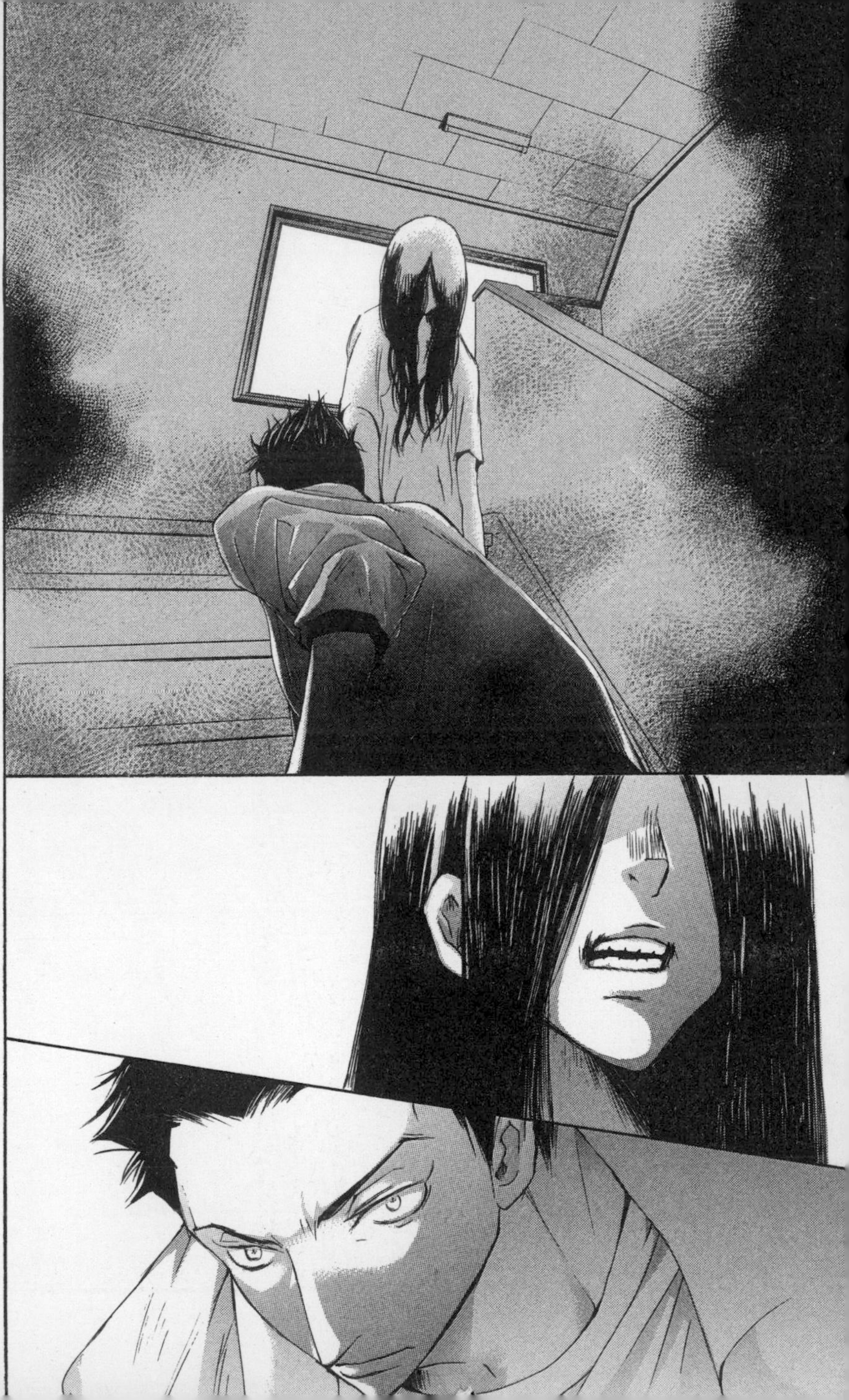

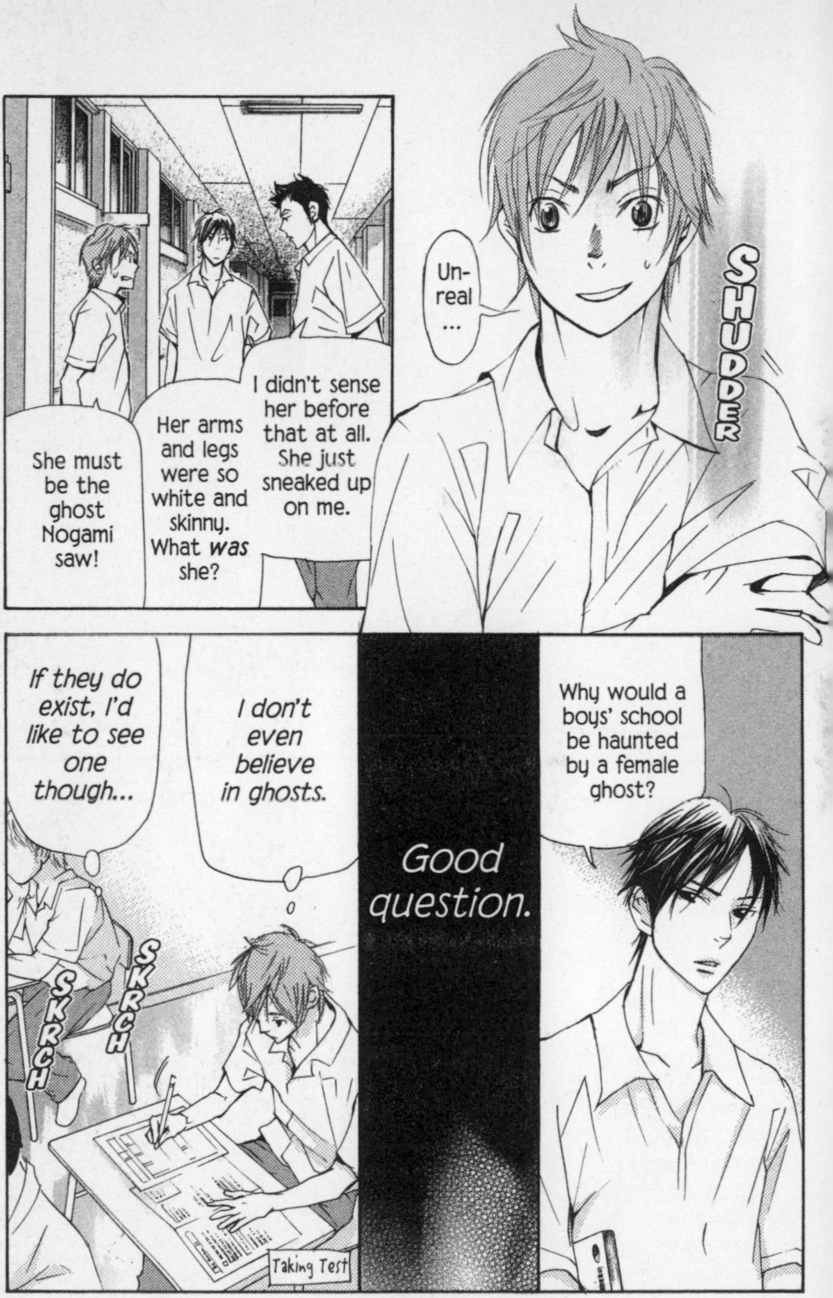
Un-real...
SHUDDER
I didn't sense her before that at all. She just sneaked up on me.
Her arms and legs were so white and skinny. What *was* she?
She must be the ghost Nogami saw!
Why would a boys' school be haunted by a female ghost?
Good question.
I don't even believe in ghosts.
If they do exist, I'd like to see one though...
SKRCH
SKRCH
Taking Test

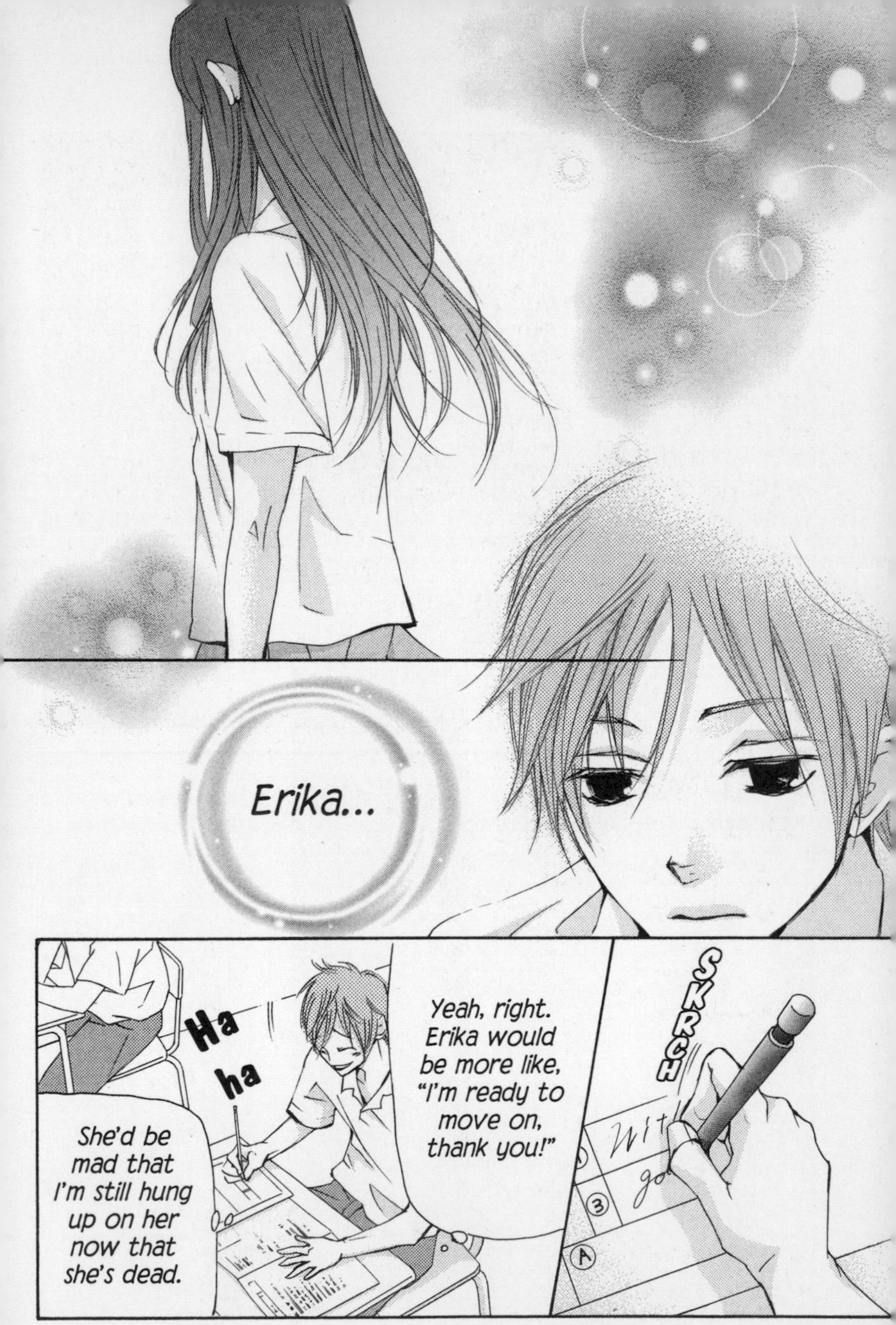
Erika...
SKRCH
Yeah, right. Erika would be more like, "I'm ready to move on, thank you!"
Ha ha
She'd be mad that I'm still hung up on her now that she's dead.

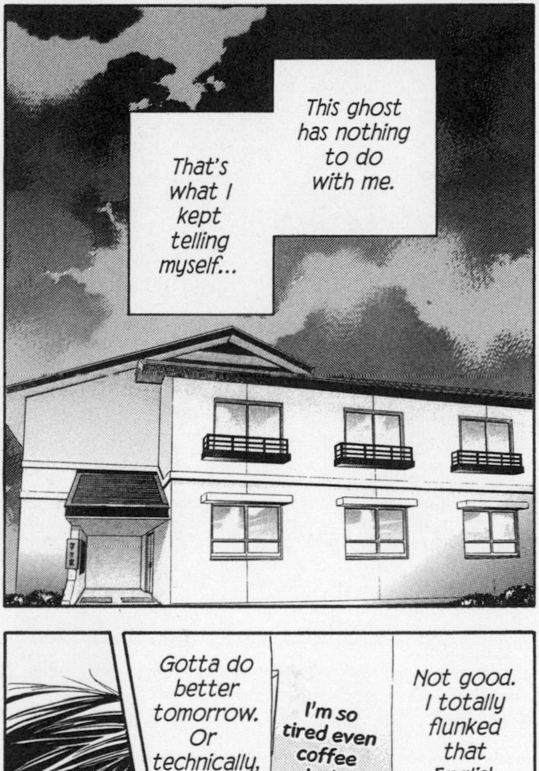
This ghost has nothing to do with me.
That's what I kept telling myself...
Not good. I totally flunked that English test.
I'm so tired even coffee isn't helping.
Gotta do better tomorrow. Or technically, today...
PLUNK
BZZ

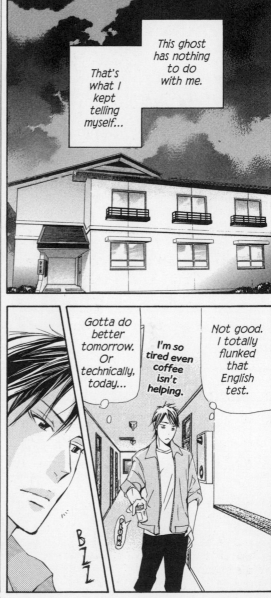

## 1/3 Filler Corner

## A Collection of Words That Shocked Me

For this volume's pointless filler corners, I want to tell you about some things I'd heard that made me want to say, "What?!" in response.
In other words, please enjoy Mitsuo Aida*-esque words that might sear into your heart...

**Part ①**

**Hey, want to take care of some axolotls?**

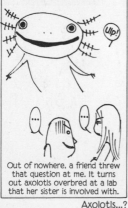

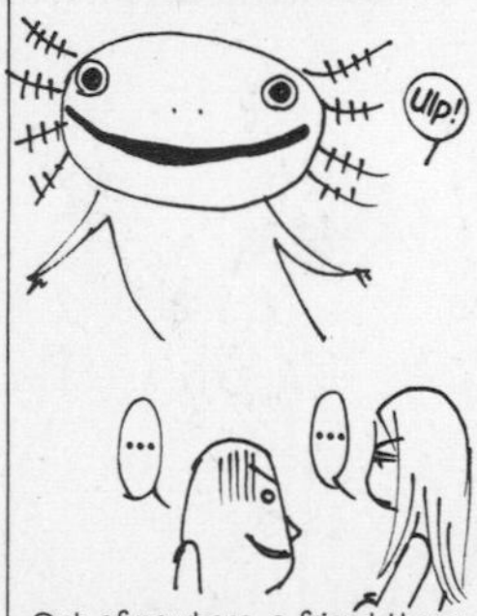
Ulp!
...
...

Out of nowhere, a friend threw that question at me. It turns out axolotls overbred at a lab that her sister is involved with.

Axolotls...?

*Mitsuo Aida is a Japanese calligrapher and poet.

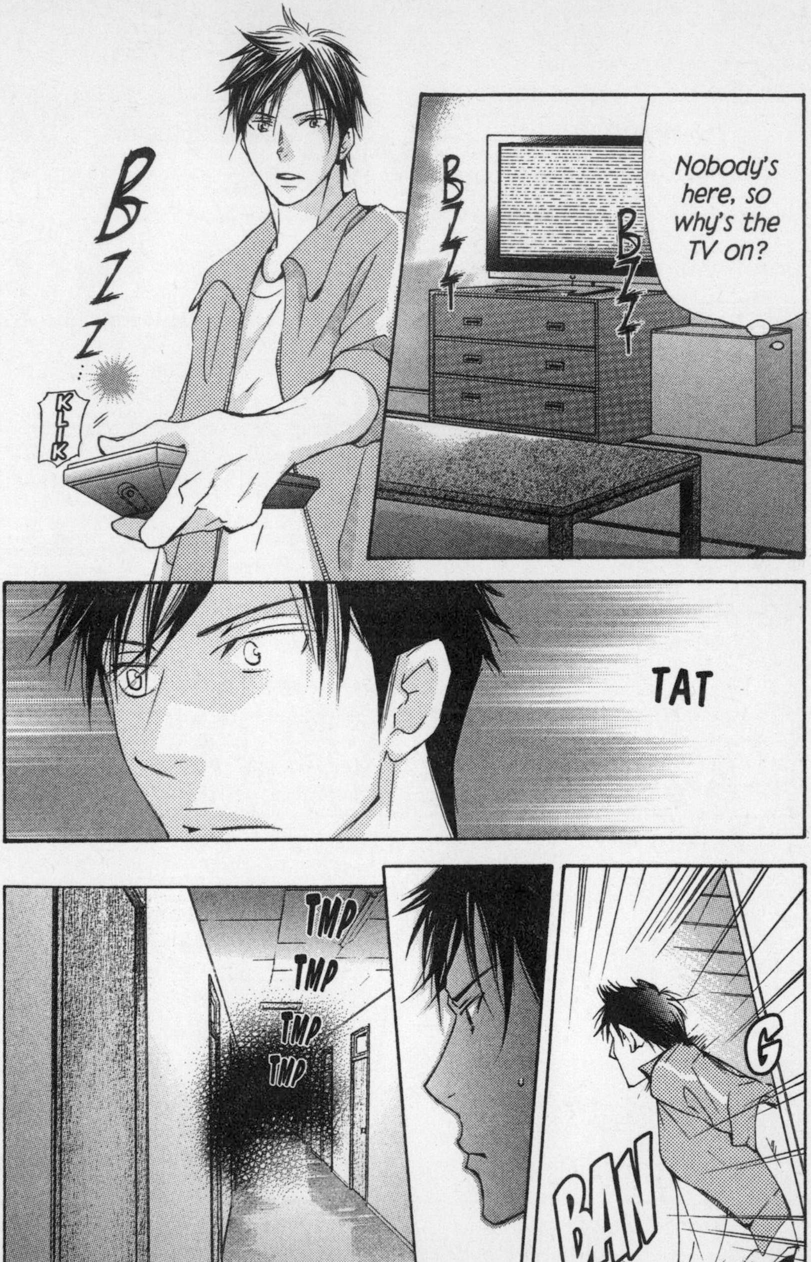
BZZT
BZZT
Nobody's here, so why's the TV on?
BZZZ
KLIK
TAT
G
BAN
TMP
TMP
TMP
TMP

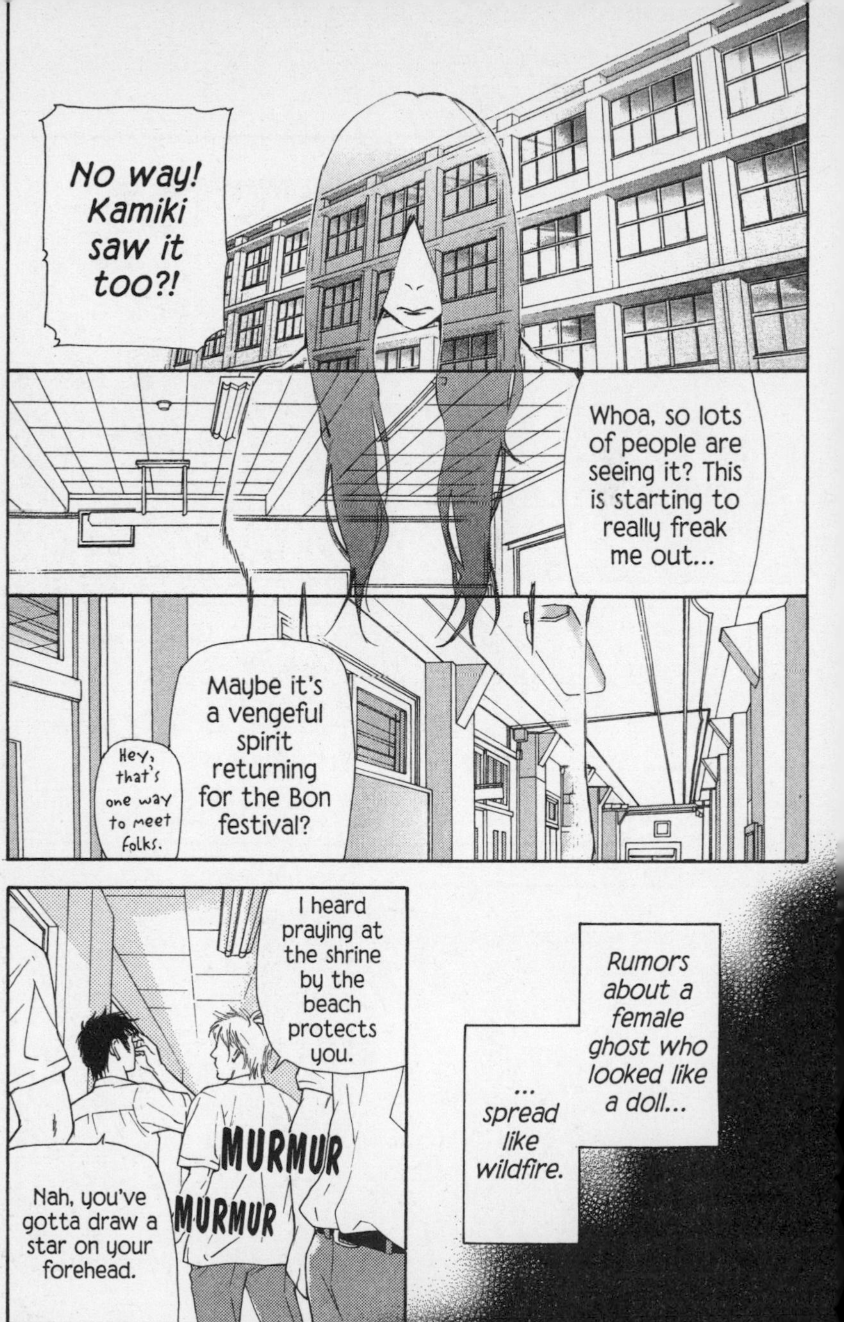
No way! Kamiki saw it too?!
Whoa, so lots of people are seeing it? This is starting to really freak me out...
Maybe it's a vengeful spirit returning for the Bon festival?
Hey, that's one way to meet folks.
Rumors about a female ghost who looked like a doll...
... spread like wildfire.
I heard praying at the shrine by the beach protects you.
MURMUR
MURMUR
Nah, you've gotta draw a star on your forehead.

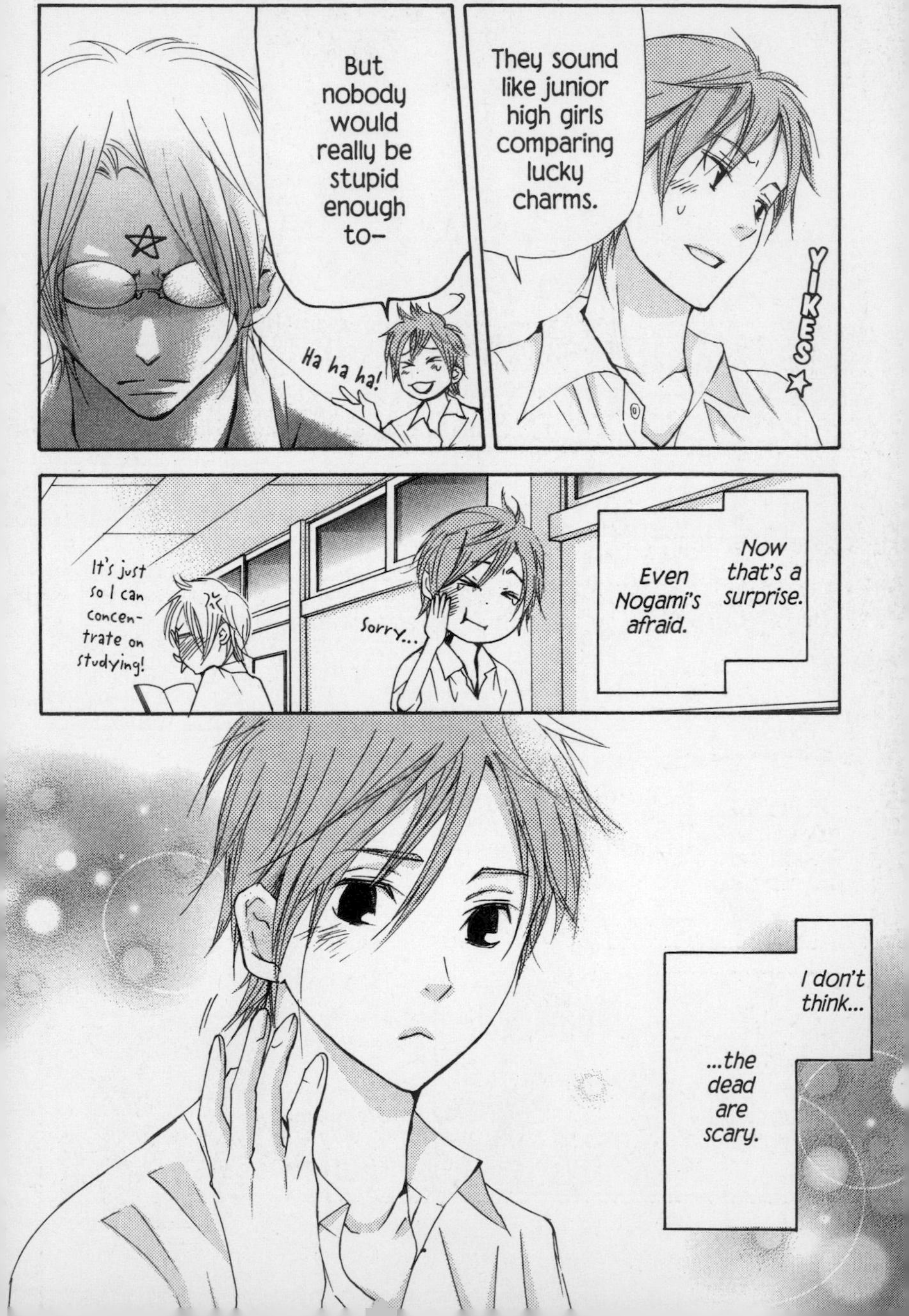
They sound like junior high girls comparing lucky charms.
YIKES☆
But nobody would really be stupid enough to–
Ha ha ha!
Now that's a surprise.
Even Nogami's afraid.
Sorry...
It's just so I can concen-trate on studying!
I don't think...
...the dead are scary.

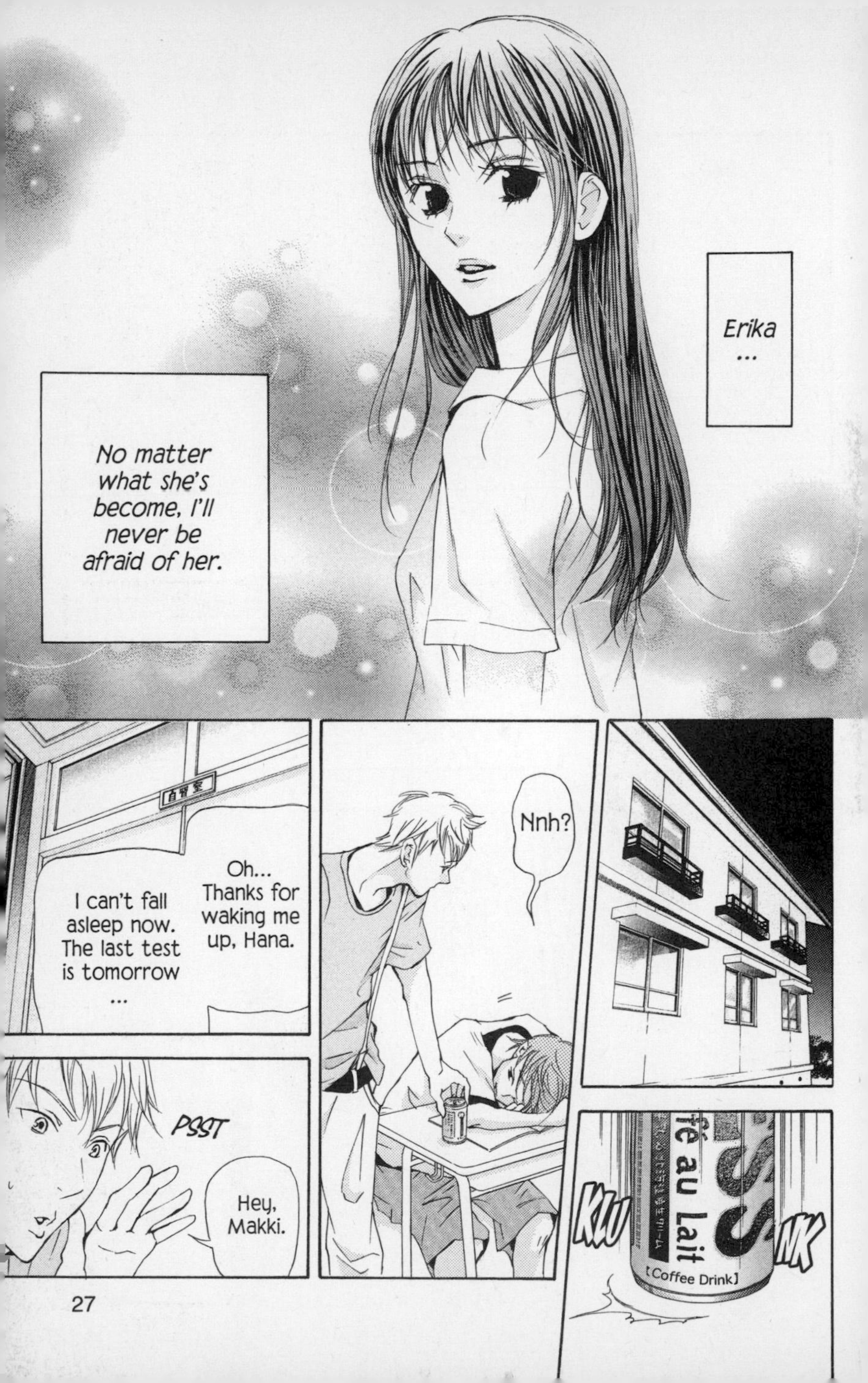
Erika ...
No matter what she's become, I'll never be afraid of her.
KLU NK
fé au Lait
【Coffee Drink】
Nnh?
Oh... Thanks for waking me up, Hana.
I can't fall asleep now. The last test is tomorrow ...
PSST
Hey, Makki.

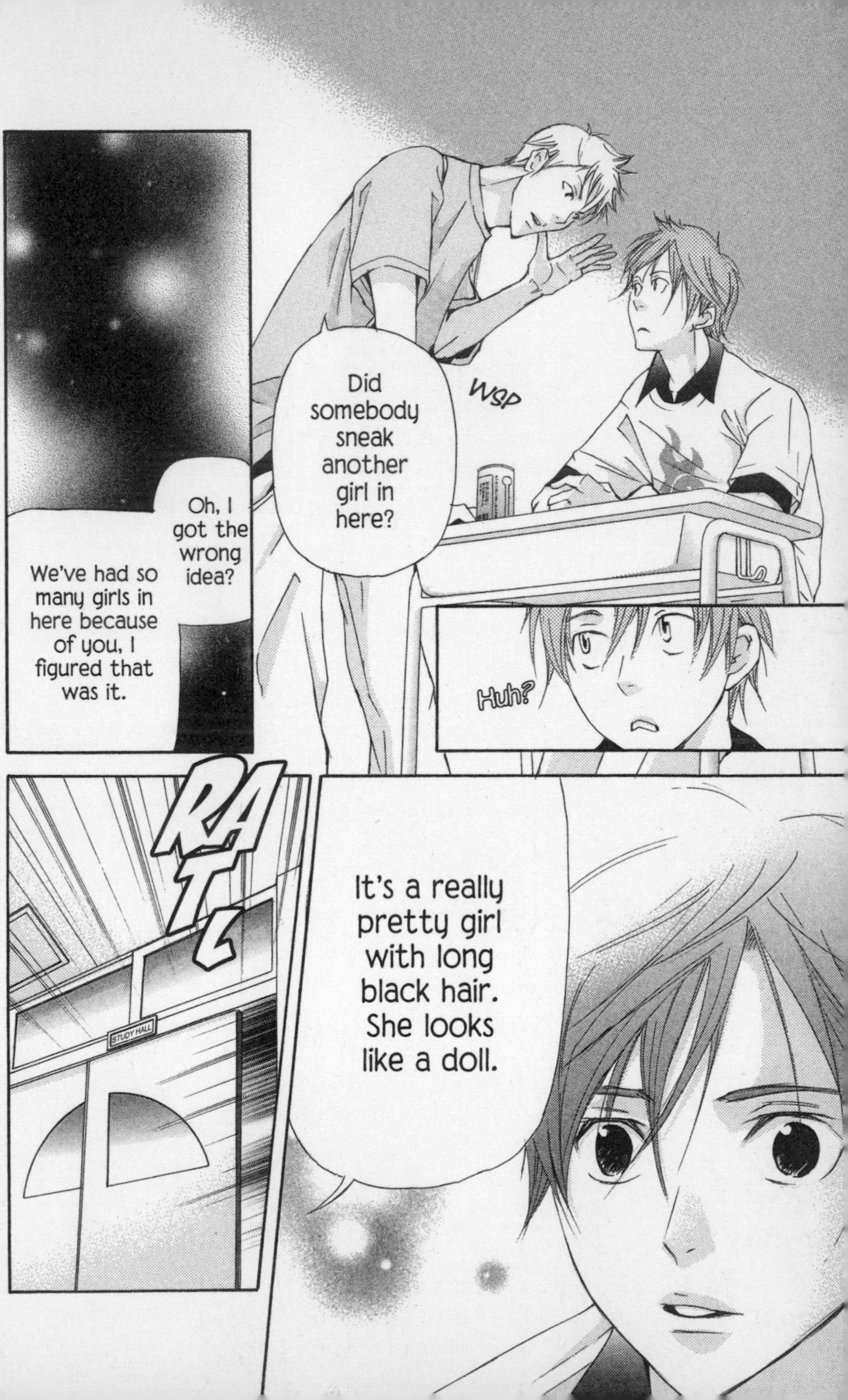
Did somebody sneak another girl in here?
WSP
Huh?
Oh, I got the wrong idea?
We've had so many girls in here because of you, I figured that was it.
It's a really pretty girl with long black hair. She looks like a doll.
RATL
STUDY HALL

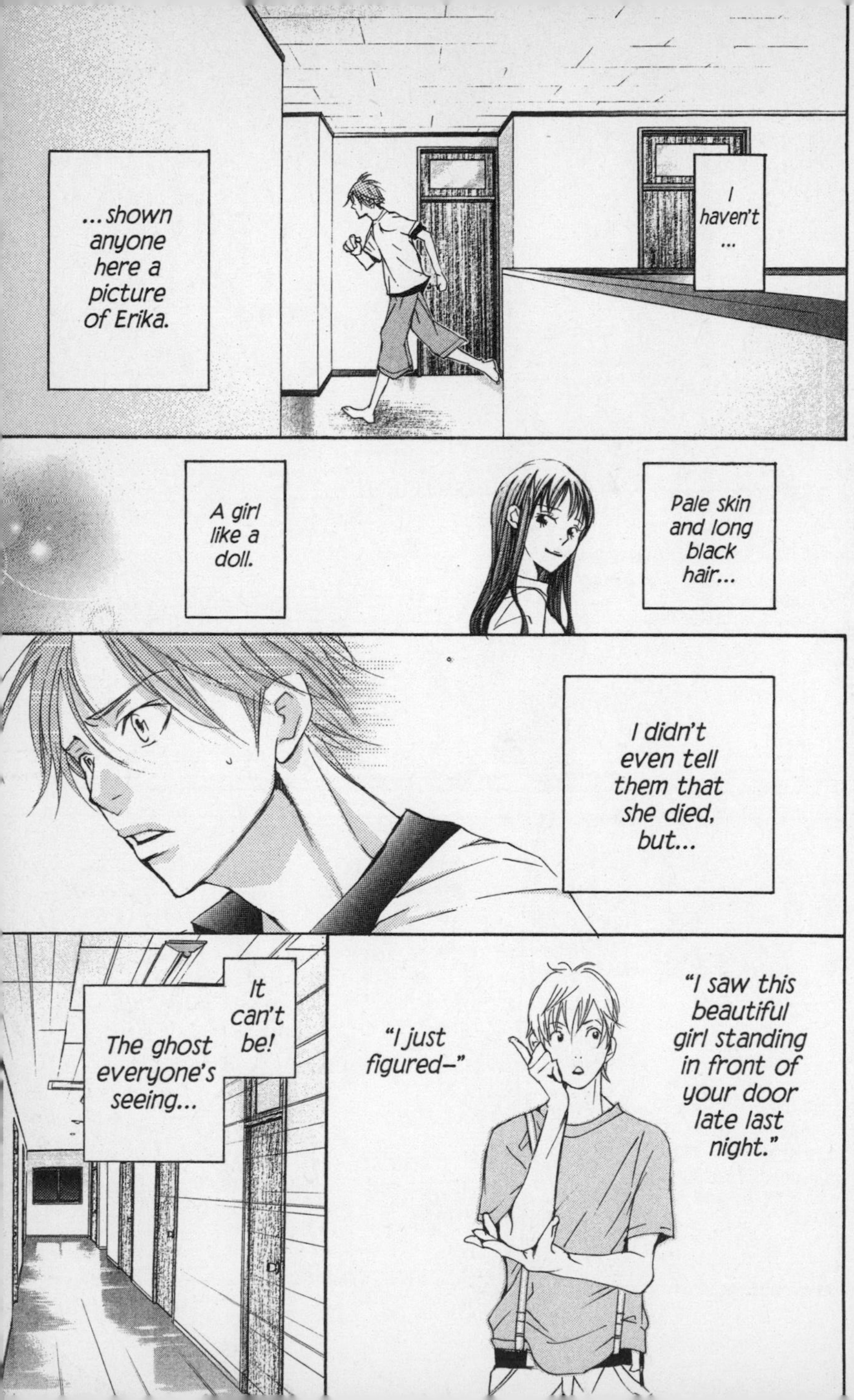

I haven't ...
...shown anyone here a picture of Erika.
Pale skin and long black hair...
A girl like a doll.
I didn't even tell them that she died, but...
"I saw this beautiful girl standing in front of your door late last night."
"I just figured–"
It can't be!
The ghost everyone's seeing...

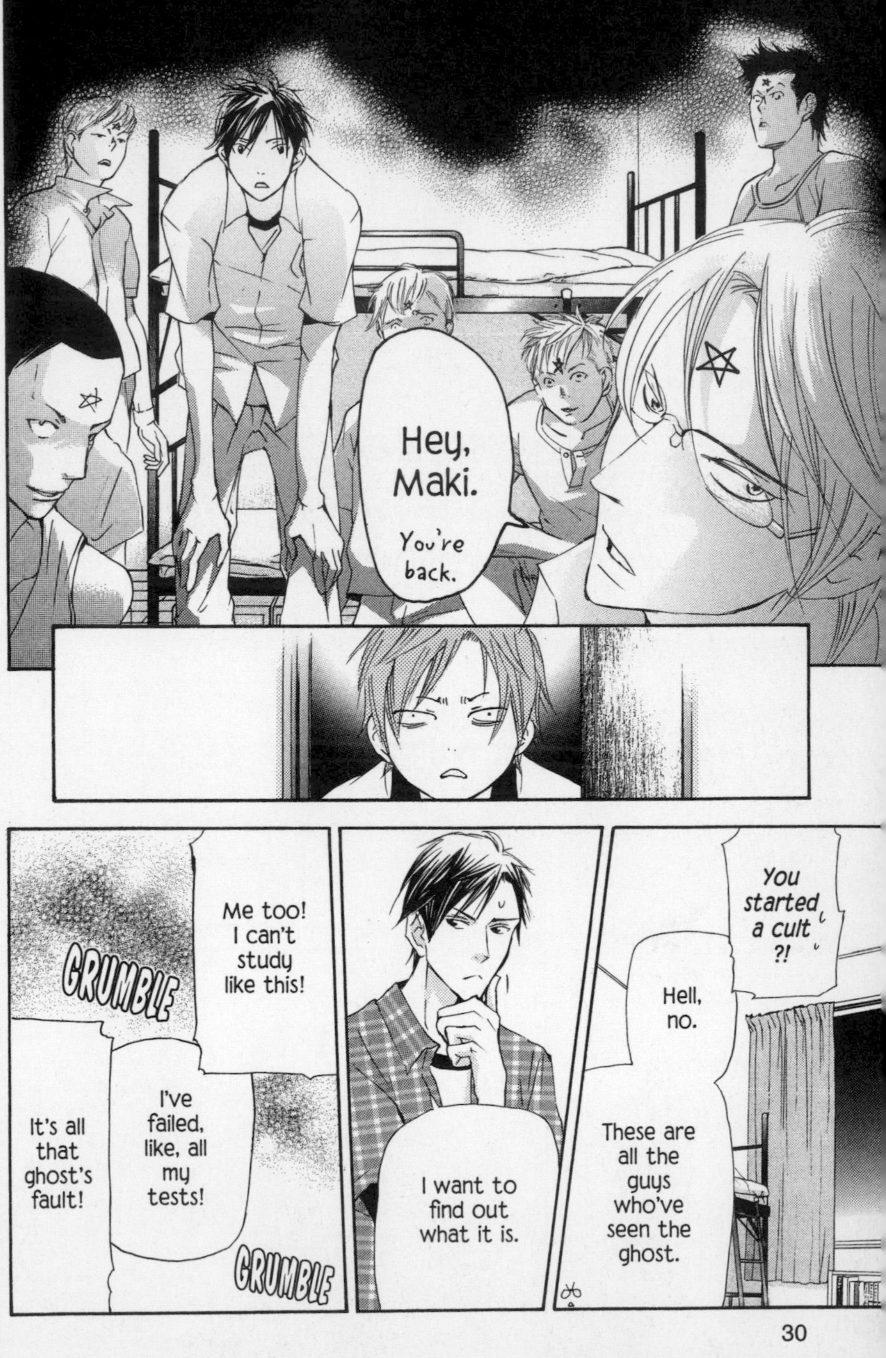
Hey, Maki.
You're back.
You started a cult ?!
Hell, no.
These are all the guys who've seen the ghost.
I want to find out what it is.
Me too! I can't study like this!
GRUMBLE
I've failed, like, all my tests!
It's all that ghost's fault!
GRUMBLE

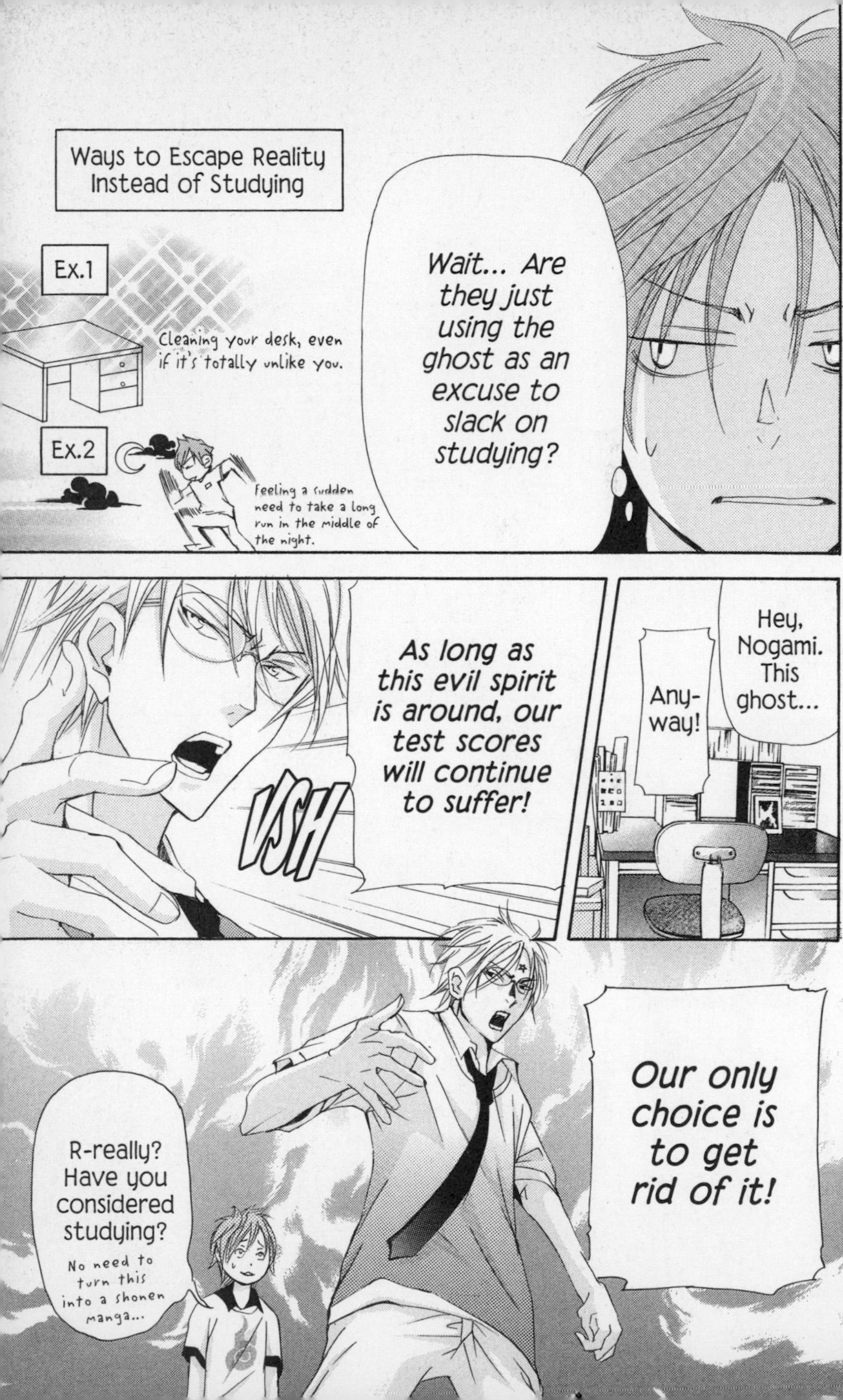
Wait... Are they just using the ghost as an excuse to slack on studying?
Ways to Escape Reality Instead of Studying
Ex.1
Cleaning your desk, even if it's totally unlike you.
Ex.2
Feeling a sudden need to take a long run in the middle of the night.
Hey, Nogami. This ghost...
Any-way!
As long as this evil spirit is around, our test scores will continue to suffer!
VSH
Our only choice is to get rid of it!
R-really? Have you considered studying?
No need to turn this into a shonen manga...

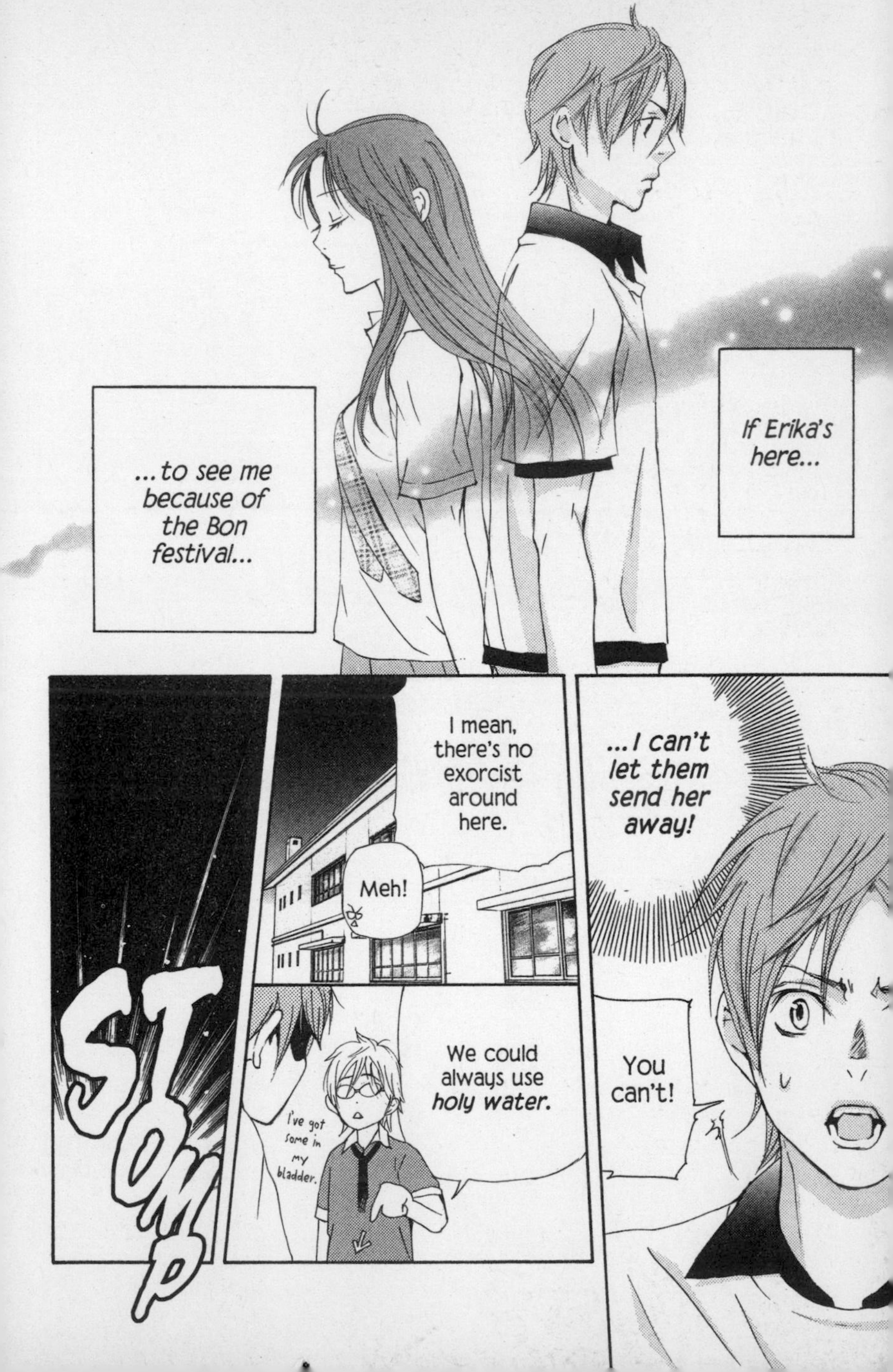
If Erika's here...
...to see me because of the Bon festival...
...I can't let them send her away!
You can't!
I mean, there's no exorcist around here.
Meh!
We could always use holy water.
I've got some in my bladder.
STOMP

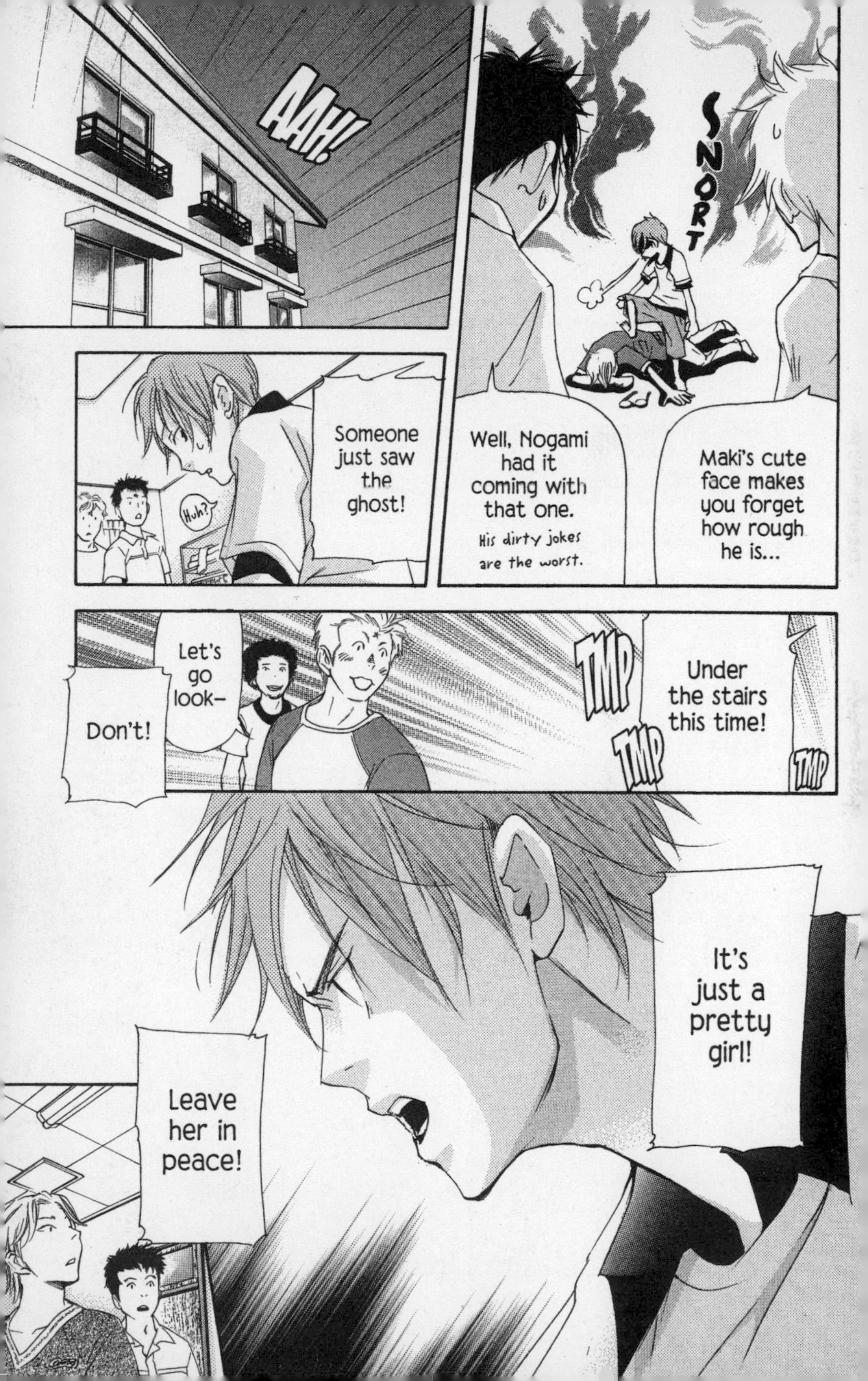
SNORT
Maki's cute face makes you forget how rough he is...
Well, Nogami had it coming with that one.
His dirty jokes are the worst.
AAH!!
Someone just saw the ghost!
Huh?
TMP
TMP
TMP
Under the stairs this time!
Let's go look—
Don't!
It's just a pretty girl!
Leave her in peace!

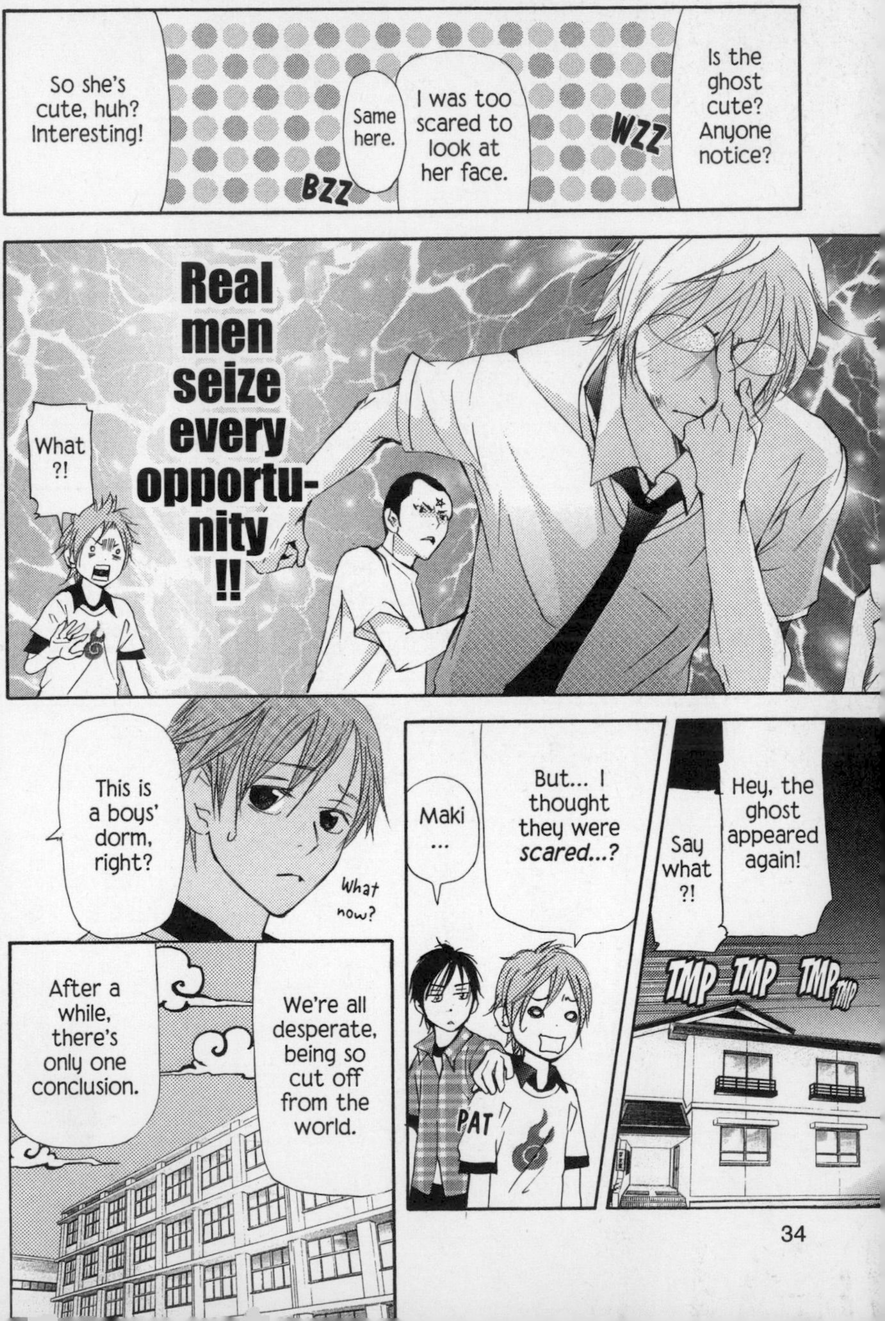

Is the ghost cute? Anyone notice?
WZZ
I was too scared to look at her face.
Same here.
BZZ
So she's cute, huh? Interesting!
Real men seize every opportunity!!
What?!
Hey, the ghost appeared again!
Say what?!
TMP TMP TMP TMP
But... I thought they were *scared...?*
Maki ...
PAT
This is a boys' dorm, right?
What now?
We're all desperate, being so cut off from the world.
After a while, there's only one conclusion.

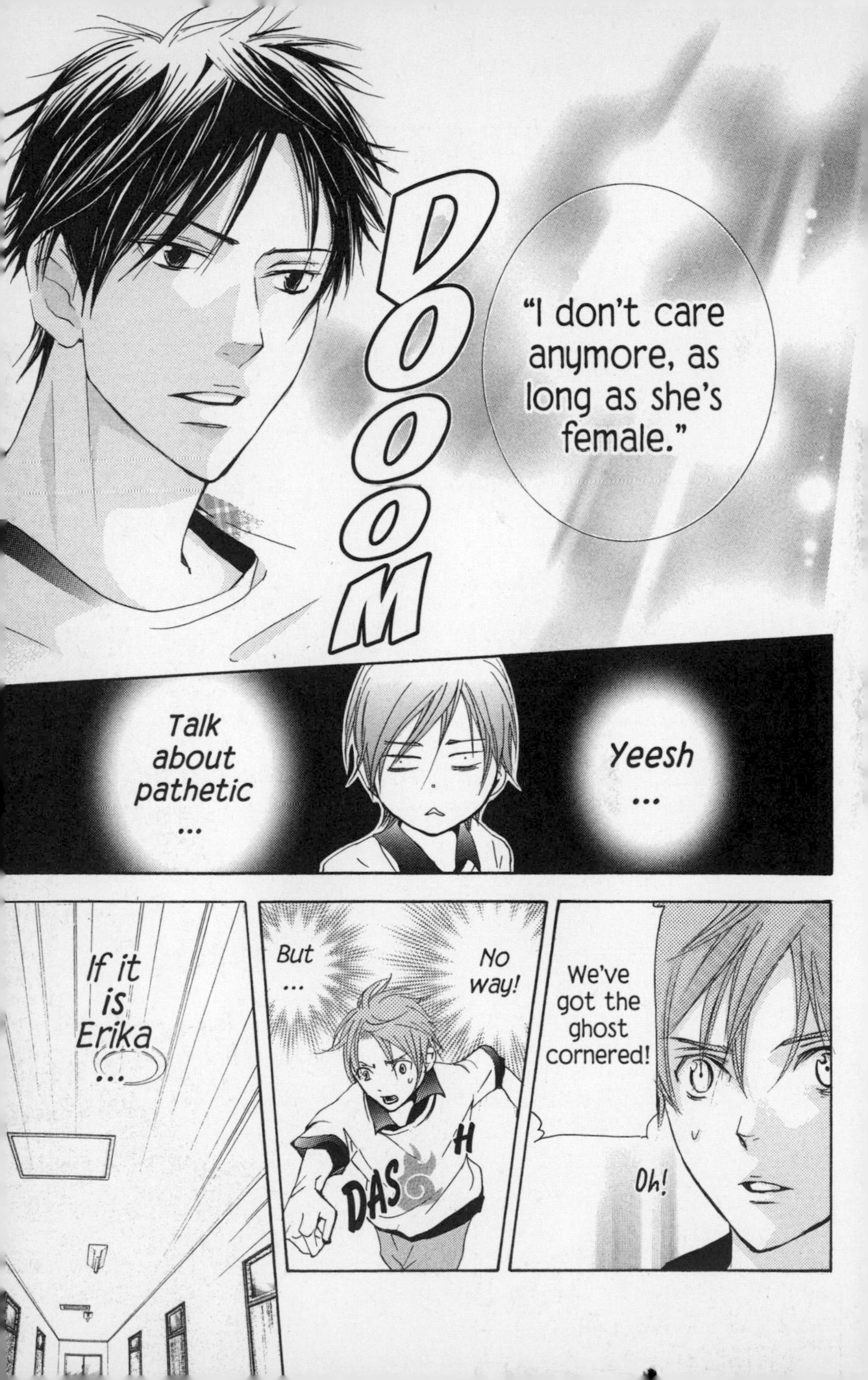
"I don't care anymore, as long as she's female."
DOOOOM
Yeesh ...
Talk about pathetic ...
We've got the ghost cornered!
Oh!
No way!
But ...
DASH
If it is Erika ...

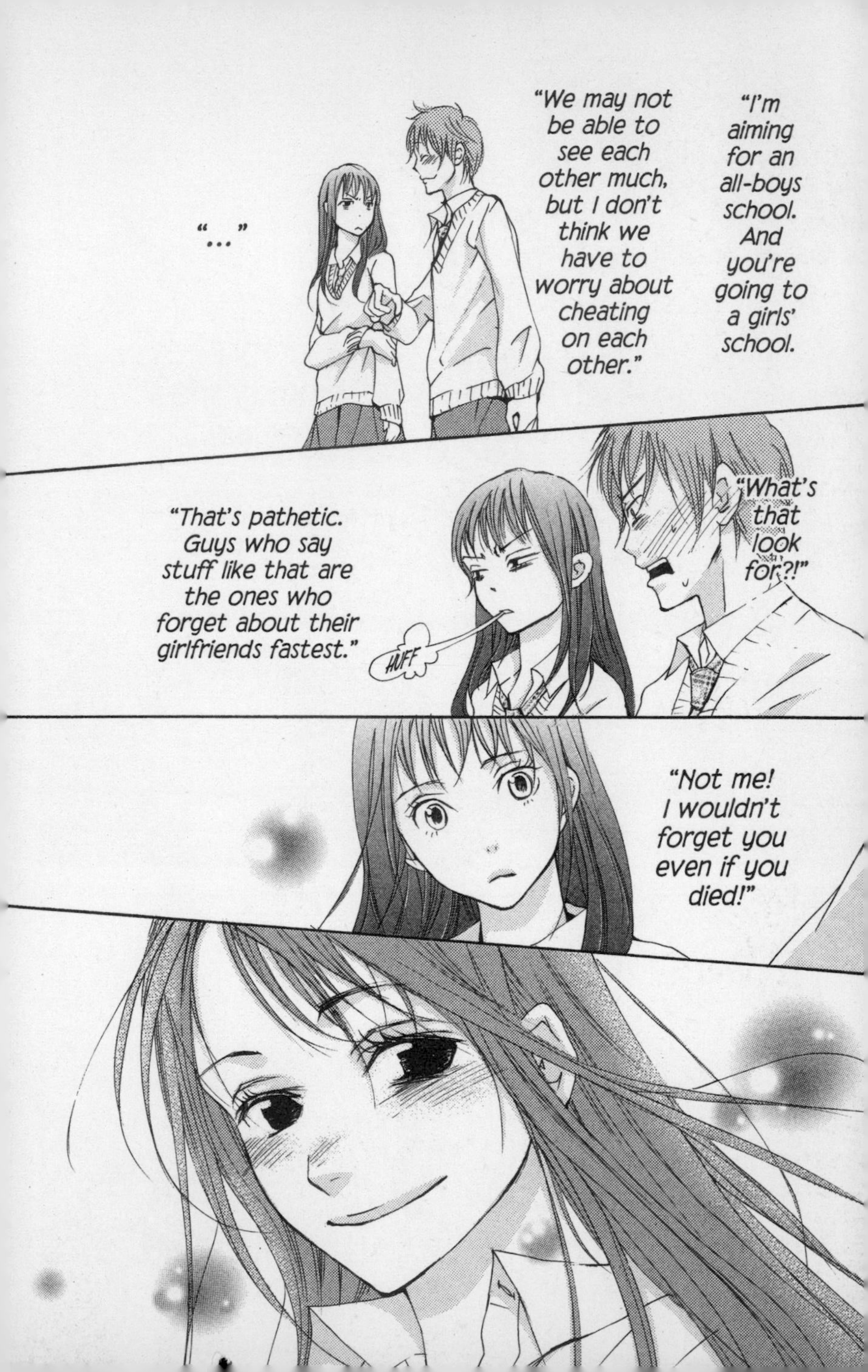
"I'm aiming for an all-boys school. And you're going to a girls' school.
"We may not be able to see each other much, but I don't think we have to worry about cheating on each other."
"..."
"What's that look for?!"
"That's pathetic. Guys who say stuff like that are the ones who forget about their girlfriends fastest."
HUFF
"Not me! I wouldn't forget you even if you died!"

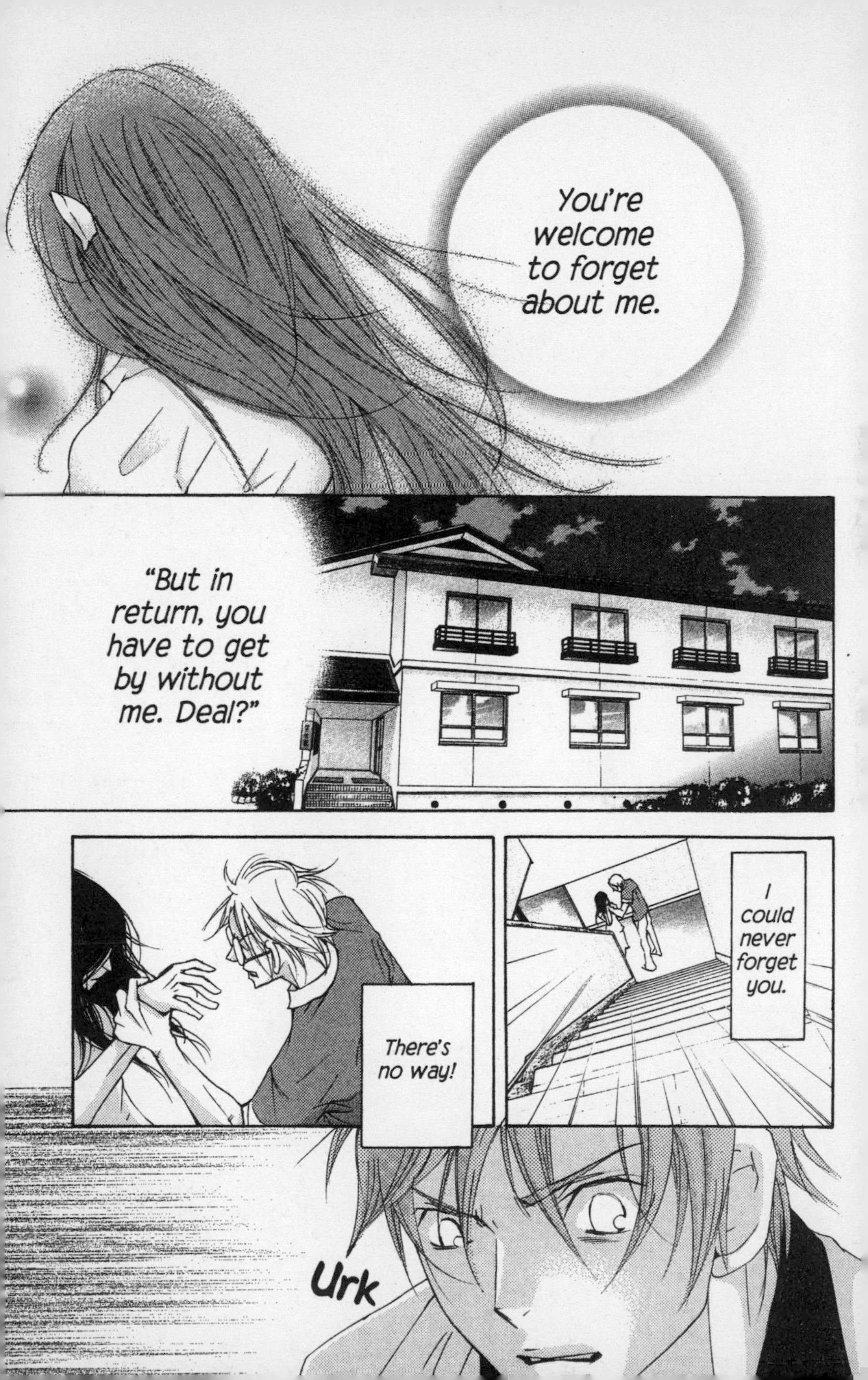
You're welcome to forget about me.
"But in return, you have to get by without me. Deal?"
I could never forget you.
There's no way!
Urk

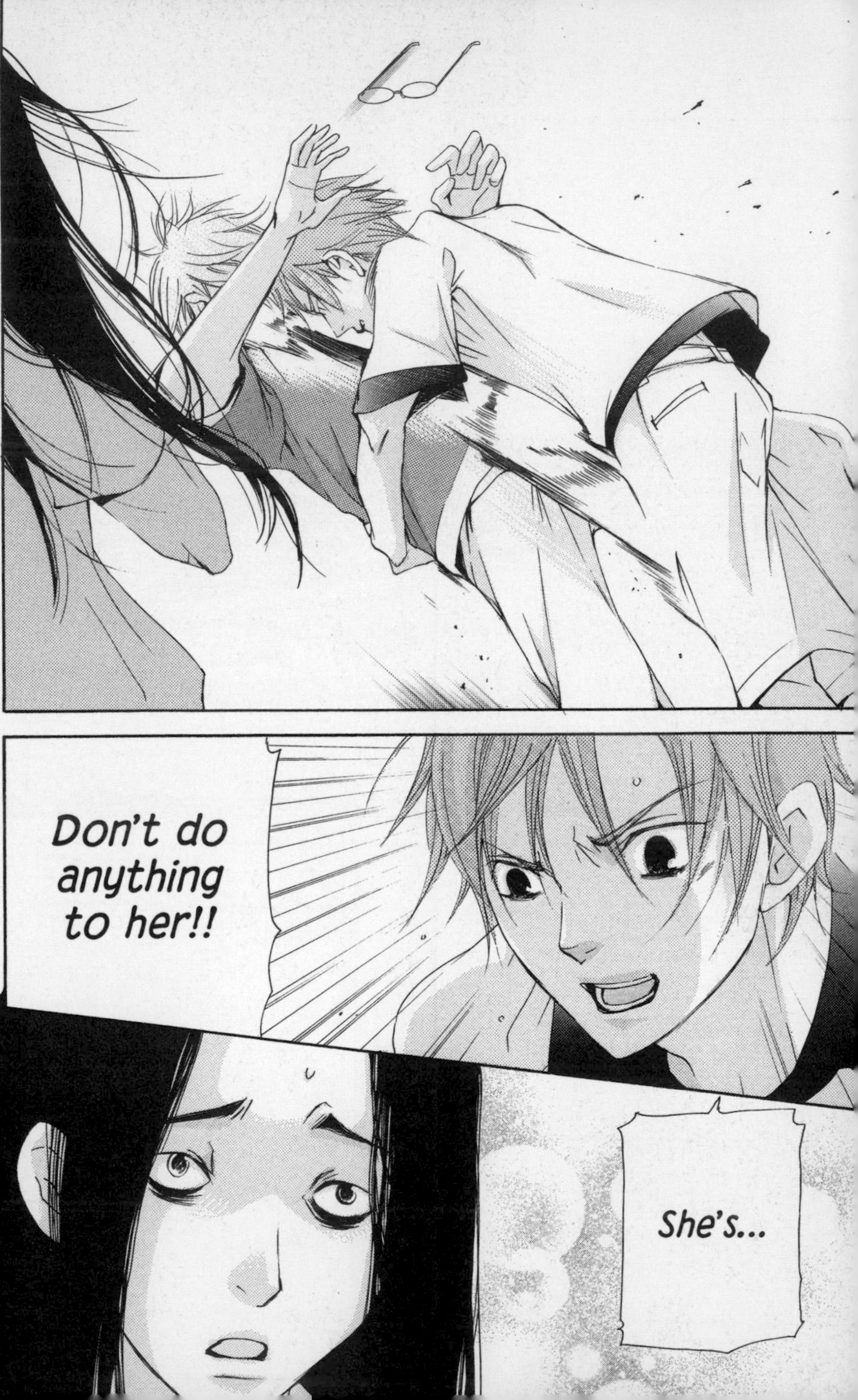
Don't do anything to her!!
She's...

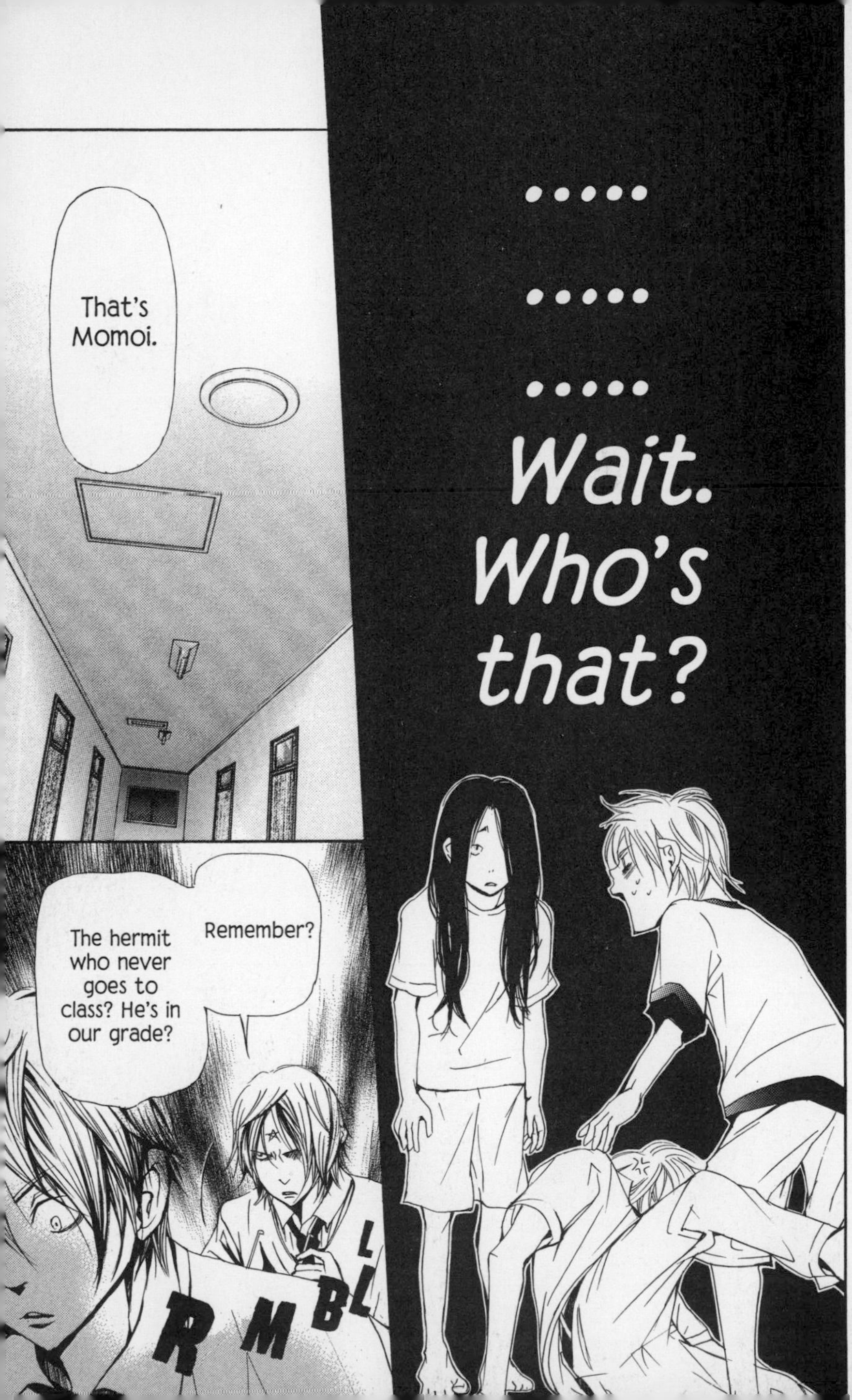
.....
.....
.....
Wait. Who's that?
That's Momoi.
Remember?
The hermit who never goes to class? He's in our grade?
RMBLL

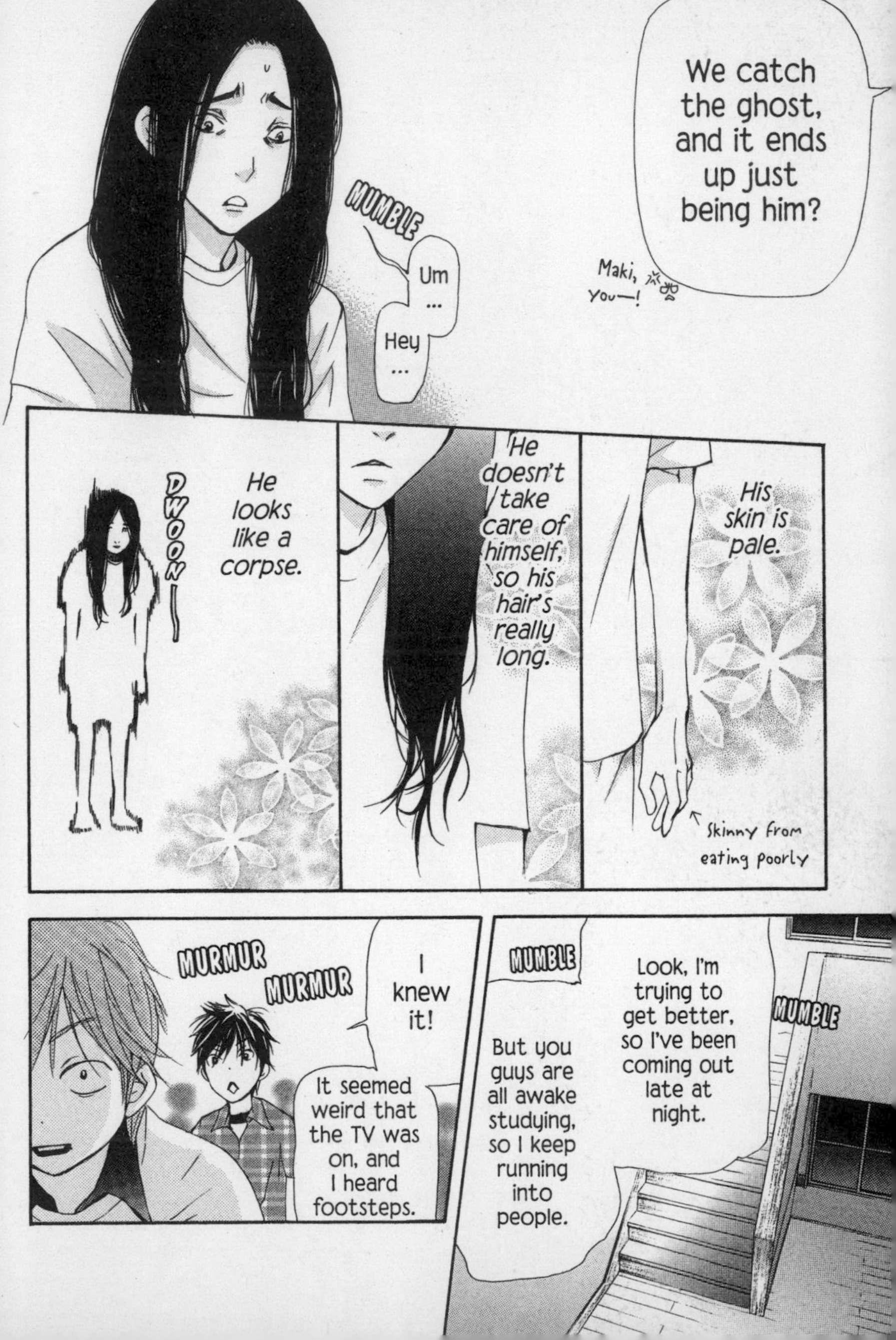
We catch the ghost, and it ends up just being him?
Maki, you—!
MUMBLE
Um ...
Hey ...
His skin is pale.
Skinny from eating poorly
He doesn't take care of himself, so his hair's really long.
He looks like a corpse.
DWOON
MUMBLE
Look, I'm trying to get better, so I've been coming out late at night.
MUMBLE
But you guys are all awake studying, so I keep running into people.
I knew it!
It seemed weird that the TV was on, and I heard footsteps.
MURMUR
MURMUR

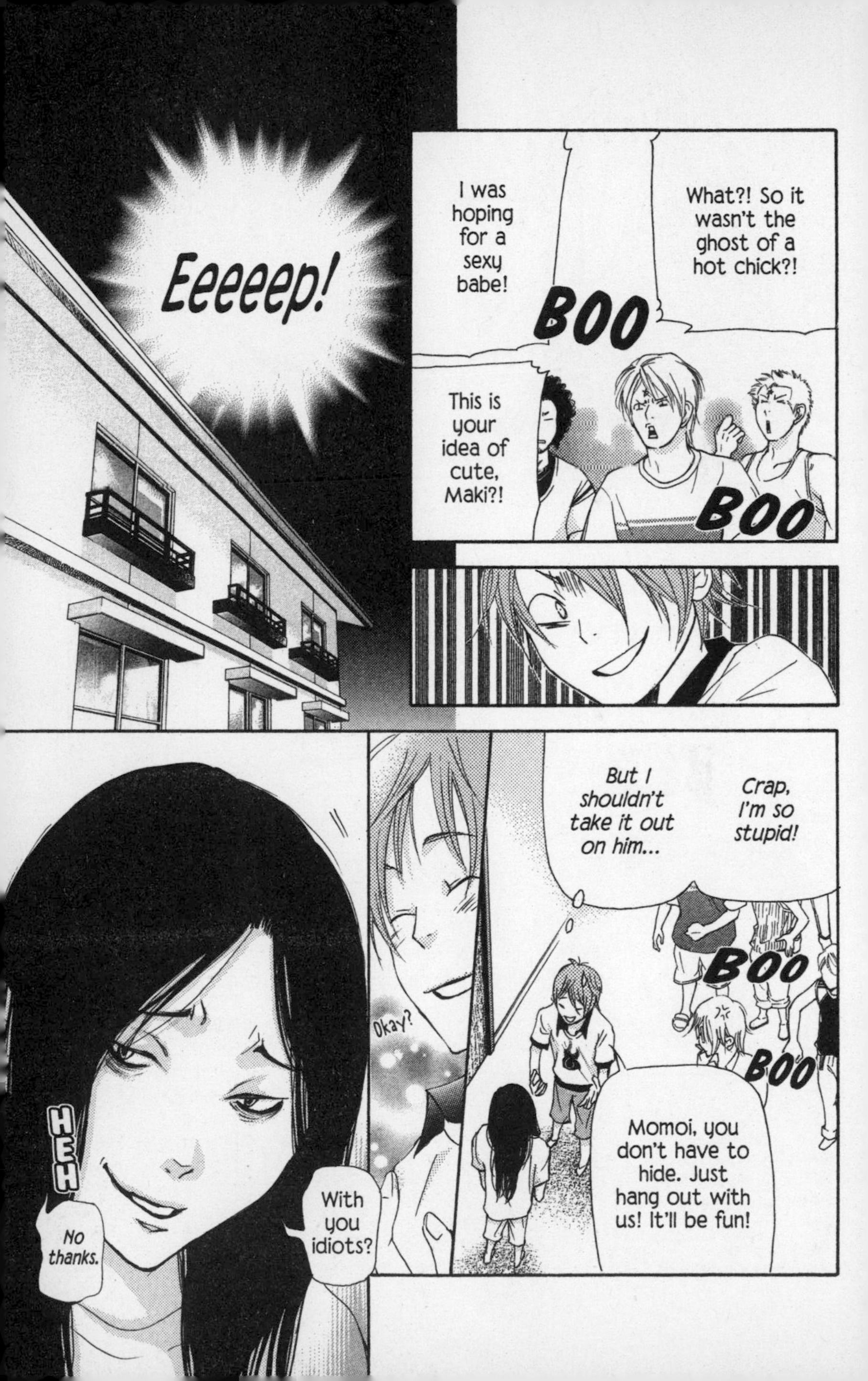
What?! So it wasn't the ghost of a hot chick?!
I was hoping for a sexy babe!
BOO
This is your idea of cute, Maki?!
BOO
Eeeeep!
Crap, I'm so stupid!
But I shouldn't take it out on him...
BOO
BOO
Momoi, you don't have to hide. Just hang out with us! It'll be fun!
Okay?
With you idiots?
HEH
No thanks.

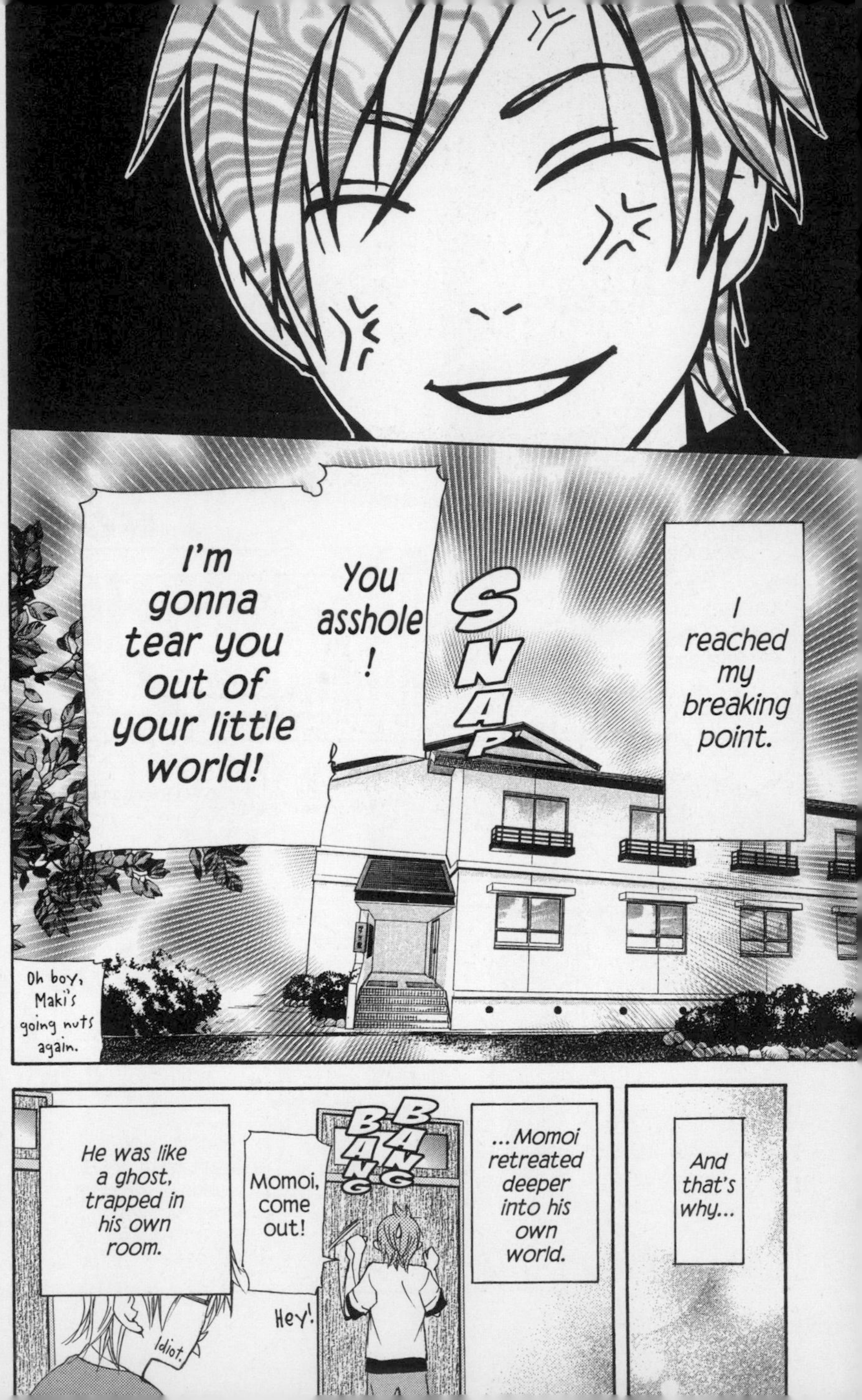
I reached my breaking point.
SNAP
You asshole!
I'm gonna tear you out of your little world!
Oh boy, Maki's going nuts again.
And that's why...
...Momoi retreated deeper into his own world.
BANG BANG
Momoi, come out!
Hey!
He was like a ghost, trapped in his own room.
Idiot.

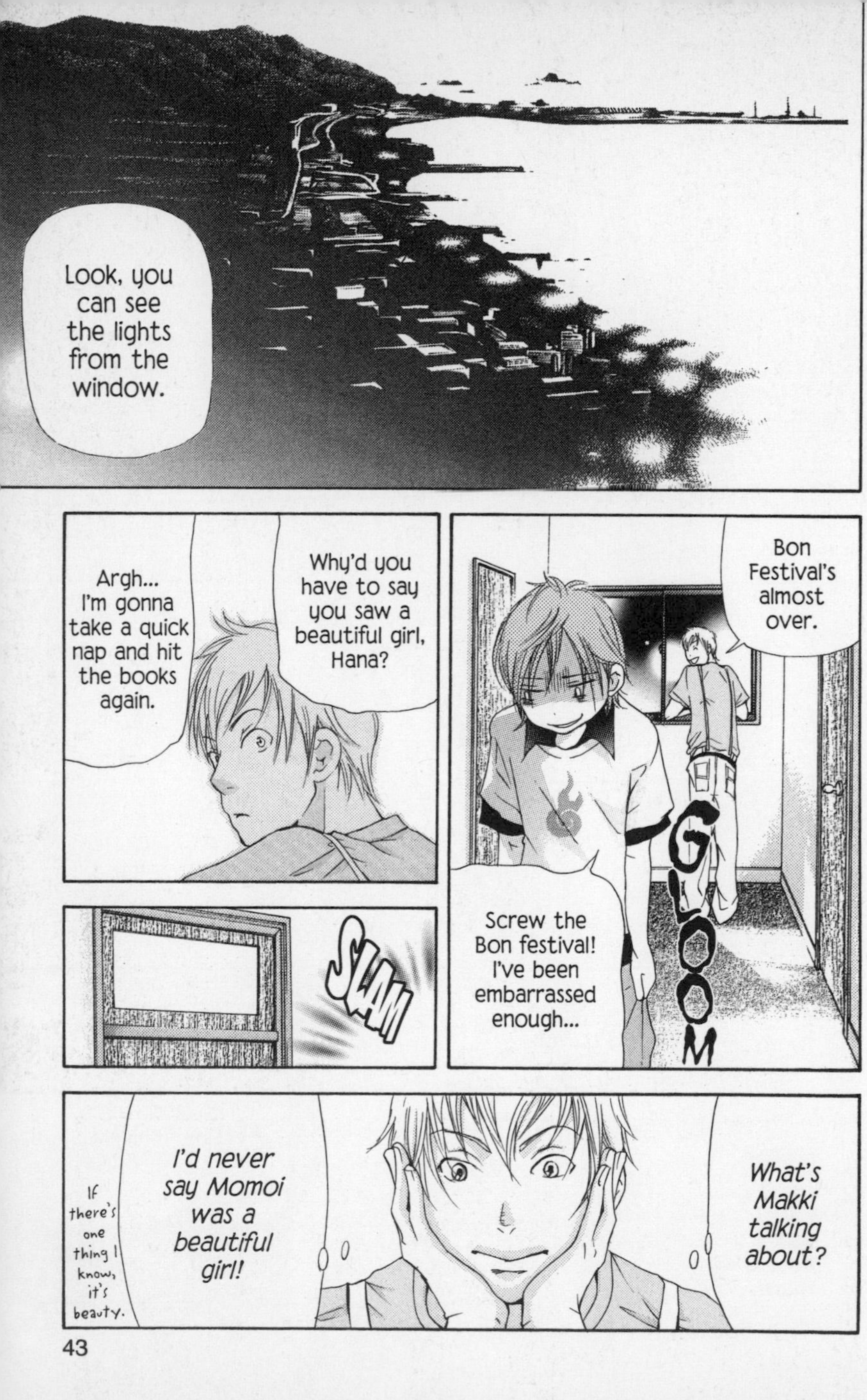
Look, you can see the lights from the window.
Bon Festival's almost over.
GLOOM
Screw the Bon festival! I've been embarrassed enough...
Why'd you have to say you saw a beautiful girl, Hana?
Argh... I'm gonna take a quick nap and hit the books again.
SLAM
What's Makki talking about?
I'd never say Momoi was a beautiful girl!
If there's one thing I know, it's beauty.

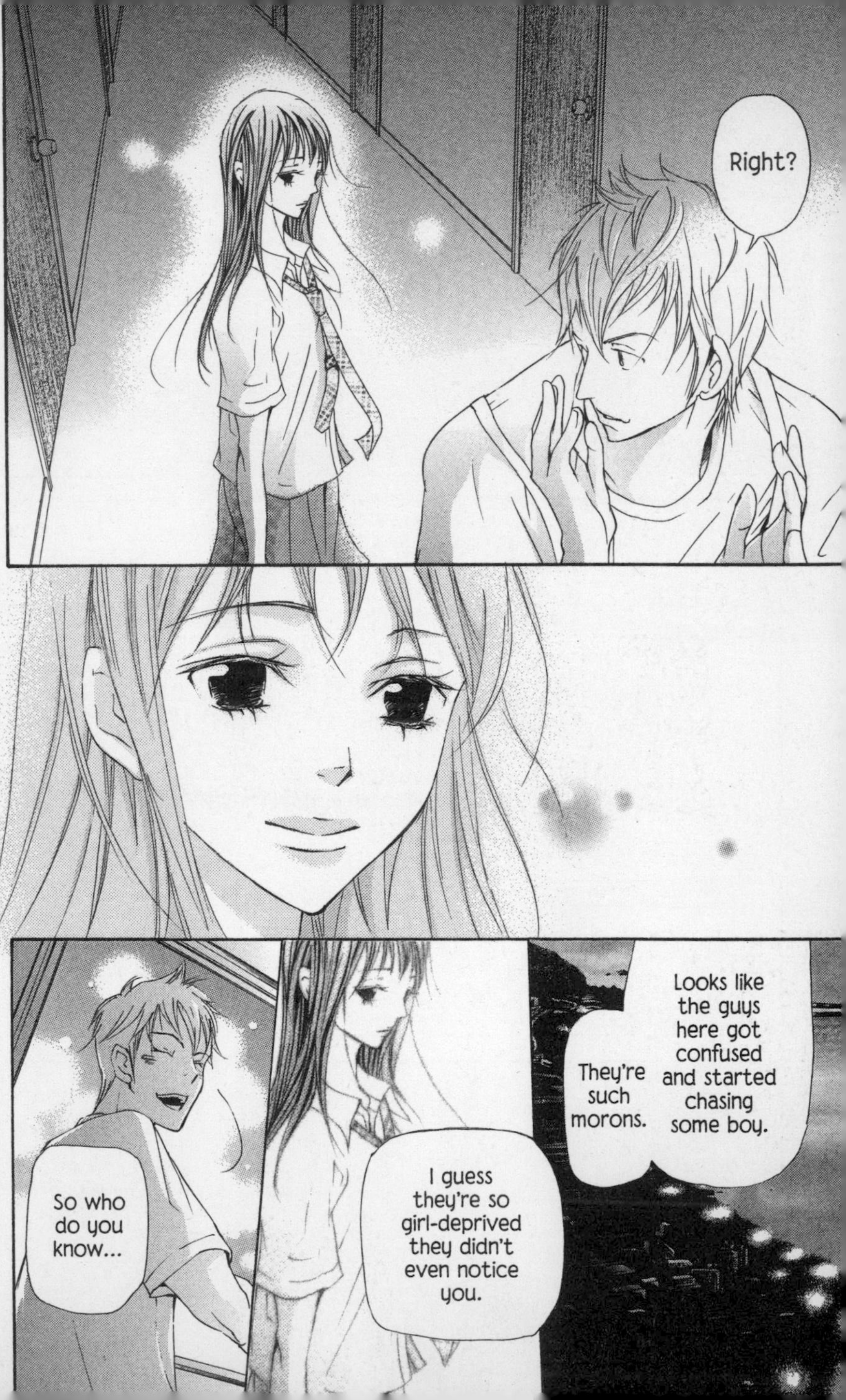
Right?
Looks like the guys here got confused and started chasing some boy.
They're such morons.
I guess they're so girl-deprived they didn't even notice you.
So who do you know...

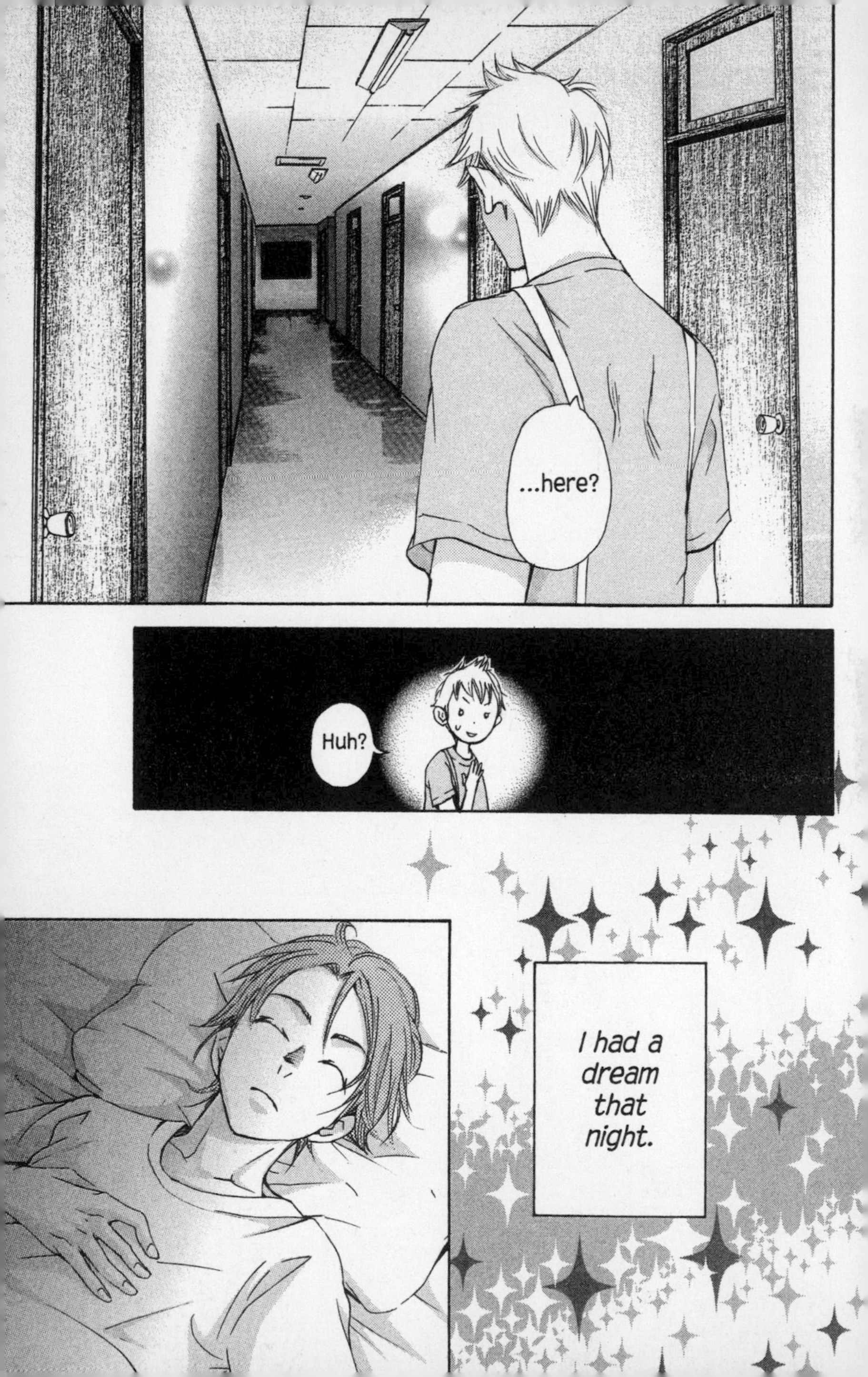
...here?
Huh?
I had a dream that night.

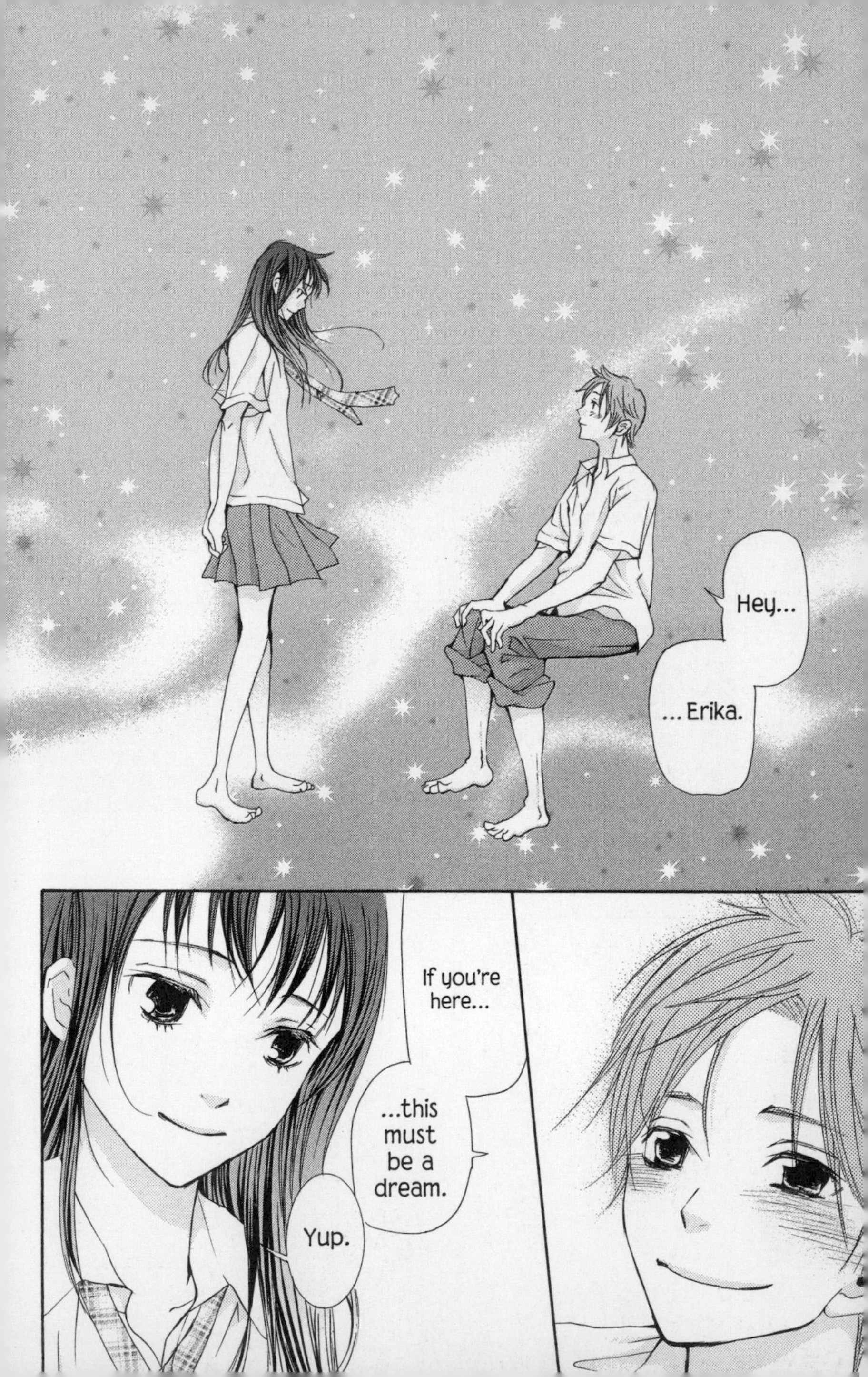
Hey...
... Erika.
If you're here...
...this must be a dream.
Yup.

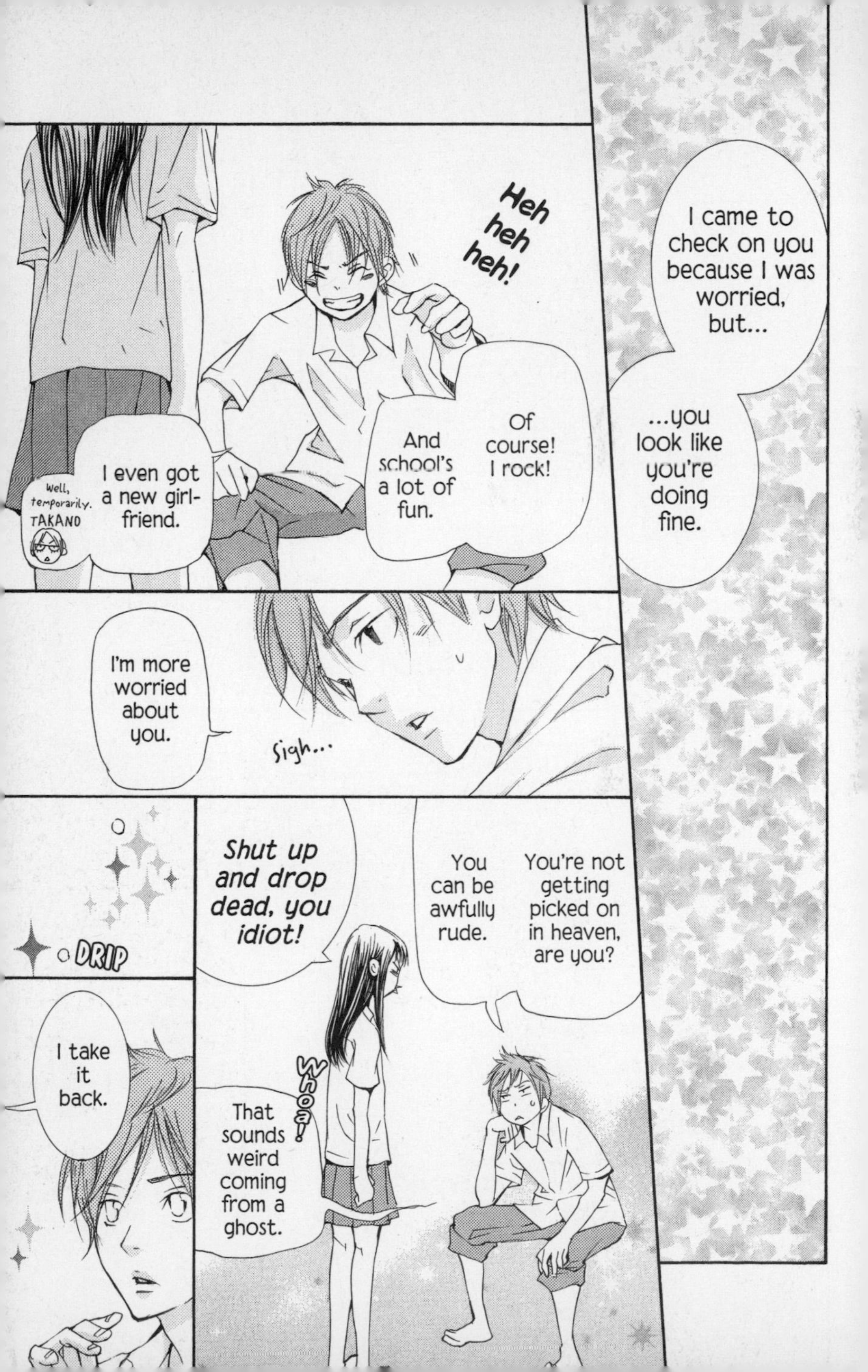
I came to check on you because I was worried, but...
...you look like you're doing fine.
Of course! I rock!
And school's a lot of fun.
Heh heh heh!
I even got a new girl-friend.
Well, temporarily. TAKANO
I'm more worried about you.
Sigh...
You're not getting picked on in heaven, are you?
You can be awfully rude.
Shut up and drop dead, you idiot!
Whoa!
That sounds weird coming from a ghost.
DRIP
I take it back.

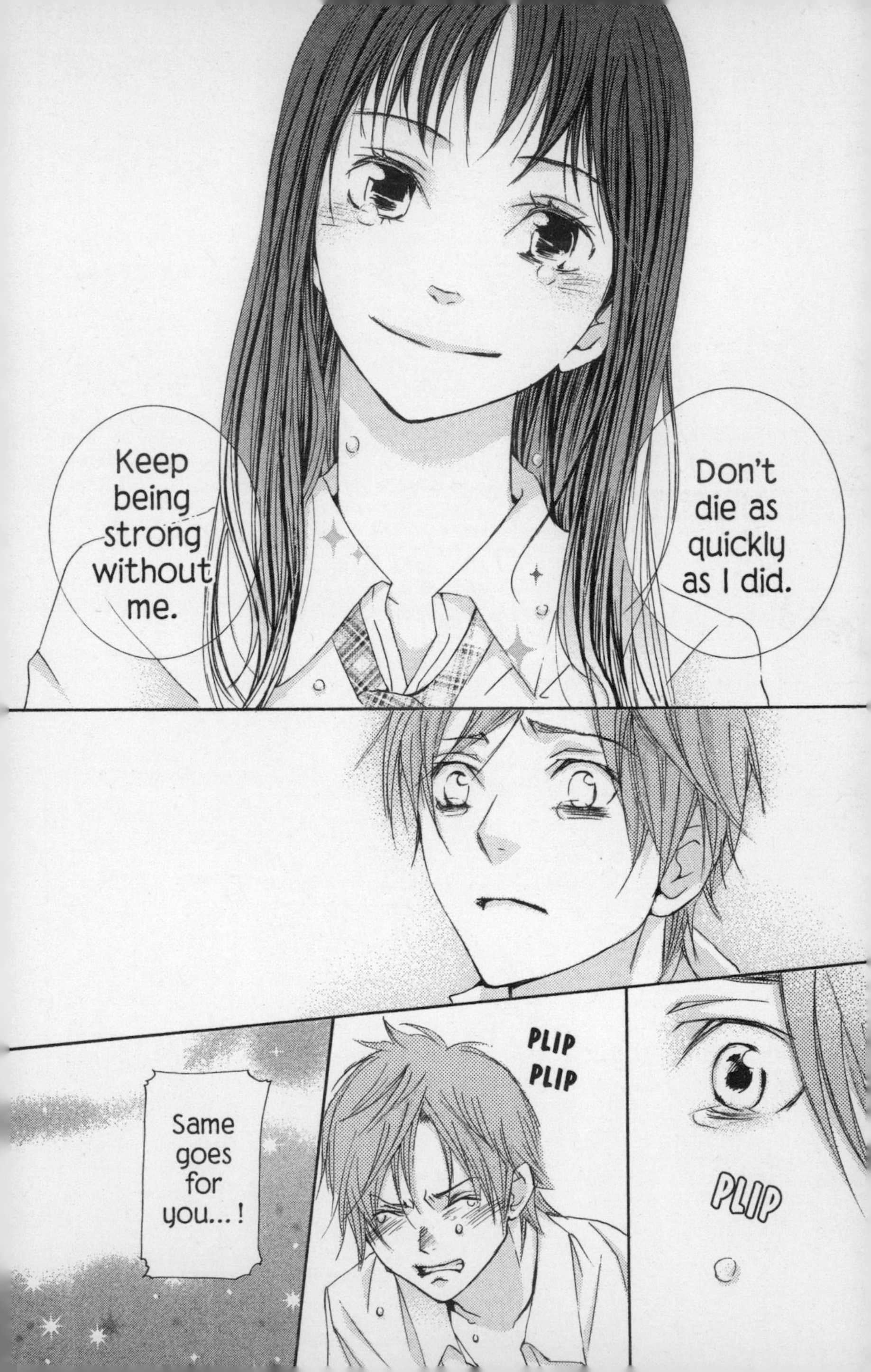
Don't die as quickly as I did.
Keep being strong without me.
PLIP
PLIP PLIP
Same goes for you...!

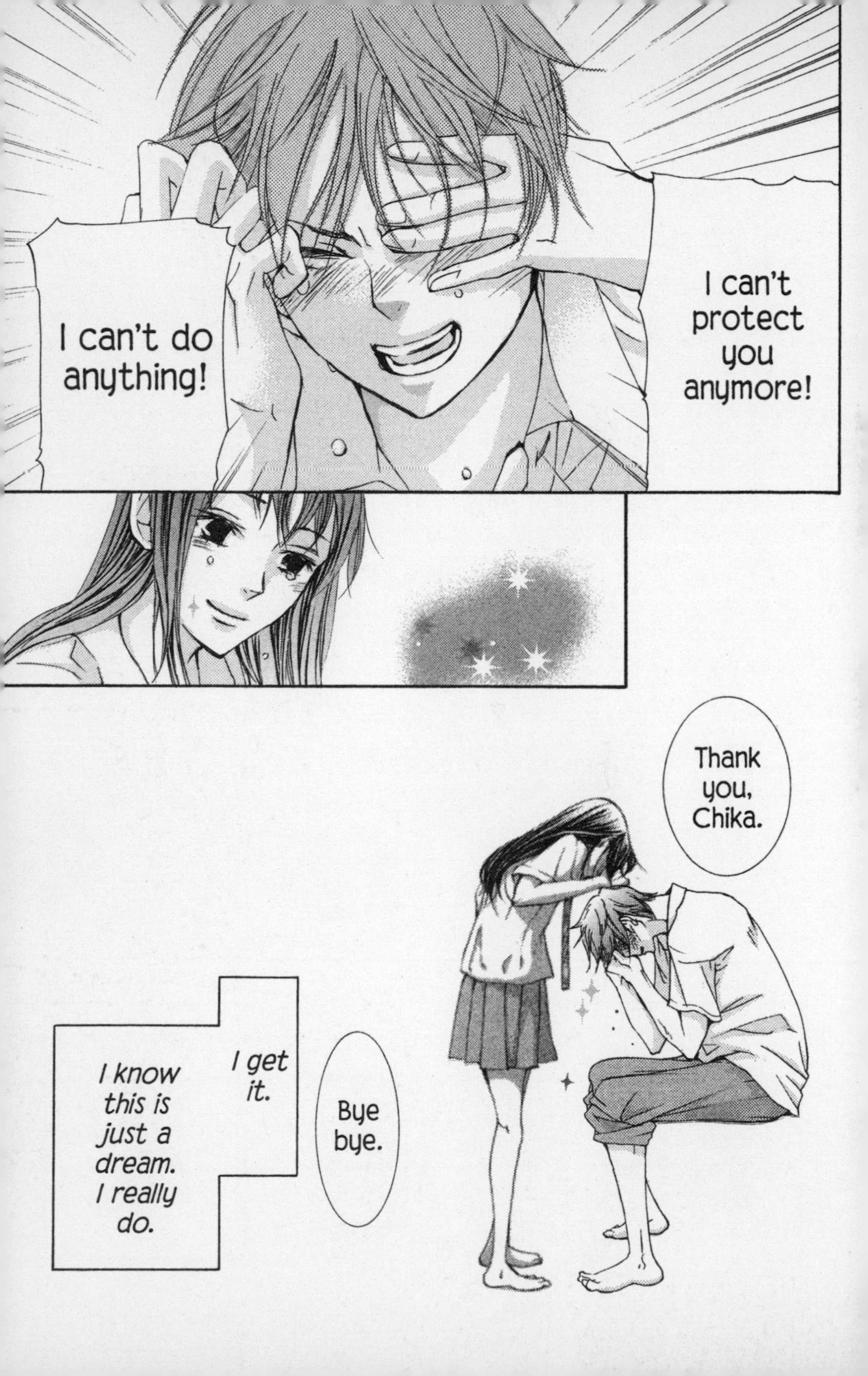
I can't protect you anymore!
I can't do anything!
Thank you, Chika.
Bye bye.
I get it.
I know this is just a dream. I really do.

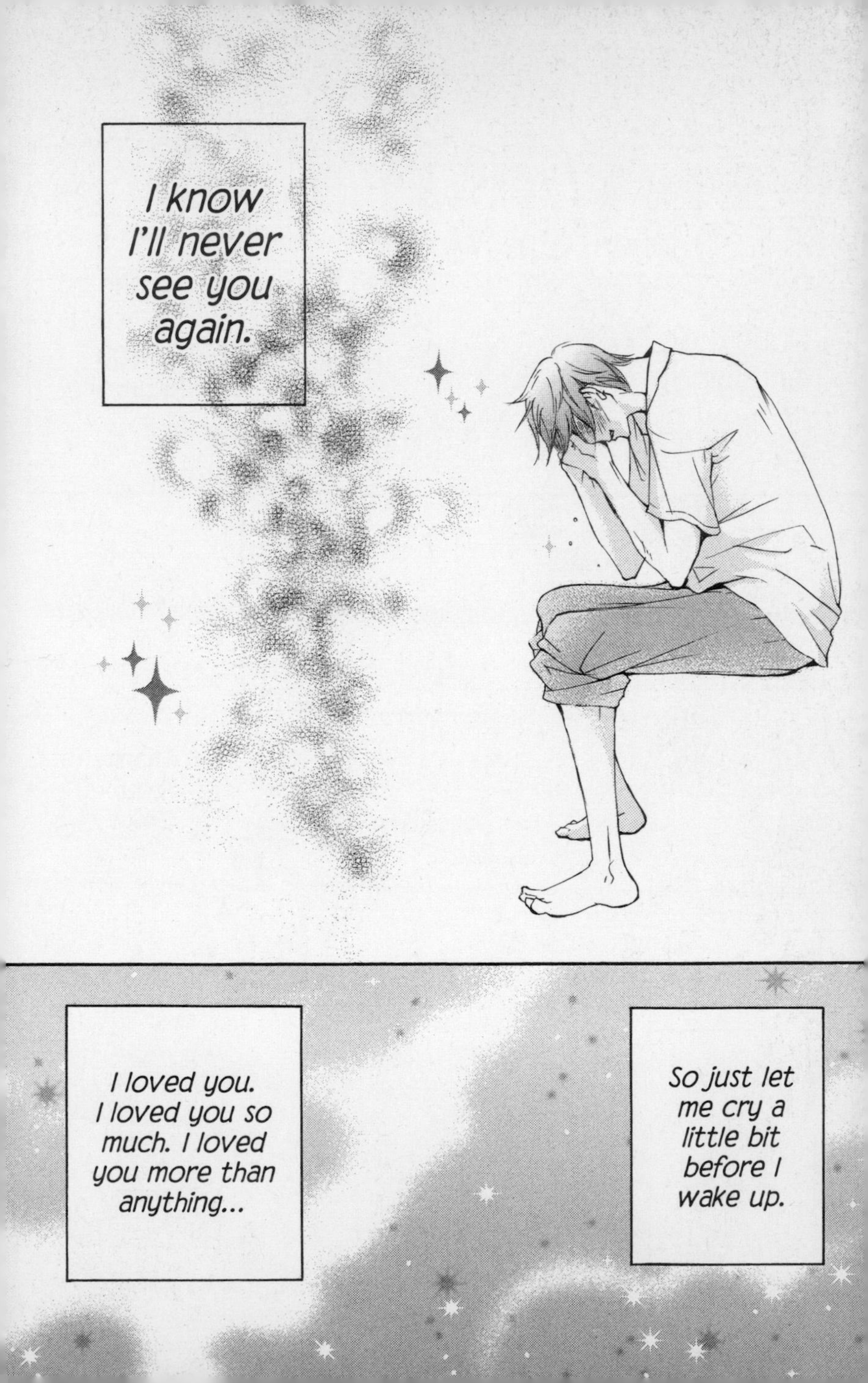
I know I'll never see you again.
So just let me cry a little bit before I wake up.
I loved you. I loved you so much. I loved you more than anything...

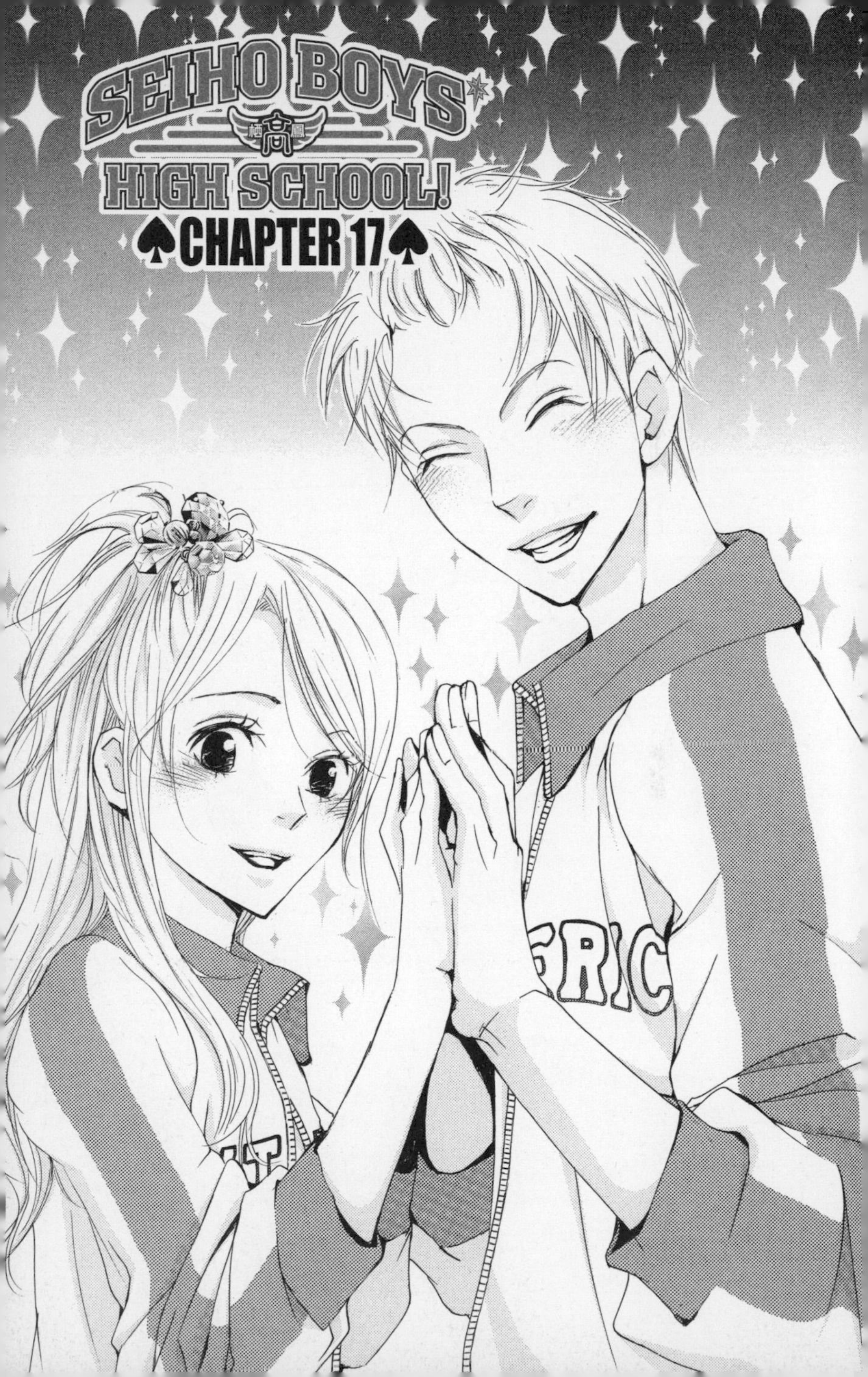
SEIHO BOYS' HIGH SCHOOL!
CHAPTER 17
FRIC

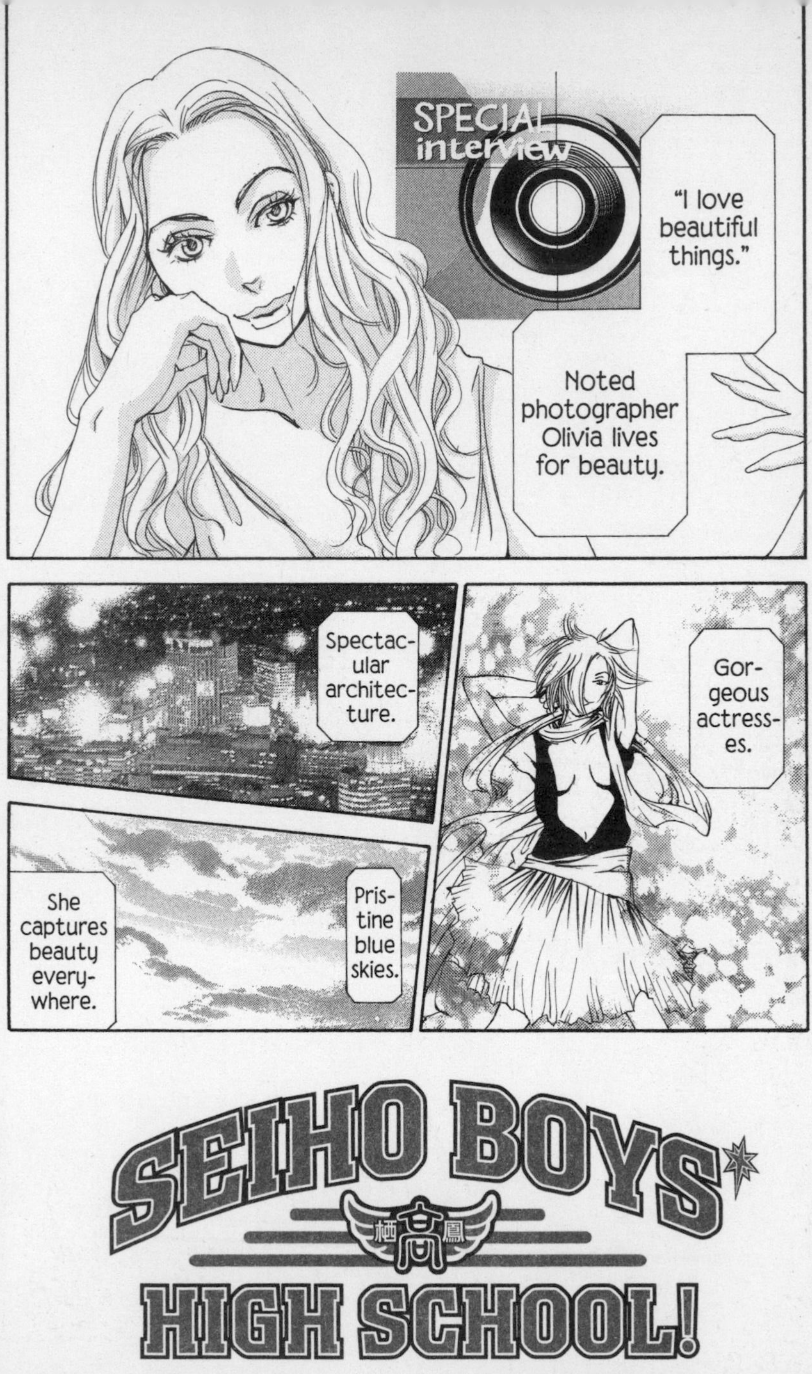
SPECIAL interview
"I love beautiful things."
Noted photographer Olivia lives for beauty.
Gorgeous actresses.
Spectacular architecture.
Pristine blue skies.
She captures beauty everywhere.

# SEIHO BOYS HIGH SCHOOL!

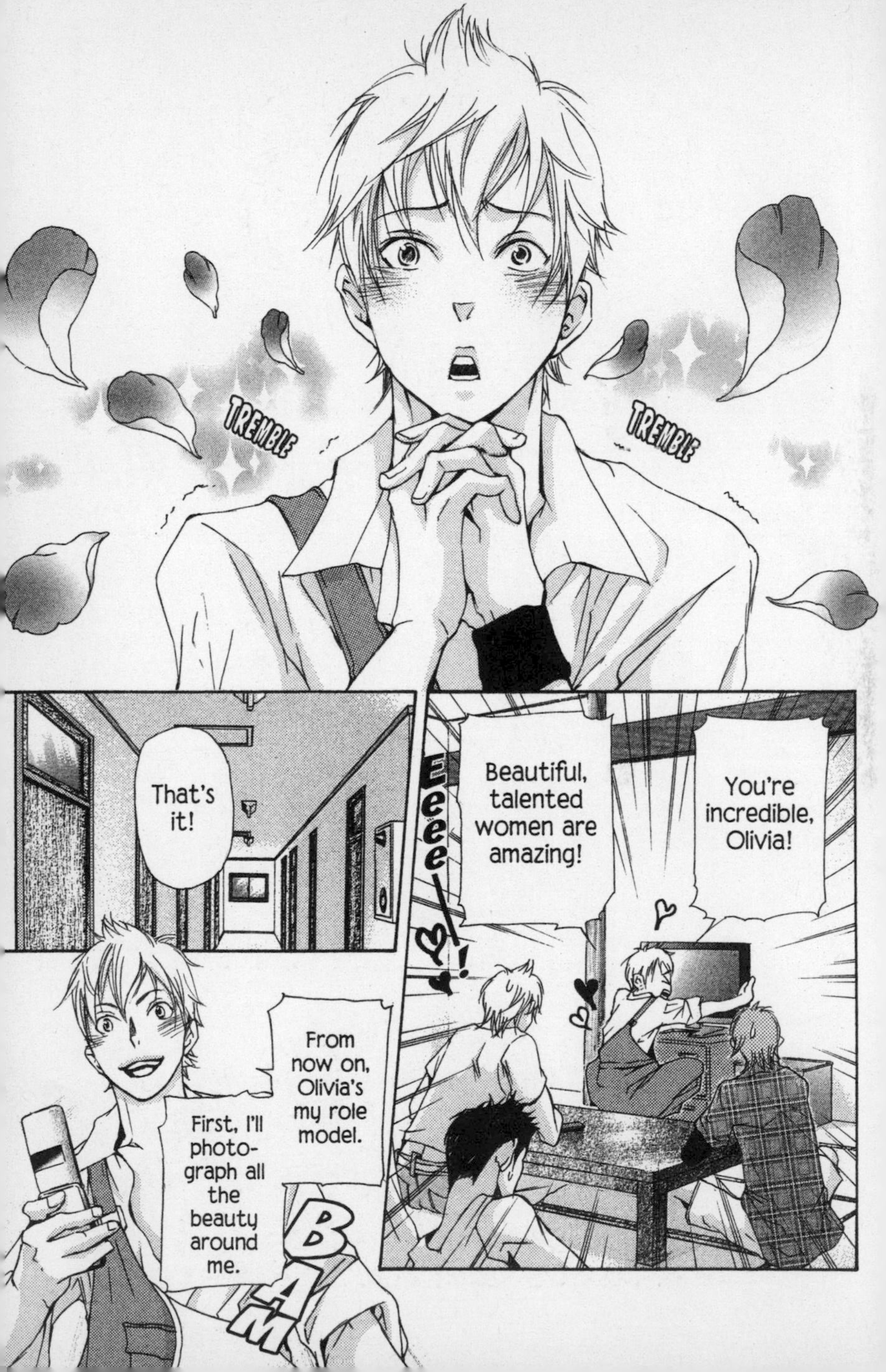
TREMBLE
TREMBLE
You're incredible, Olivia!
Beautiful, talented women are amazing!
Eeeee—!
That's it!
From now on, Olivia's my role model.
First, I'll photograph all the beauty around me.
BAM

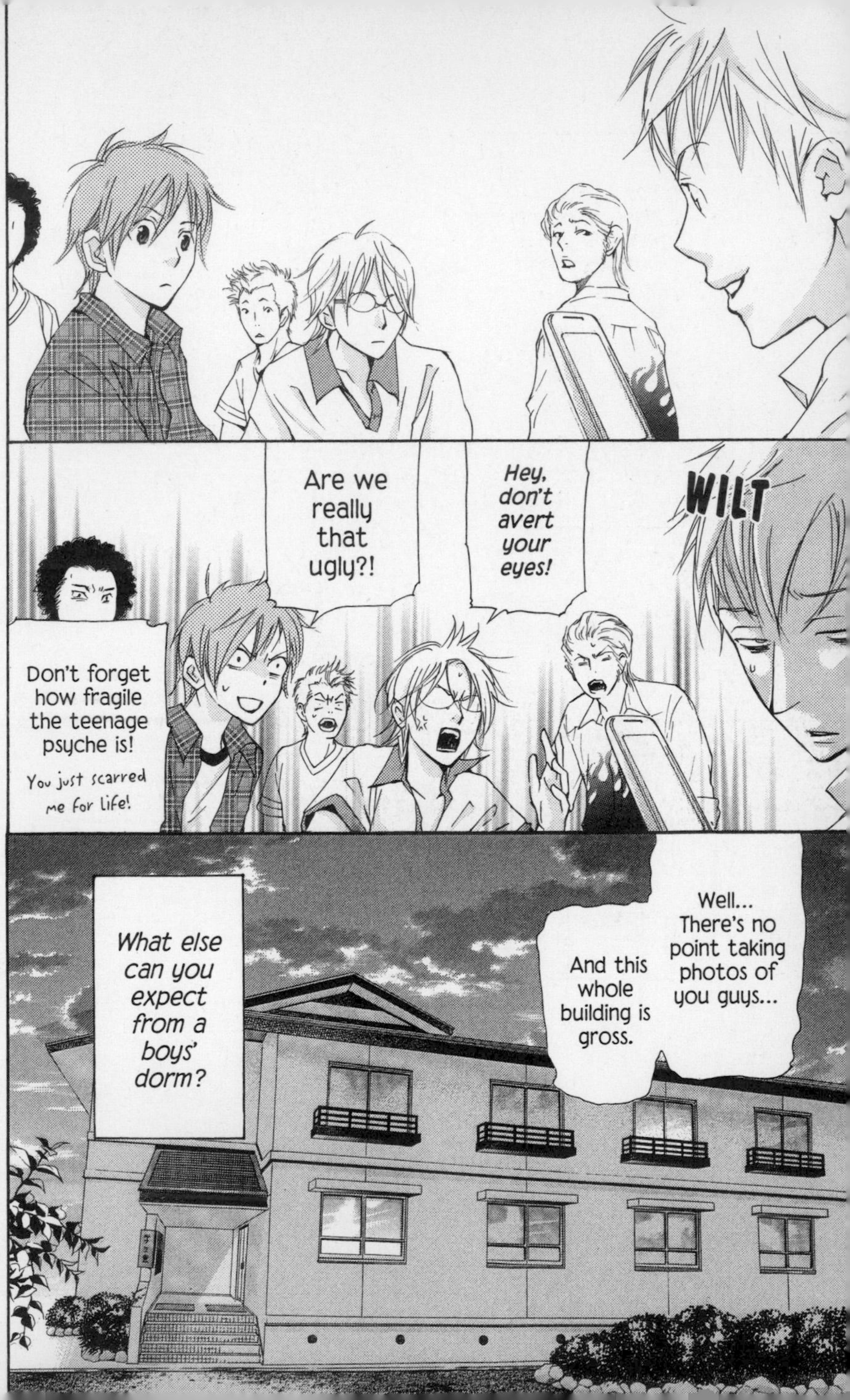
WILT
Hey, don't avert your eyes!
Are we really that ugly?!
Don't forget how fragile the teenage psyche is!
You just scarred me for life!
Well... There's no point taking photos of you guys...
And this whole building is gross.
What else can you expect from a boys' dorm?

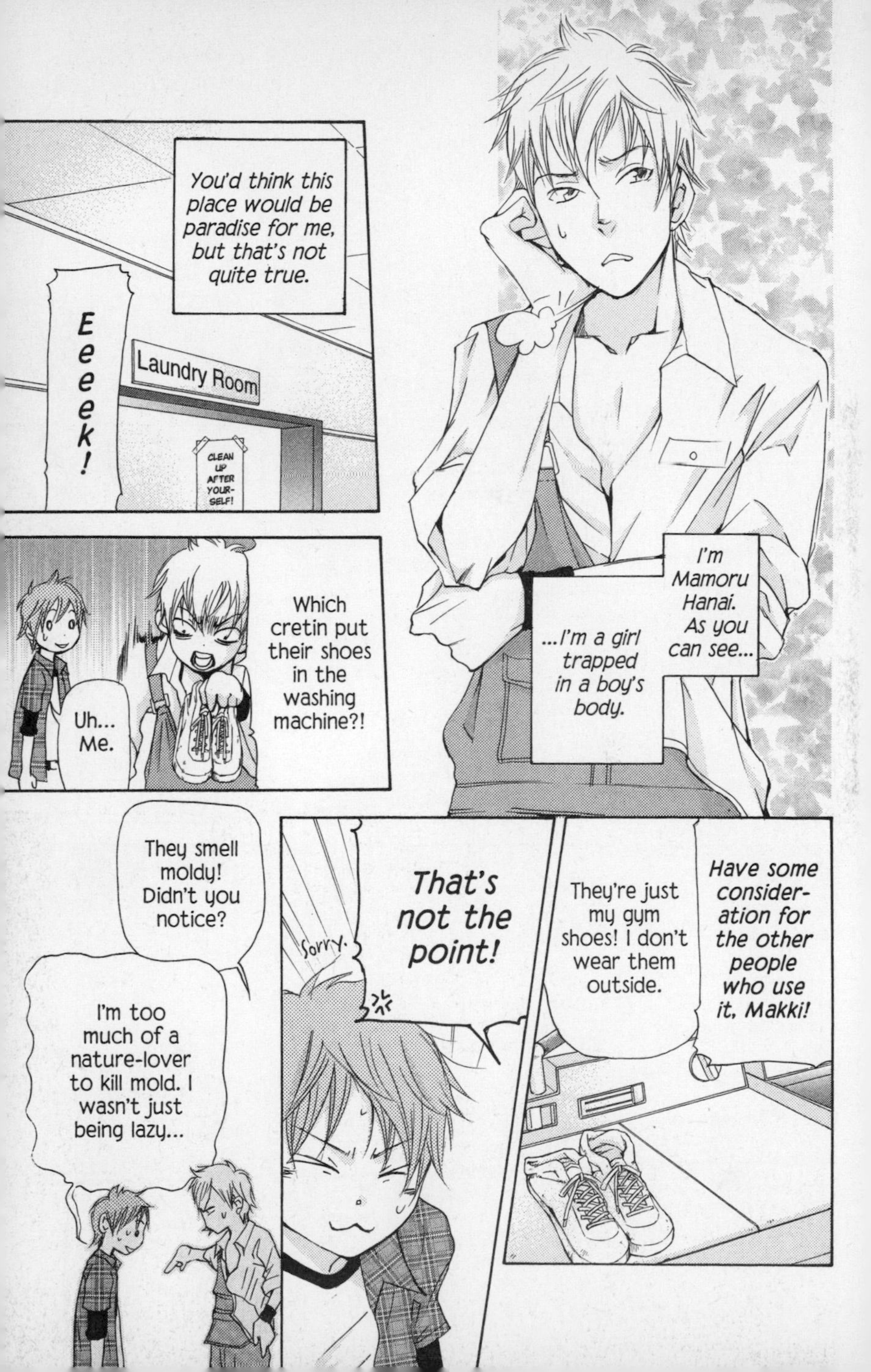
I'm Mamoru Hanai. As you can see...
...I'm a girl trapped in a boy's body.
You'd think this place would be paradise for me, but that's not quite true.
Eeeek!
Laundry Room
CLEAN UP AFTER YOURSELF!
Which cretin put their shoes in the washing machine?!
Uh... Me.
Have some consider-ation for the other people who use it, Makki!
They're just my gym shoes! I don't wear them outside.
That's not the point!
Sorry.
They smell moldy! Didn't you notice?
I'm too much of a nature-lover to kill mold. I wasn't just being lazy...

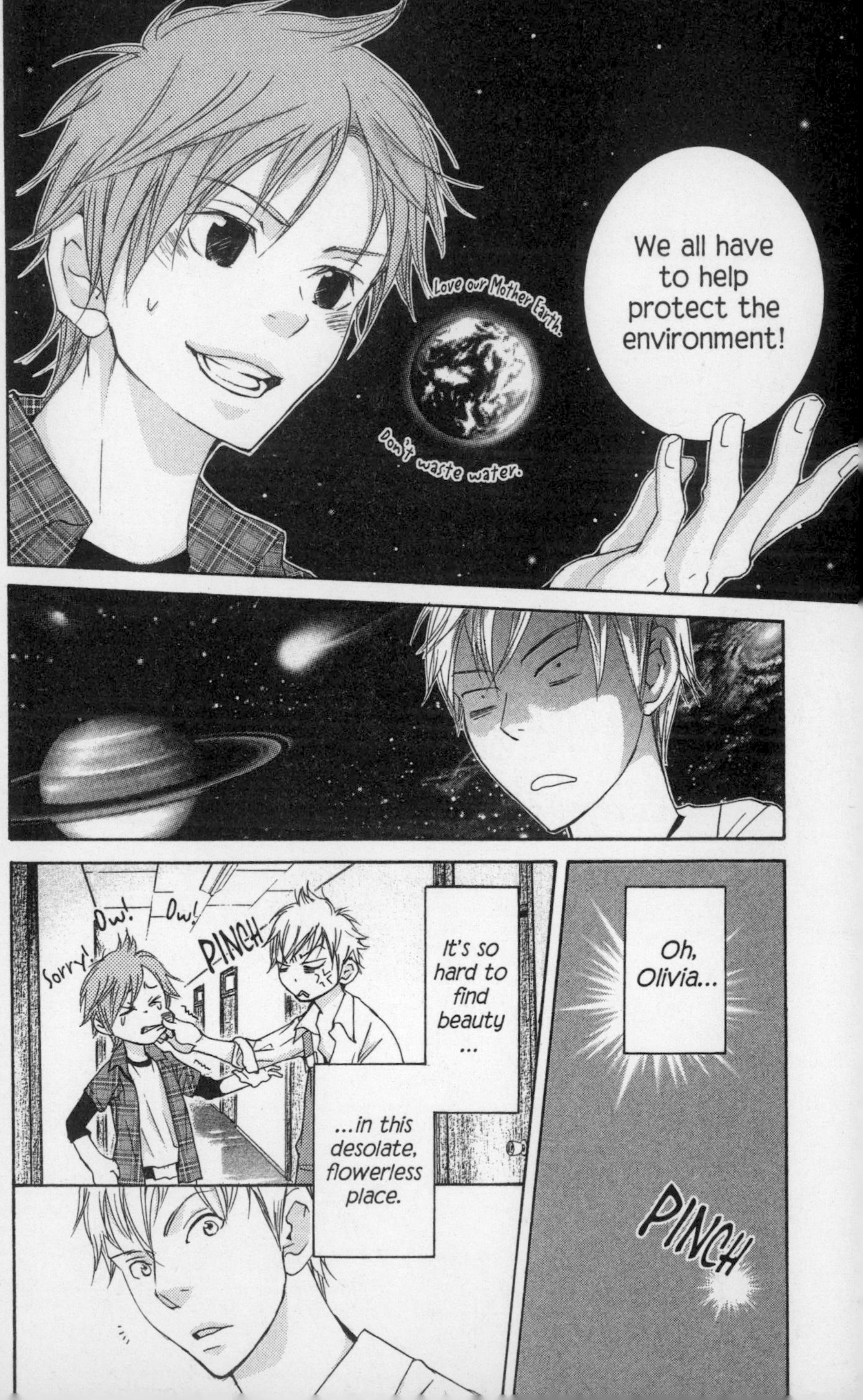
We all have to help protect the environment!
Love our Mother Earth.
Don't waste water.
Oh, Olivia...
PINCH
It's so hard to find beauty ...
Ow! Ow!
PINCH
Sorry!
...in this desolate, flowerless place.

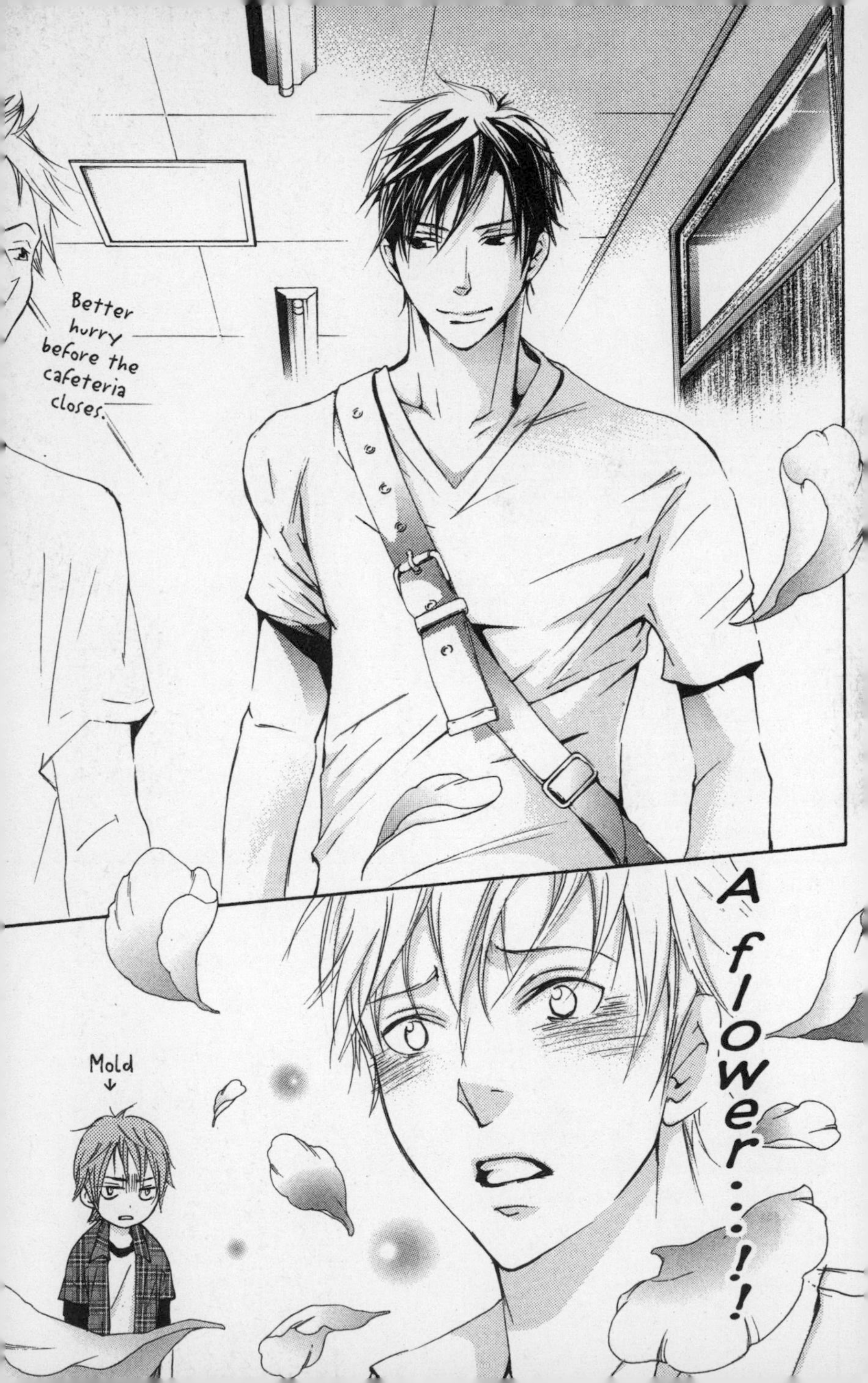
Better hurry before the cafeteria closes.
A flower...!!
Mold

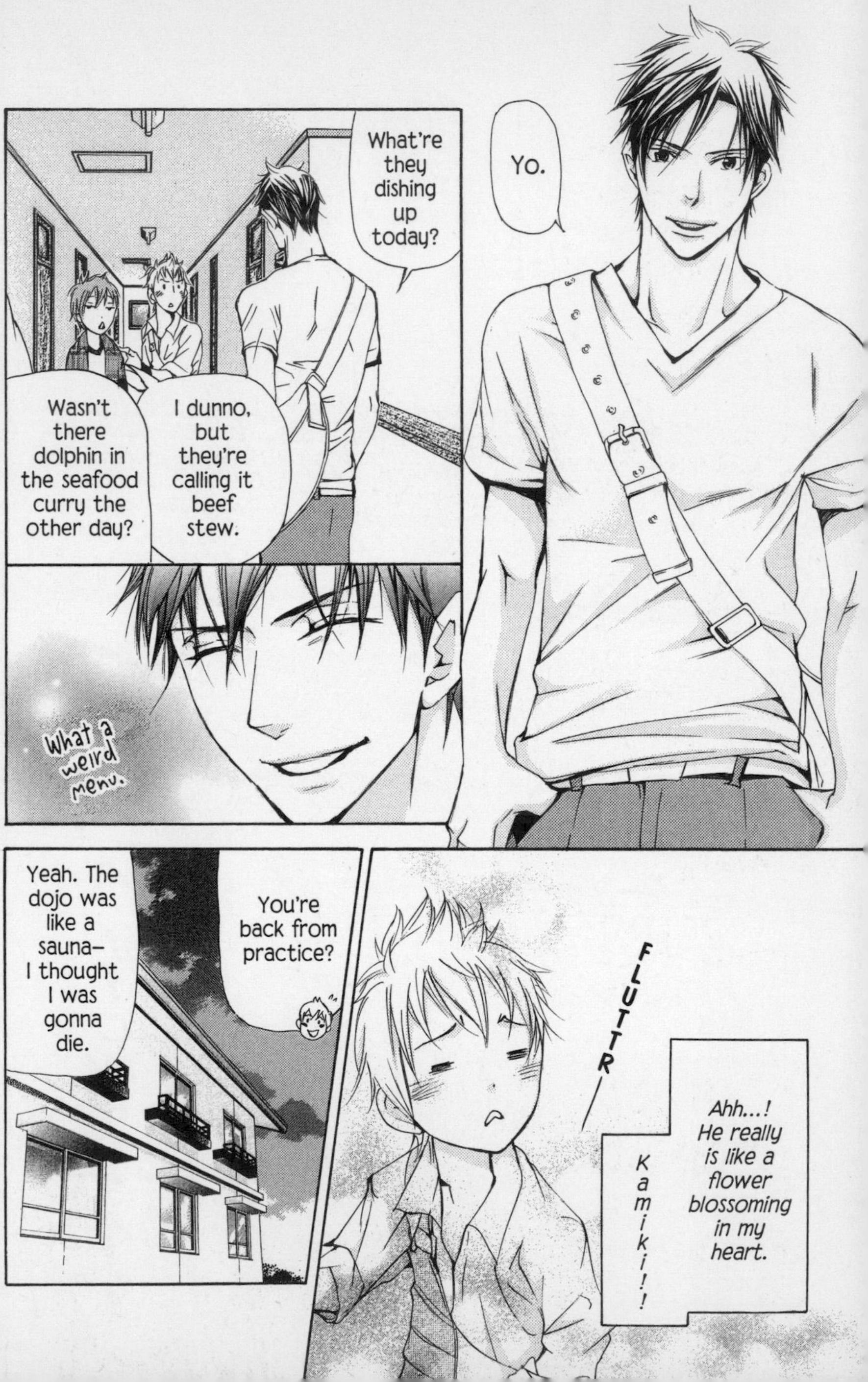
Yo.
What're they dishing up today?
I dunno, but they're calling it beef stew.
Wasn't there dolphin in the seafood curry the other day?
What a weird menu.
FLUTTR
Kamiki!!
Ahh...! He really is like a flower blossoming in my heart.
You're back from practice?
Yeah. The dojo was like a sauna— I thought I was gonna die.

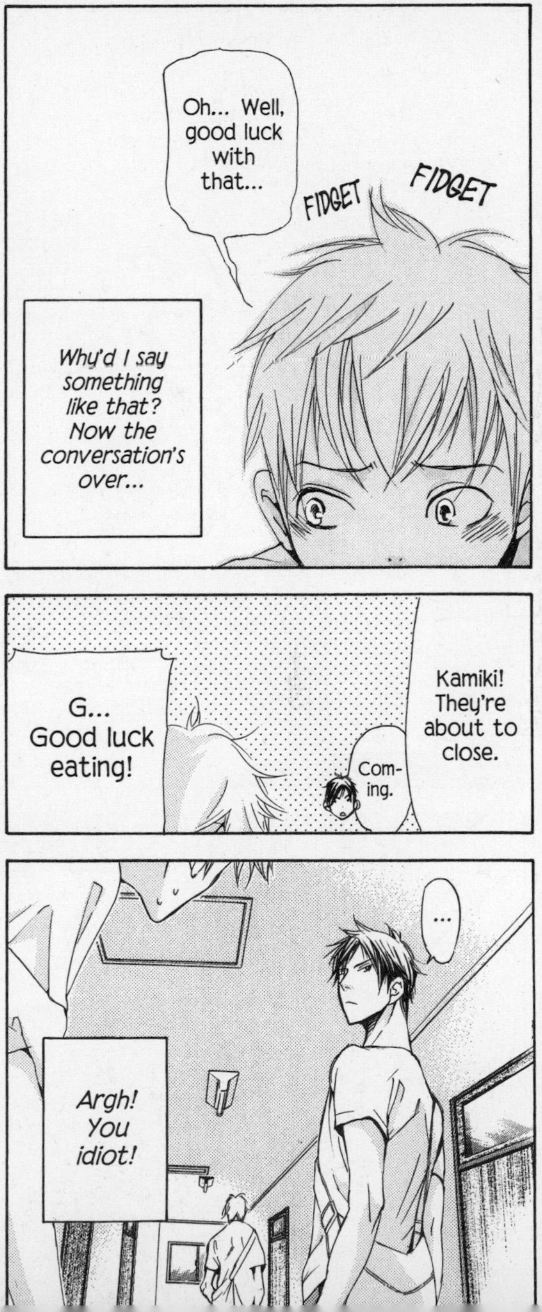
Oh... Well, good luck with that...
FIDGET
FIDGET
Why'd I say something like that? Now the conversation's over...
Kamiki! They're about to close.
Com-ing.
G... Good luck eating!
...
Argh! You idiot!

1/3 Filler Corner

A Collection of Words That Shocked Me

**Part ②**

I saw this written on the packaging of a rose hip teabag.

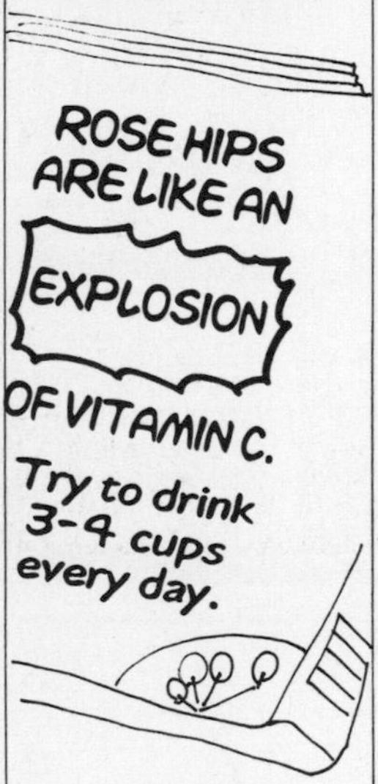
ROSE HIPS ARE LIKE AN
EXPLOSION
OF VITAMIN C.
Try to drink 3-4 cups every day.

That's impossible.

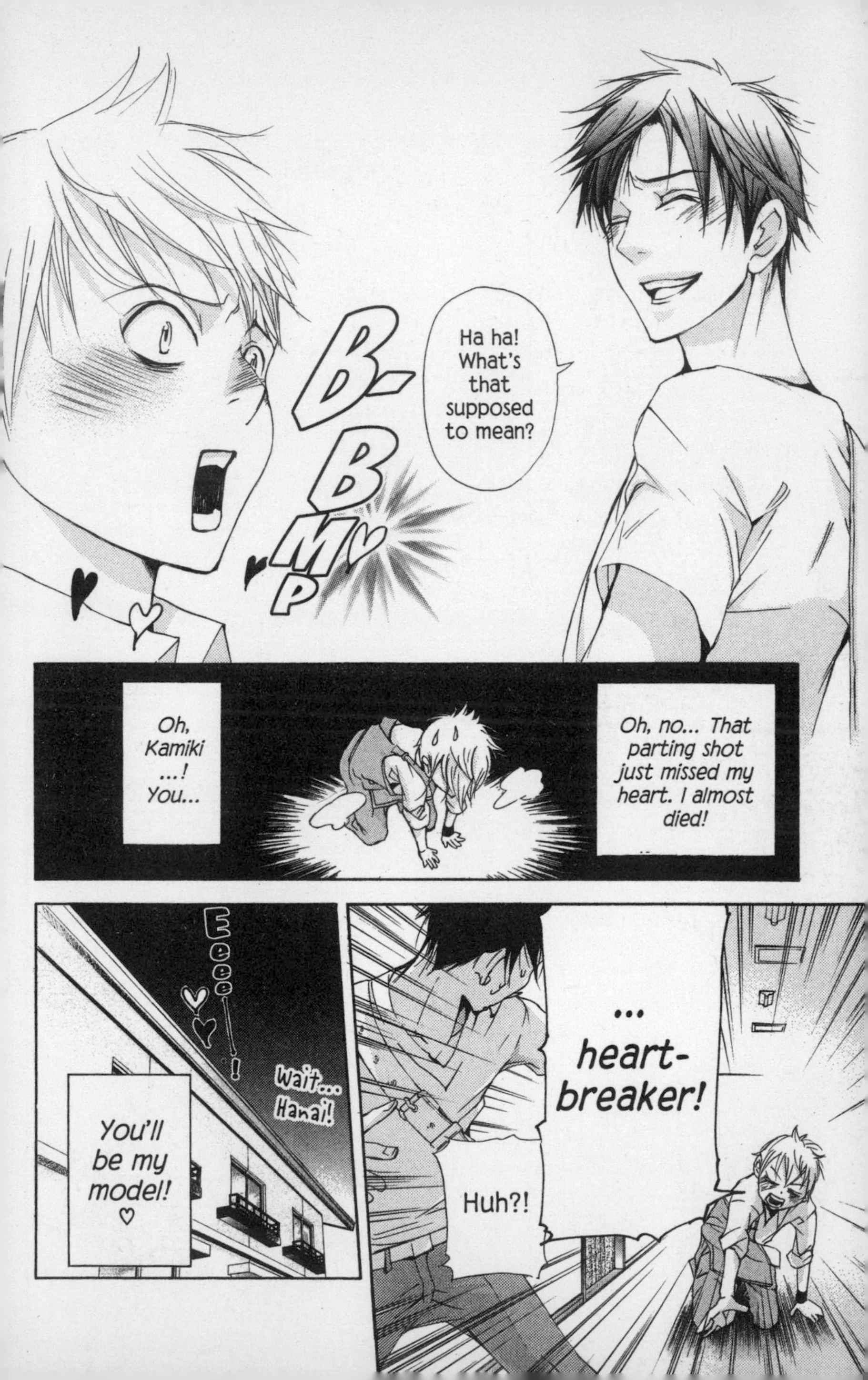
Ha ha! What's that supposed to mean?
B-B-BMP
Oh, no... That parting shot just missed my heart. I almost died!
Oh, Kamiki ...! You...
... heart-breaker!
Huh?!
Eeee—!
Wait... Hanai!
You'll be my model! ♡

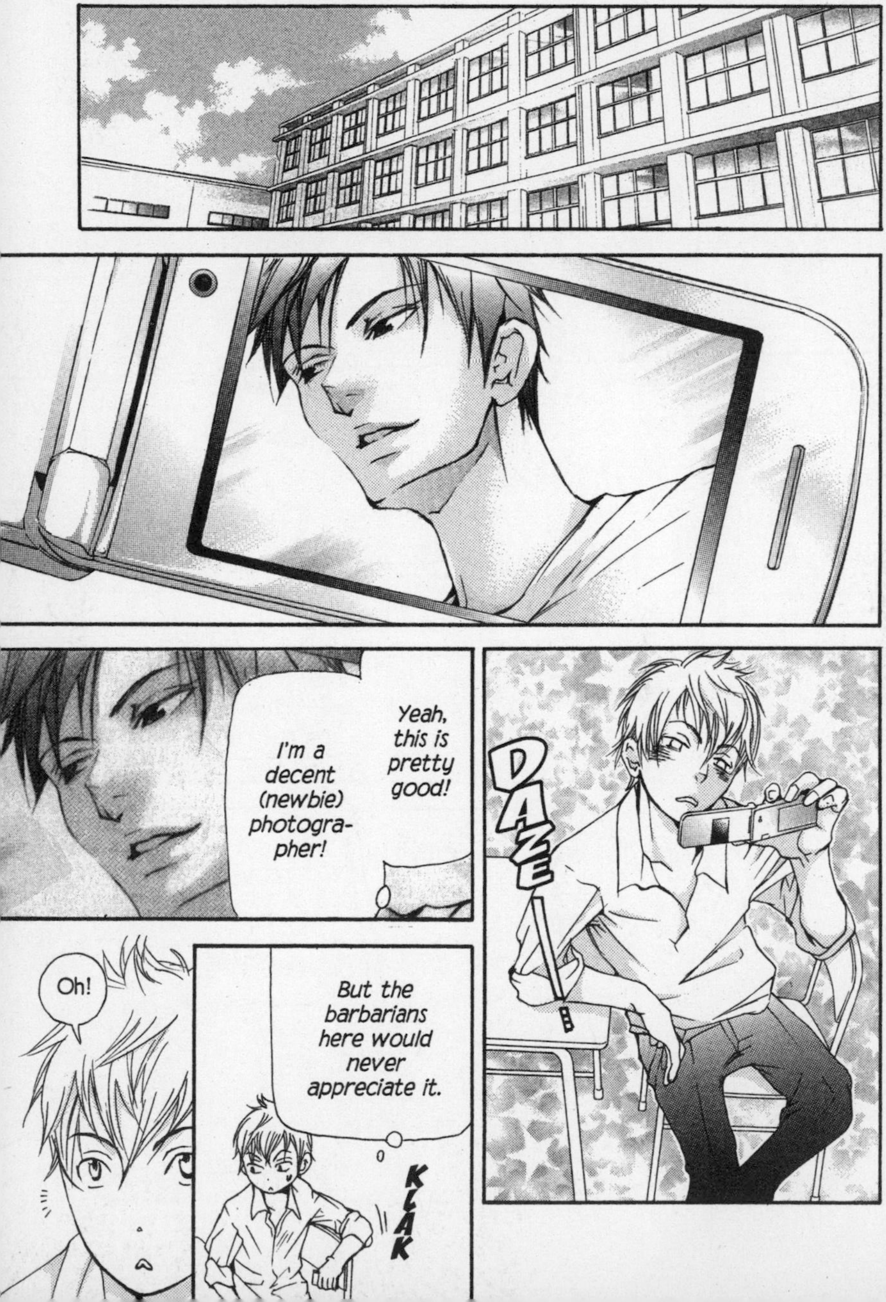
DAZE
Yeah, this is pretty good!
I'm a decent (newbie) photographer!
But the barbarians here would never appreciate it.
KLAK
Oh!

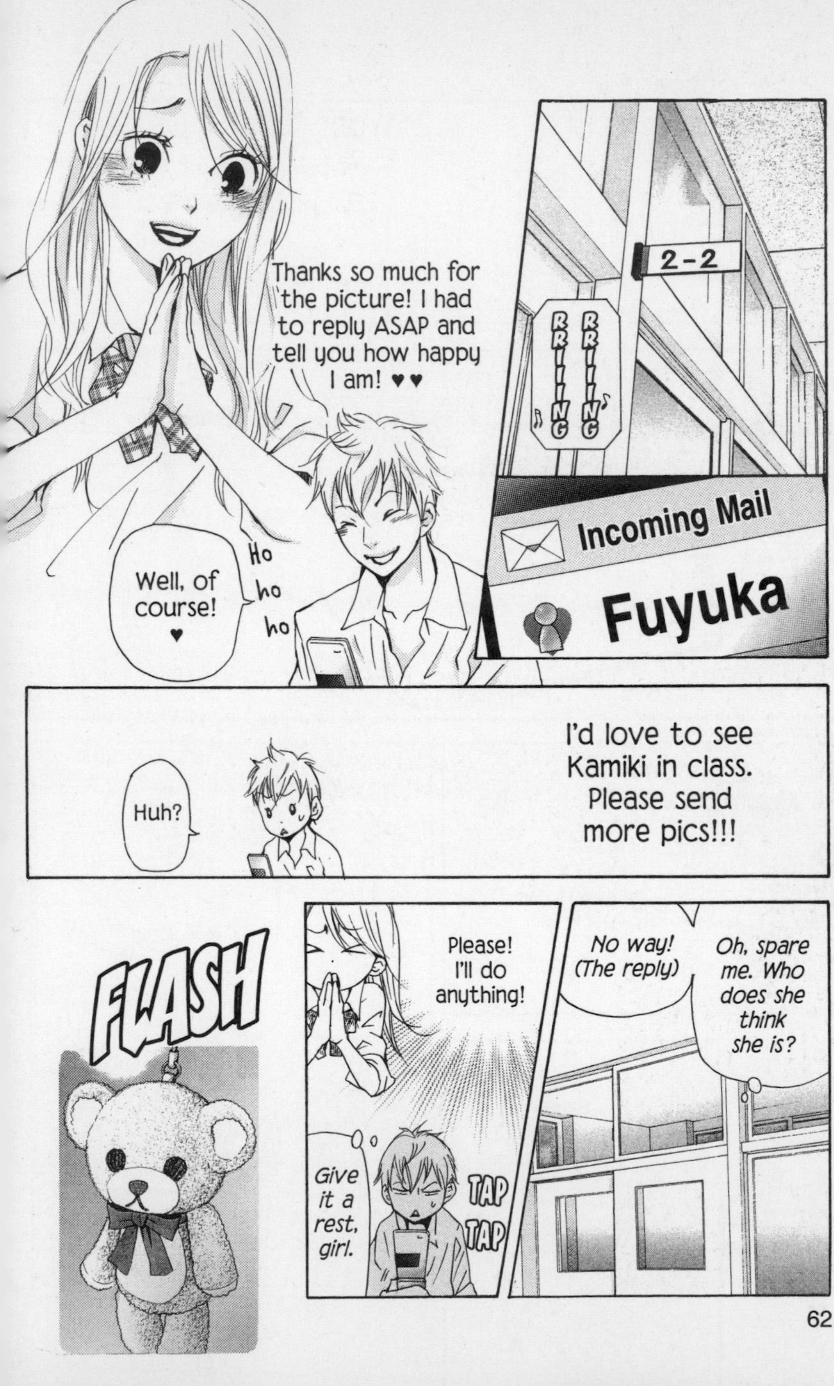
2-2
RRIING RRIING
Incoming Mail
Fuyuka
Thanks so much for the picture! I had to reply ASAP and tell you how happy I am! ♥♥
Well, of course! ♥
Ho ho ho
I'd love to see Kamiki in class. Please send more pics!!!
Huh?
No way! (The reply)
Oh, spare me. Who does she think she is?
Please! I'll do anything!
Give it a rest, girl.
TAP TAP
FLASH

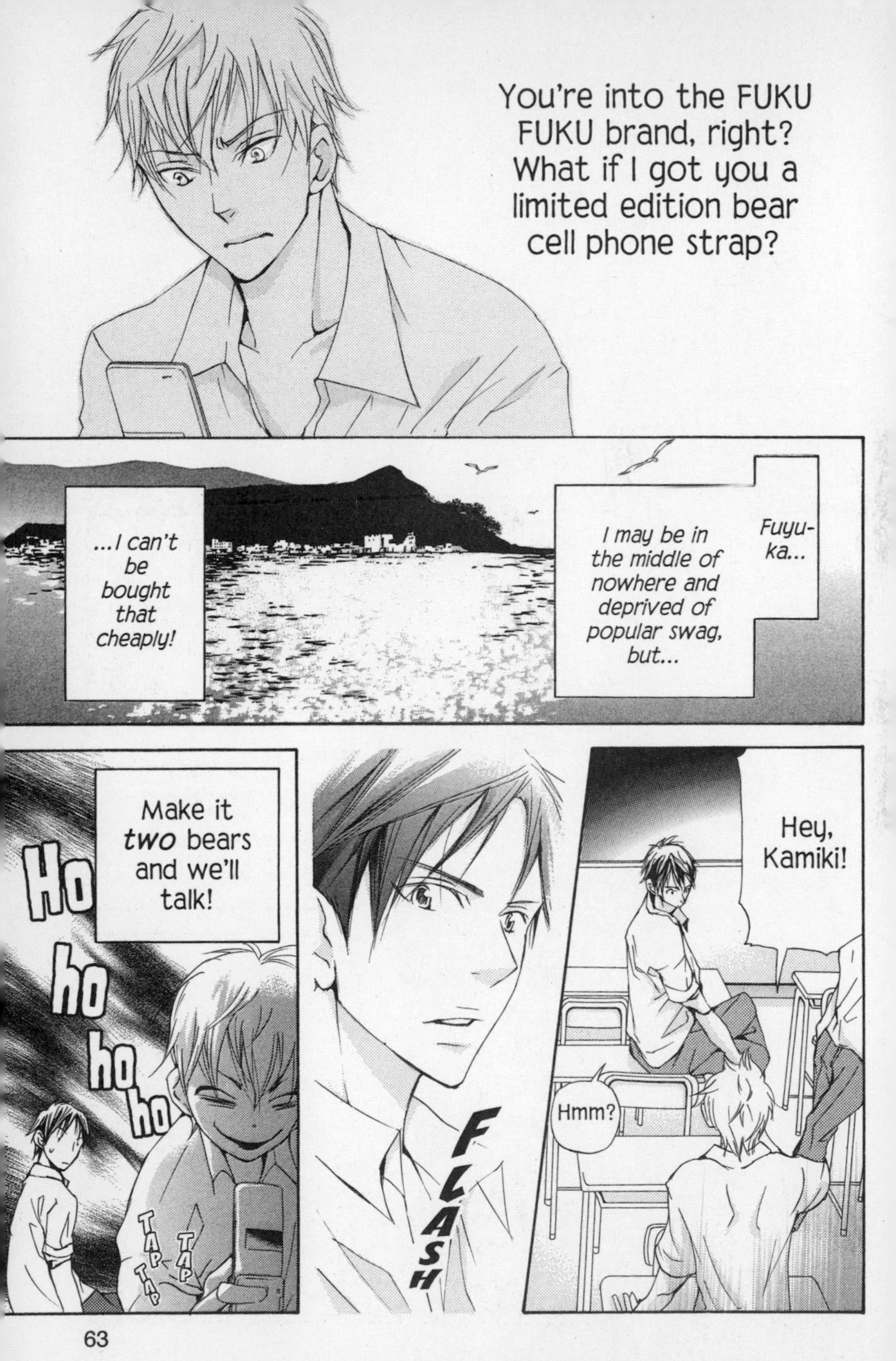
You're into the FUKU FUKU brand, right? What if I got you a limited edition bear cell phone strap?
Fuyu-ka...
I may be in the middle of nowhere and deprived of popular swag, but...
...I can't be bought that cheaply!
Hey, Kamiki!
Hmm?
FLASH
Make it *two* bears and we'll talk!
Ho ho ho ho
TAP TAP TAP TAP

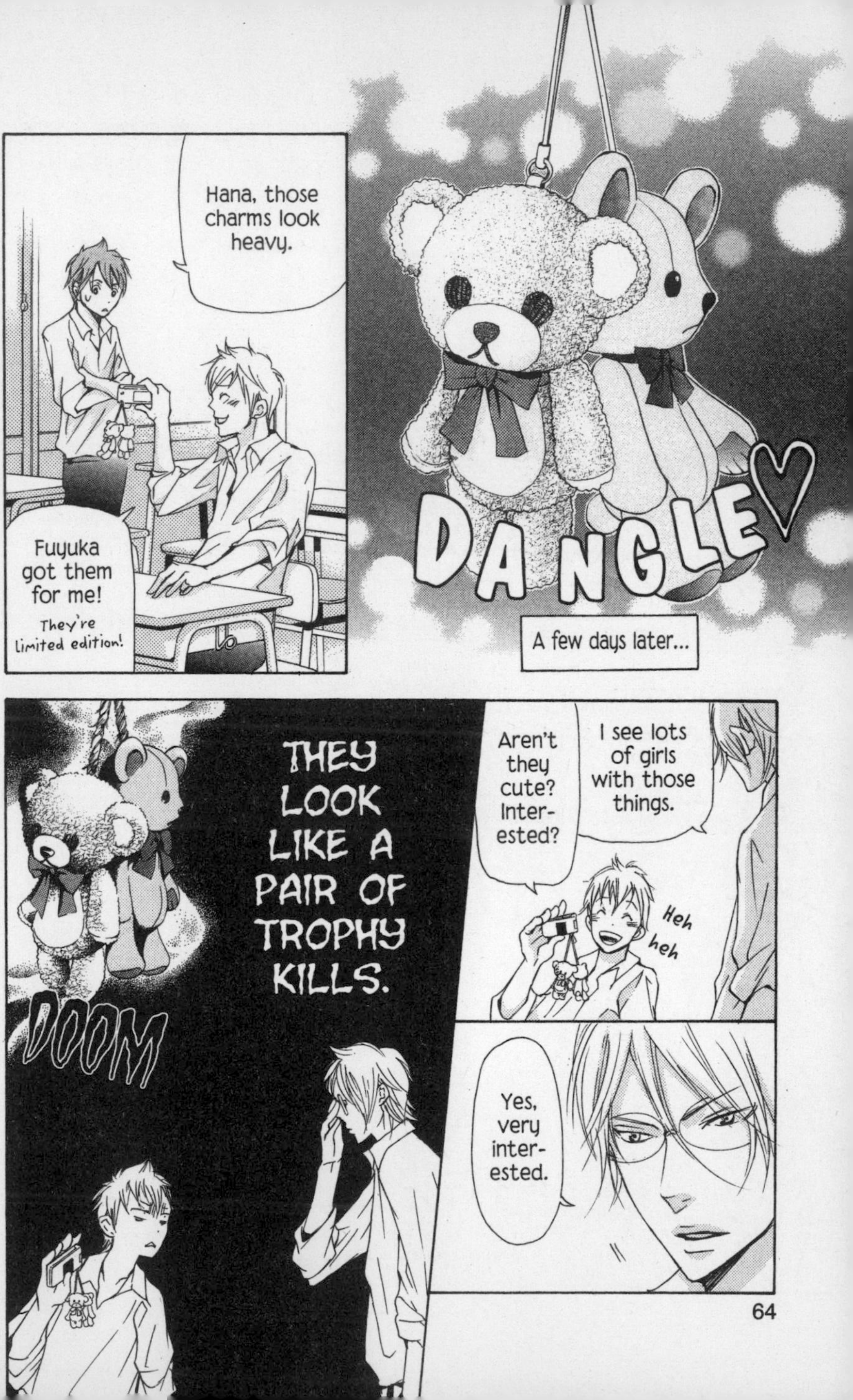
DANGLE♡
A few days later...
Hana, those charms look heavy.
Fuyuka got them for me!
They're limited edition!
I see lots of girls with those things.
Aren't they cute? Inter-ested?
Heh heh
Yes, very inter-ested.
THEY LOOK LIKE A PAIR OF TROPHY KILLS.
DOOM

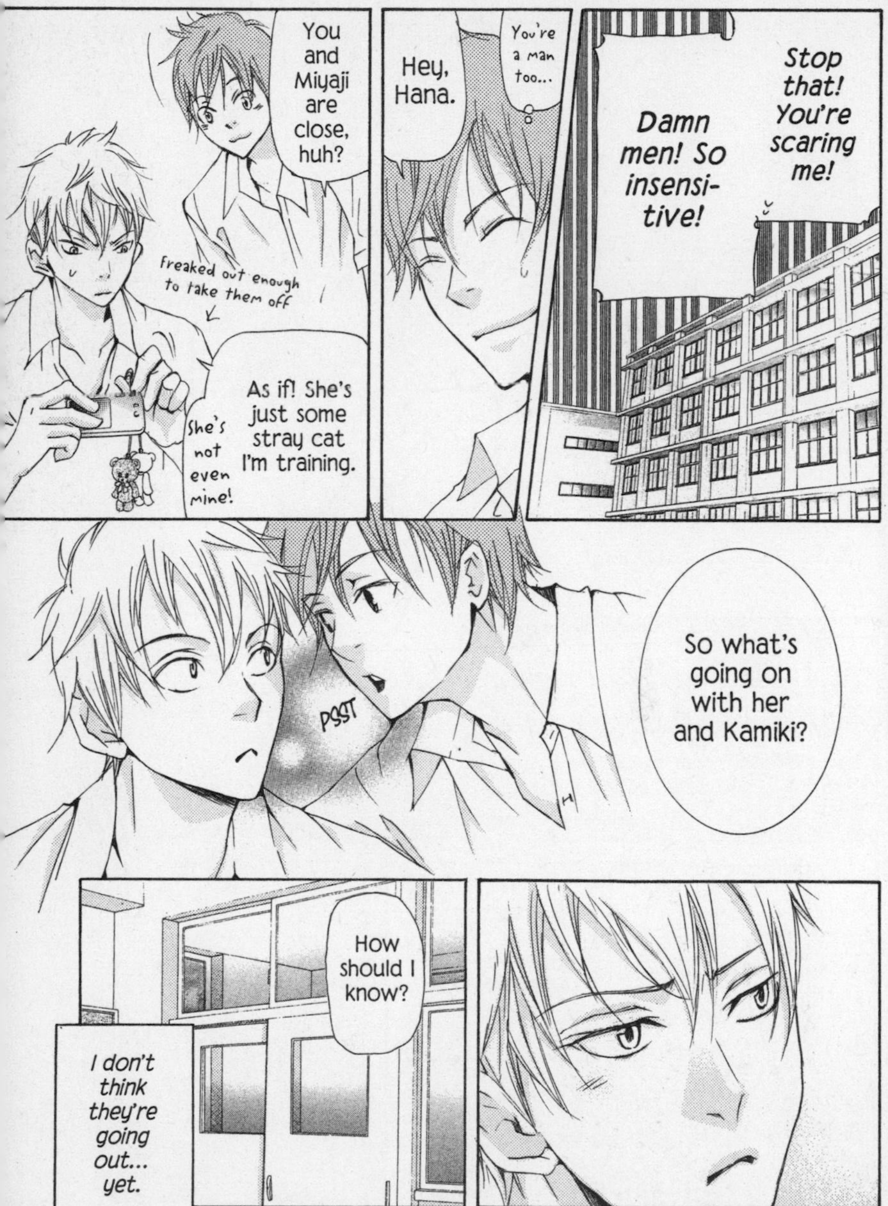
Stop that! You're scaring me!
Damn men! So insensitive!
You're a man too...
Hey, Hana.
You and Miyaji are close, huh?
freaked out enough to take them off
As if! She's just some stray cat I'm training.
She's not even mine!
So what's going on with her and Kamiki?
PSST
How should I know?
I don't think they're going out... yet.

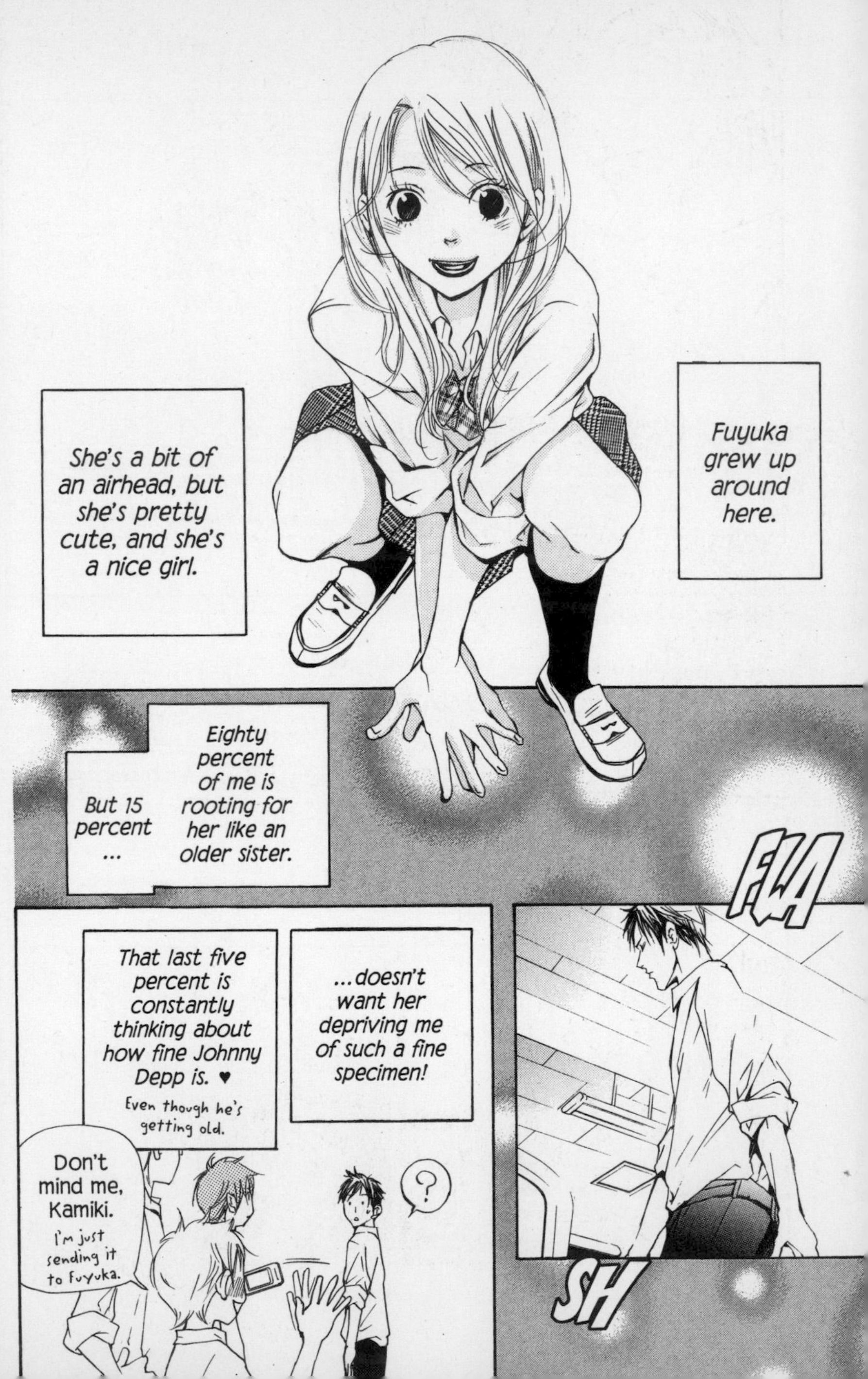
Fuyuka grew up around here.
She's a bit of an airhead, but she's pretty cute, and she's a nice girl.
Eighty percent of me is rooting for her like an older sister.
But 15 percent ...
FWA
SH
...doesn't want her depriving me of such a fine specimen!
That last five percent is constantly thinking about how fine Johnny Depp is. ♥
Even though he's getting old.
?
Don't mind me, Kamiki.
I'm just sending it to Fuyuka.

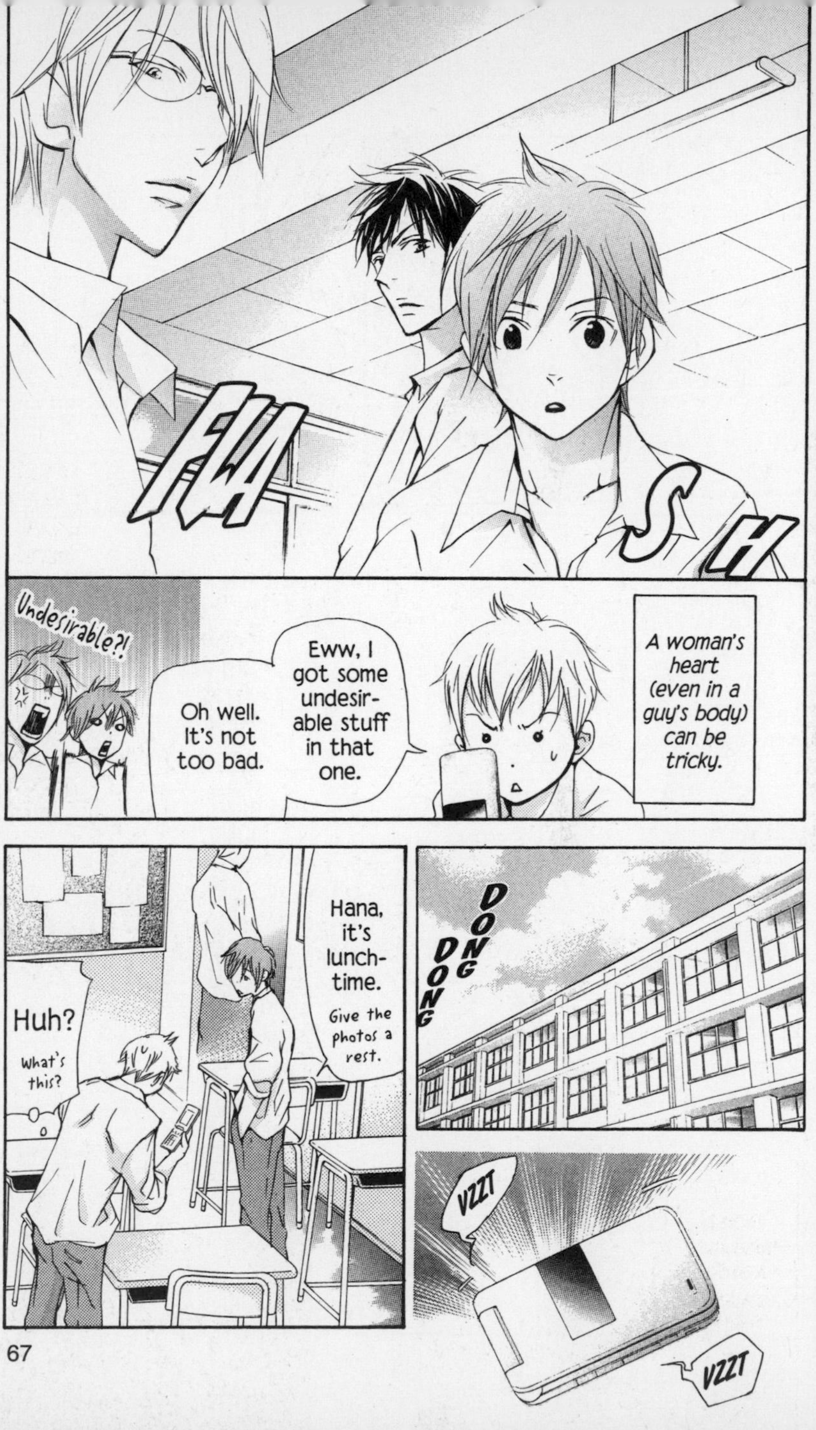
FWASH
A woman's heart (even in a guy's body) can be tricky.
Eww, I got some undesirable stuff in that one.
Oh well. It's not too bad.
Undesirable?!
DONG DONG
DONG
VZZT
VZZT
Hana, it's lunchtime.
Give the photos a rest.
Huh?
What's this?

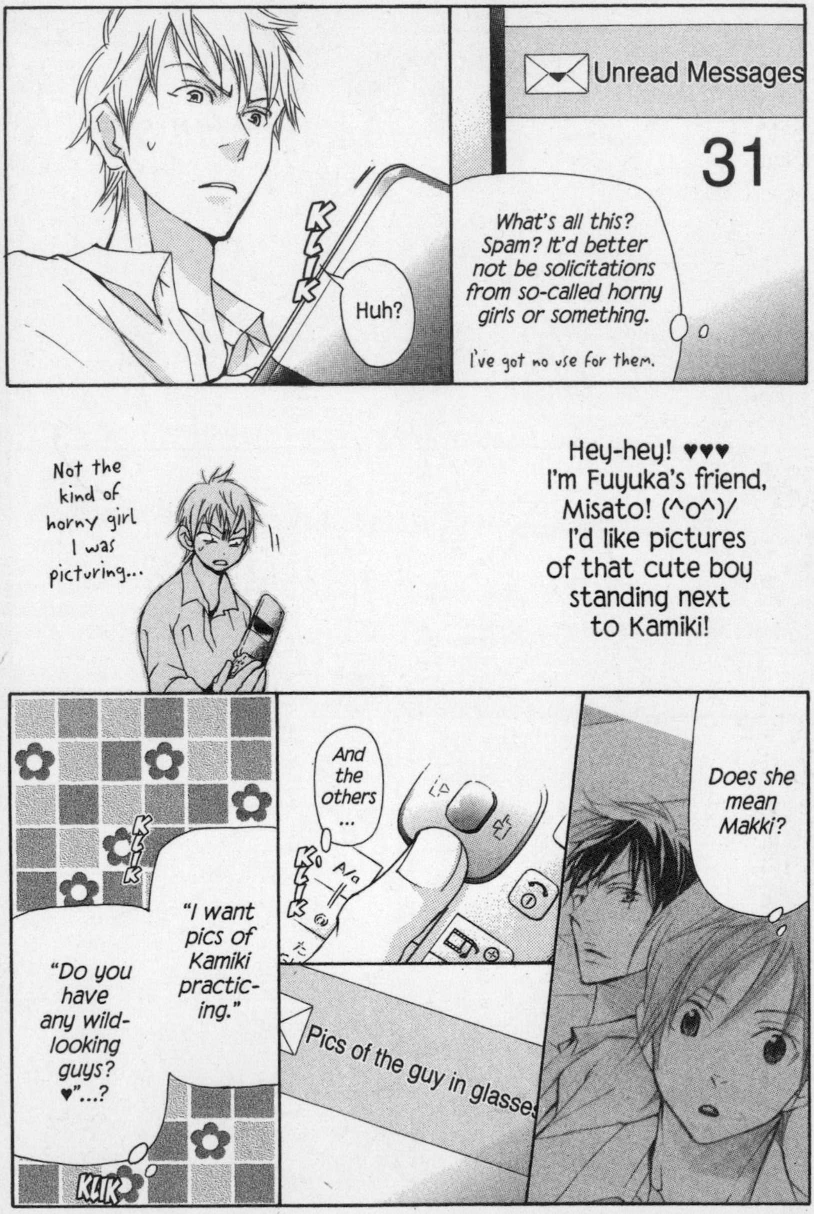
Unread Messages
31
What's all this? Spam? It'd better not be solicitations from so-called horny girls or something.
I've got no use for them.
KLIK KLIK
Huh?
Hey-hey! ♥♥♥ I'm Fuyuka's friend, Misato! (^o^)/ I'd like pictures of that cute boy standing next to Kamiki!
Not the kind of horny girl I was picturing...
Does she mean Makki?
And the others...
KLIK
Pics of the guy in glasses
"I want pics of Kamiki practicing."
"Do you have any wild-looking guys? ♥"...?
KLIK
KLIK

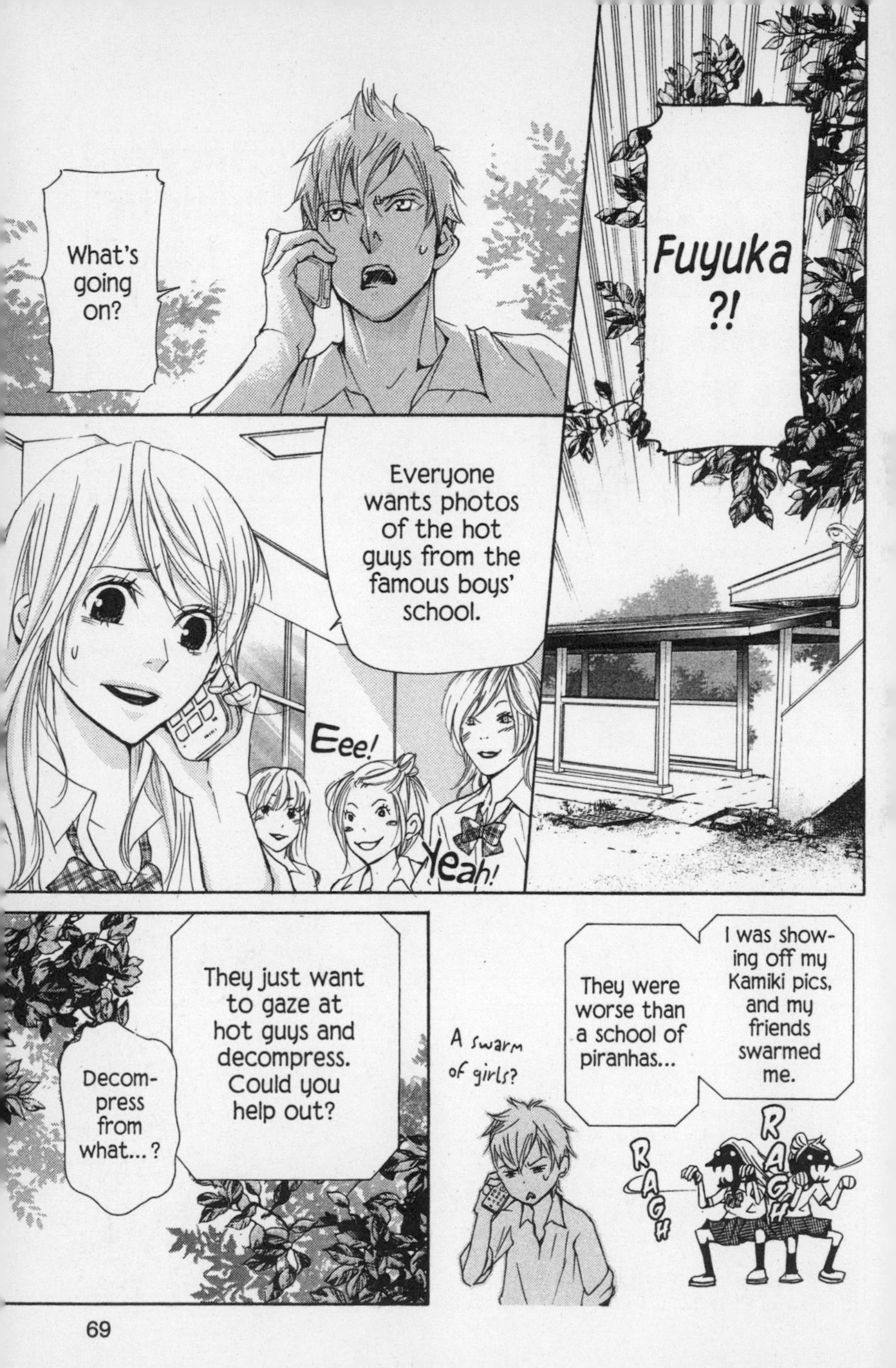

Fuyuka ?!
What's going on?
Everyone wants photos of the hot guys from the famous boys' school.
Eee!
Yeah!
I was showing off my Kamiki pics, and my friends swarmed me.
They were worse than a school of piranhas...
A swarm of girls?
RAGH
RAGH
They just want to gaze at hot guys and decompress. Could you help out?
Decompress from what...?

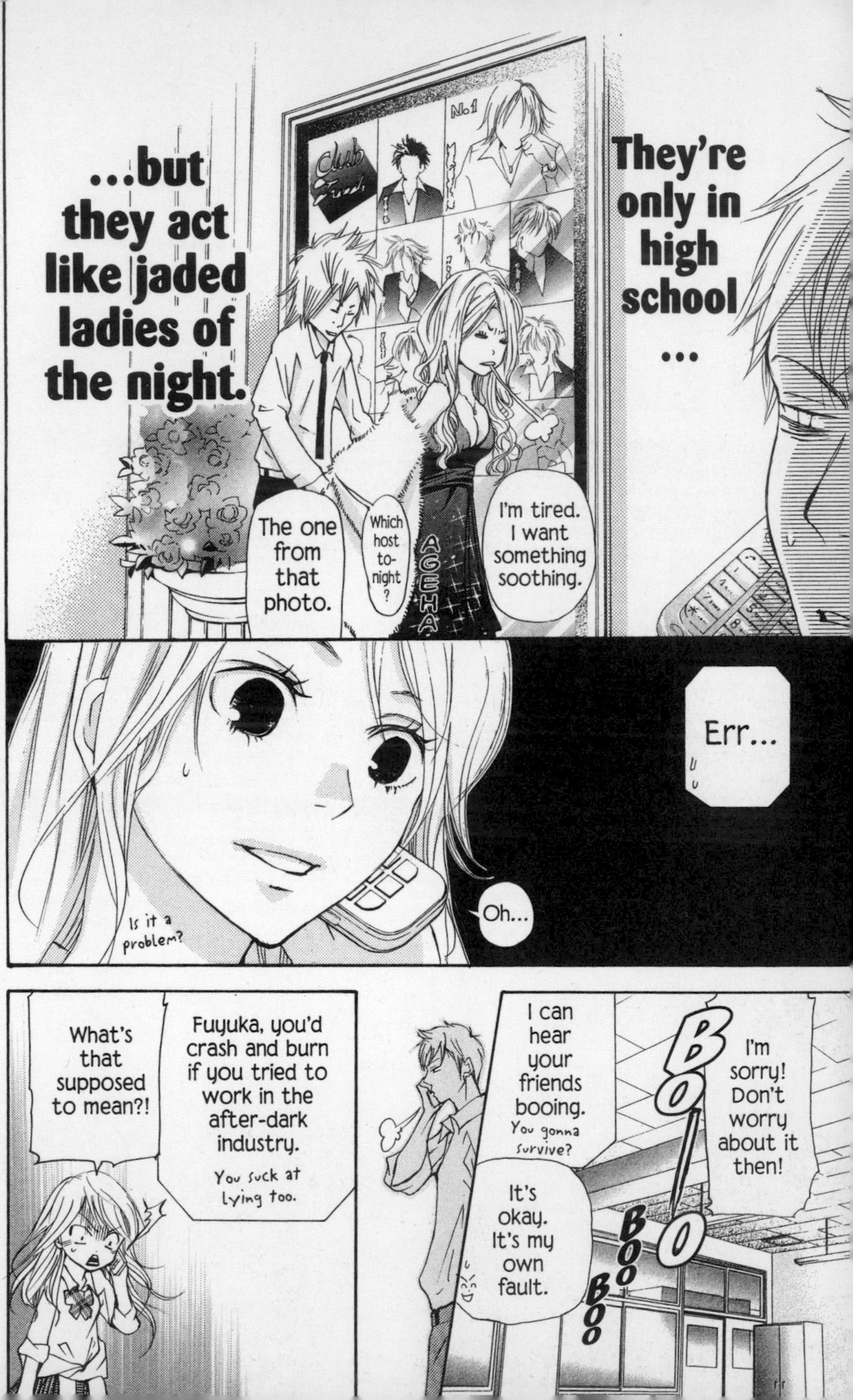
They're only in high school...
...but they act like jaded ladies of the night.
No.1
I'm tired. I want something soothing.
AGEHA
Which host to-night?
The one from that photo.
Err...
Oh...
Is it a problem?
I'm sorry! Don't worry about it then!
BOO BOO BOO BOO
I can hear your friends booing.
You gonna survive?
It's okay. It's my own fault.
Fuyuka, you'd crash and burn if you tried to work in the after-dark industry.
You suck at lying too.
What's that supposed to mean?!

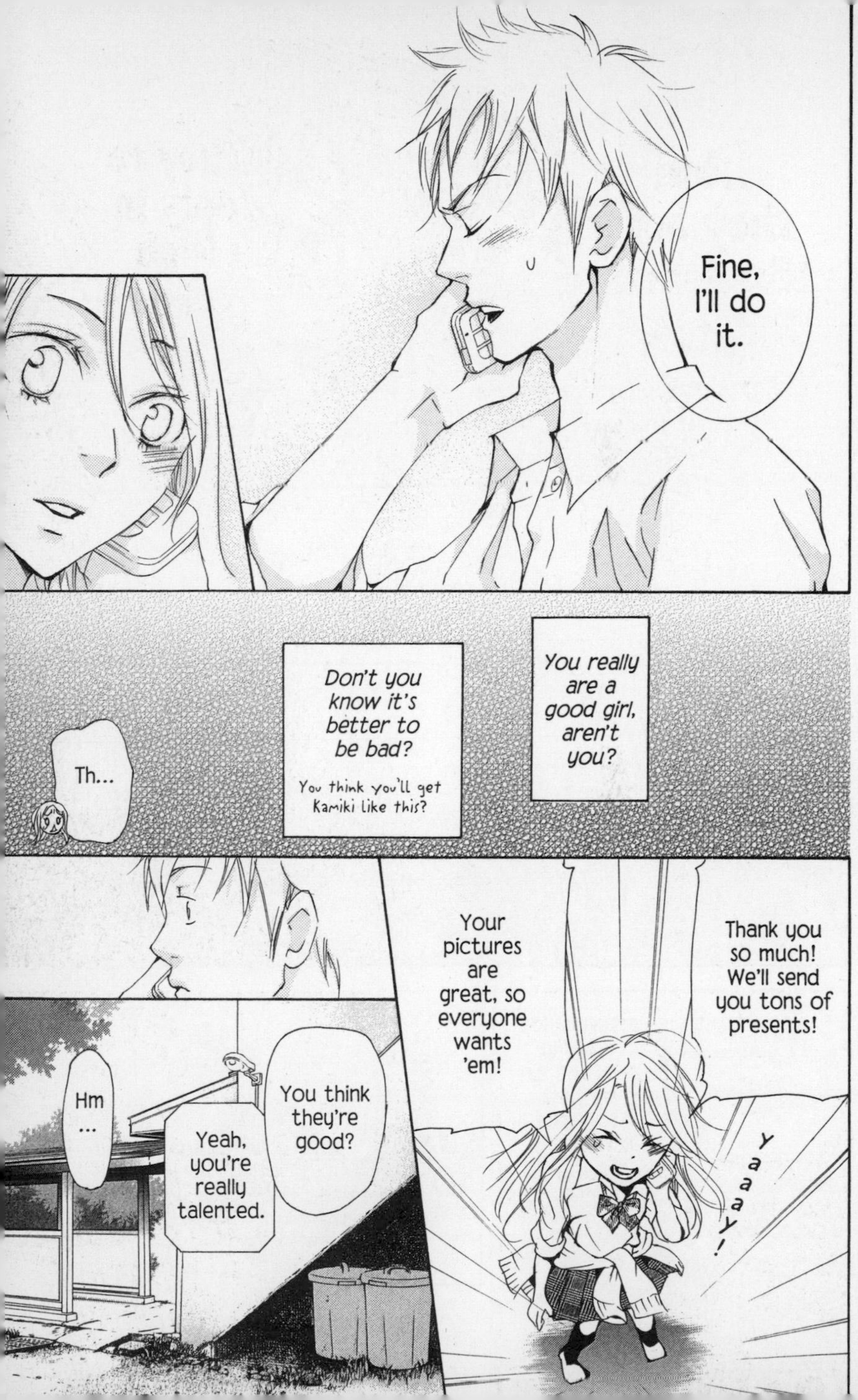
Fine, I'll do it.
You really are a good girl, aren't you?
Don't you know it's better to be bad?
You think you'll get Kamiki like this?
Th...
Thank you so much! We'll send you tons of presents!
Your pictures are great, so everyone wants 'em!
Yaaaay!
You think they're good?
Yeah, you're really talented.
Hm...

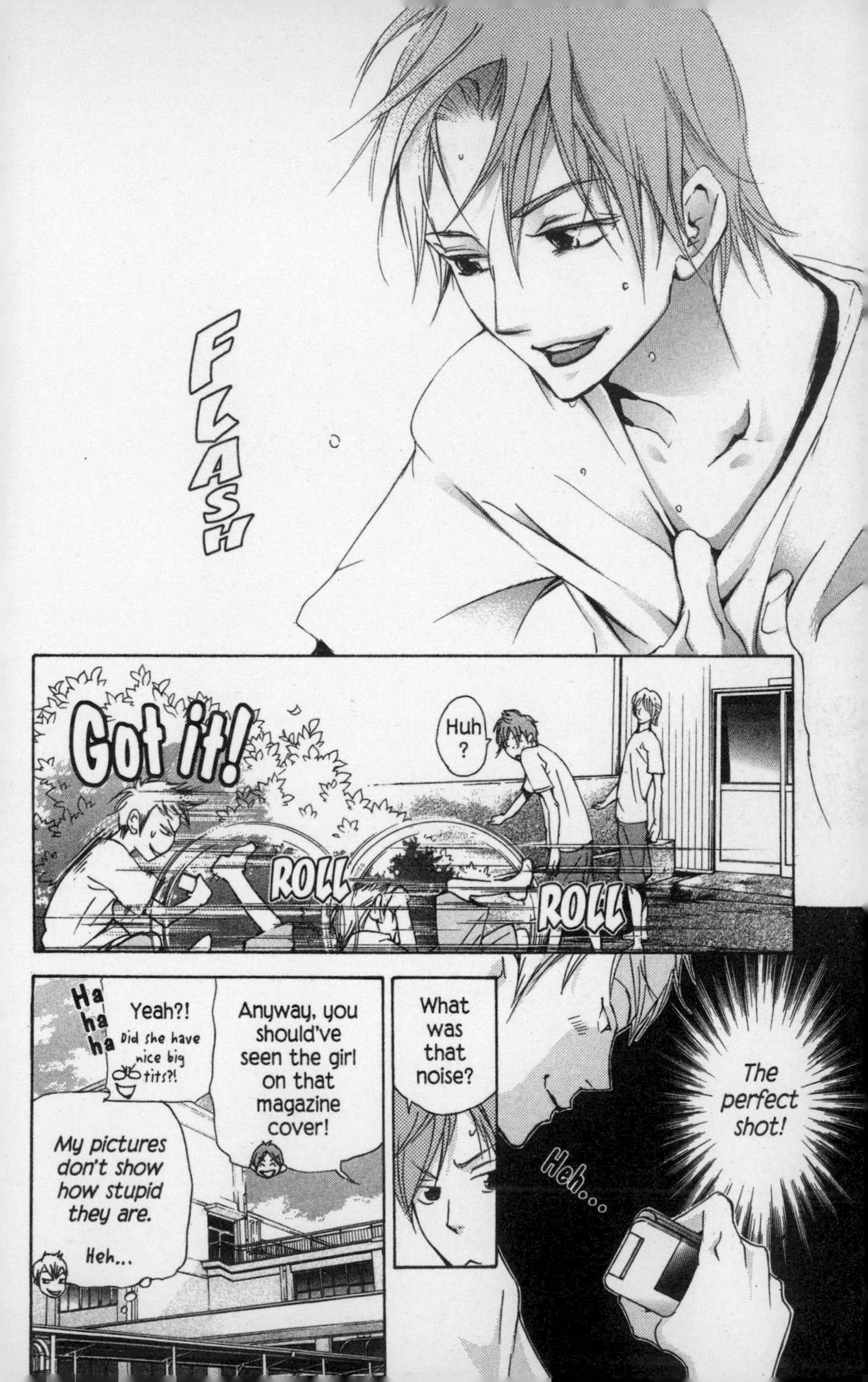
FLASH
Huh?
Got it!
ROLL
ROLL
The perfect shot!
Heh...
What was that noise?
Anyway, you should've seen the girl on that magazine cover!
Yeah?! Did she have nice big tits?!
Ha ha ha
My pictures don't show how stupid they are.
Heh...

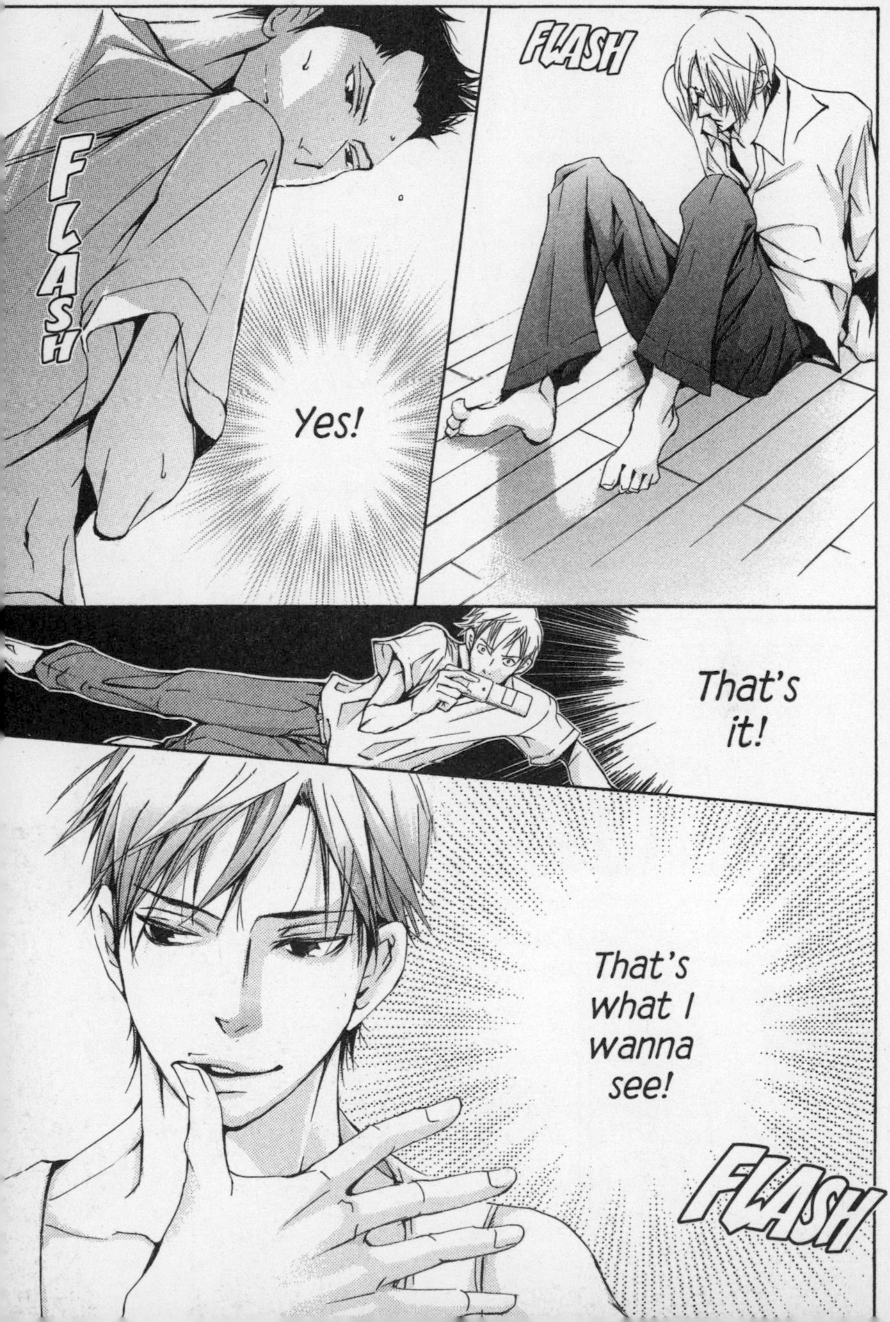
FLASH
FLASH
Yes!
That's it!
That's what I wanna see!
FLASH

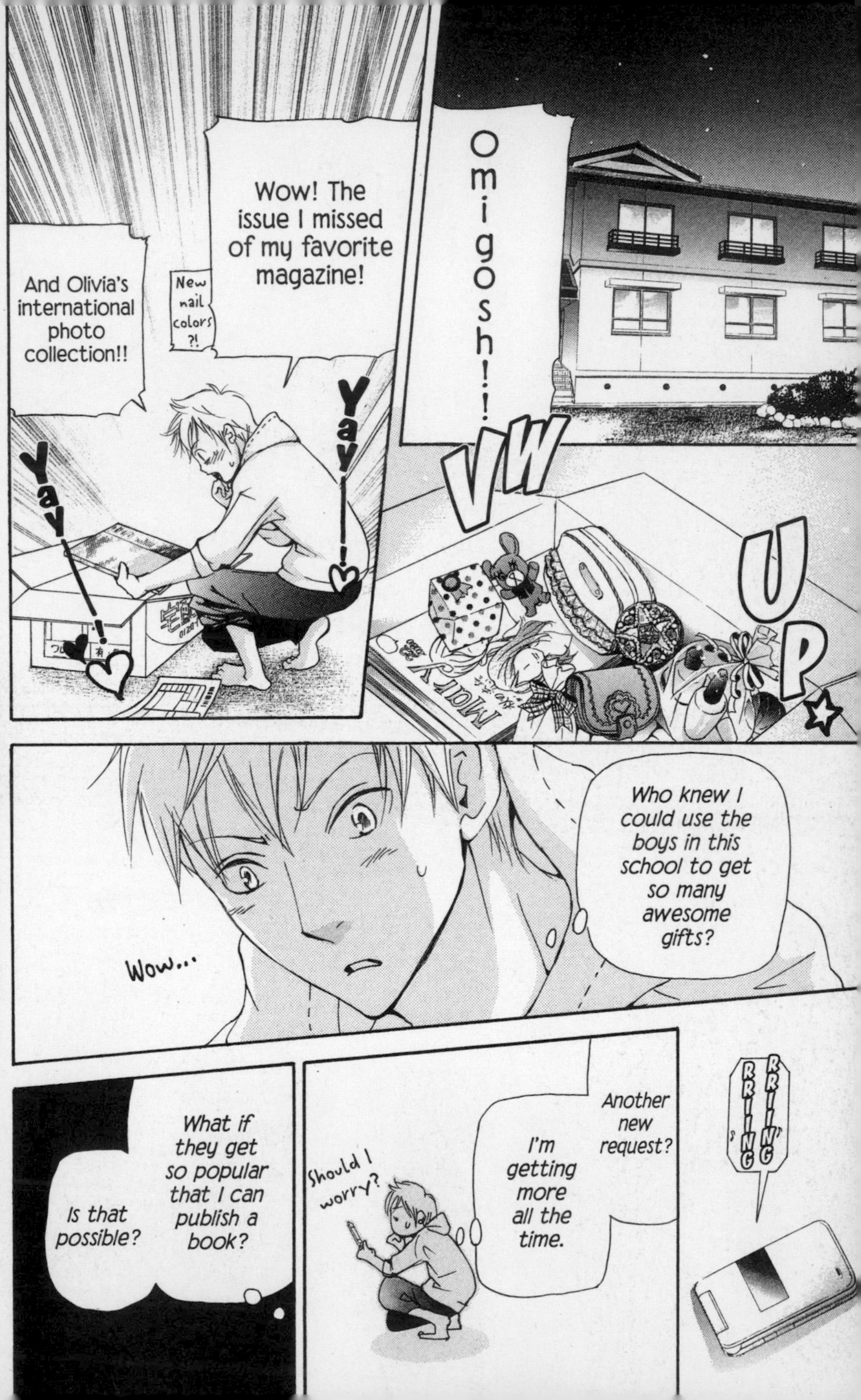
Omigosh!!!
VW
UP
Wow! The issue I missed of my favorite magazine!
New nail colors?!
And Olivia's international photo collection!!
Yay!
Yay!
Who knew I could use the boys in this school to get so many awesome gifts?
Wow...
RRING
RRING
Another new request?
I'm getting more all the time.
Should I worry?
What if they get so popular that I can publish a book?
Is that possible?

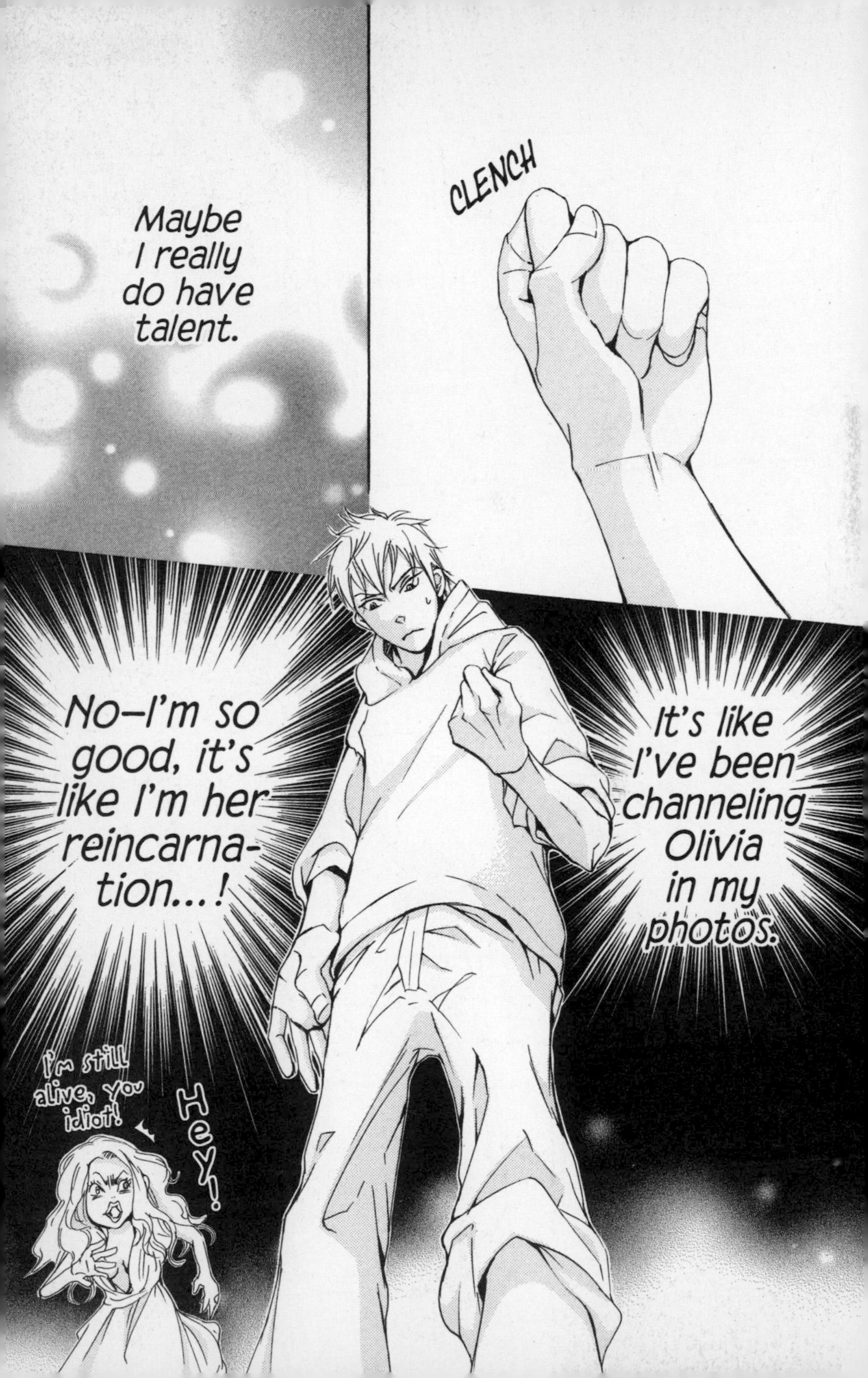
CLENCH
Maybe I really do have talent.
It's like I've been channeling Olivia in my photos.
No–I'm so good, it's like I'm her reincarnation...!
HEY!
I'm still alive, you idiot!

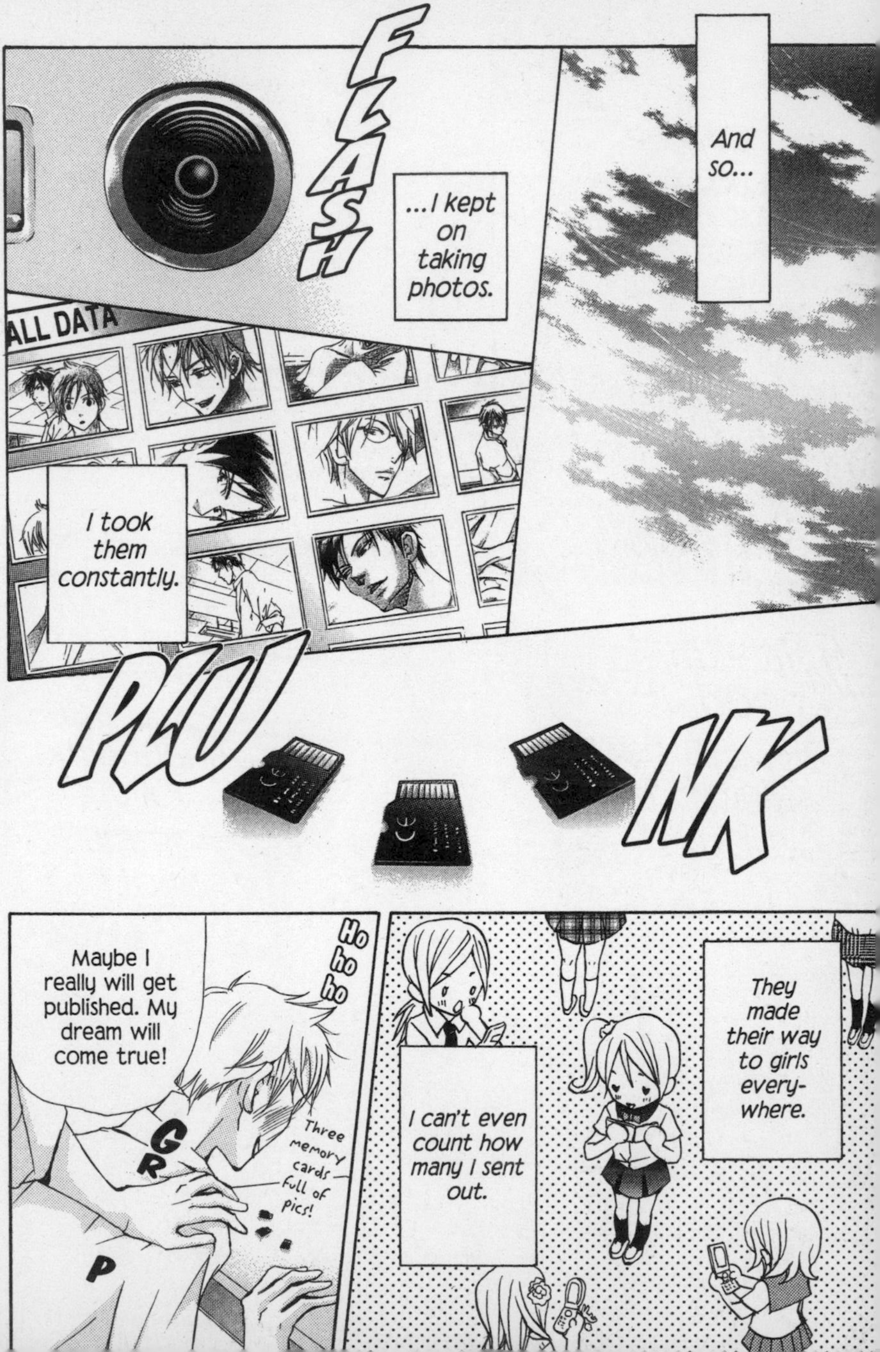
And so...
FLASH
...I kept on taking photos.
ALL DATA
I took them constantly.
PLUNK
They made their way to girls every-where.
I can't even count how many I sent out.
Ho ho ho
Maybe I really will get published. My dream will come true!
Three memory cards full of pics!
GRP

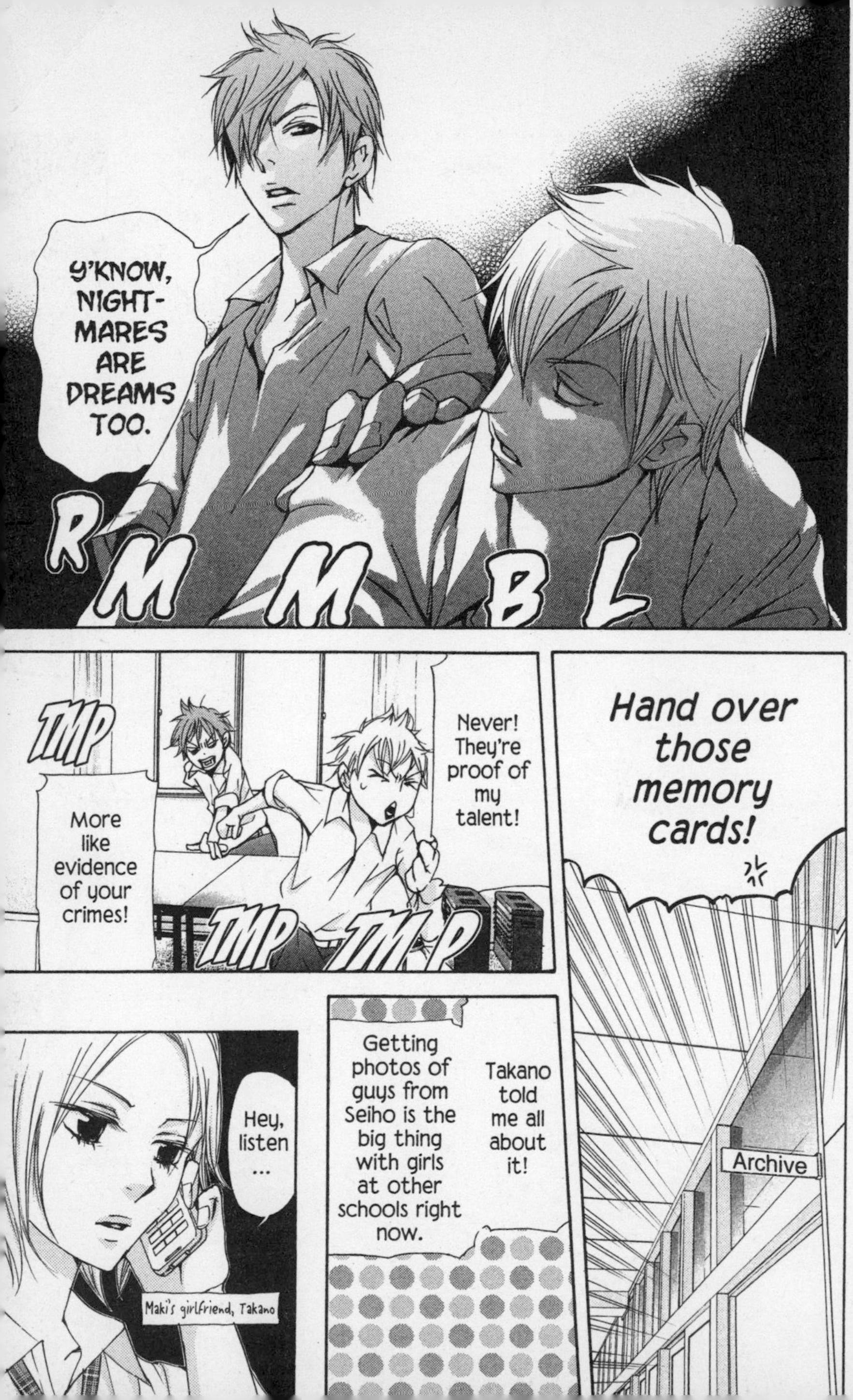
Y'KNOW, NIGHT-MARES ARE DREAMS TOO.
RMMBL
Hand over those memory cards!
Archive
Never! They're proof of my talent!
TMP
More like evidence of your crimes!
TMP TMP
Getting photos of guys from Seiho is the big thing with girls at other schools right now.
Takano told me all about it!
Hey, listen...
Maki's girlfriend, Takano

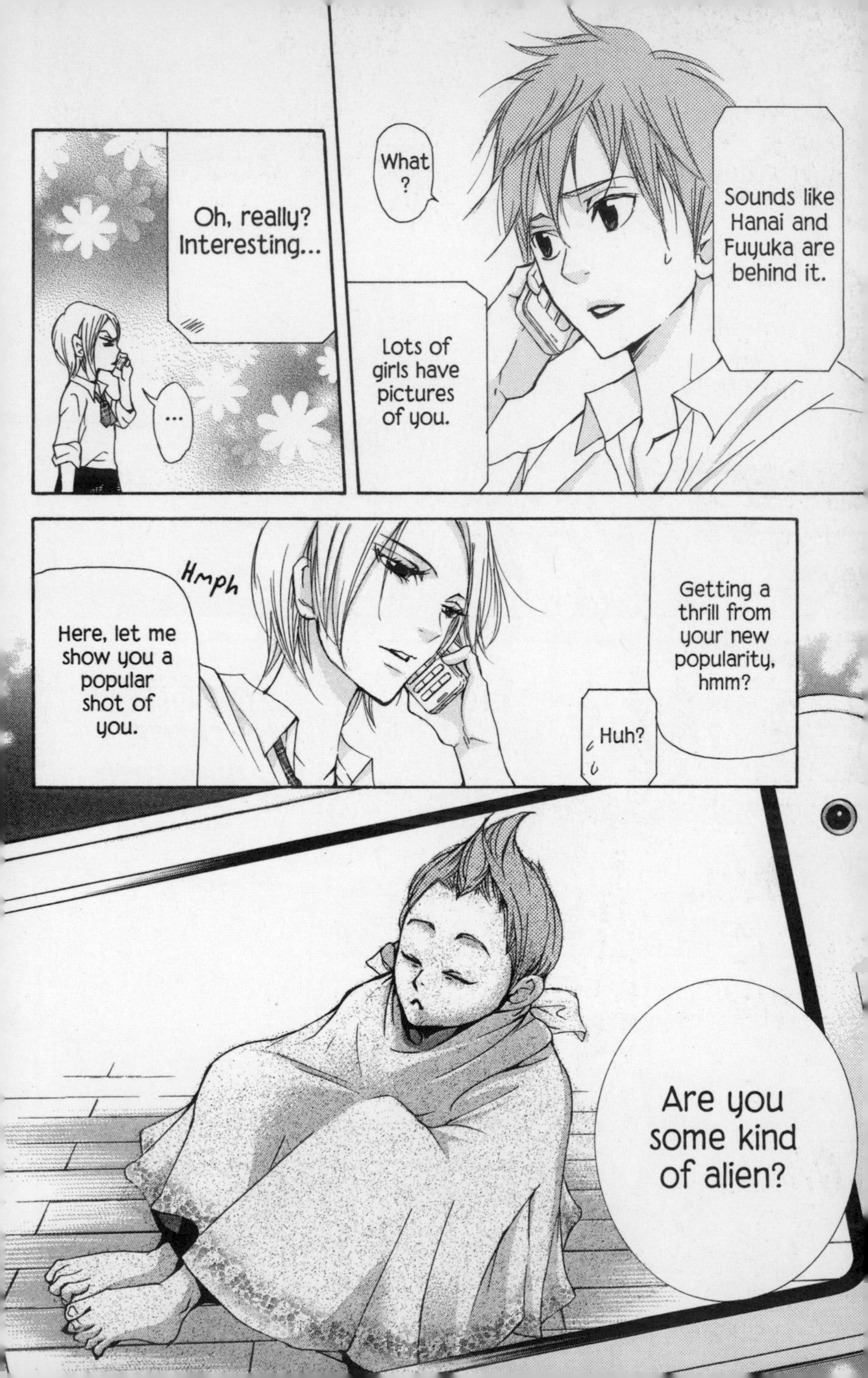
Sounds like Hanai and Fuyuka are behind it.
What?
Lots of girls have pictures of you.
Oh, really? Interesting...
...
Getting a thrill from your new popularity, hmm?
Huh?
Hmph
Here, let me show you a popular shot of you.
Are you some kind of alien?

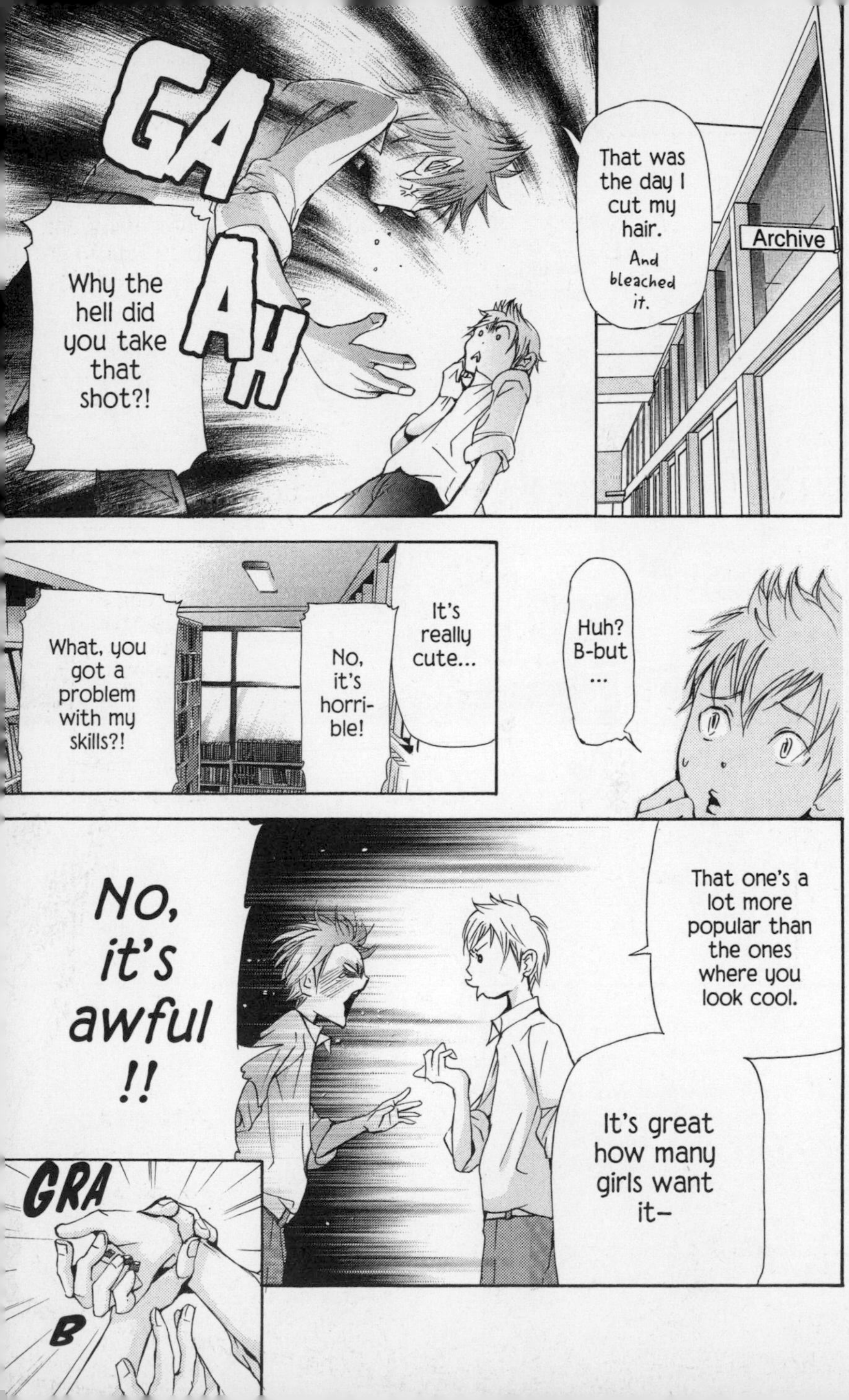
That was the day I cut my hair.
And bleached it.
Archive
GAAH
Why the hell did you take that shot?!
Huh? B-but ...
It's really cute...
No, it's horrible!
What, you got a problem with my skills?!
That one's a lot more popular than the ones where you look cool.
It's great how many girls want it–
No, it's awful!!
GRAB

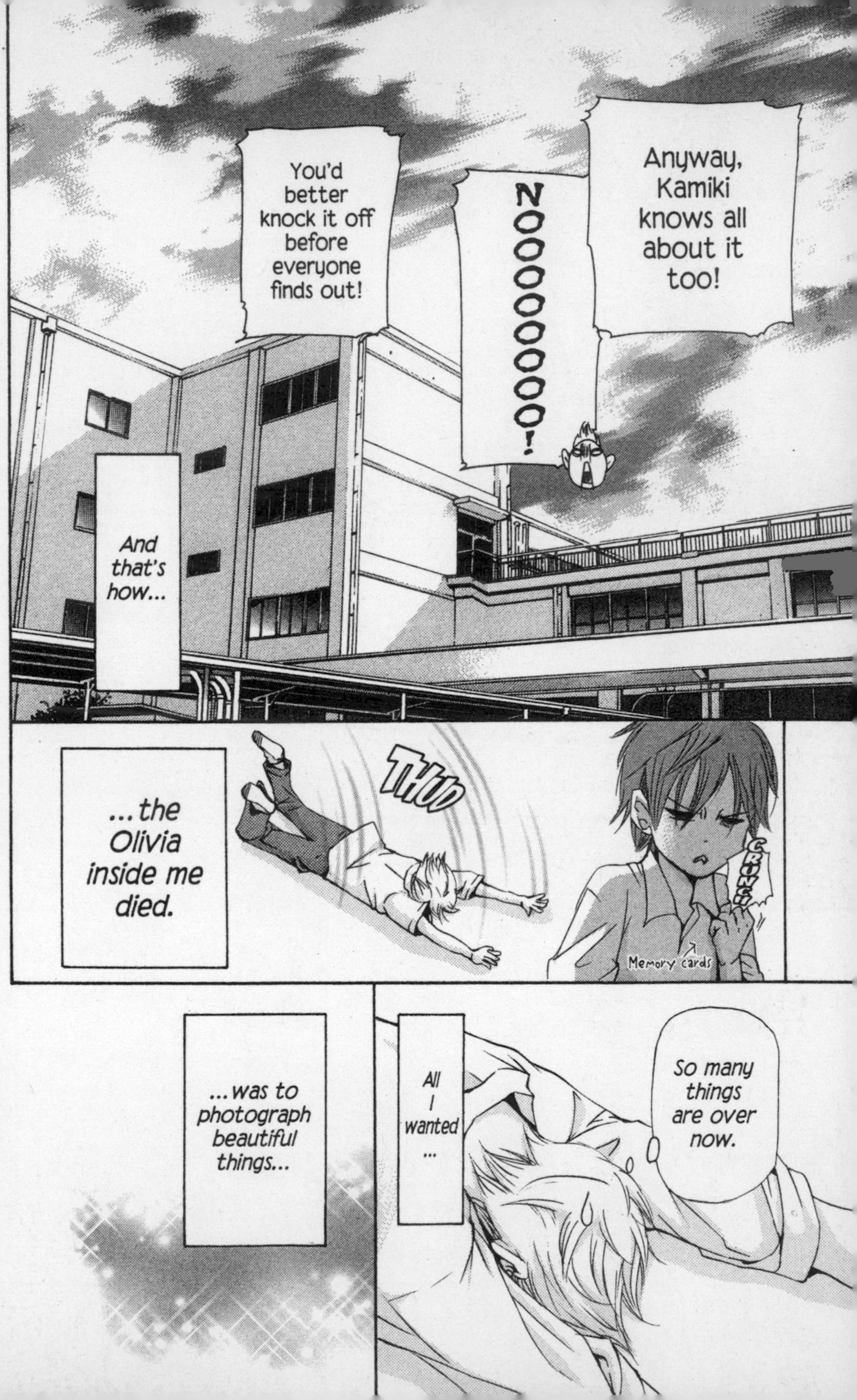
Anyway, Kamiki knows all about it too!
NOOOOOOOO!
You'd better knock it off before everyone finds out!
And that's how...
CRUNCH
Memory cards
THUD
...the Olivia inside me died.
So many things are over now.
All I wanted...
...was to photograph beautiful things...

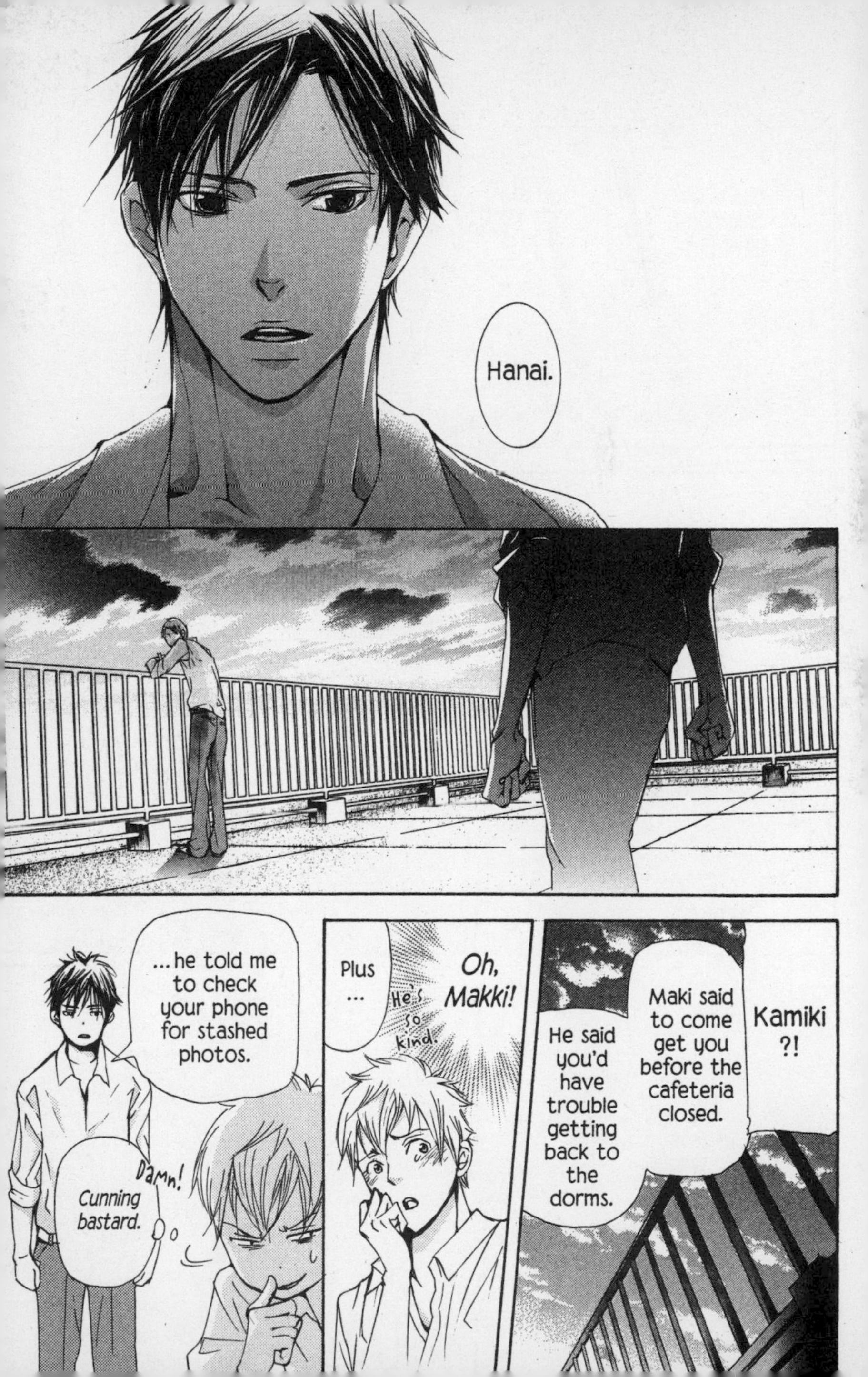
Hanai.
Kamiki ?!
Maki said to come get you before the cafeteria closed.
He said you'd have trouble getting back to the dorms.
Oh, Makki!
He's so kind.
Plus ...
...he told me to check your phone for stashed photos.
Damn!
Cunning bastard.

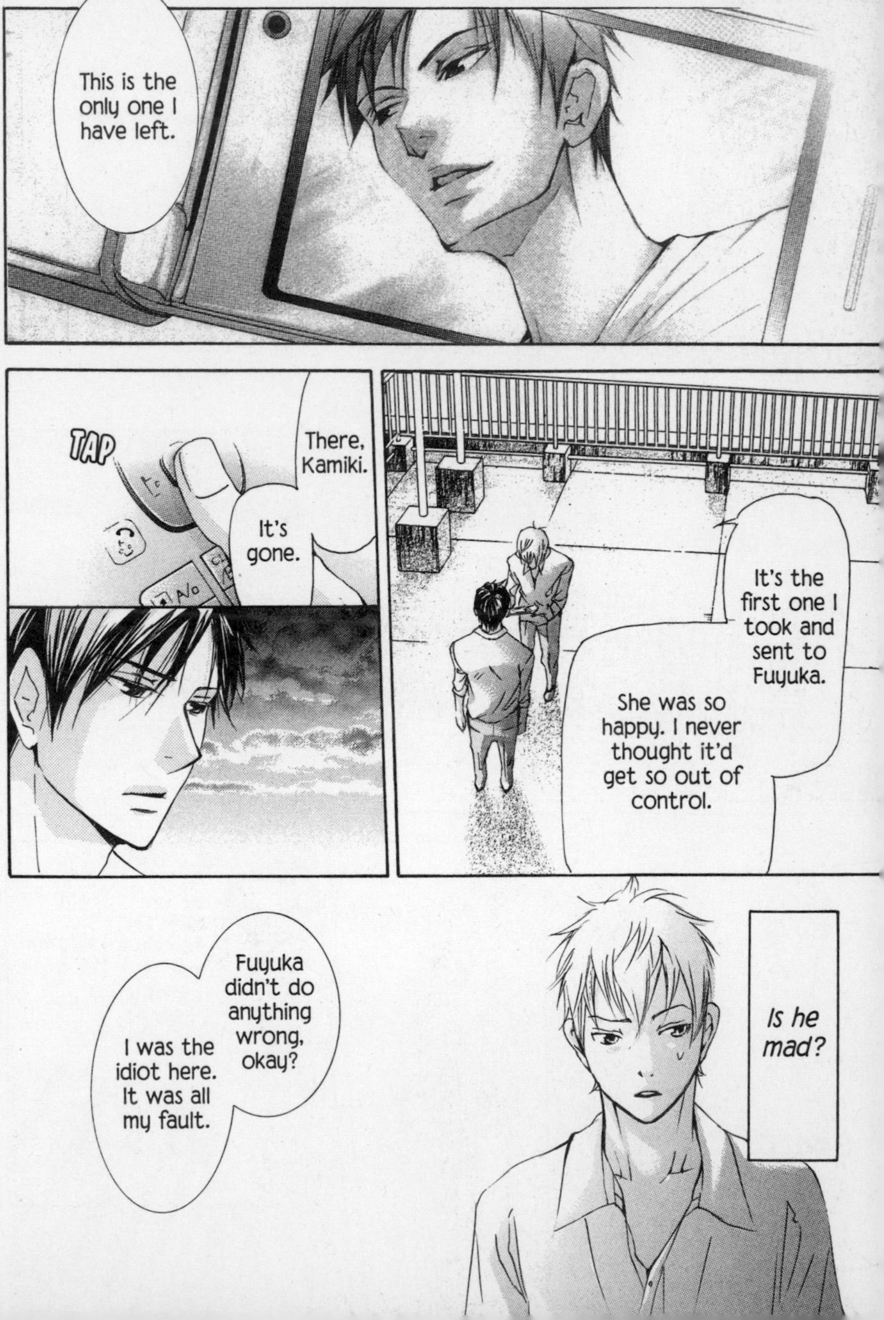
This is the only one I have left.
It's the first one I took and sent to Fuyuka.
She was so happy. I never thought it'd get so out of control.
TAP
There, Kamiki.
It's gone.
Is he mad?
Fuyuka didn't do anything wrong, okay?
I was the idiot here. It was all my fault.

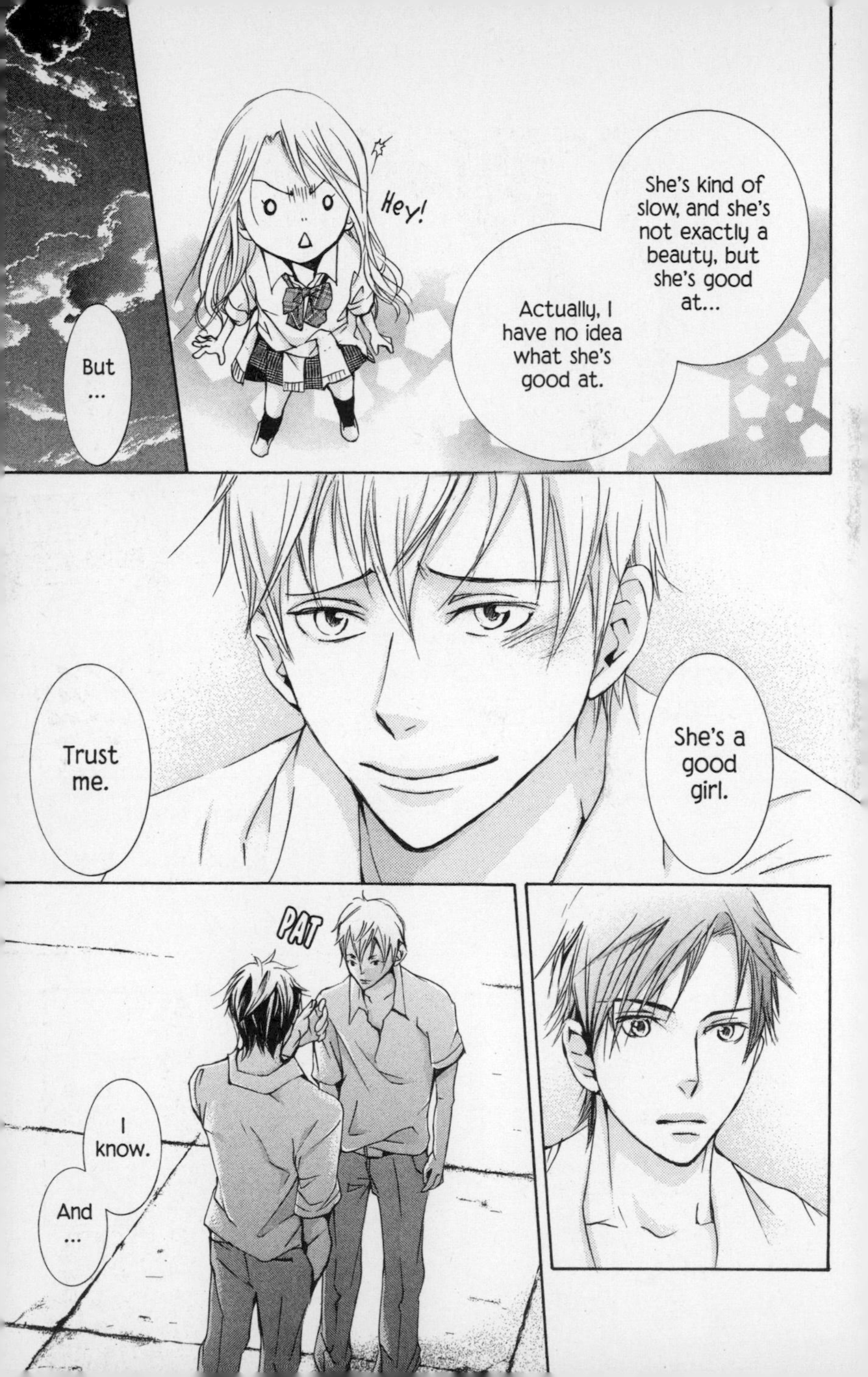
She's kind of slow, and she's not exactly a beauty, but she's good at...
Actually, I have no idea what she's good at.
Hey!
But ...
She's a good girl.
Trust me.
PAT
I know.
And ...

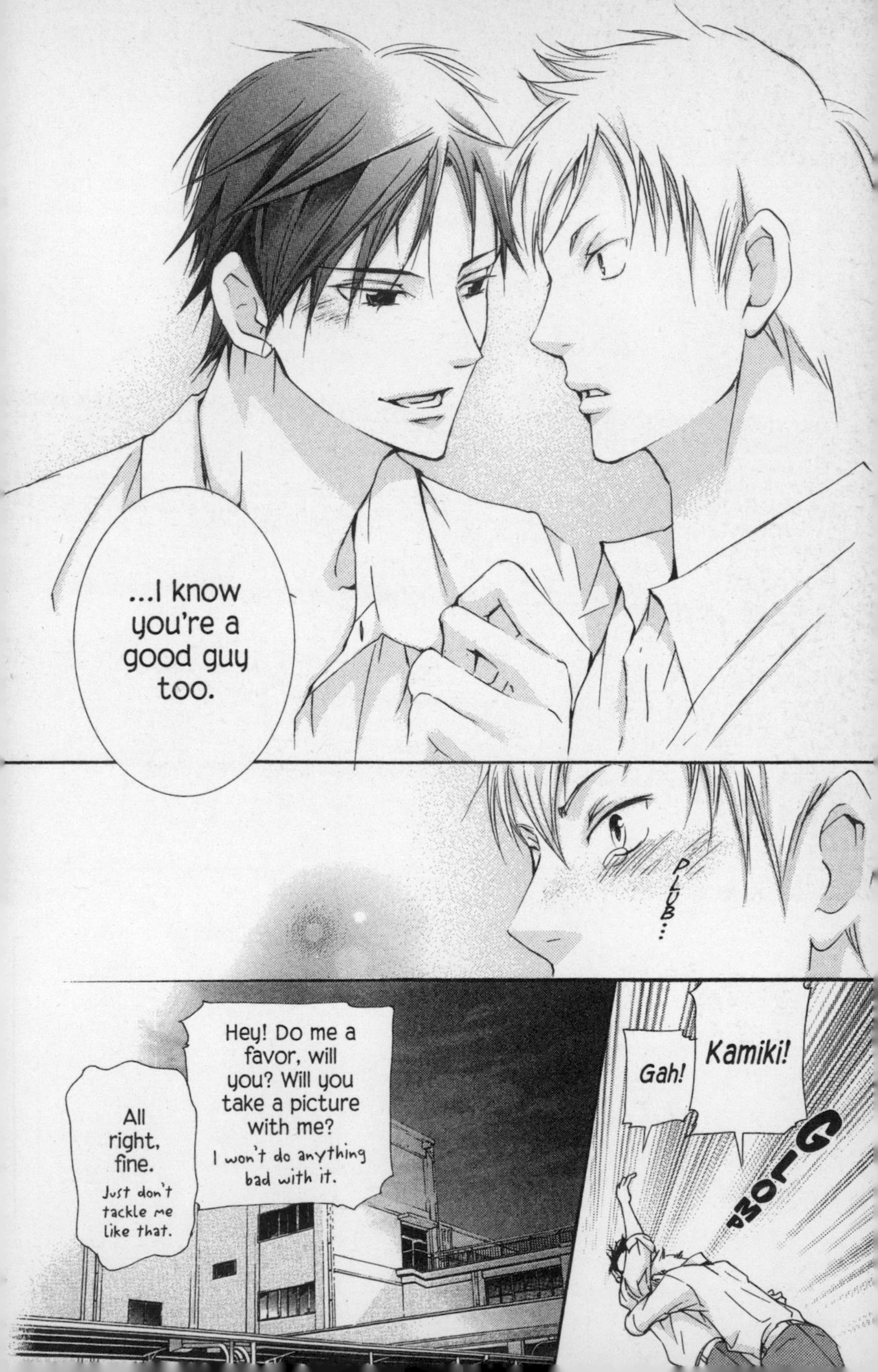
...I know you're a good guy too.
PLUB...
Kamiki!
Gah!
GLOMP
Hey! Do me a favor, will you? Will you take a picture with me?
I won't do anything bad with it.
All right, fine.
Just don't tackle me like that.

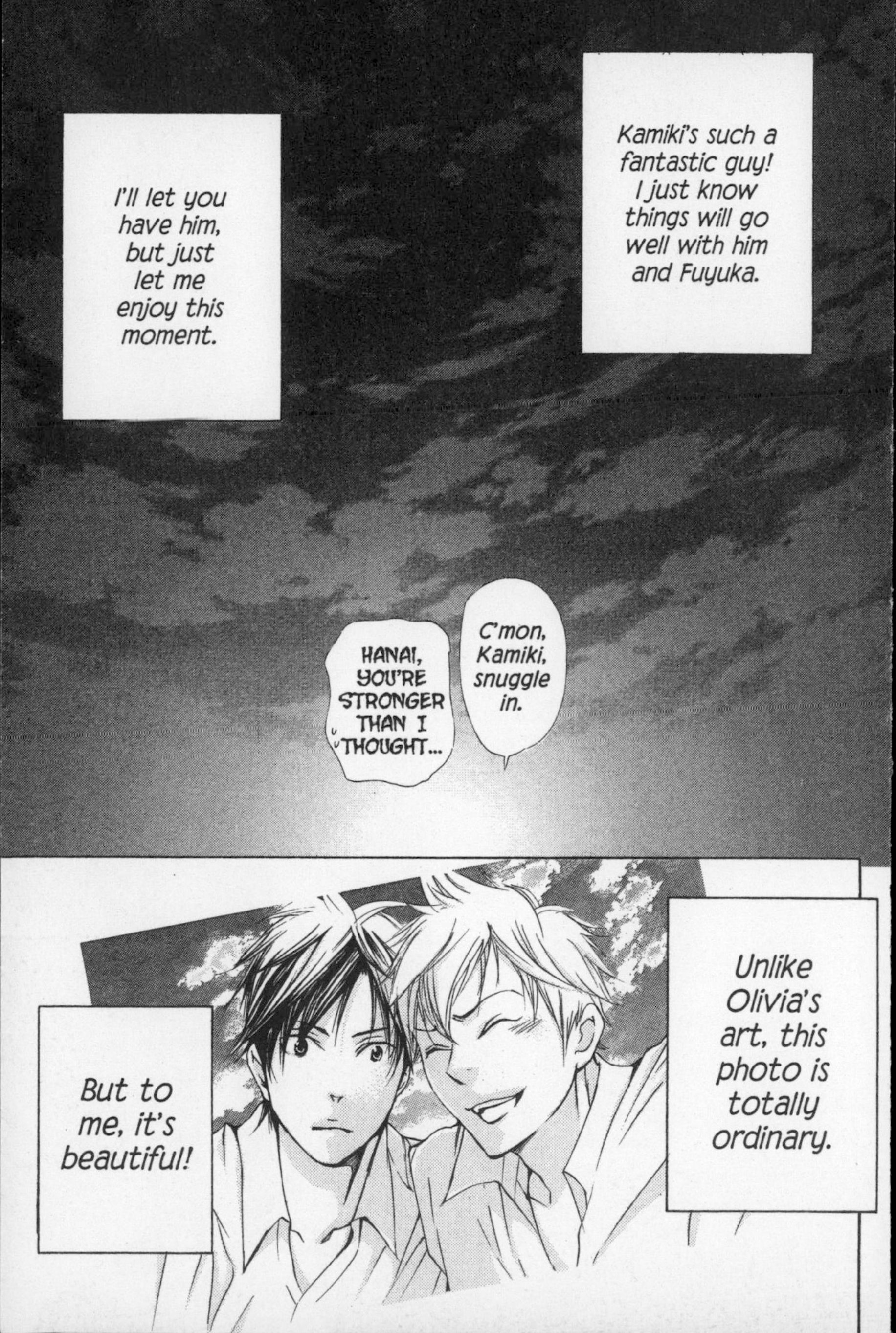
Kamiki's such a fantastic guy! I just know things will go well with him and Fuyuka.
I'll let you have him, but just let me enjoy this moment.
C'mon, Kamiki, snuggle in.
HANAI, YOU'RE STRONGER THAN I THOUGHT...
Unlike Olivia's art, this photo is totally ordinary.
But to me, it's beautiful!

# SEIHO BOYS HIGH SCHOOL!

## ♠CHAPTER 18♠

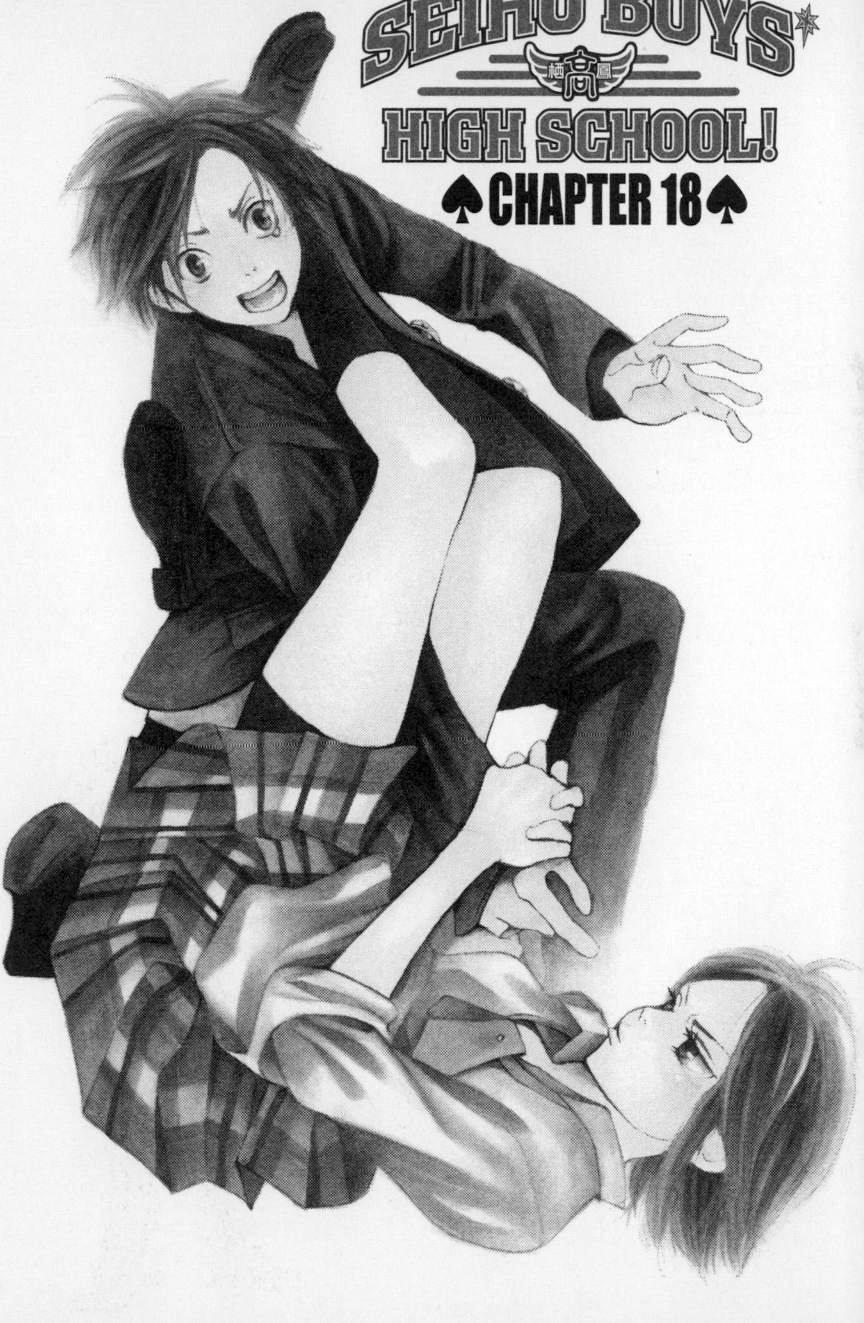

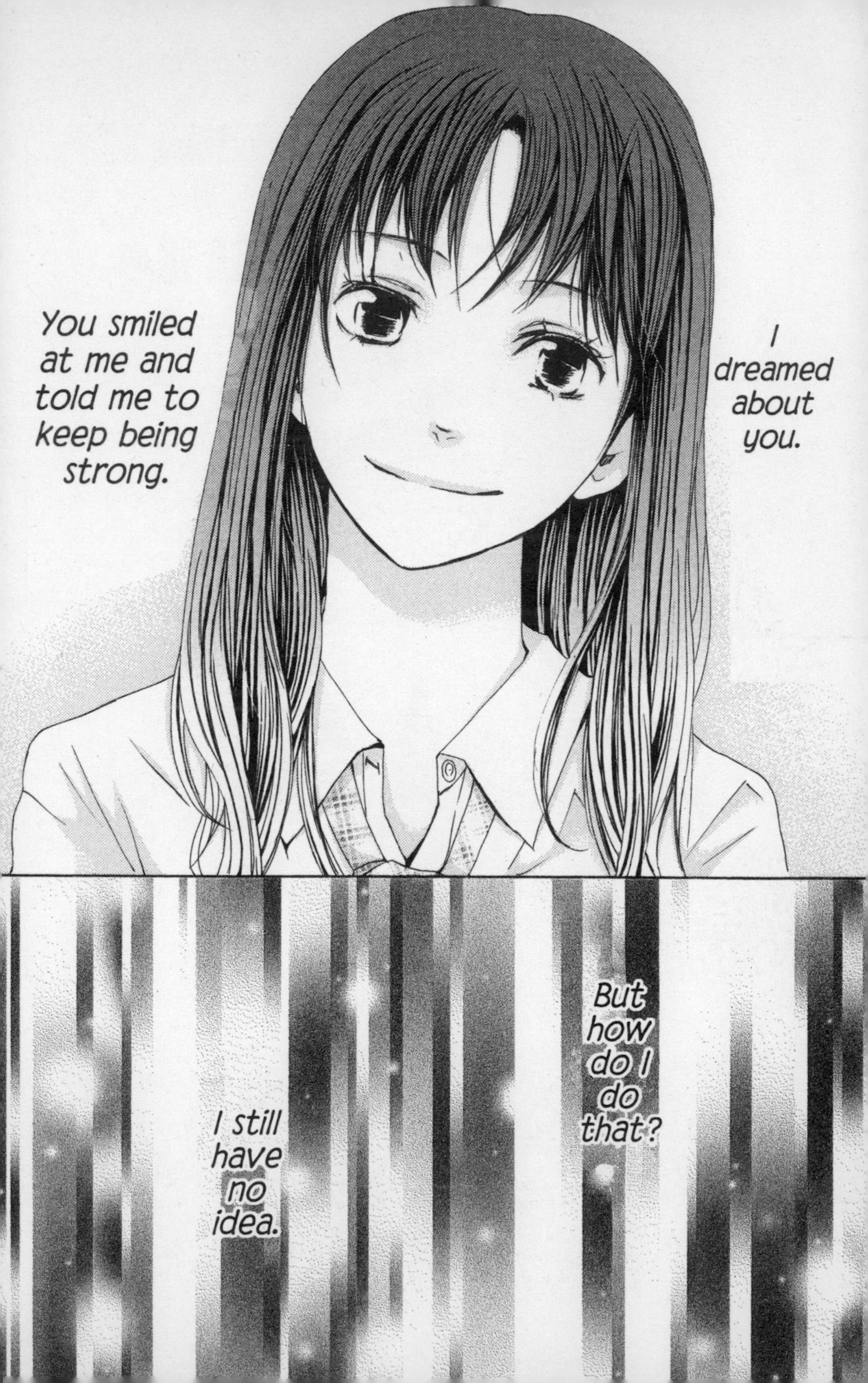
I dreamed about you.
You smiled at me and told me to keep being strong.
But how do I do that?
I still have no idea.

Uh-huh. Yeah.
Really?
That's good to know.
Sunday it is then.

# SEIHO BOYS HIGH SCHOOL!

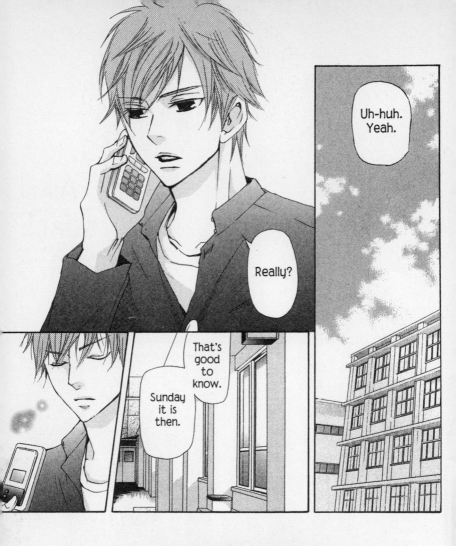

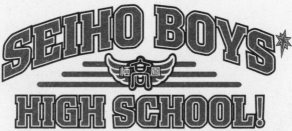

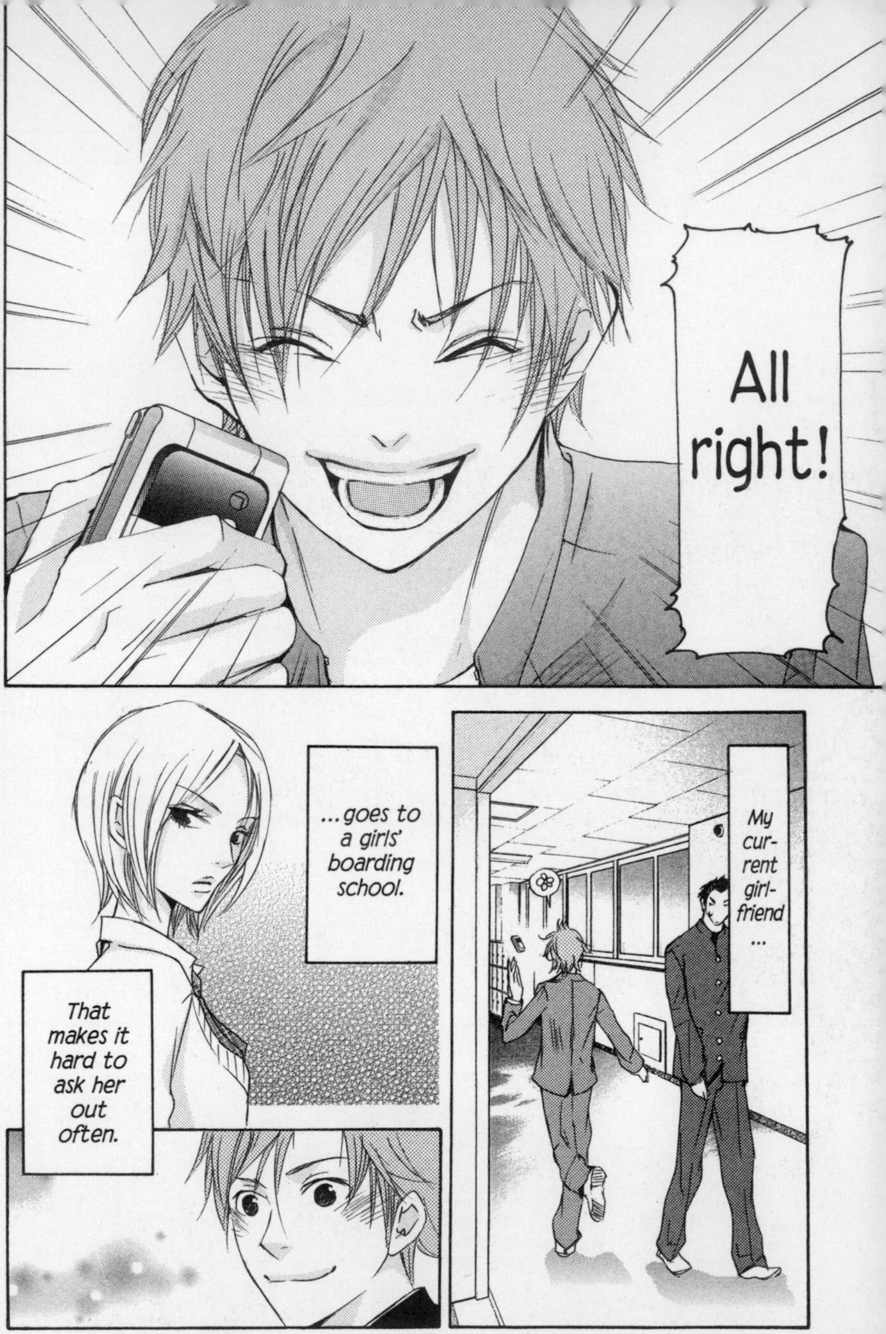
All right!
My current girlfriend...
...goes to a girls' boarding school.
That makes it hard to ask her out often.

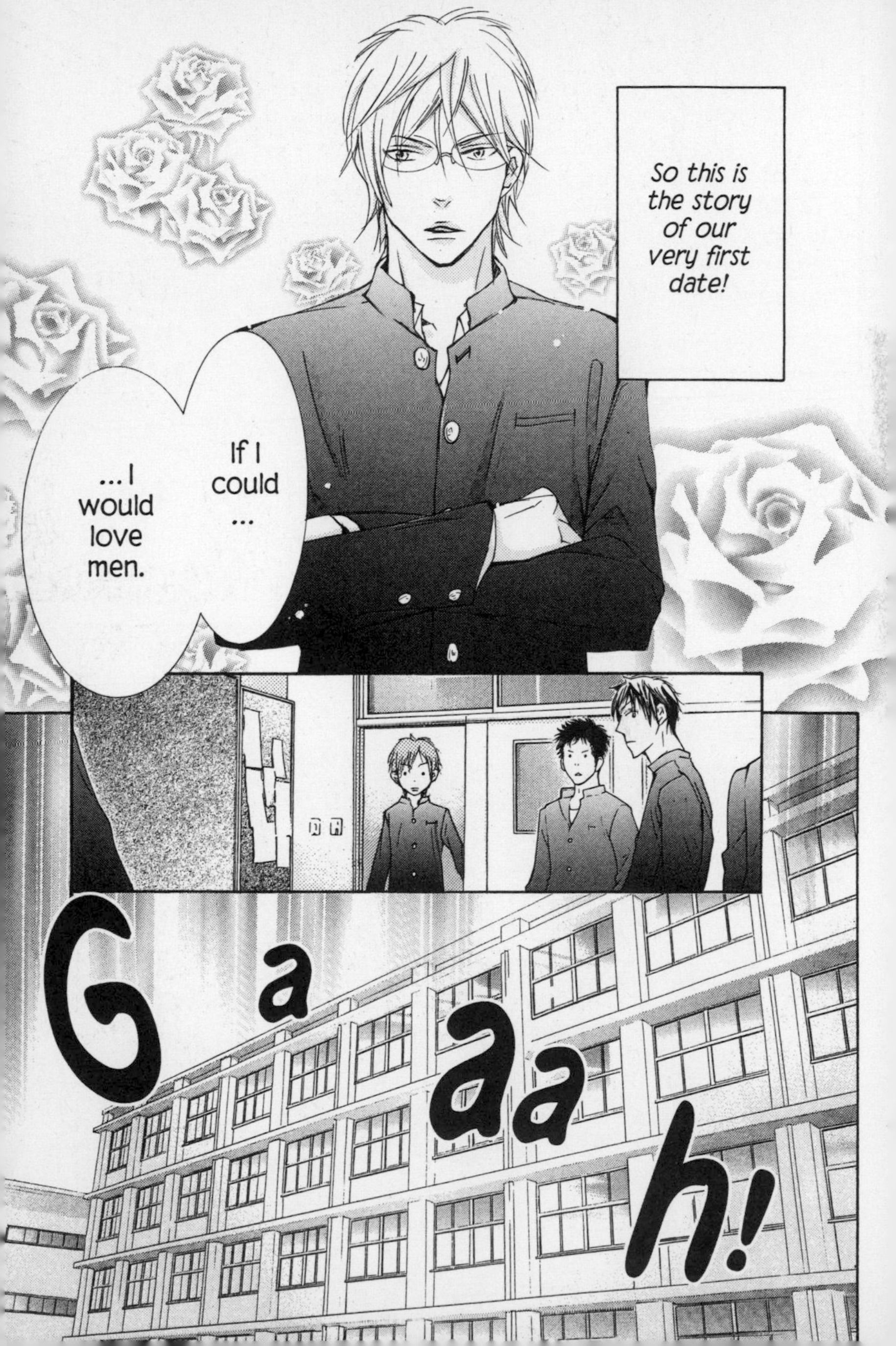
So this is the story of our very first date!
If I could ...
... I would love men.
Gaaaah!

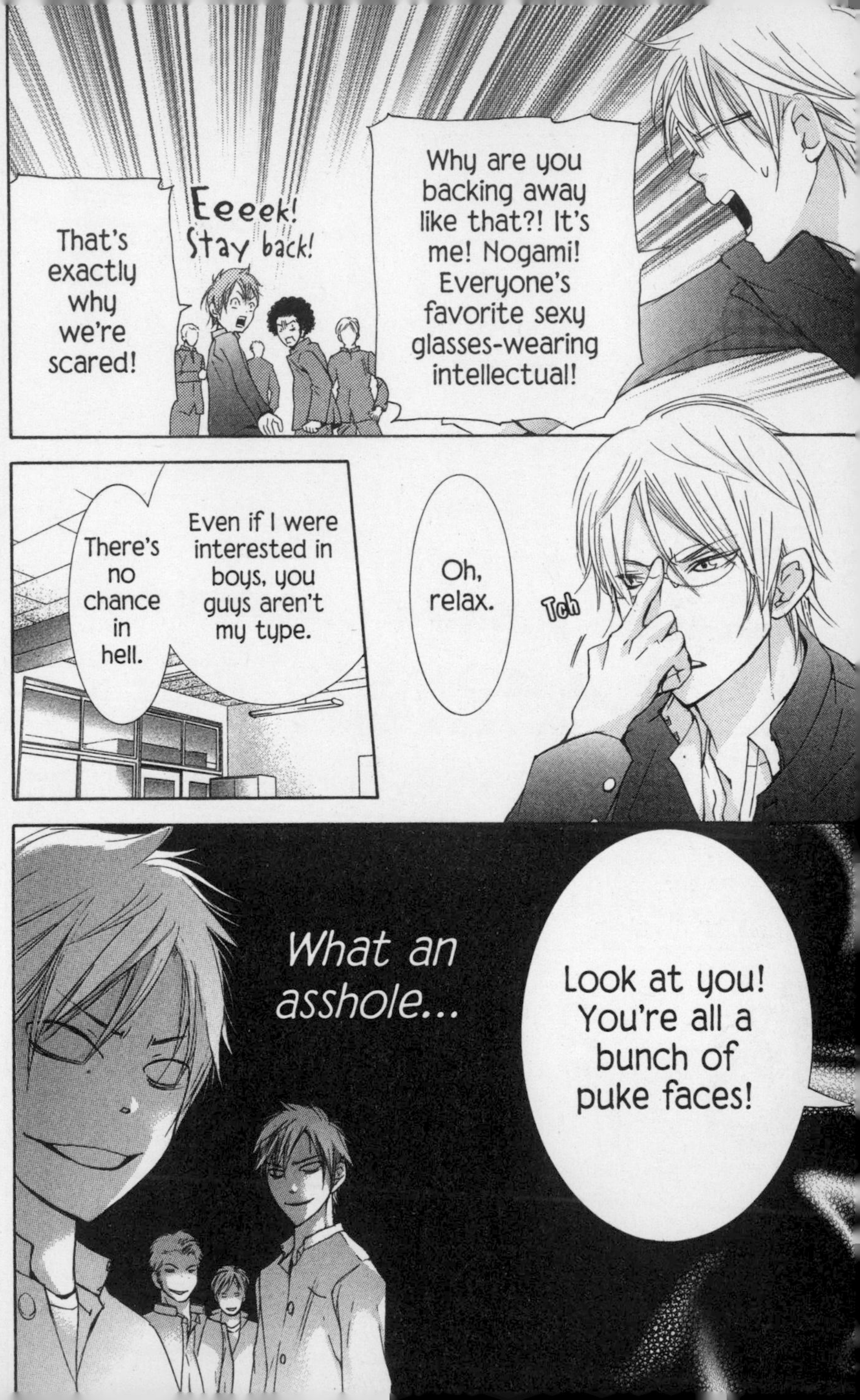
Why are you backing away like that?! It's me! Nogami! Everyone's favorite sexy glasses-wearing intellectual!
Eeeek! Stay back!
That's exactly why we're scared!
Tch
Oh, relax.
Even if I were interested in boys, you guys aren't my type.
There's no chance in hell.
Look at you! You're all a bunch of puke faces!
What an asshole...

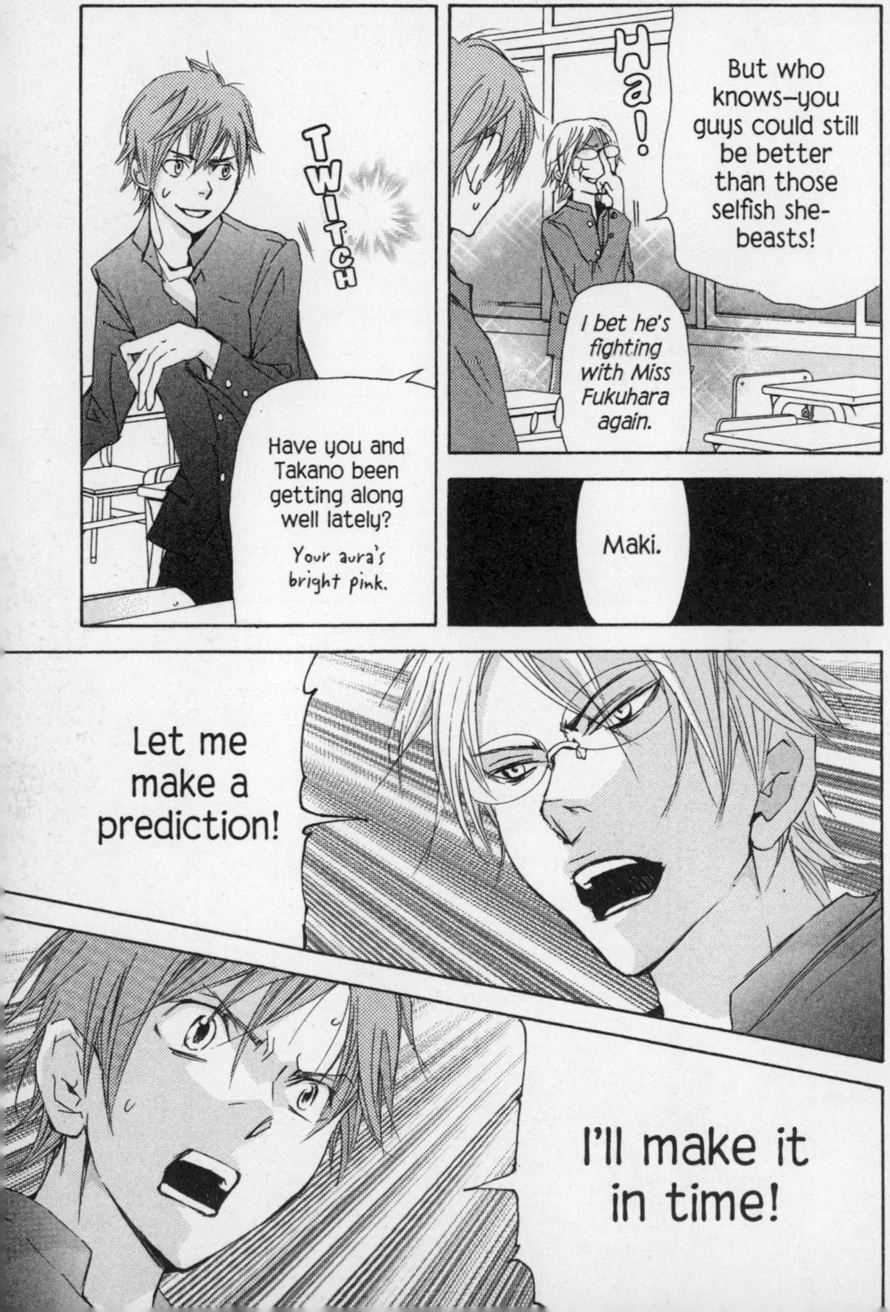
Ha!
But who knows—you guys could still be better than those selfish she-beasts!
I bet he's fighting with Miss Fukuhara again.
Maki.
TWITCH
Have you and Takano been getting along well lately?
Your aura's bright pink.
Let me make a prediction!
I'll make it in time!

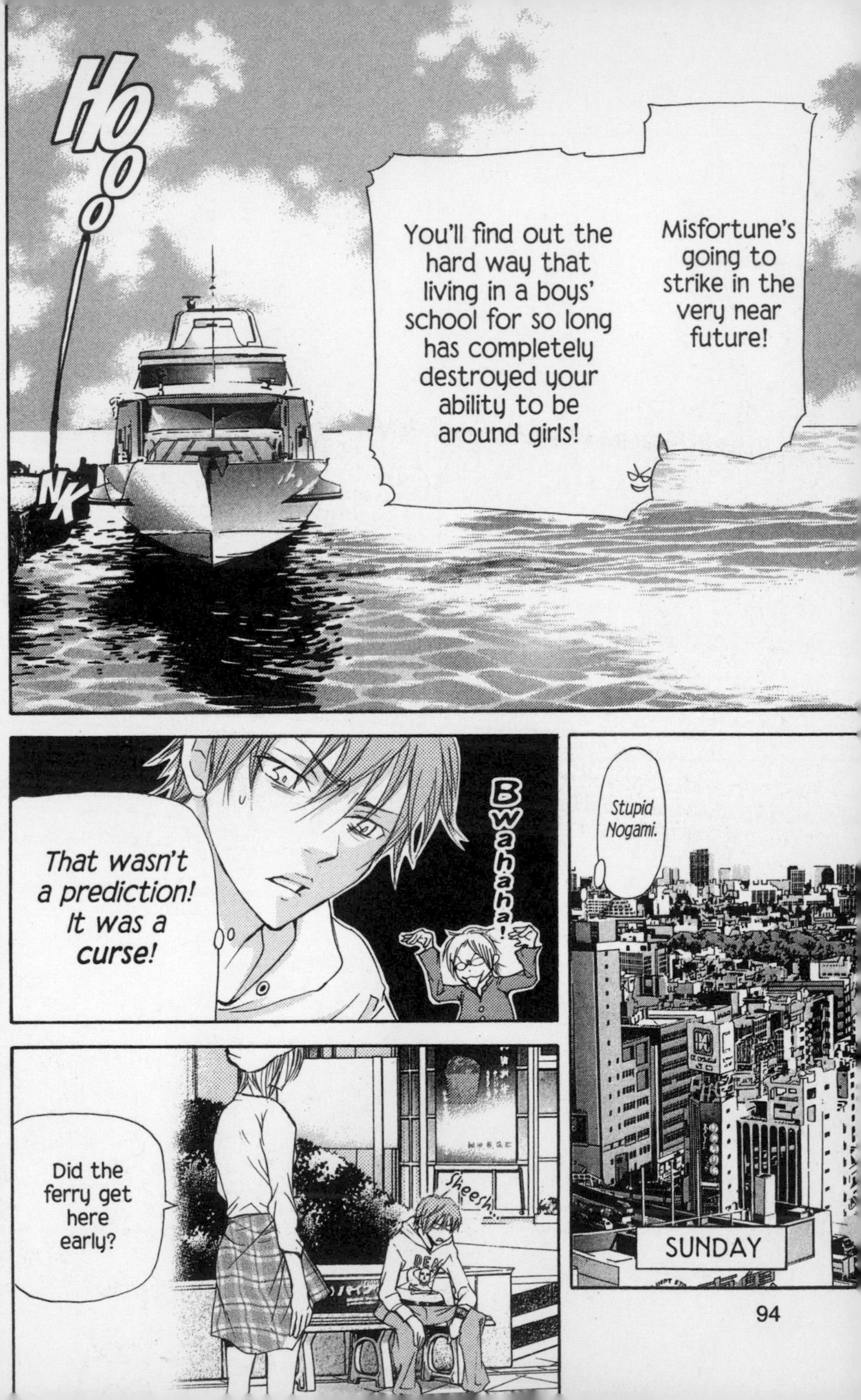
HOoooo
NK
Misfortune's going to strike in the very near future!
You'll find out the hard way that living in a boys' school for so long has completely destroyed your ability to be around girls!
Stupid Nogami.
SUNDAY
Bwahaha!
That wasn't a prediction! It was a curse!
Sheesh...
Did the ferry get here early?

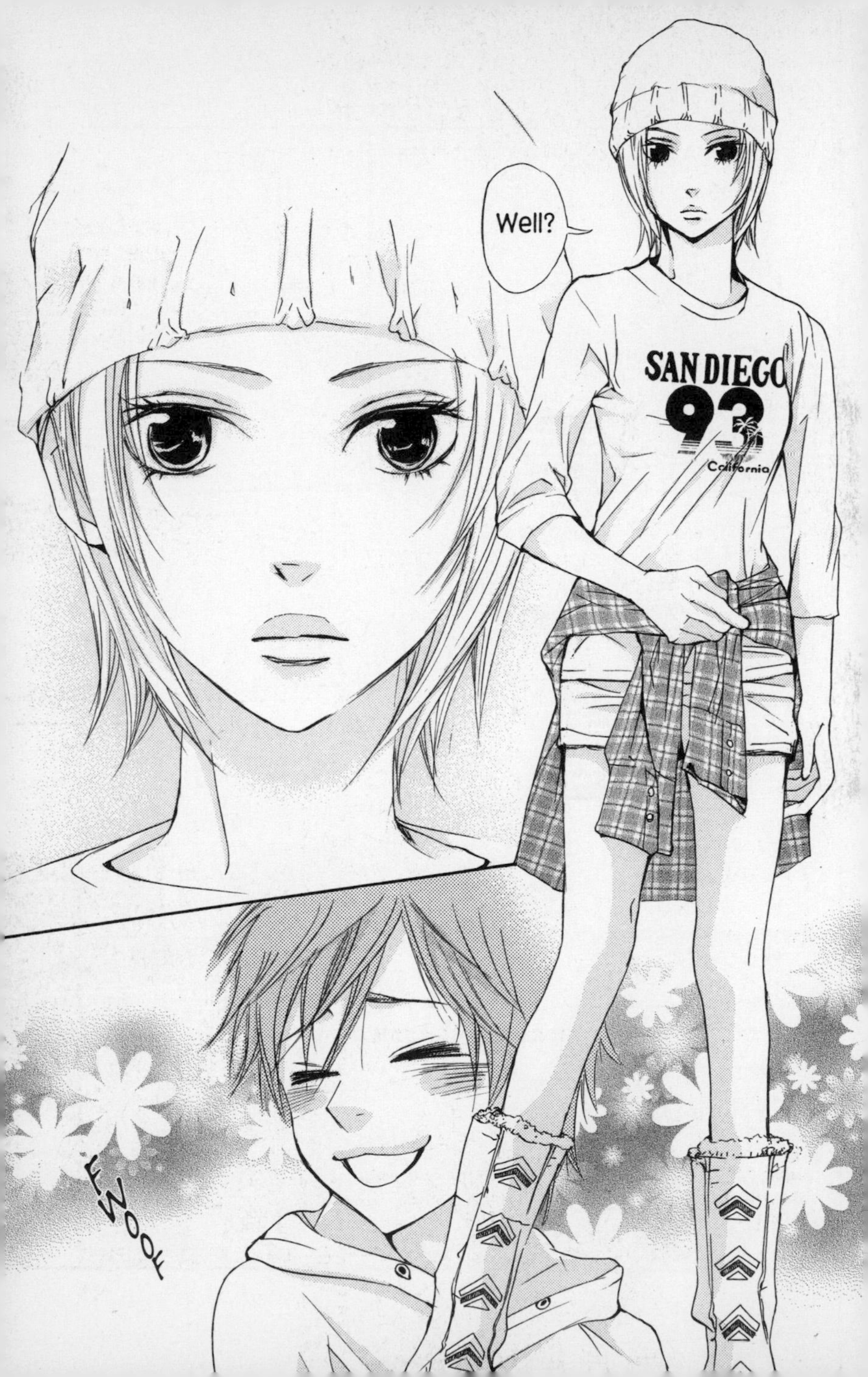
Well?
SAN DIEGO
93
California

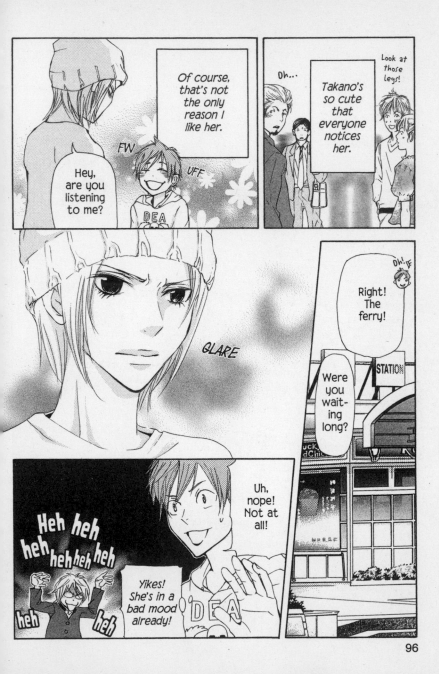

Oh...
Takano's so cute that everyone notices her.
Look at those legs!
Of course, that's not the only reason I like her.
FW
UFF
Hey, are you listening to me?
Oh!
Right! The ferry!
Were you wait-ing long?
STATION
GLARE
Uh, nope! Not at all!
Yikes! She's in a bad mood already!
Heh heh heh heh heh heh
heh
heh

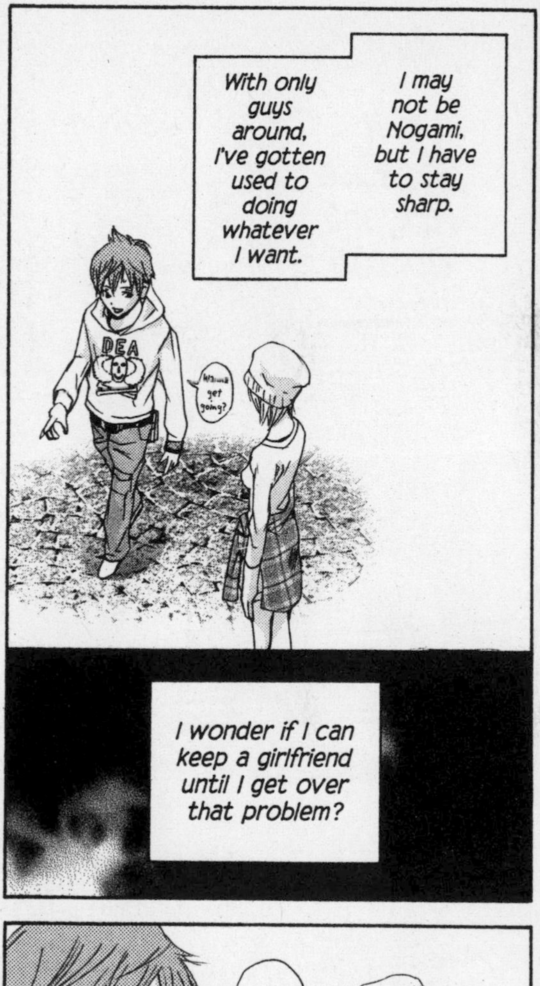
I may not be Nogami, but I have to stay sharp.
With only guys around, I've gotten used to doing whatever I want.
get going?
DEA
I wonder if I can keep a girlfriend until I get over that problem?
What?
Oh.
SAN DIEGO

## 1/3 Filler Corner

## A Collection of Words That Shocked Me

**Part ③**

Here's an answer my friend "A" flatly gave to a fashion student's survey in Ginza.

The question was "What's your favorite brand?"

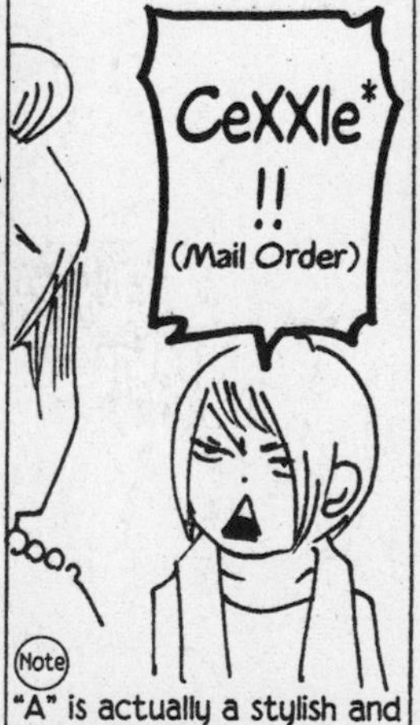
CeXXle* !!
(Mail Order)

*Not a high-end brand

Note "A" is actually a stylish and cute girl. She just felt she couldn't be bothered...

They didn't ask her any more questions after that...

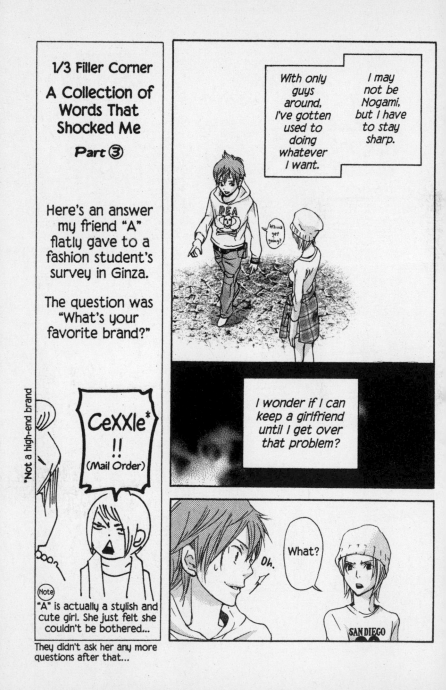

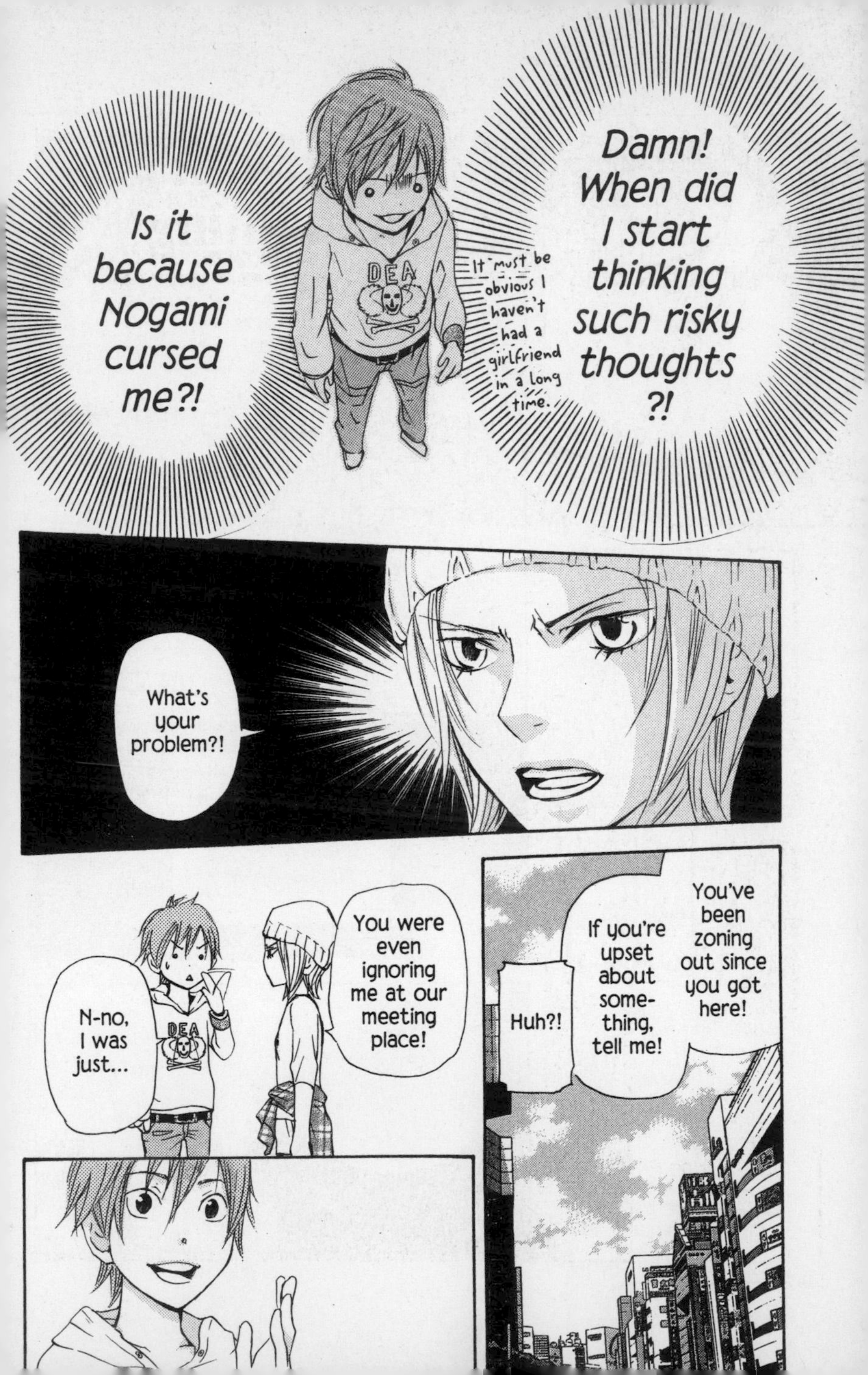
Damn! When did I start thinking such risky thoughts?!
It must be obvious I haven't had a girlfriend in a long time.
Is it because Nogami cursed me?!
What's your problem?!
You've been zoning out since you got here!
If you're upset about something, tell me!
Huh?!
You were even ignoring me at our meeting place!
N-no, I was just...

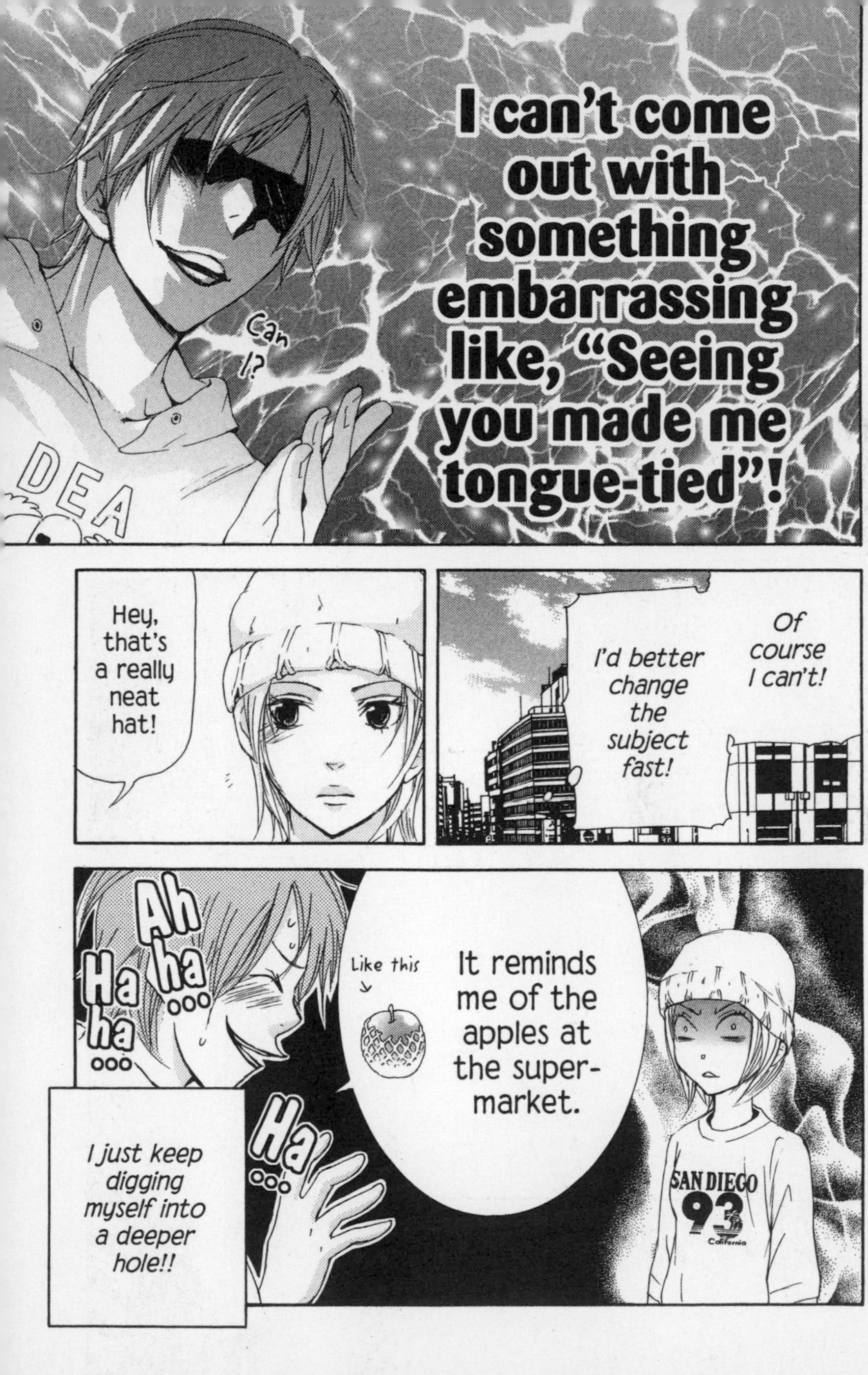
I can't come out with something embarrassing like, "Seeing you made me tongue-tied"!
Can I?
DEA
Of course I can't!
I'd better change the subject fast!
Hey, that's a really neat hat!
It reminds me of the apples at the super-market.
Like this
SAN DIECO 93 California
Ah ha ooo
Ha ha ooo
Ha ooo
I just keep digging myself into a deeper hole!!

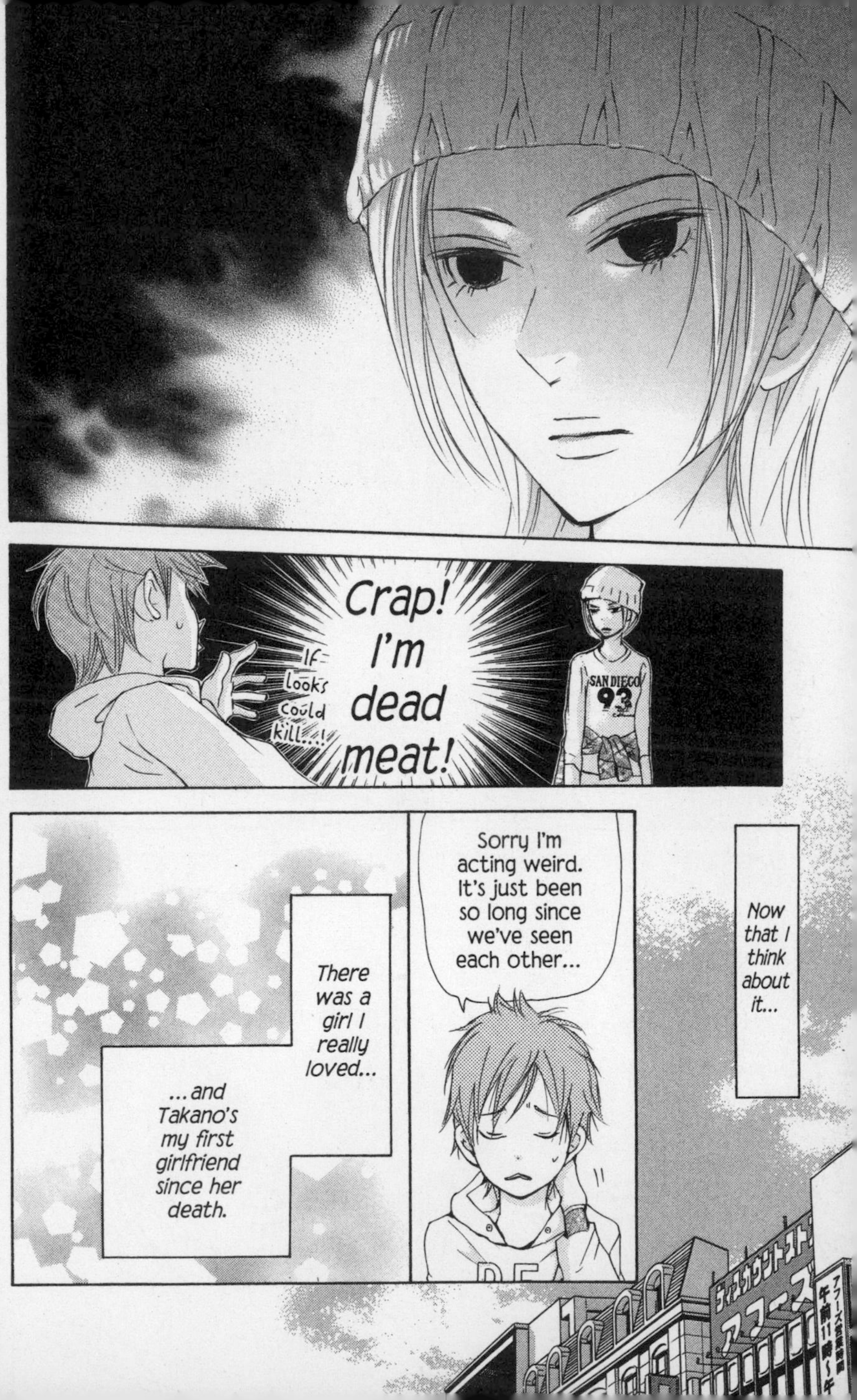
Crap! I'm dead meat!
If looks could kill...!
Now that I think about it...
Sorry I'm acting weird. It's just been so long since we've seen each other...
There was a girl I really loved...
...and Takano's my first girlfriend since her death.

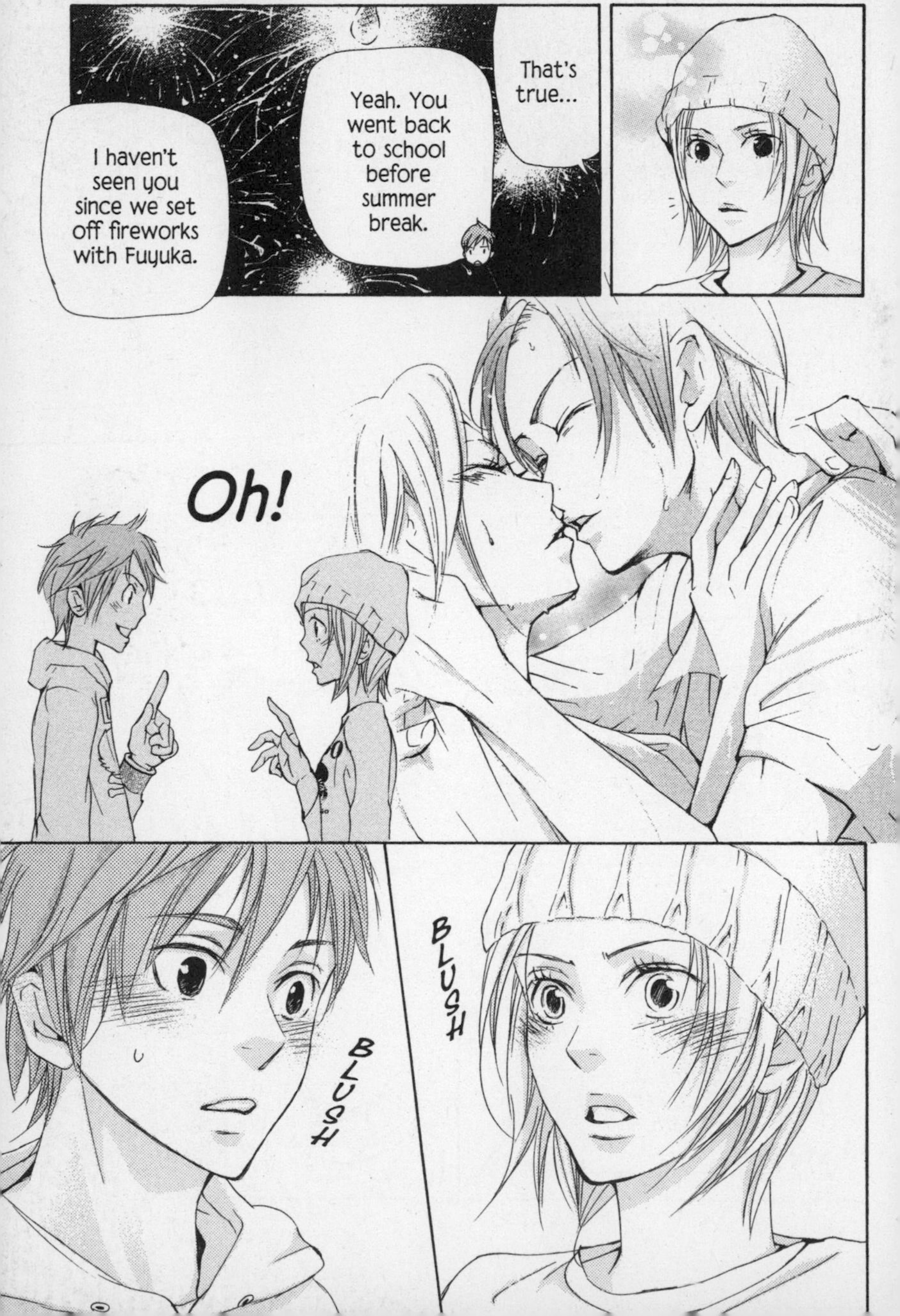
That's true...
Yeah. You went back to school before summer break.
I haven't seen you since we set off fireworks with Fuyuka.
Oh!
BLUSH
BLUSH

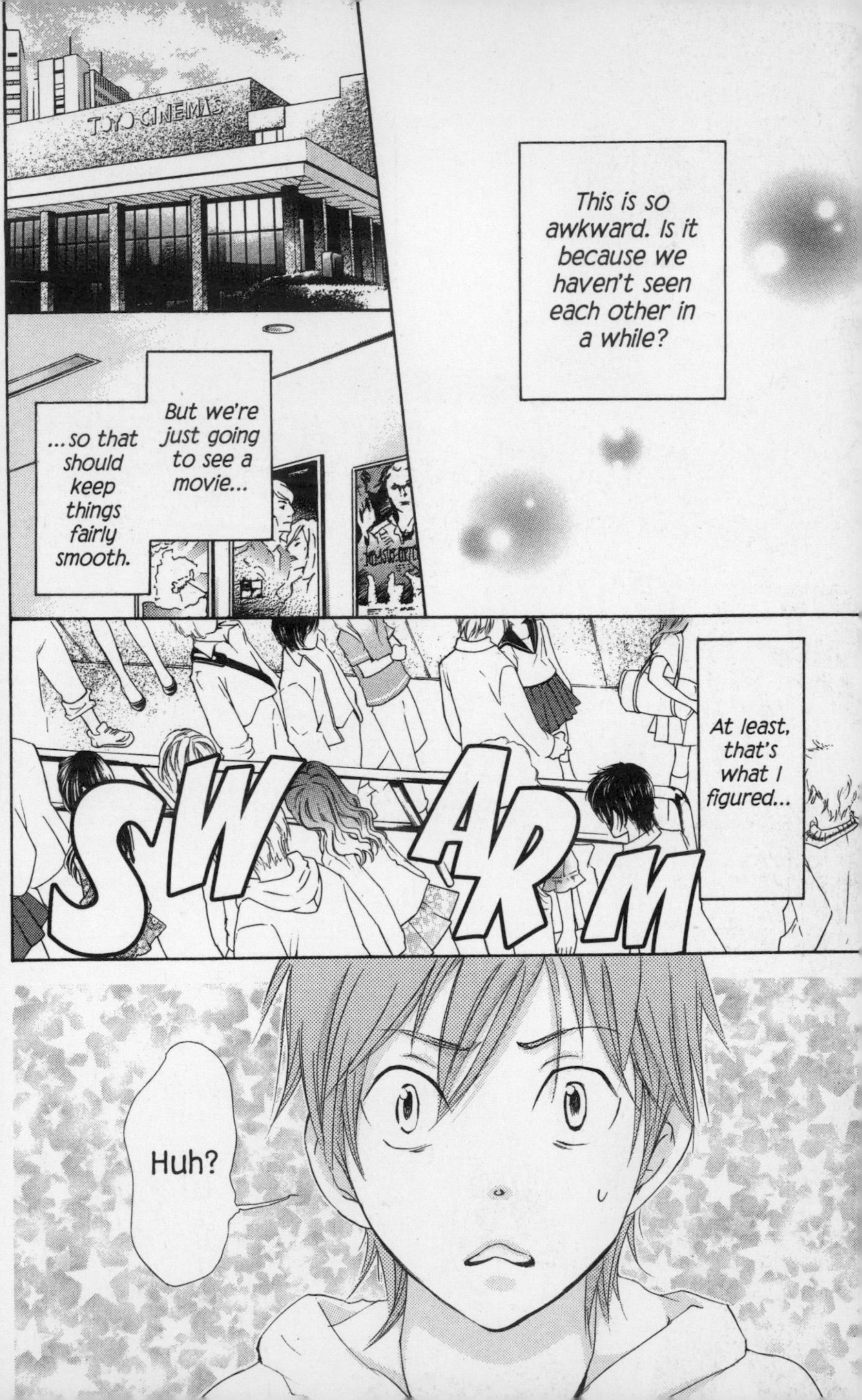
TOYO CINEMAS
This is so awkward. Is it because we haven't seen each other in a while?
But we're just going to see a movie...
...so that should keep things fairly smooth.
At least, that's what I figured...
SWARM
Huh?

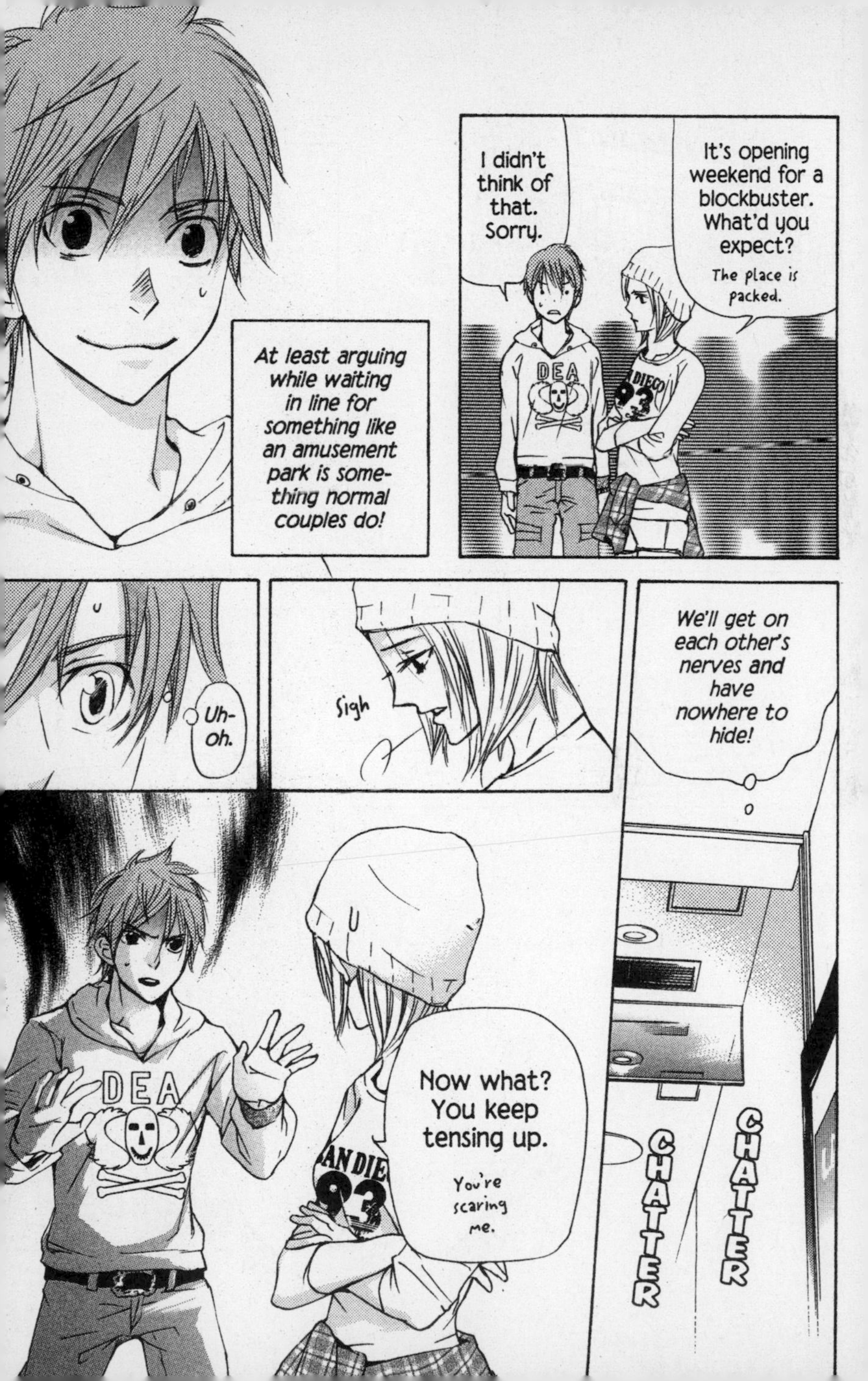
It's opening weekend for a blockbuster. What'd you expect?
The place is packed.
I didn't think of that. Sorry.
At least arguing while waiting in line for something like an amusement park is something normal couples do!
We'll get on each other's nerves and have nowhere to hide!
Sigh
Uh-oh.
CHATTER
CHATTER
Now what? You keep tensing up.
You're scaring me.

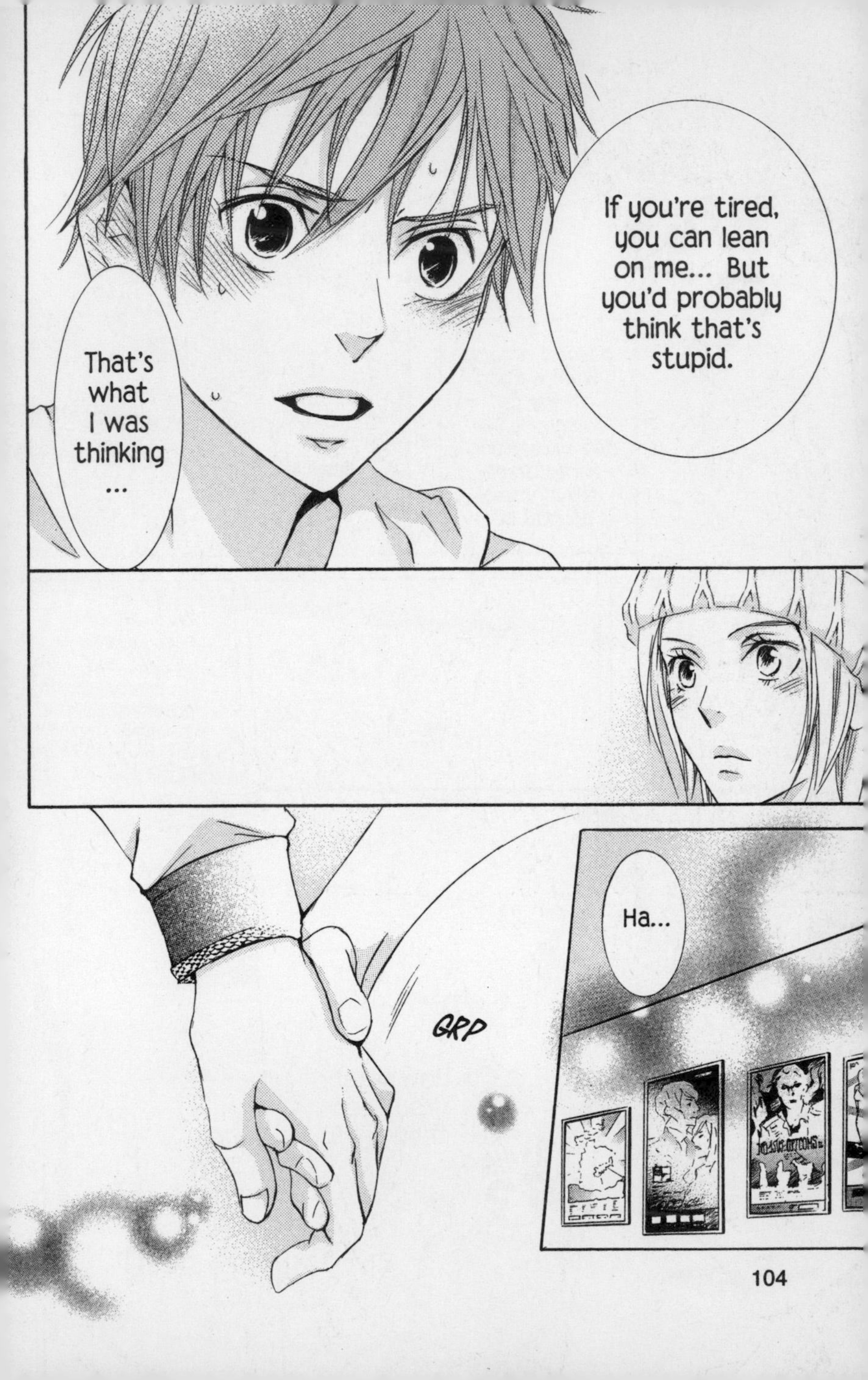
If you're tired, you can lean on me... But you'd probably think that's stupid.
That's what I was thinking ...
Ha...
GRP

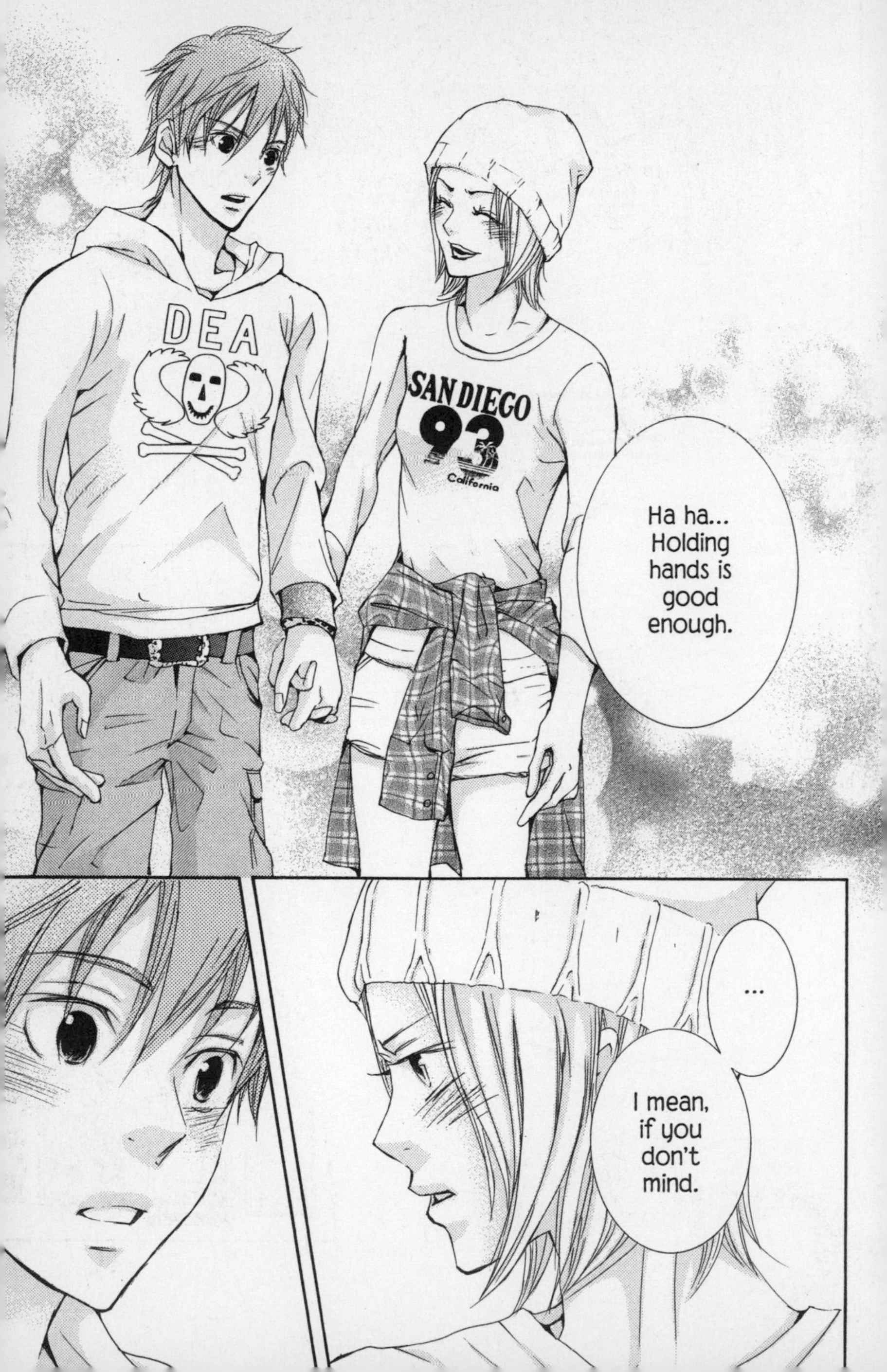
SAN DIEGO
93
California
DEA
Ha ha... Holding hands is good enough.
...
I mean, if you don't mind.

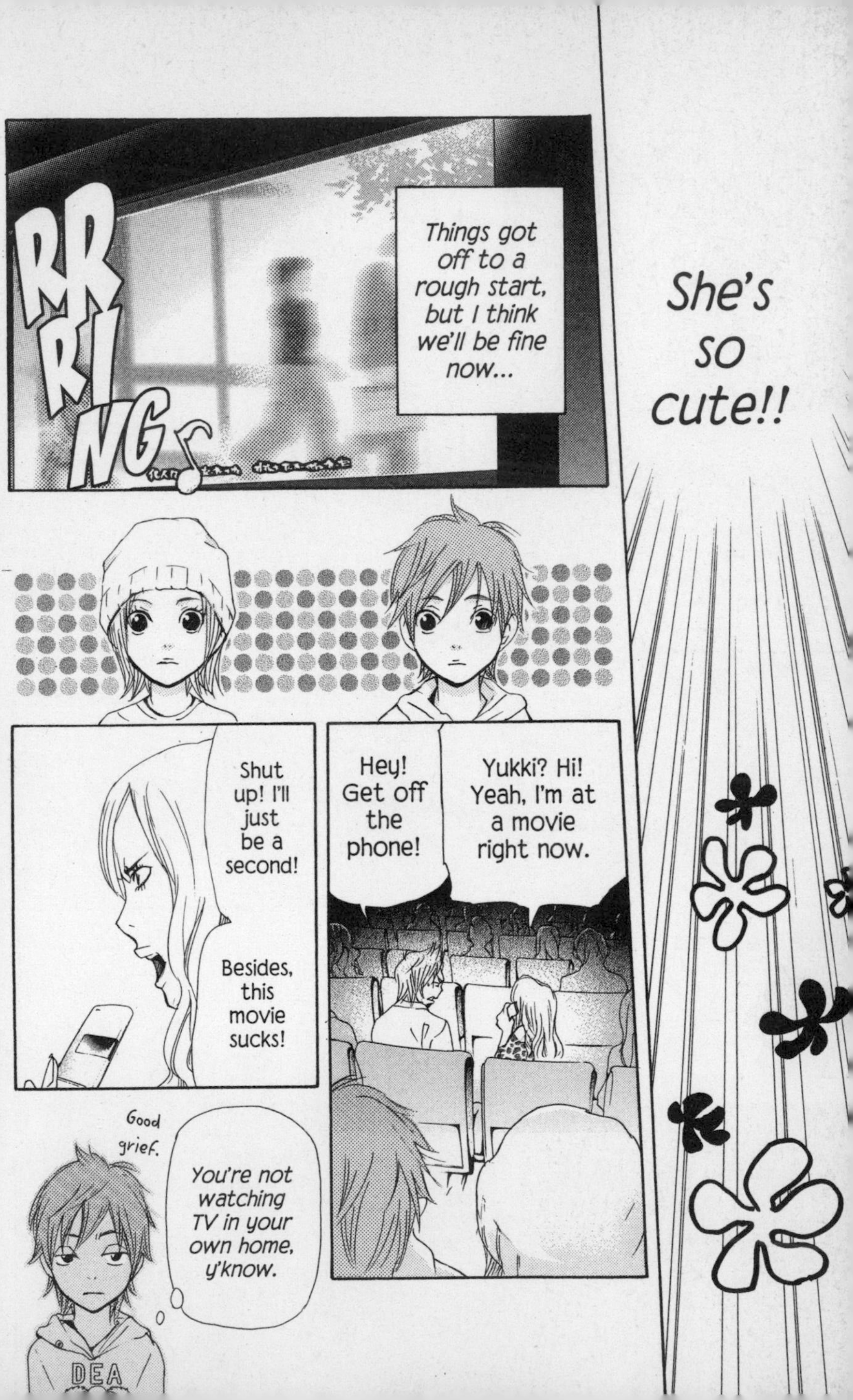
She's so cute!!
Things got off to a rough start, but I think we'll be fine now...
RRRING
Yukki? Hi! Yeah, I'm at a movie right now.
Hey! Get off the phone!
Shut up! I'll just be a second!
Besides, this movie sucks!
Good grief.
You're not watching TV in your own home, y'know.

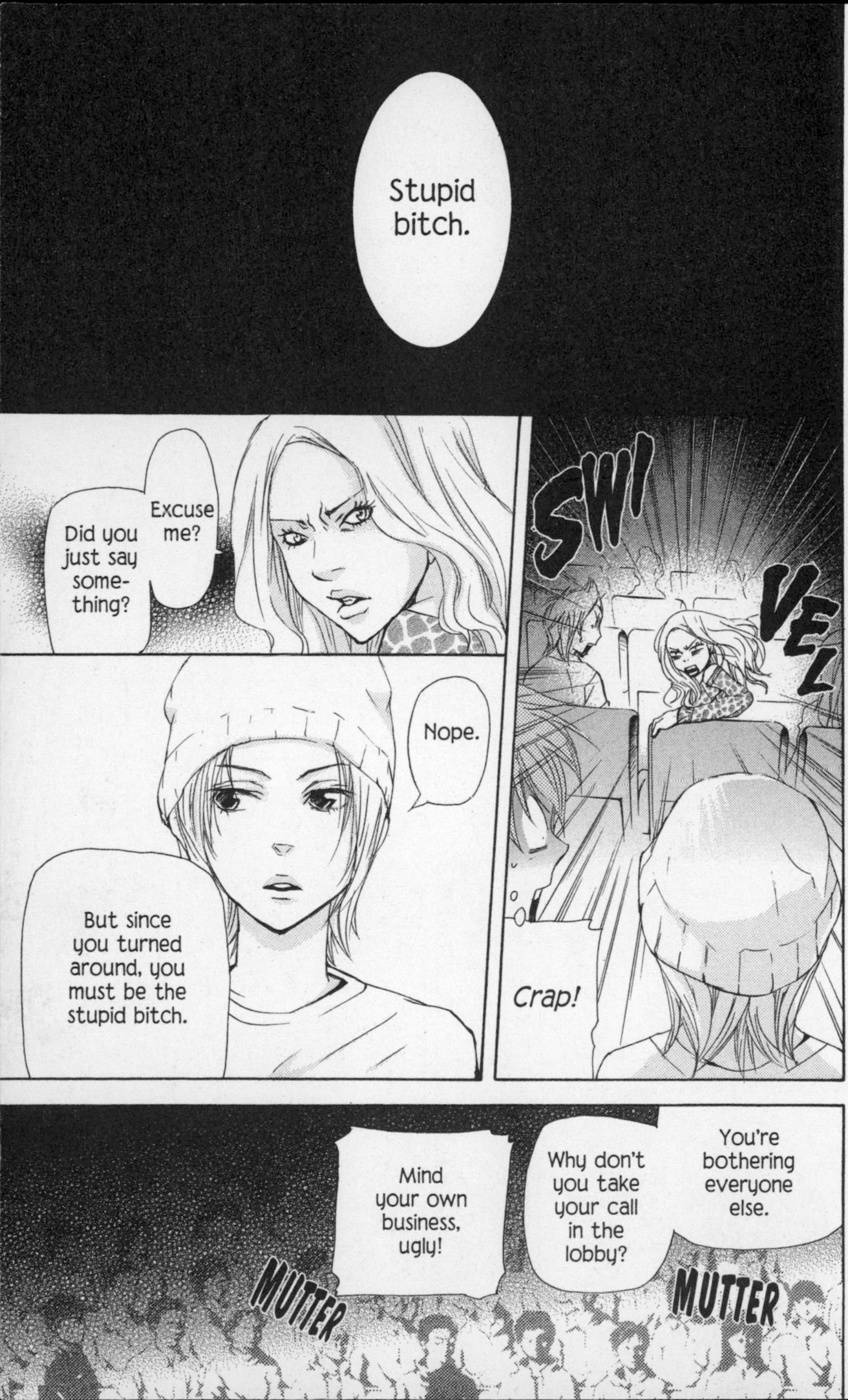
Stupid bitch.
SWIVEL
Crap!
Excuse me?
Did you just say some-thing?
Nope.
But since you turned around, you must be the stupid bitch.
You're bothering everyone else.
Why don't you take your call in the lobby?
Mind your own business, ugly!
MUTTER
MUTTER

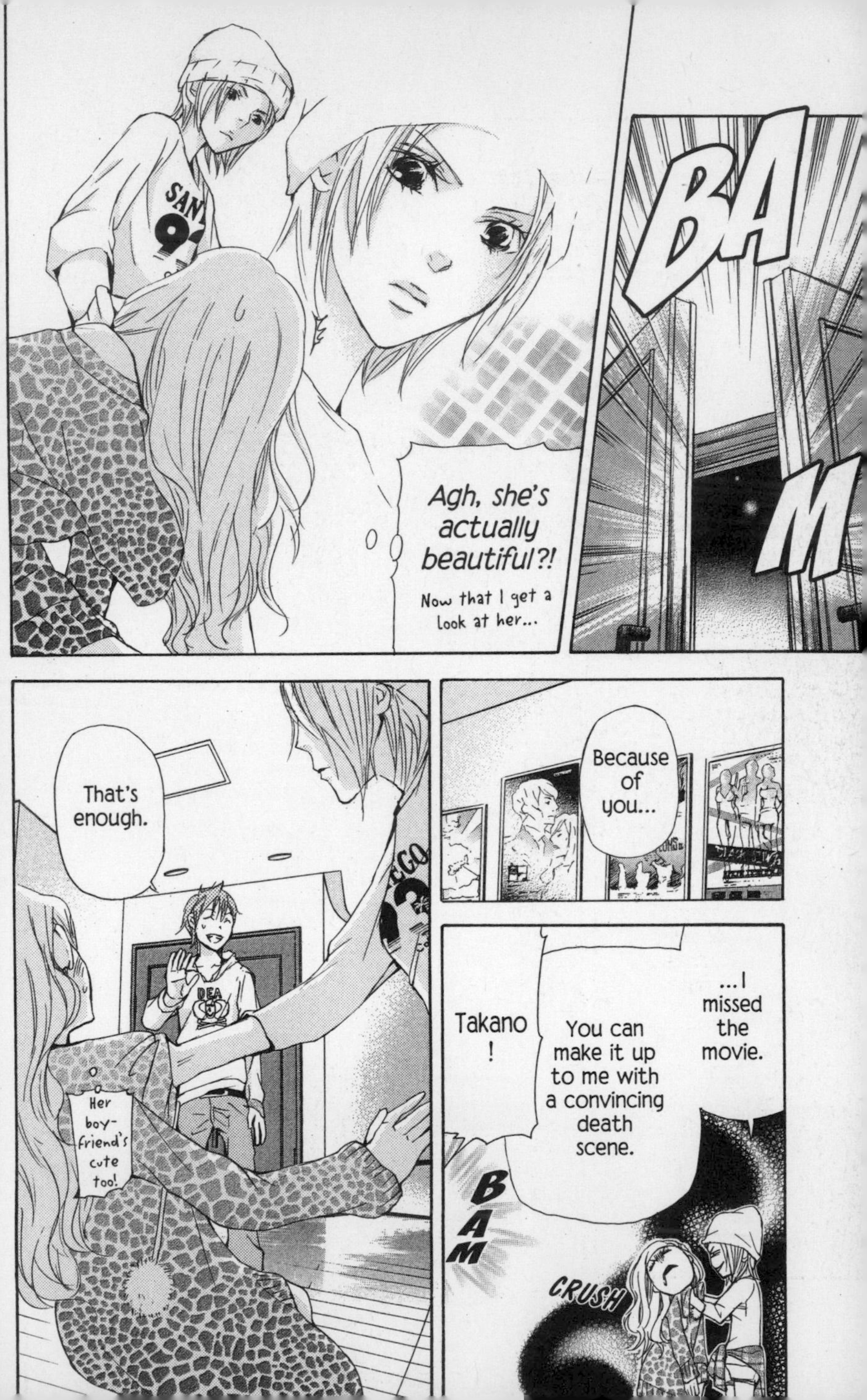
BAM
Agh, she's actually beautiful?!
Now that I get a look at her...
Because of you...
...I missed the movie.
You can make it up to me with a convincing death scene.
Takano!
BAM
CRUSH
That's enough.
Her boyfriend's cute too!

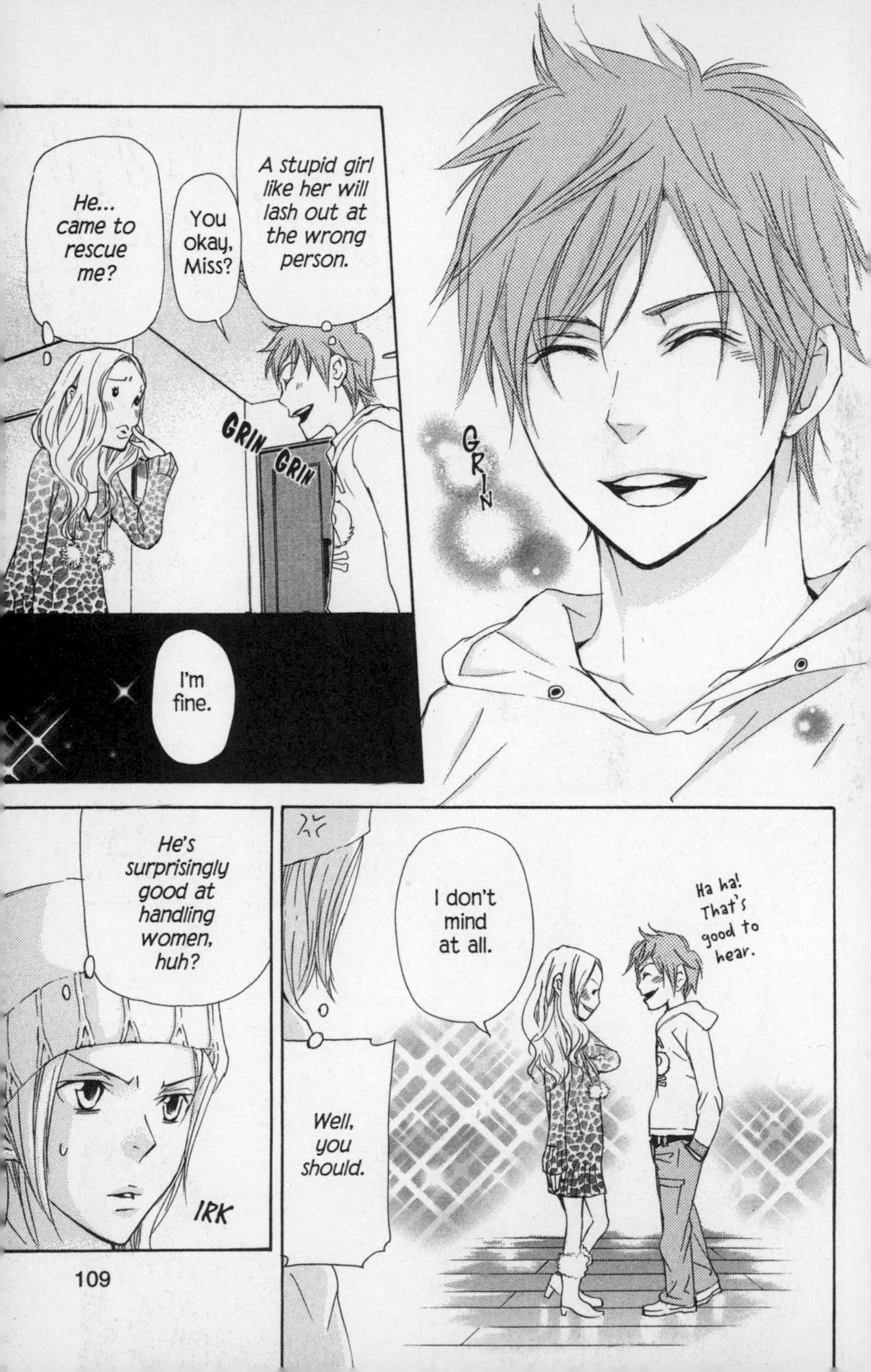
GRIN
A stupid girl like her will lash out at the wrong person.
You okay, Miss?
He... came to rescue me?
GRIN GRIN
I'm fine.
Ha ha! That's good to hear.
I don't mind at all.
Well, you should.
He's surprisingly good at handling women, huh?
IRK

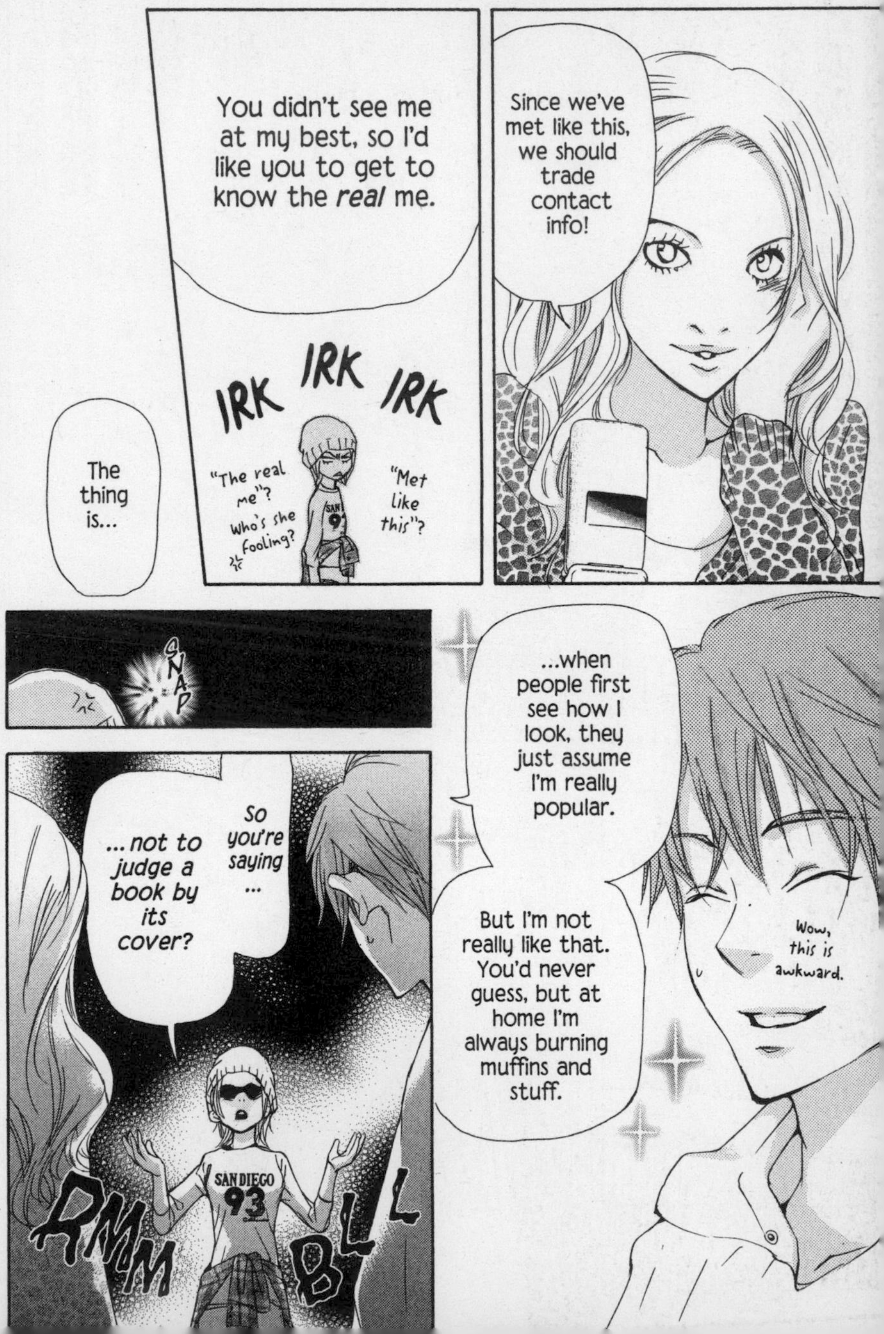
Since we've met like this, we should trade contact info!
You didn't see me at my best, so I'd like you to get to know the *real* me.
IRK IRK IRK
"Met like this"?
"The real me"? Who's she fooling?
The thing is...
...when people first see how I look, they just assume I'm really popular.
But I'm not really like that. You'd never guess, but at home I'm always burning muffins and stuff.
Wow, this is awkward.
SNAP
So you're saying...
...not to judge a book by its cover?
SAN DIEGO 93
RMMBLL

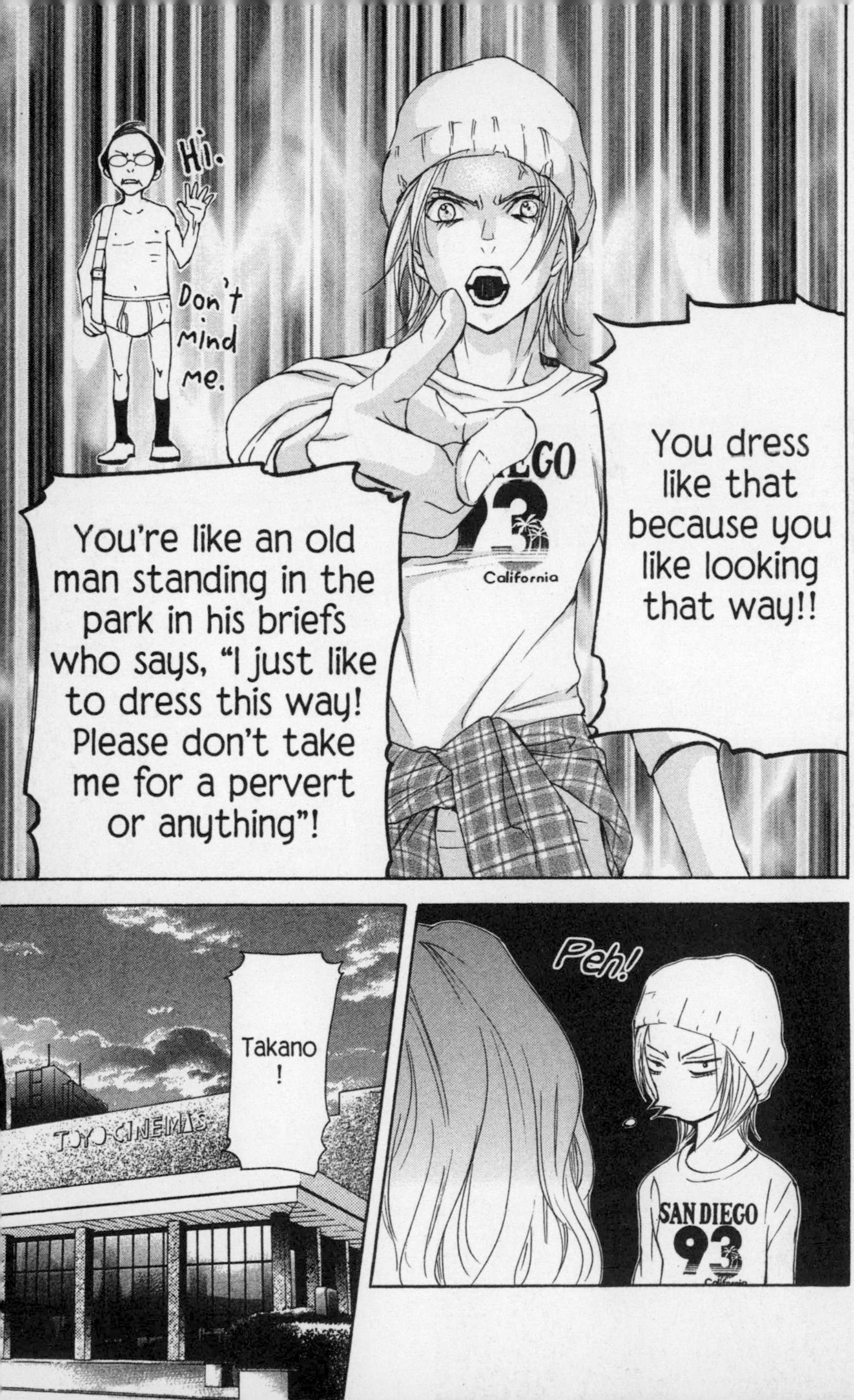
You dress like that because you like looking that way!!
You're like an old man standing in the park in his briefs who says, "I just like to dress this way! Please don't take me for a pervert or anything"!
Hi.
Don't mind me.
Peh!
SAN DIEGO 93 California
Takano !
TOYO CINEMAS

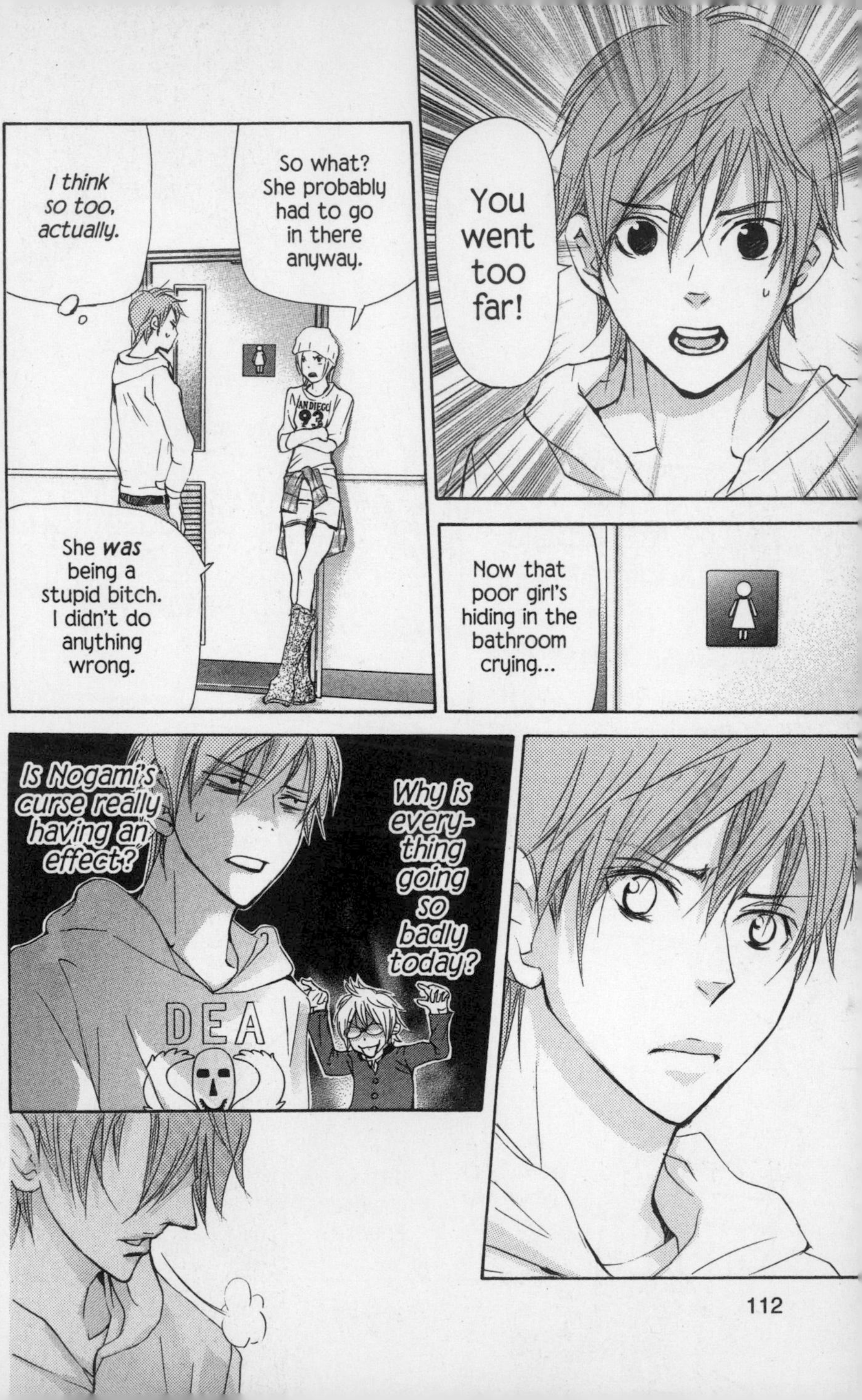
You went too far!
Now that poor girl's hiding in the bathroom crying...
So what? She probably had to go in there anyway.
*I think so too, actually.*
She *was* being a stupid bitch. I didn't do anything wrong.
Why is every-thing going so badly today?
Is Nogami's curse really having an effect?
DEA

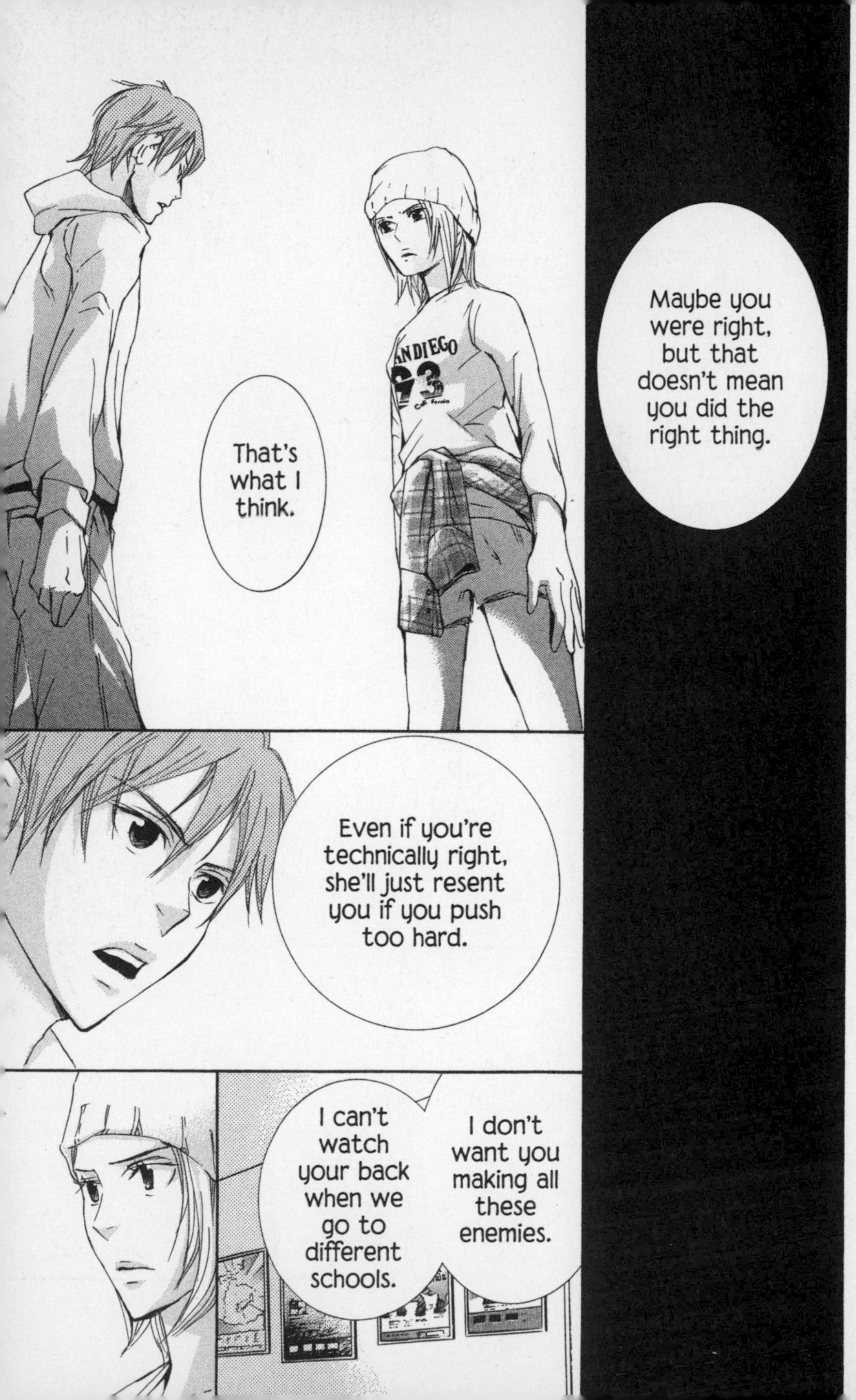
Maybe you were right, but that doesn't mean you did the right thing.
That's what I think.
Even if you're technically right, she'll just resent you if you push too hard.
I don't want you making all these enemies.
I can't watch your back when we go to different schools.

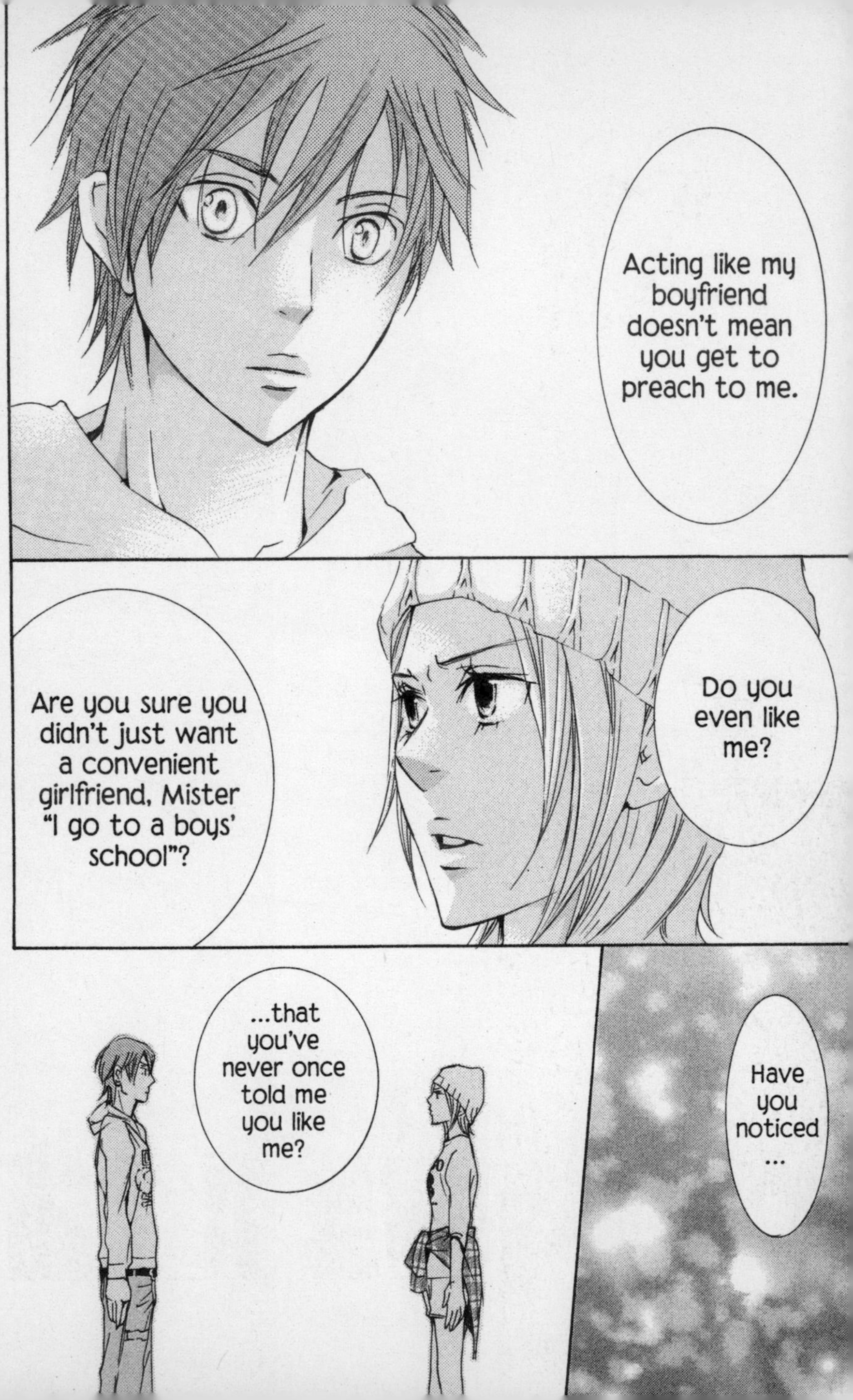
Acting like my boyfriend doesn't mean you get to preach to me.
Do you even like me?
Are you sure you didn't just want a convenient girlfriend, Mister "I go to a boys' school"?
Have you noticed ...
...that you've never once told me you like me?

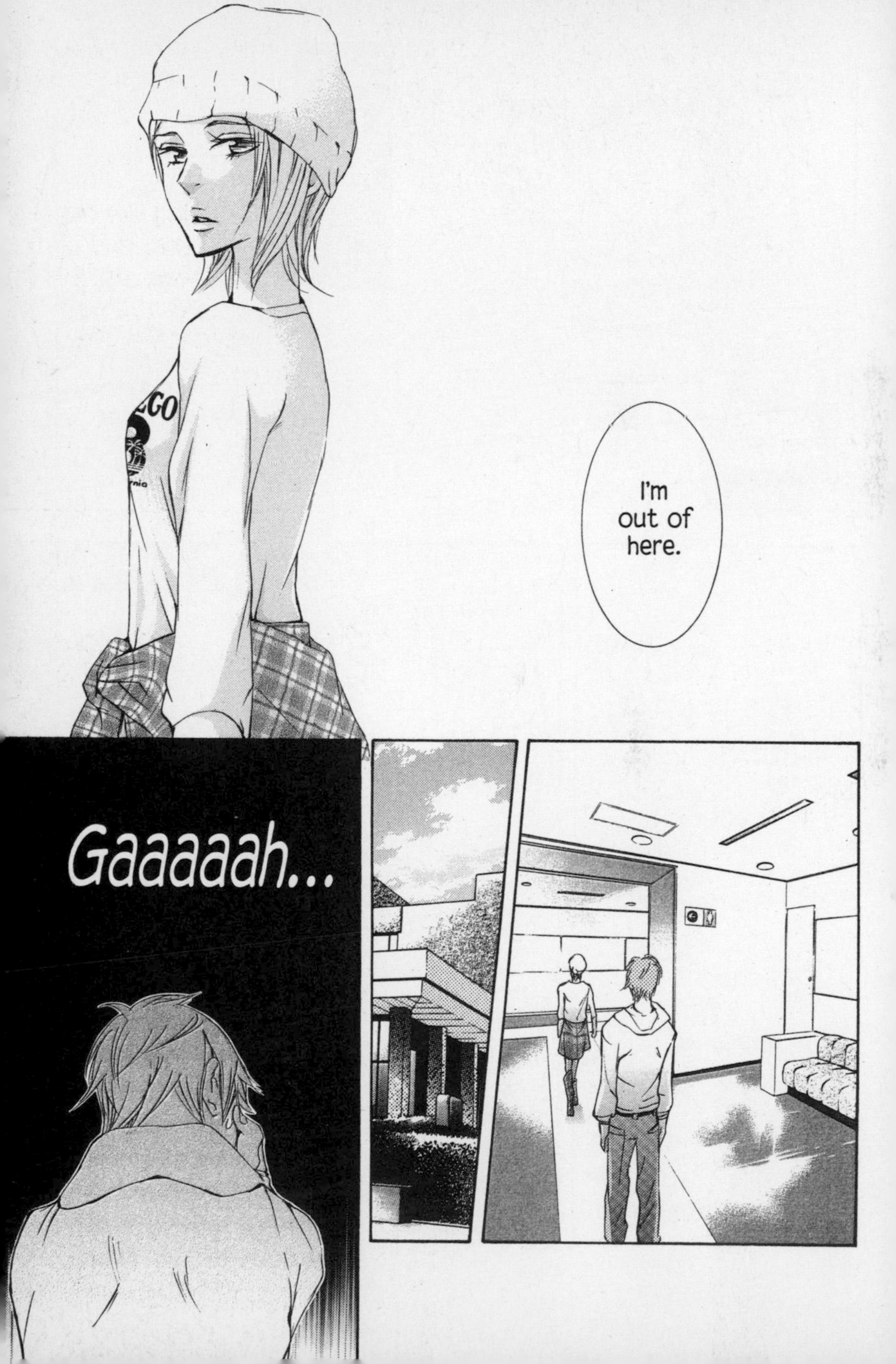
I'm out of here.
Gaaaaah...

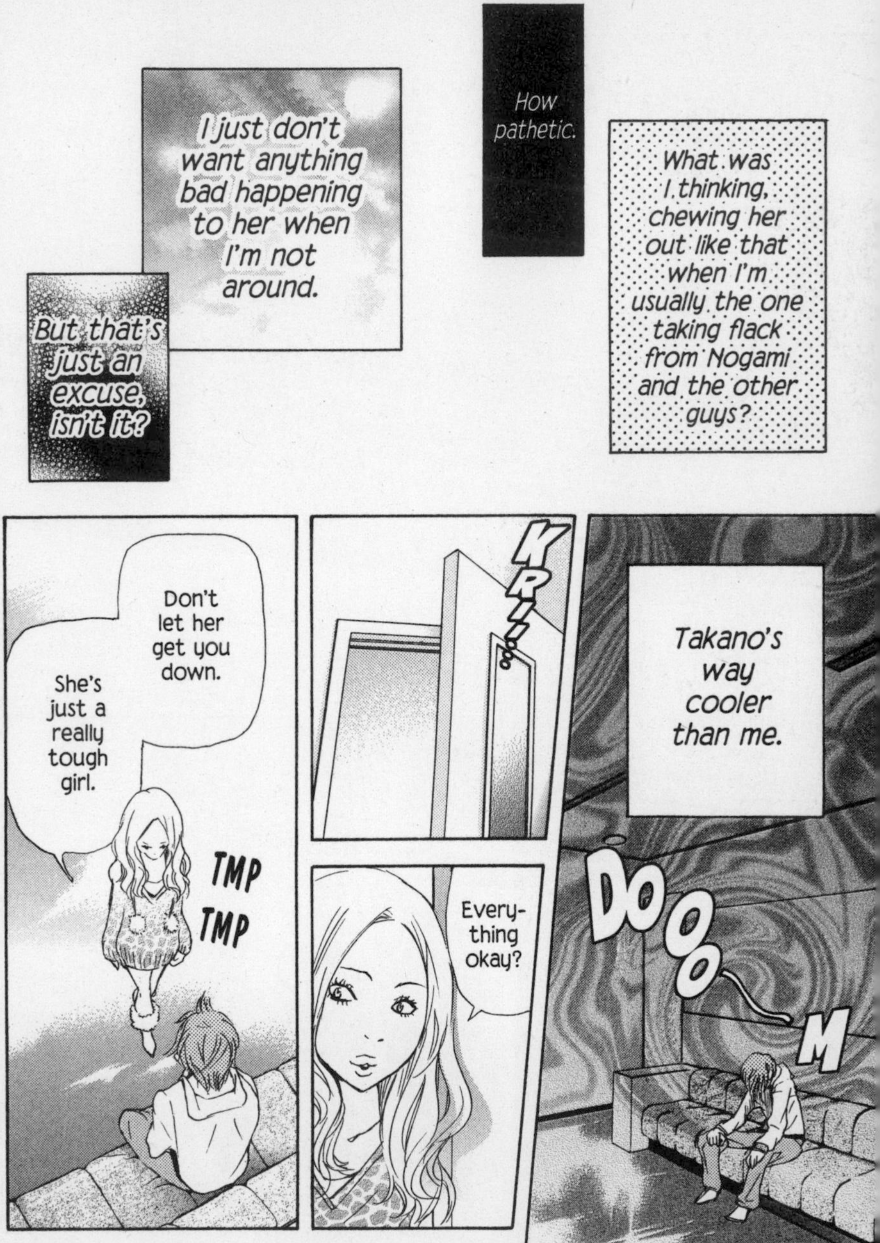
What was I thinking, chewing her out like that when I'm usually the one taking flack from Nogami and the other guys?
How pathetic.
I just don't want anything bad happening to her when I'm not around.
But that's just an excuse, isn't it?
Takano's way cooler than me.
DOOOM
KRI...
Every-thing okay?
Don't let her get you down.
She's just a really tough girl.
TMP TMP

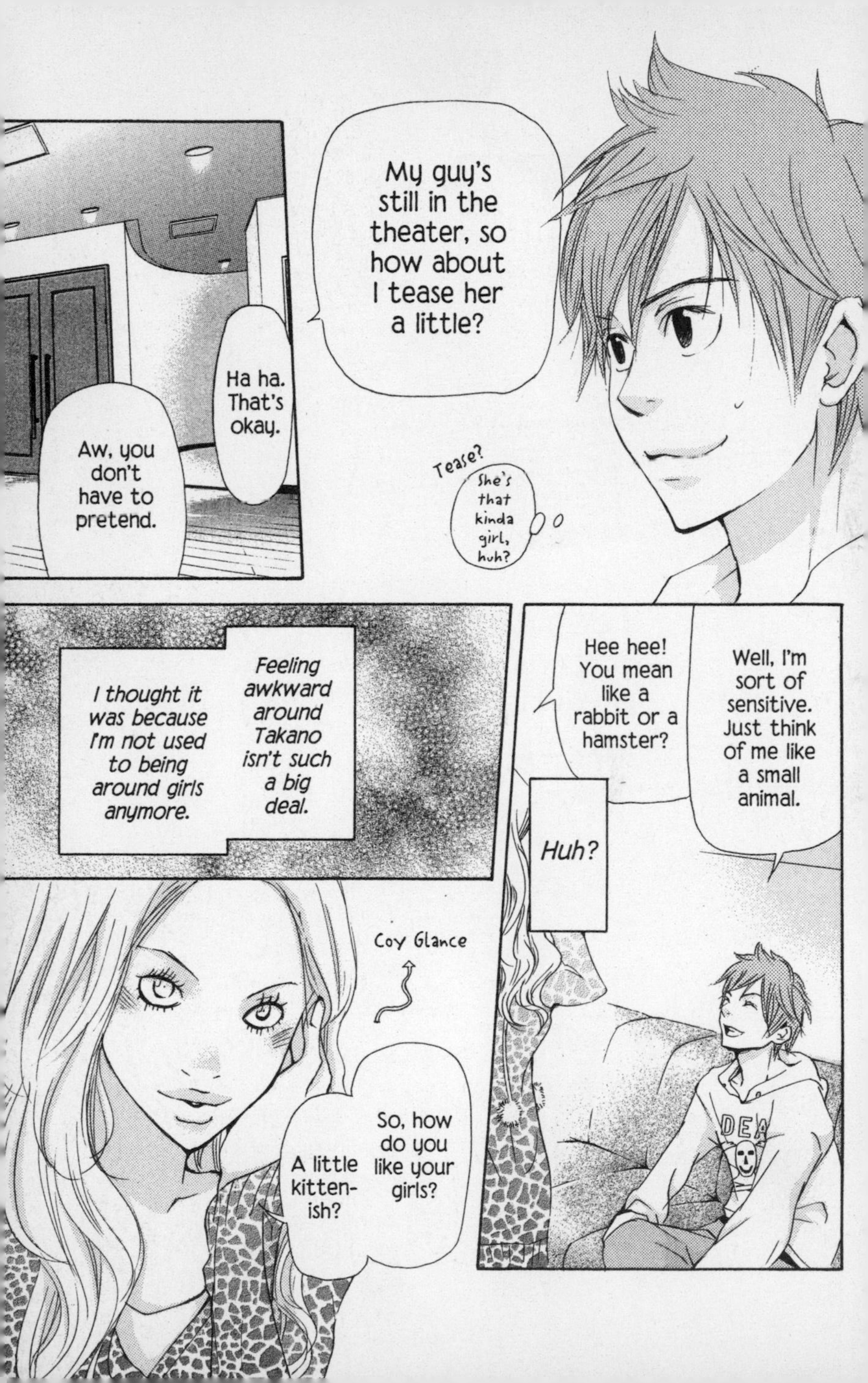
My guy's still in the theater, so how about I tease her a little?
Tease?
She's that kinda girl, huh?
Ha ha. That's okay.
Aw, you don't have to pretend.
Well, I'm sort of sensitive. Just think of me like a small animal.
Hee hee! You mean like a rabbit or a hamster?
Huh?
Feeling awkward around Takano isn't such a big deal.
I thought it was because I'm not used to being around girls anymore.
Coy Glance
So, how do you like your girls?
A little kitten-ish?

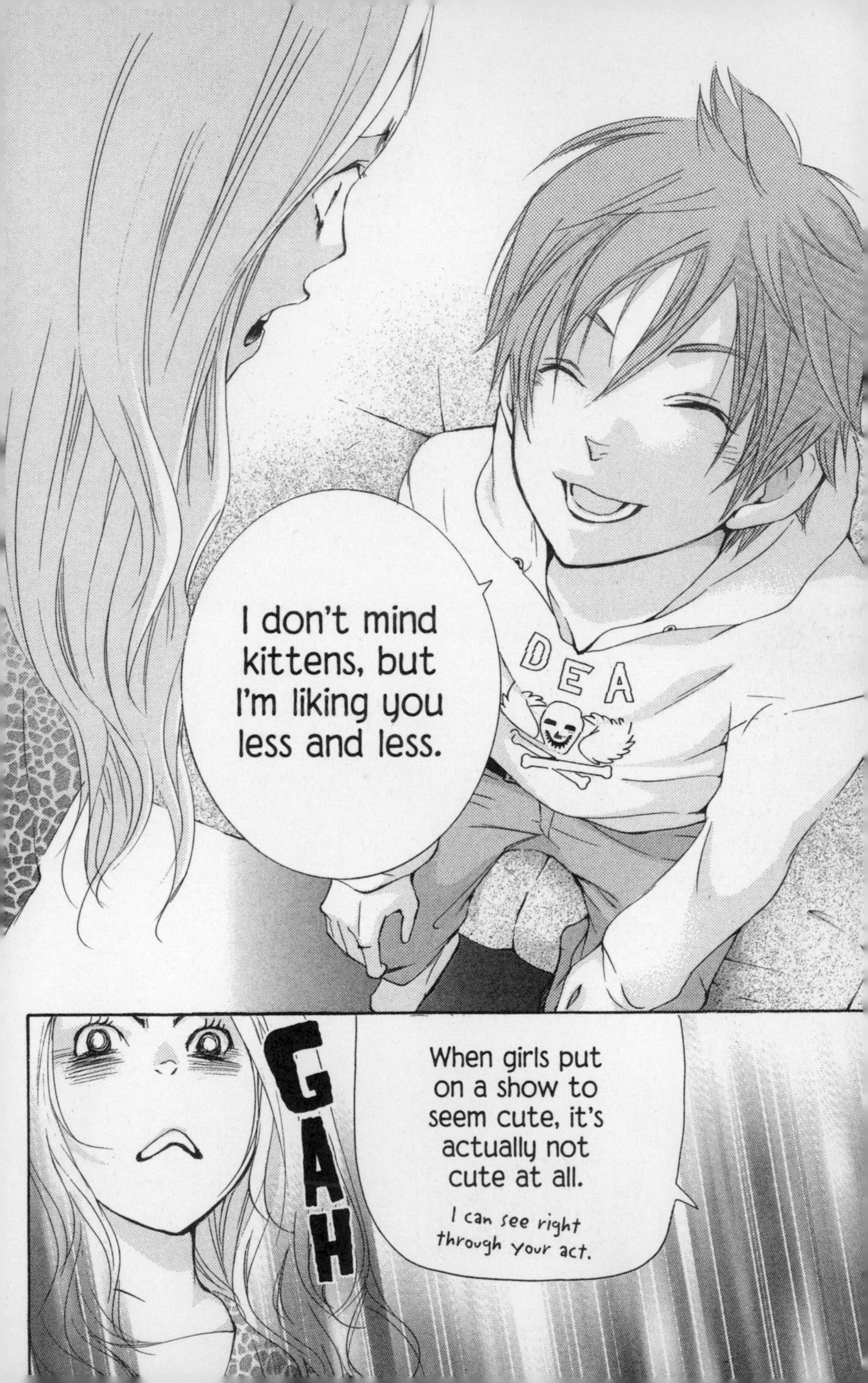
I don't mind kittens, but I'm liking you less and less.
DEA
When girls put on a show to seem cute, it's actually not cute at all.
I can see right through your act.
GAH

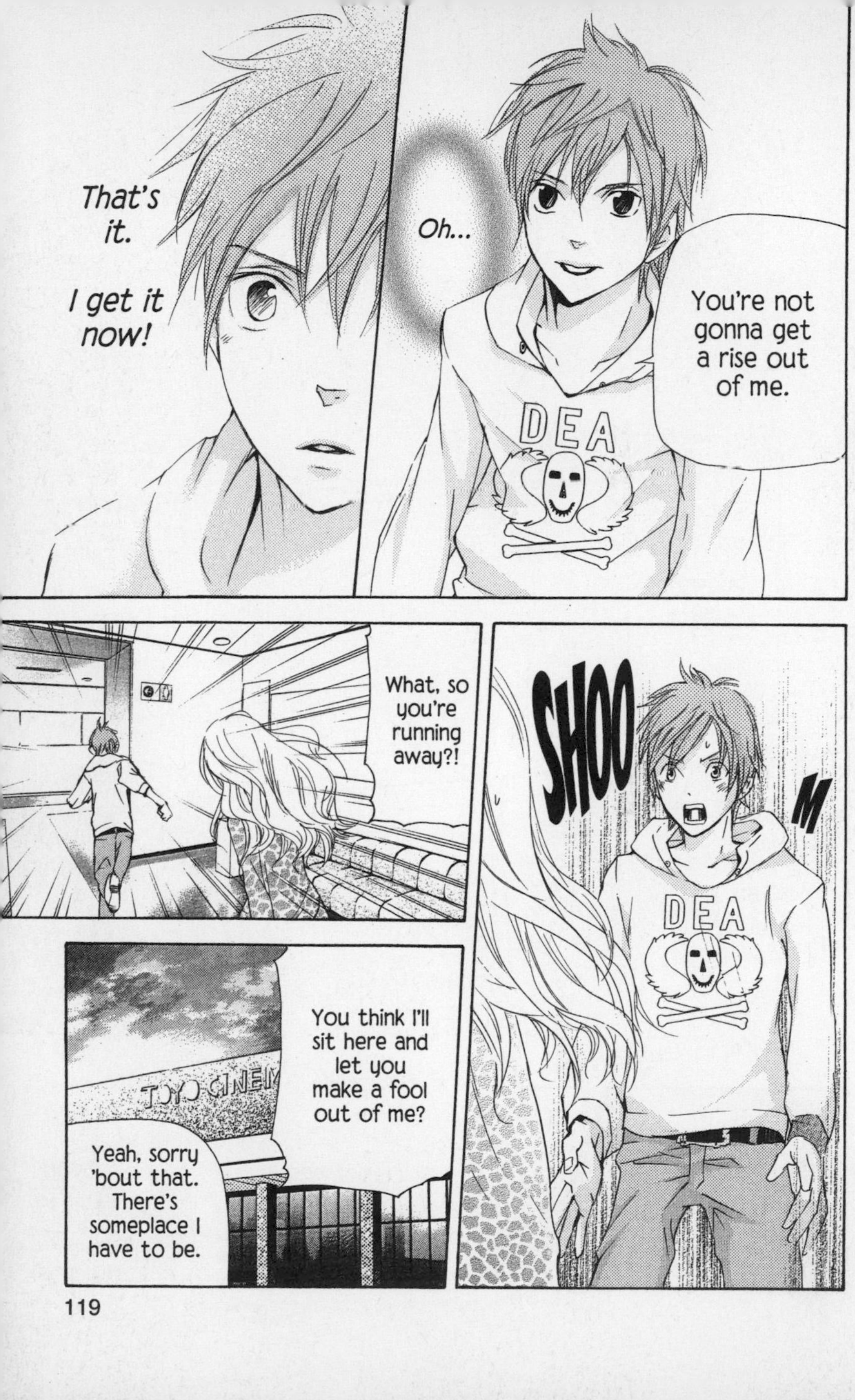
Oh...
You're not gonna get a rise out of me.
DEA
That's it.
I get it now!
SHOO M
DEA
What, so you're running away?!
You think I'll sit here and let you make a fool out of me?
TOYO CINEM
Yeah, sorry 'bout that. There's someplace I have to be.

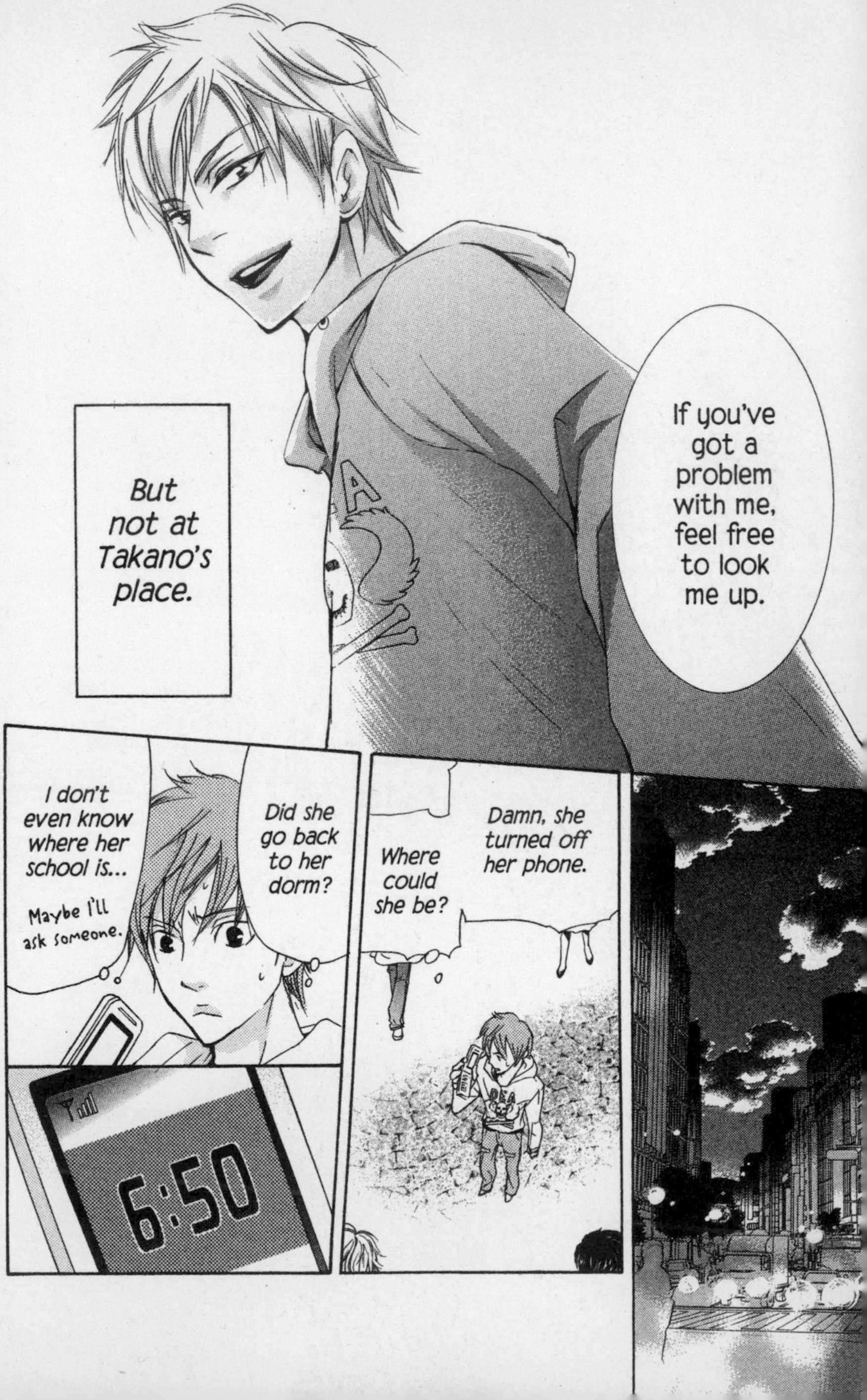
If you've got a problem with me, feel free to look me up.
But not at Takano's place.
Damn, she turned off her phone.
Where could she be?
Did she go back to her dorm?
I don't even know where her school is...
Maybe I'll ask someone.
6:50

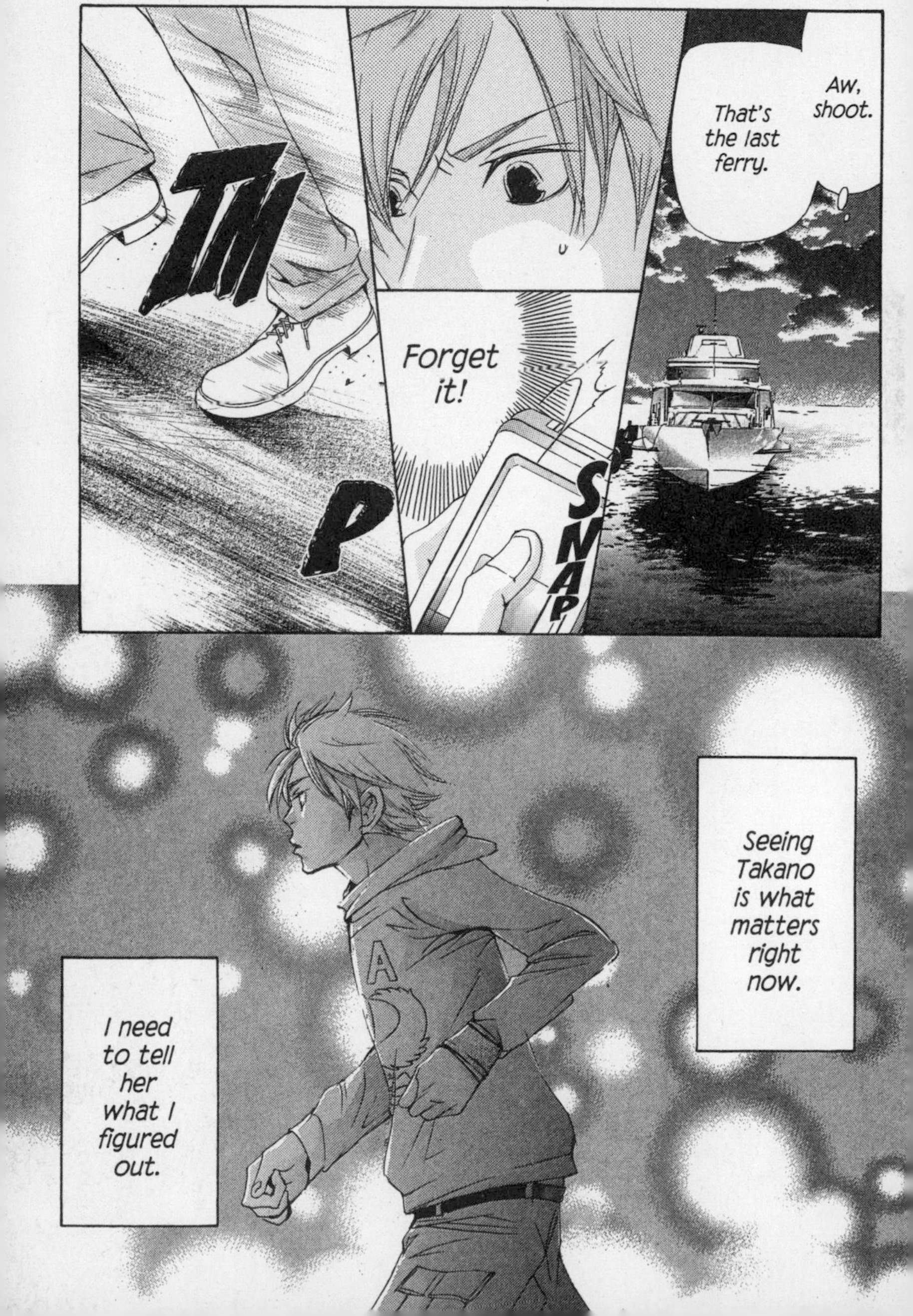
Aw, shoot.
That's the last ferry.
Forget it!
SNAP!
TMP
Seeing Takano is what matters right now.
I need to tell her what I figured out.

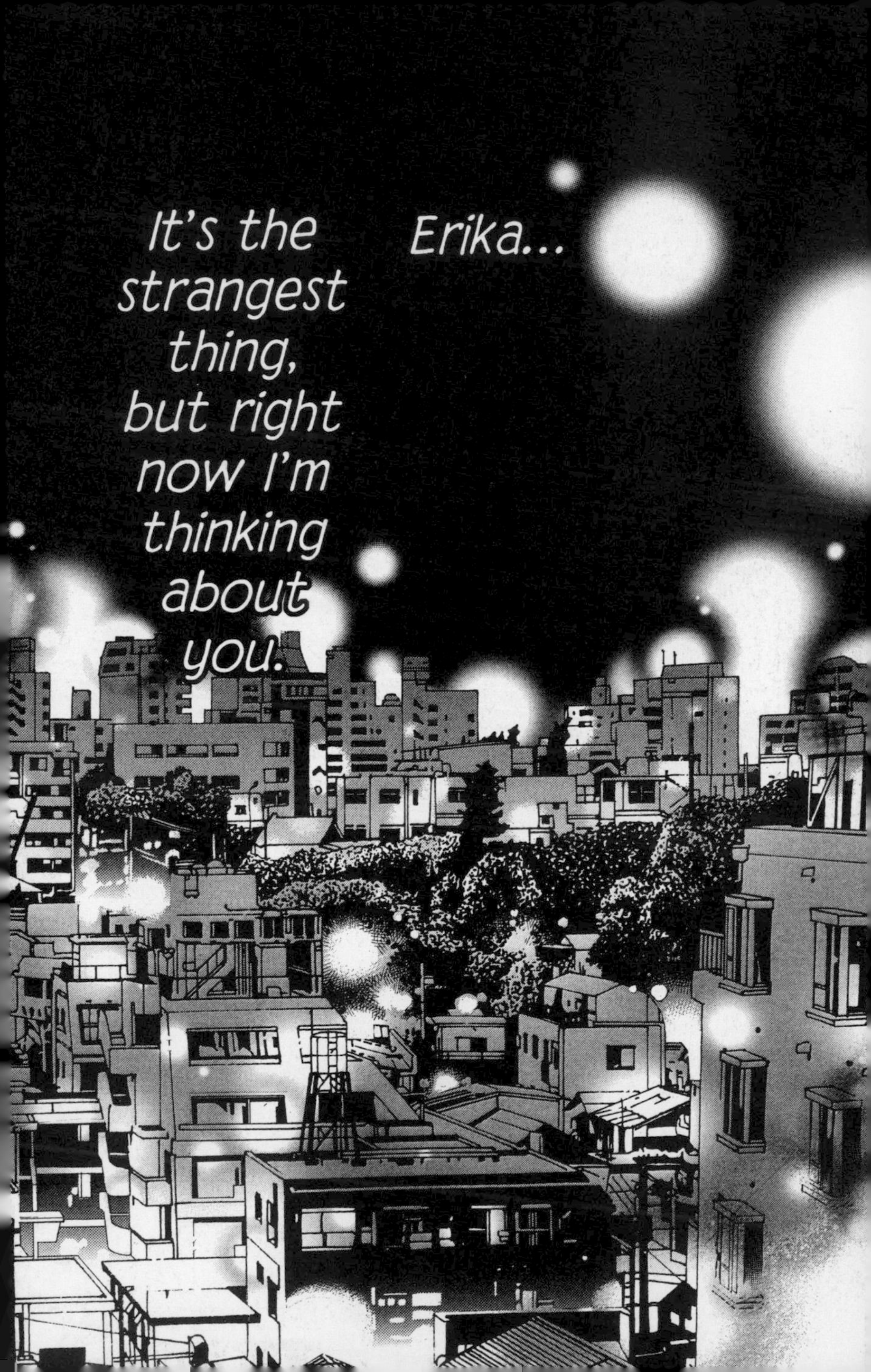
Erika...
It's the strangest thing, but right now I'm thinking about you.

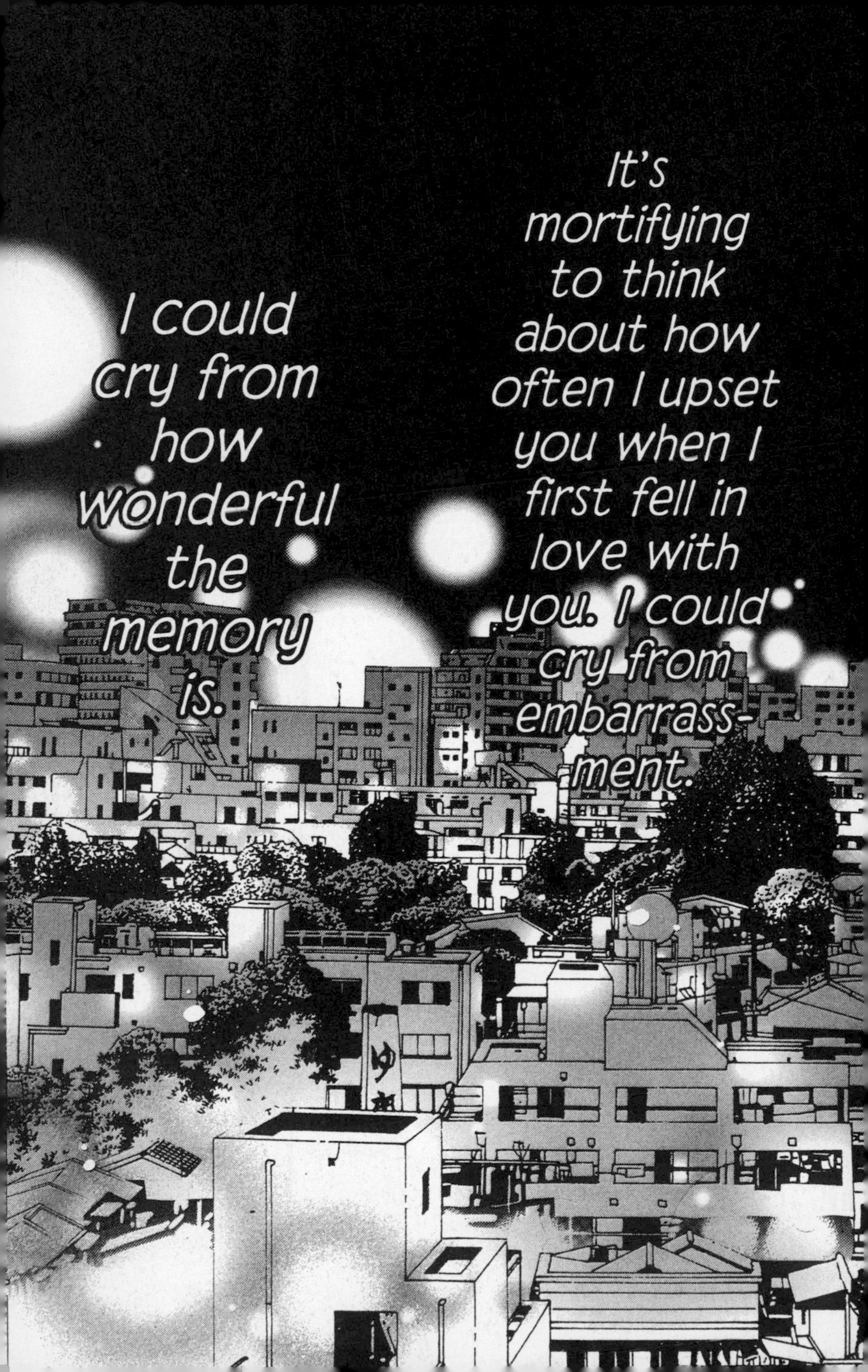
It's mortifying to think about how often I upset you when I first fell in love with you. I could cry from embarrass-ment.
I could cry from how wonderful the memory is.

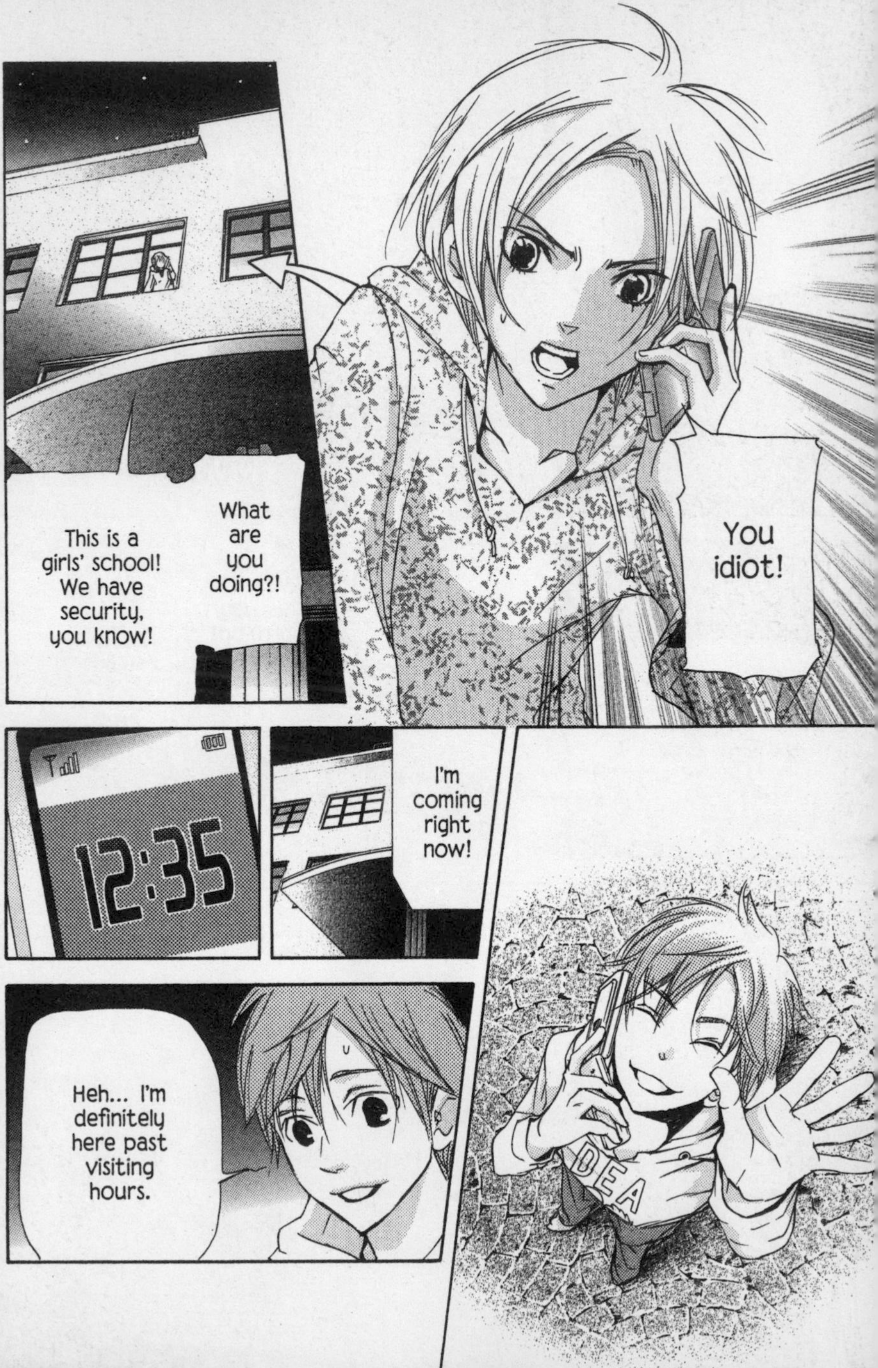
You idiot!
What are you doing?!
This is a girls' school! We have security, you know!
I'm coming right now!
12:35
Heh... I'm definitely here past visiting hours.
DEA

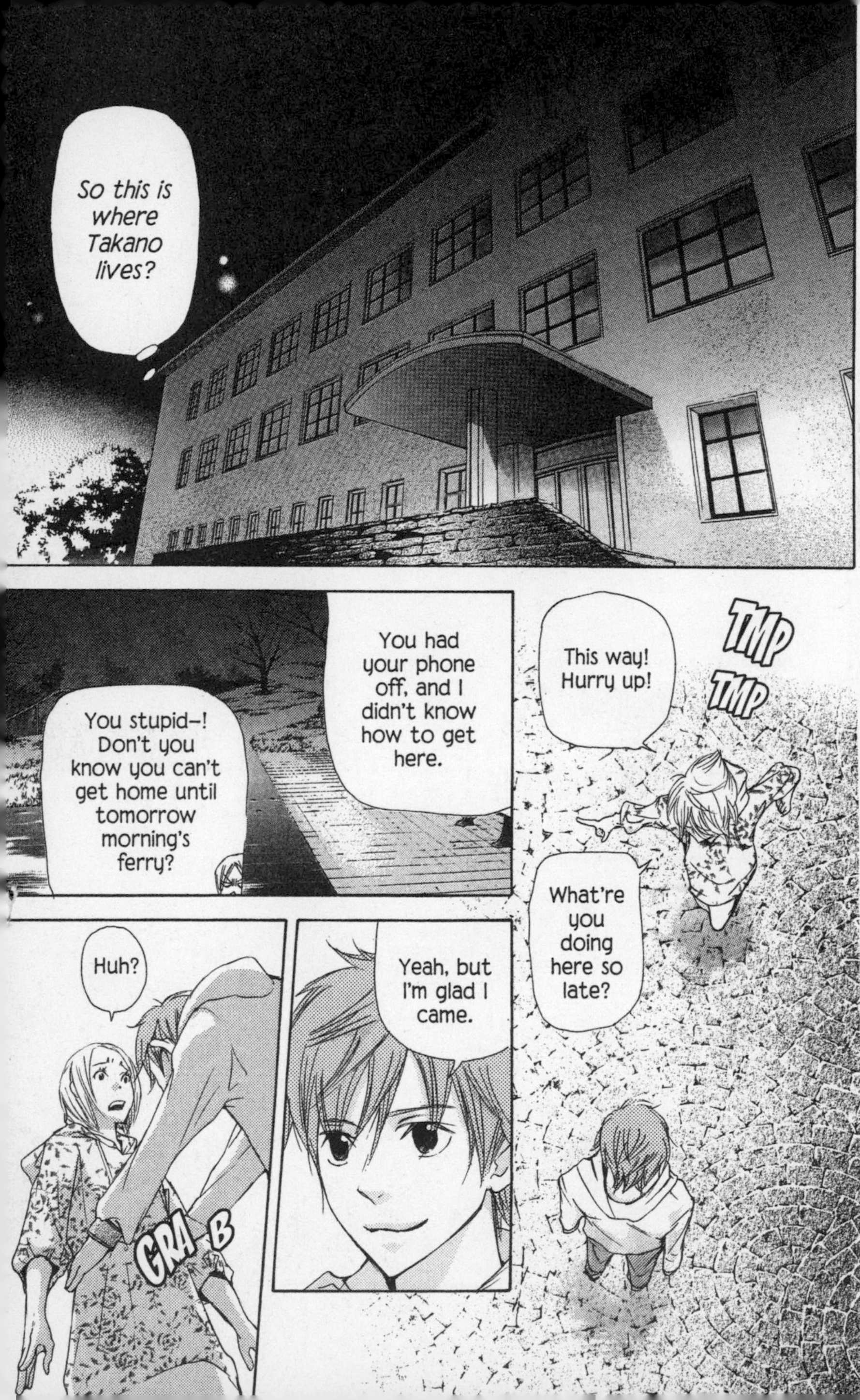
So this is where Takano lives?
TMP
TMP
This way! Hurry up!
What're you doing here so late?
You had your phone off, and I didn't know how to get here.
You stupid–! Don't you know you can't get home until tomorrow morning's ferry?
Yeah, but I'm glad I came.
Huh?
GRAB

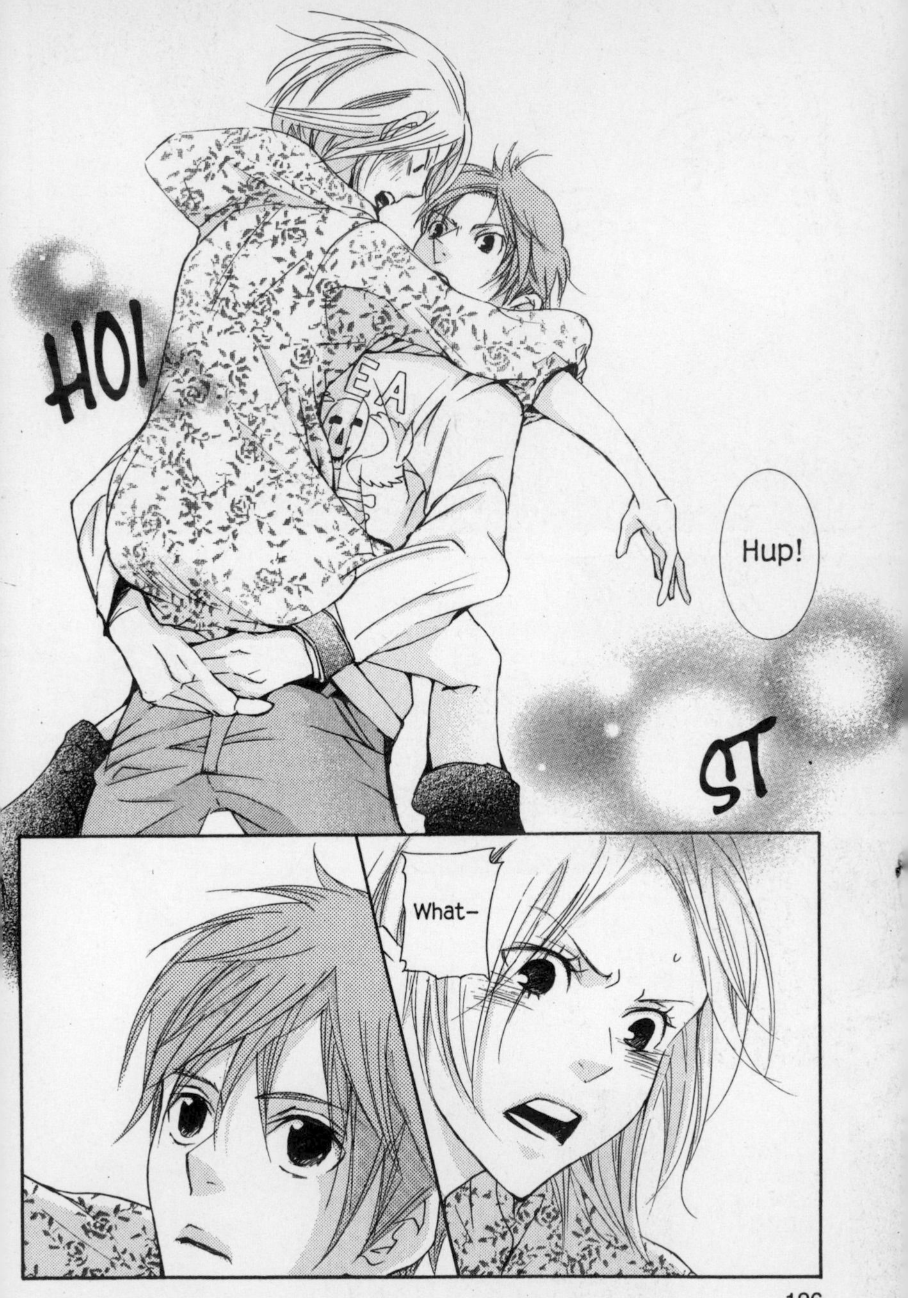
Hup!
HOI
ST
What-

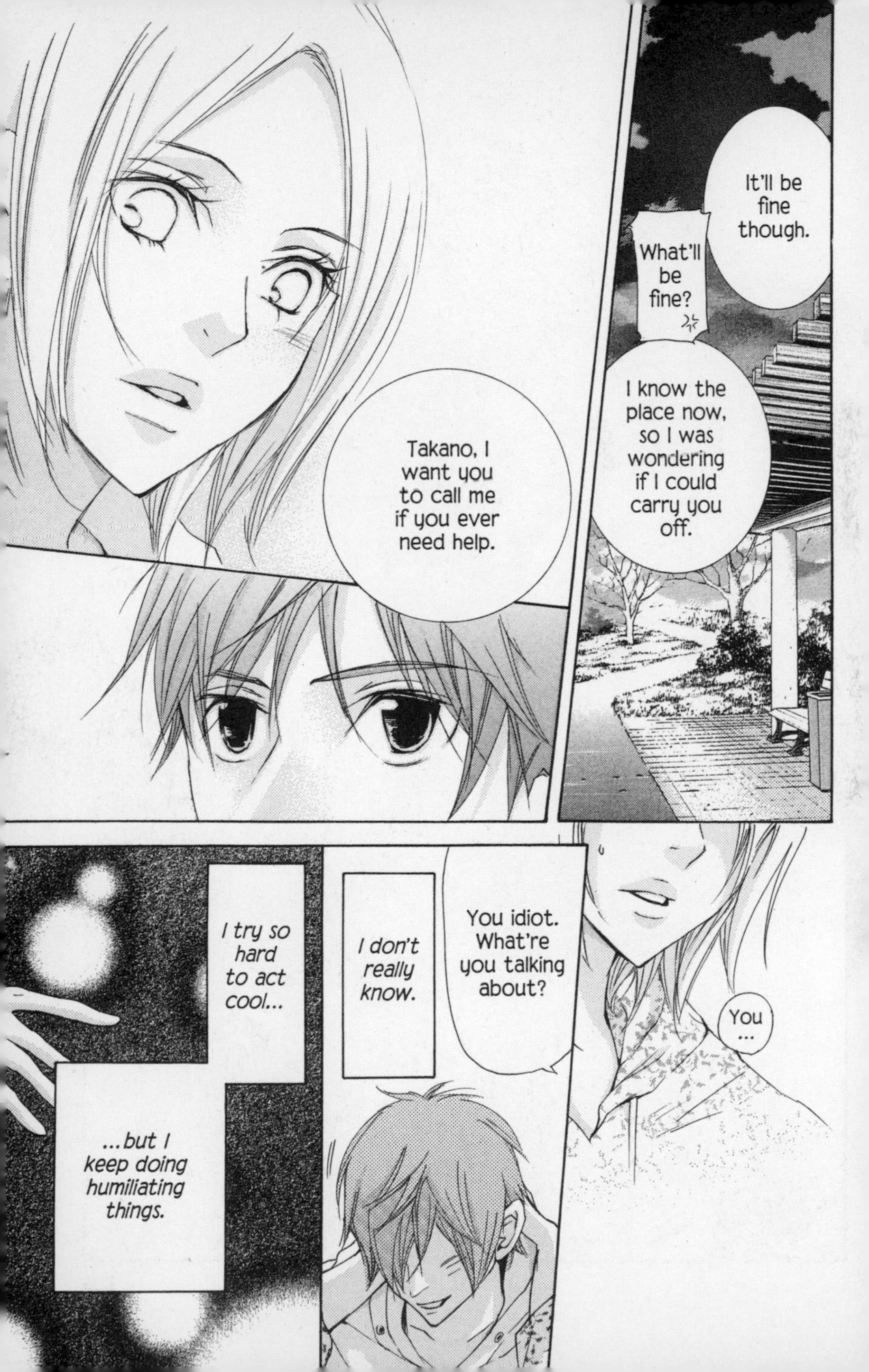
It'll be fine though.
What'll be fine?
I know the place now, so I was wondering if I could carry you off.
Takano, I want you to call me if you ever need help.
You...
You idiot. What're you talking about?
I don't really know.
I try so hard to act cool...
...but I keep doing humiliating things.

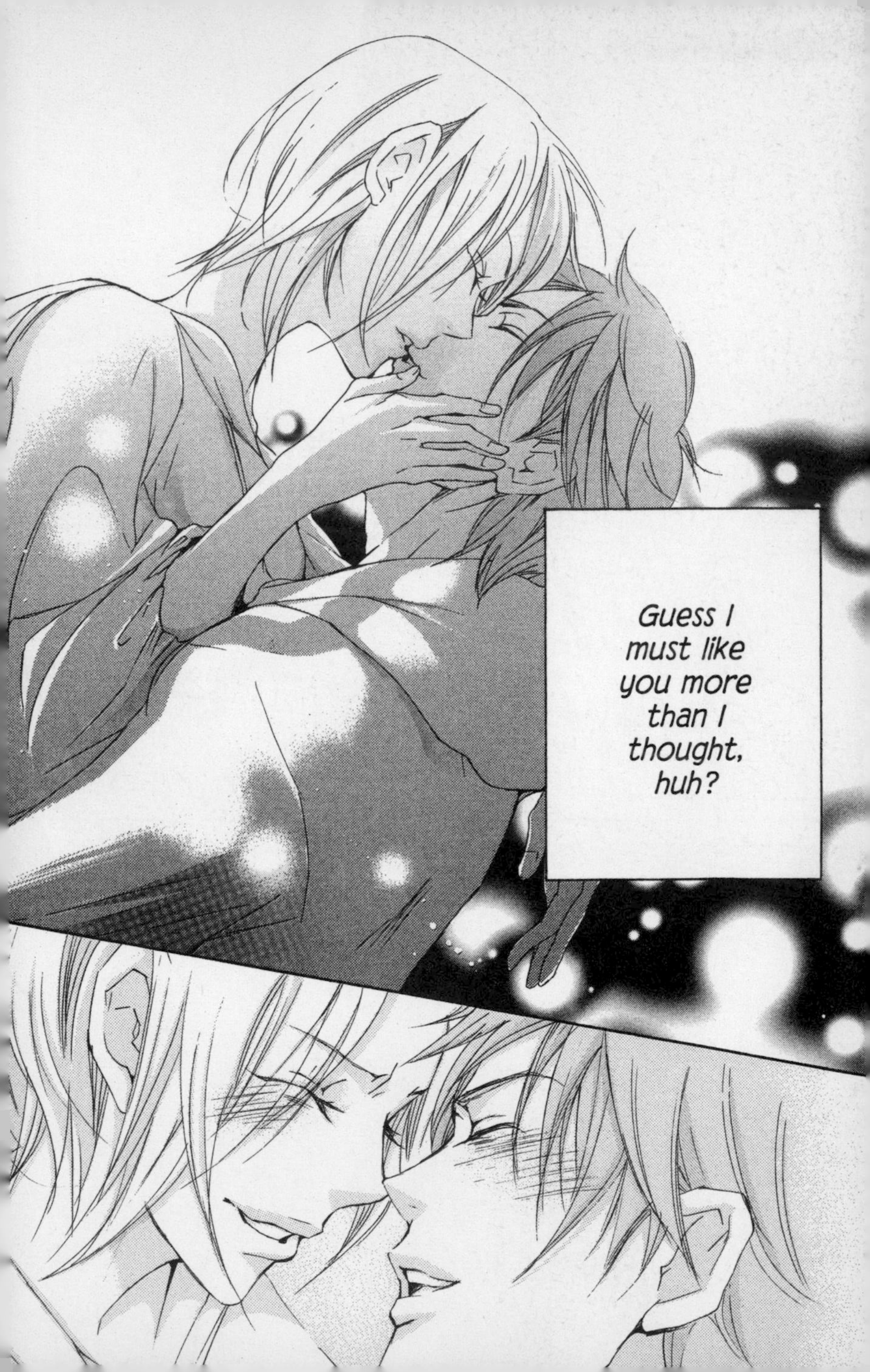
Guess I must like you more than I thought, huh?

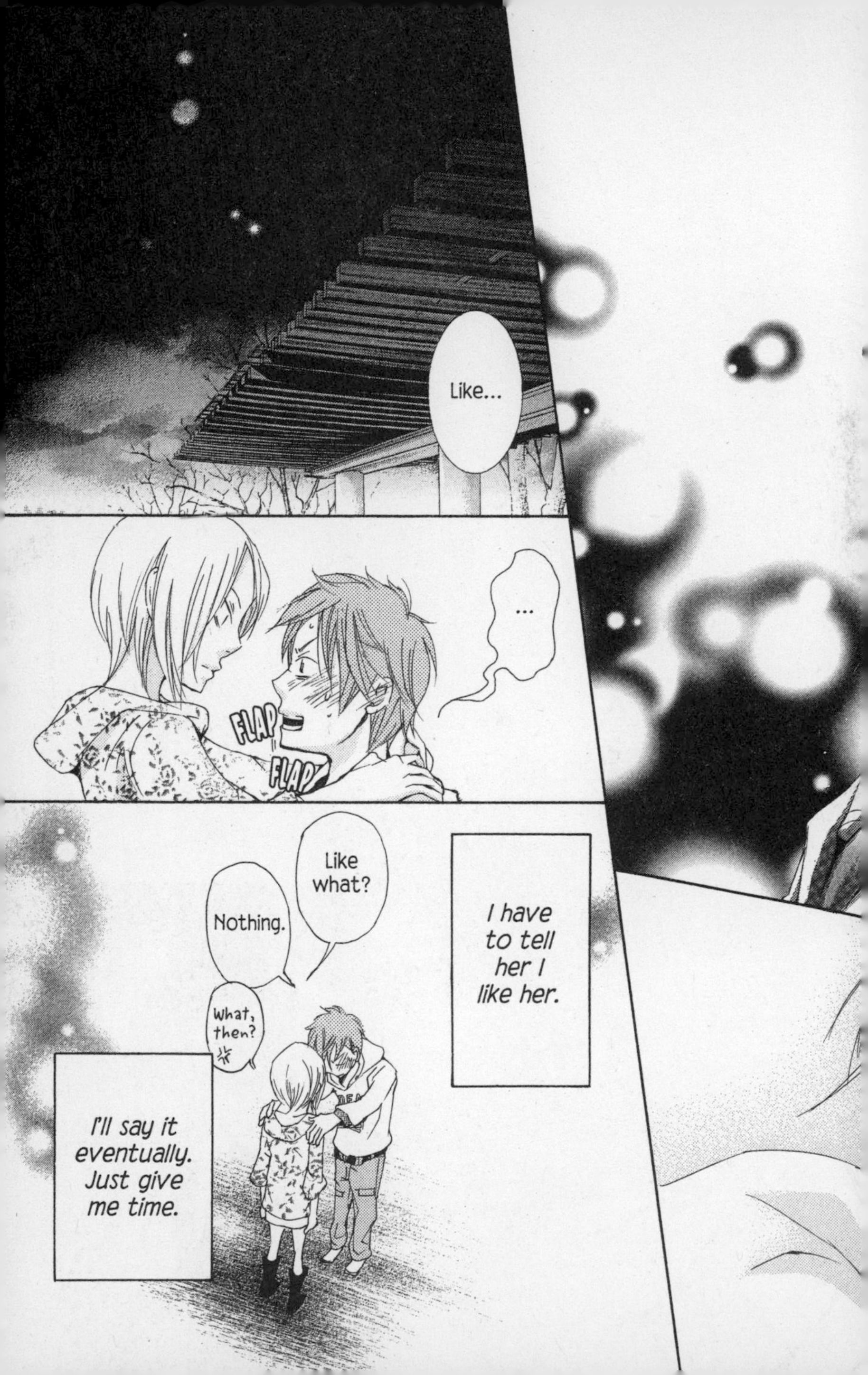
Like...
...
FLAP
FLAP
I have to tell her I like her.
Like what?
Nothing.
What, then?
I'll say it eventually. Just give me time.

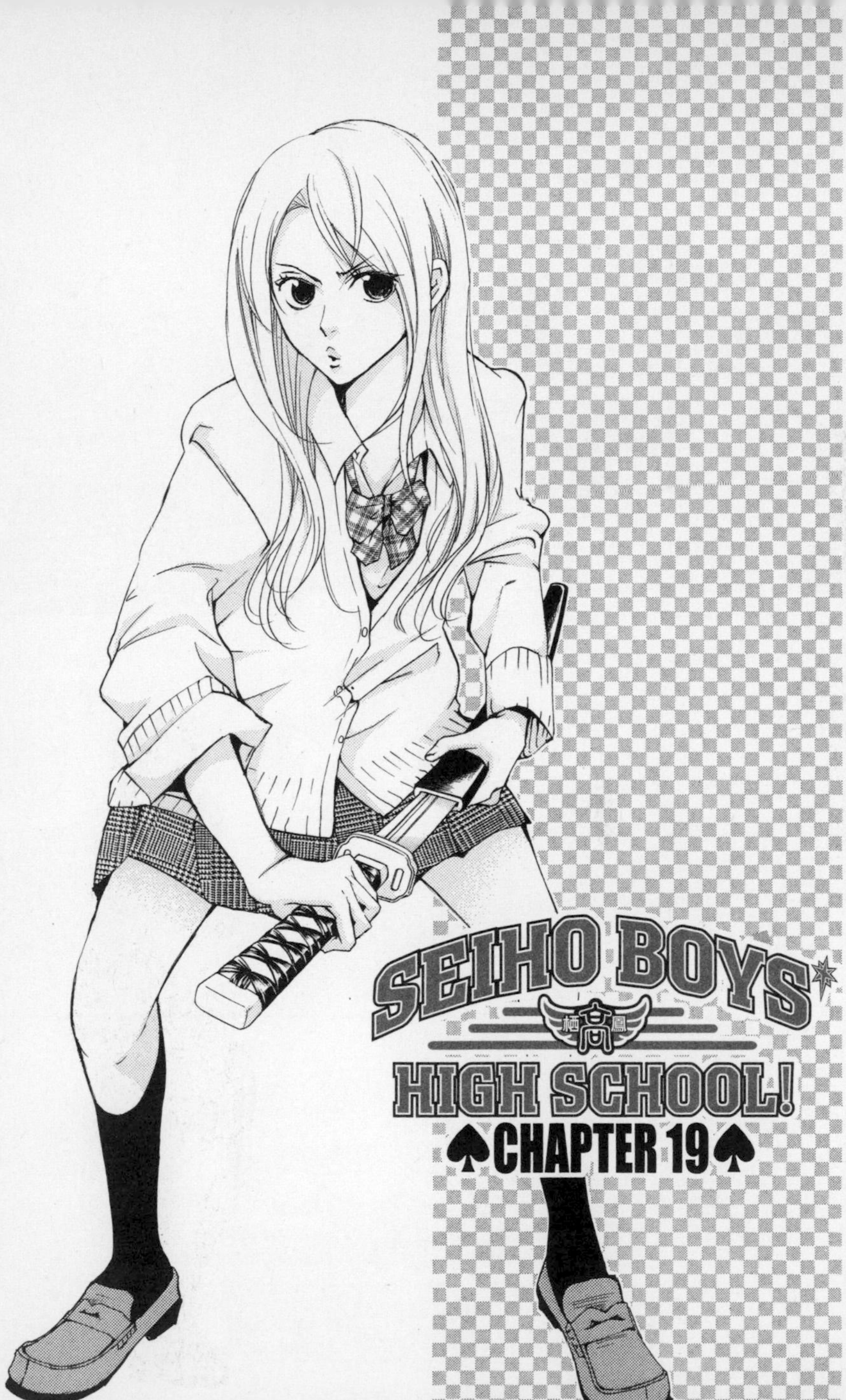
SEIHO BOYS
栖鳳高
HIGH SCHOOL!
CHAPTER 19

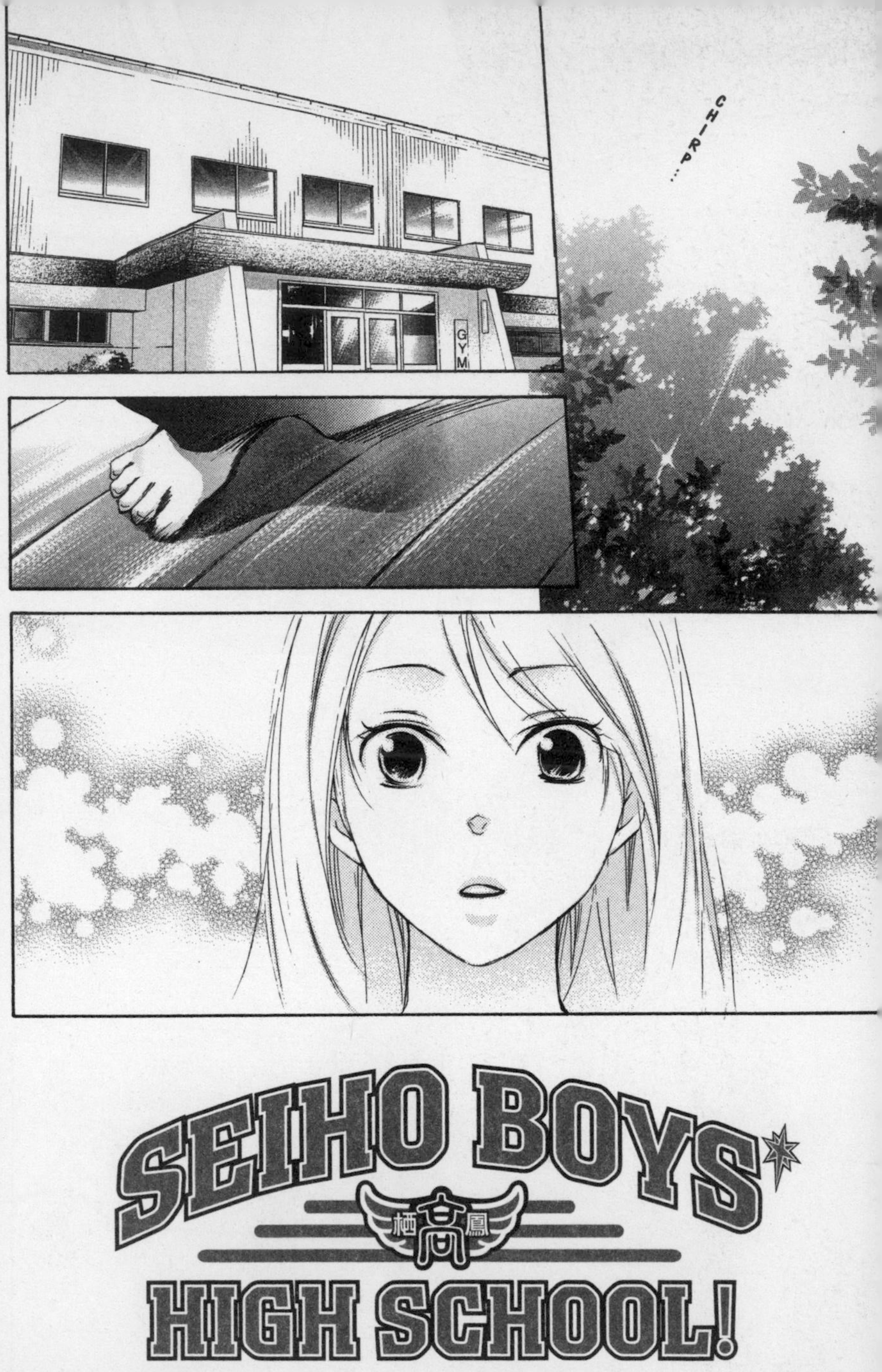
CHIRP...
GYM

# SEIHO BOYS HIGH SCHOOL!

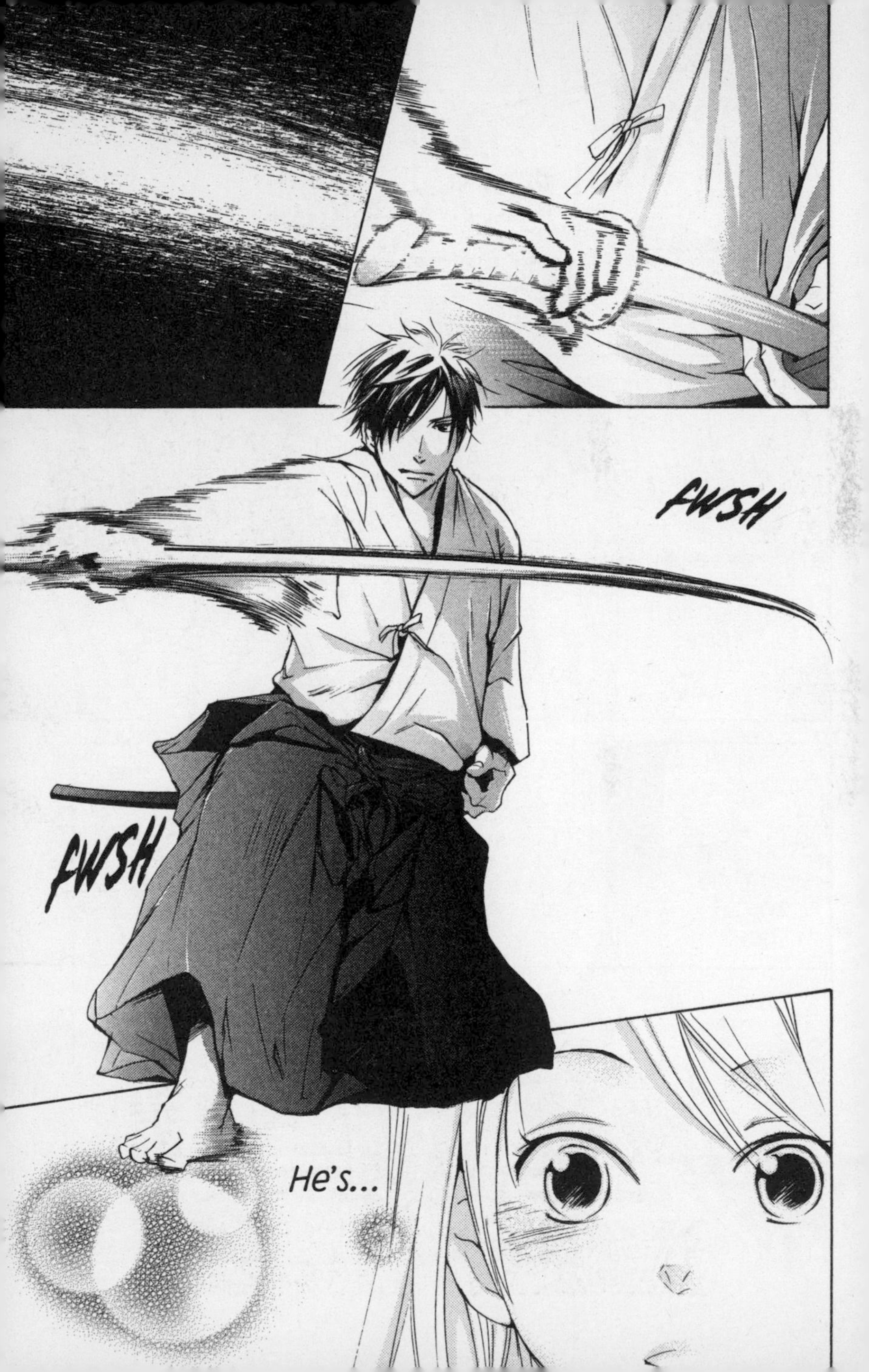
FWSH
FWSH
He's...

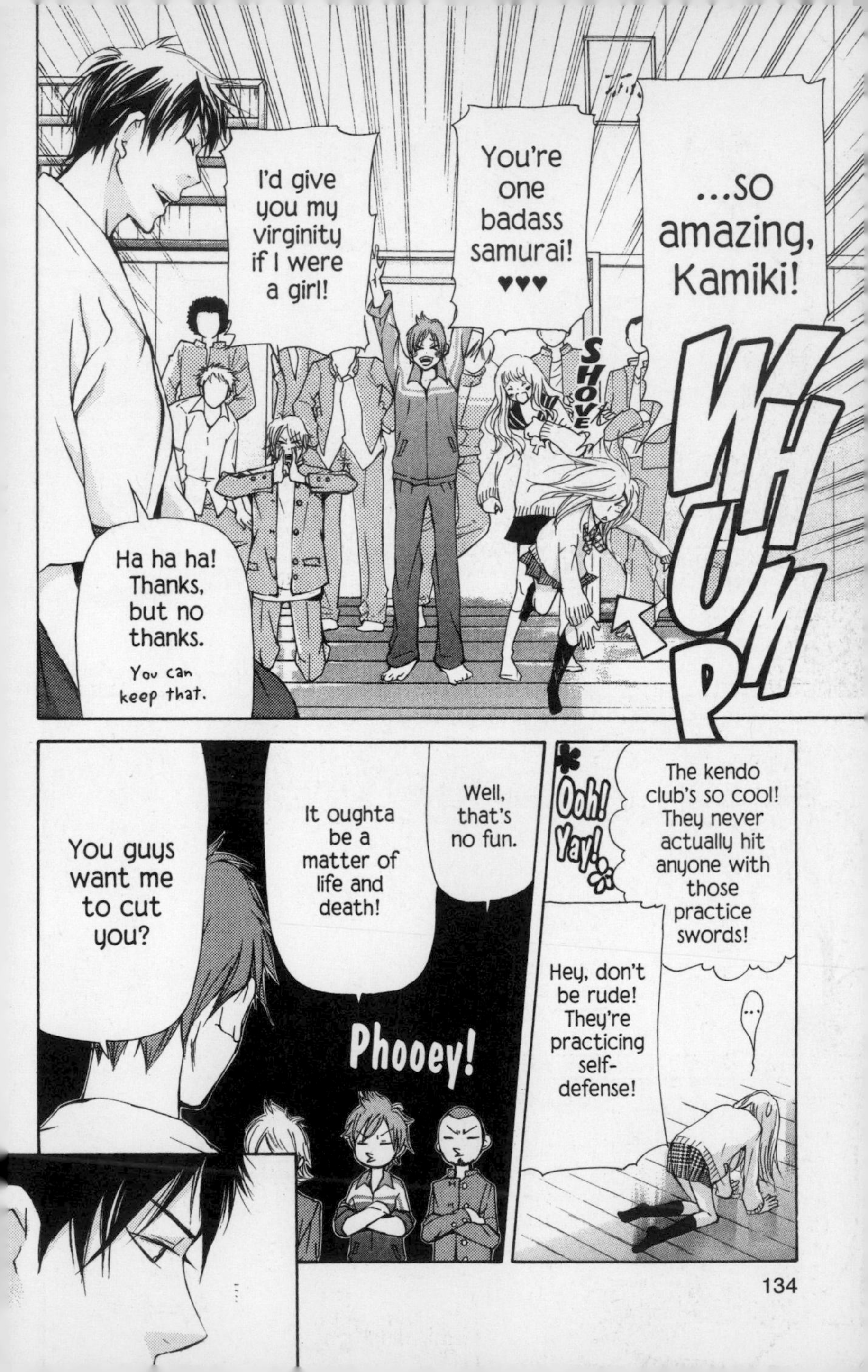
...SO amazing, Kamiki!
You're one badass samurai! ♥♥♥
I'd give you my virginity if I were a girl!
SHOVE
WHUMP
Ha ha ha! Thanks, but no thanks.
You can keep that.
Ooh! Yay!
The kendo club's so cool! They never actually hit anyone with those practice swords!
Hey, don't be rude! They're practicing self-defense!
...
Well, that's no fun.
It oughta be a matter of life and death!
Phooey!
You guys want me to cut you?
...

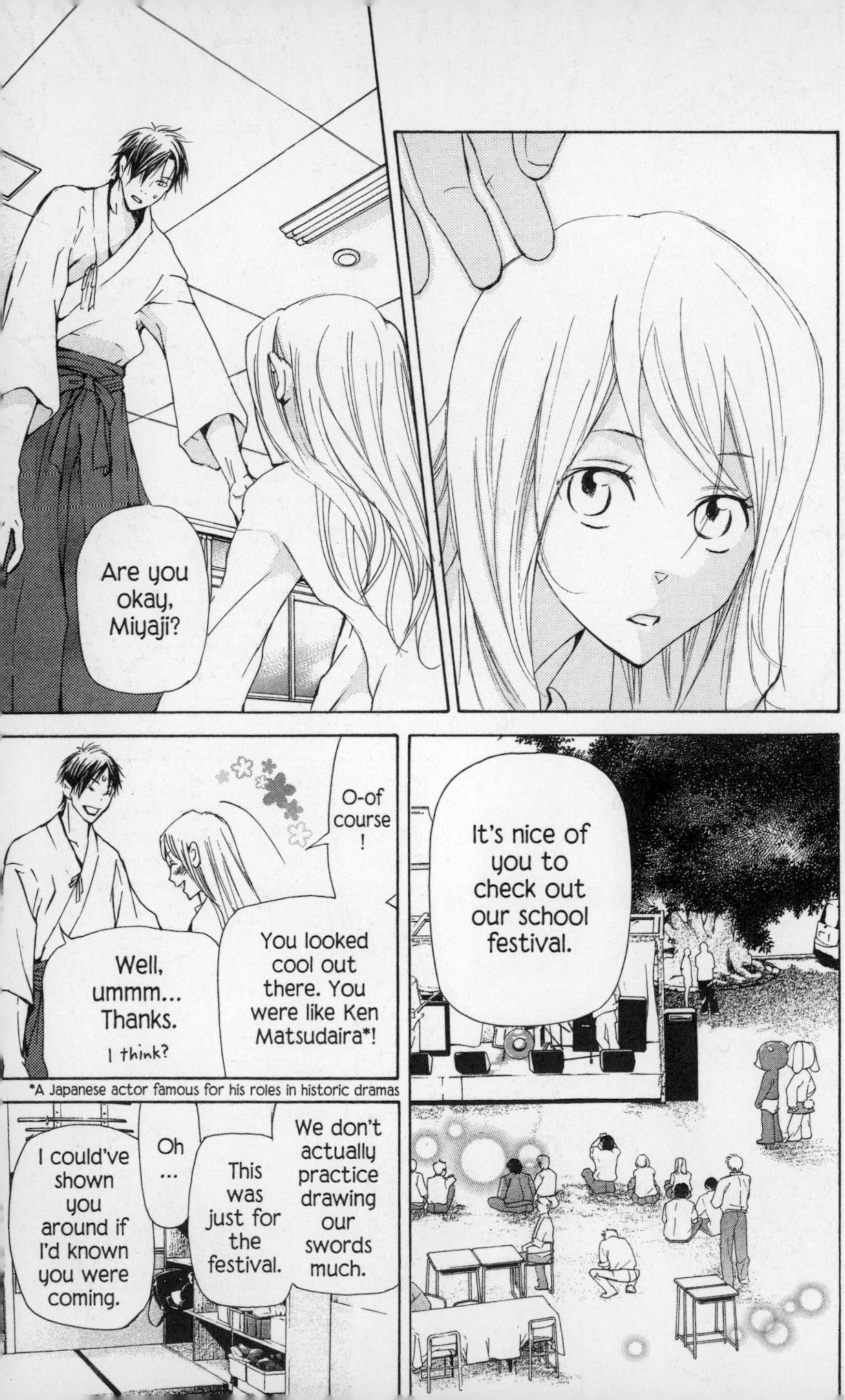
Are you okay, Miyaji?
It's nice of you to check out our school festival.
O-of course!
You looked cool out there. You were like Ken Matsudaira*!
Well, ummm... Thanks.
I think?
We don't actually practice drawing our swords much.
This was just for the festival.
Oh ...
I could've shown you around if I'd known you were coming.
*A Japanese actor famous for his roles in historic dramas

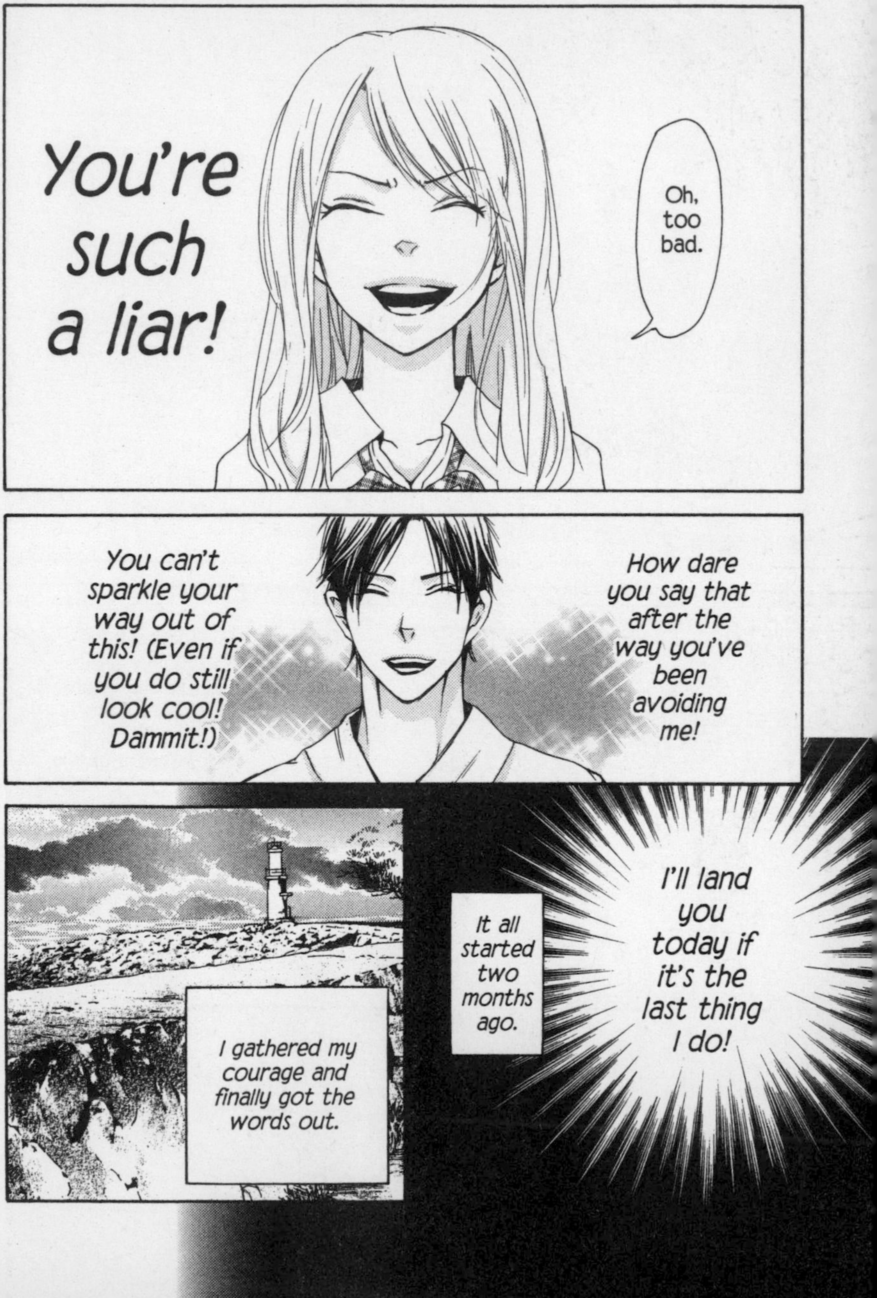
Oh, too bad.
You're such a liar!
How dare you say that after the way you've been avoiding me!
You can't sparkle your way out of this! (Even if you do still look cool! Dammit!)
I'll land you today if it's the last thing I do!
It all started two months ago.
I gathered my courage and finally got the words out.

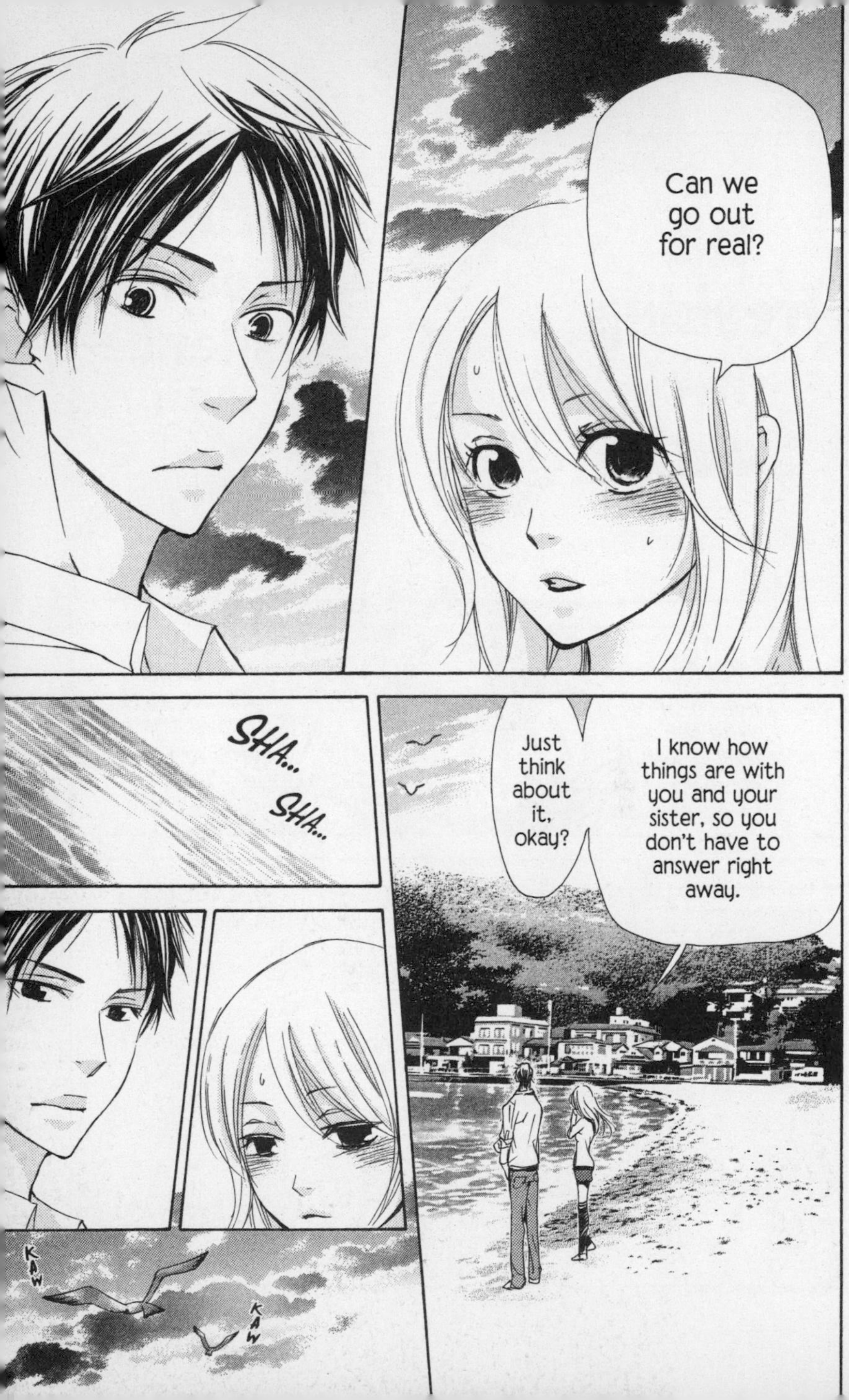
Can we go out for real?
I know how things are with you and your sister, so you don't have to answer right away.
Just think about it, okay?
SHA... SHA...
KAW
KAW

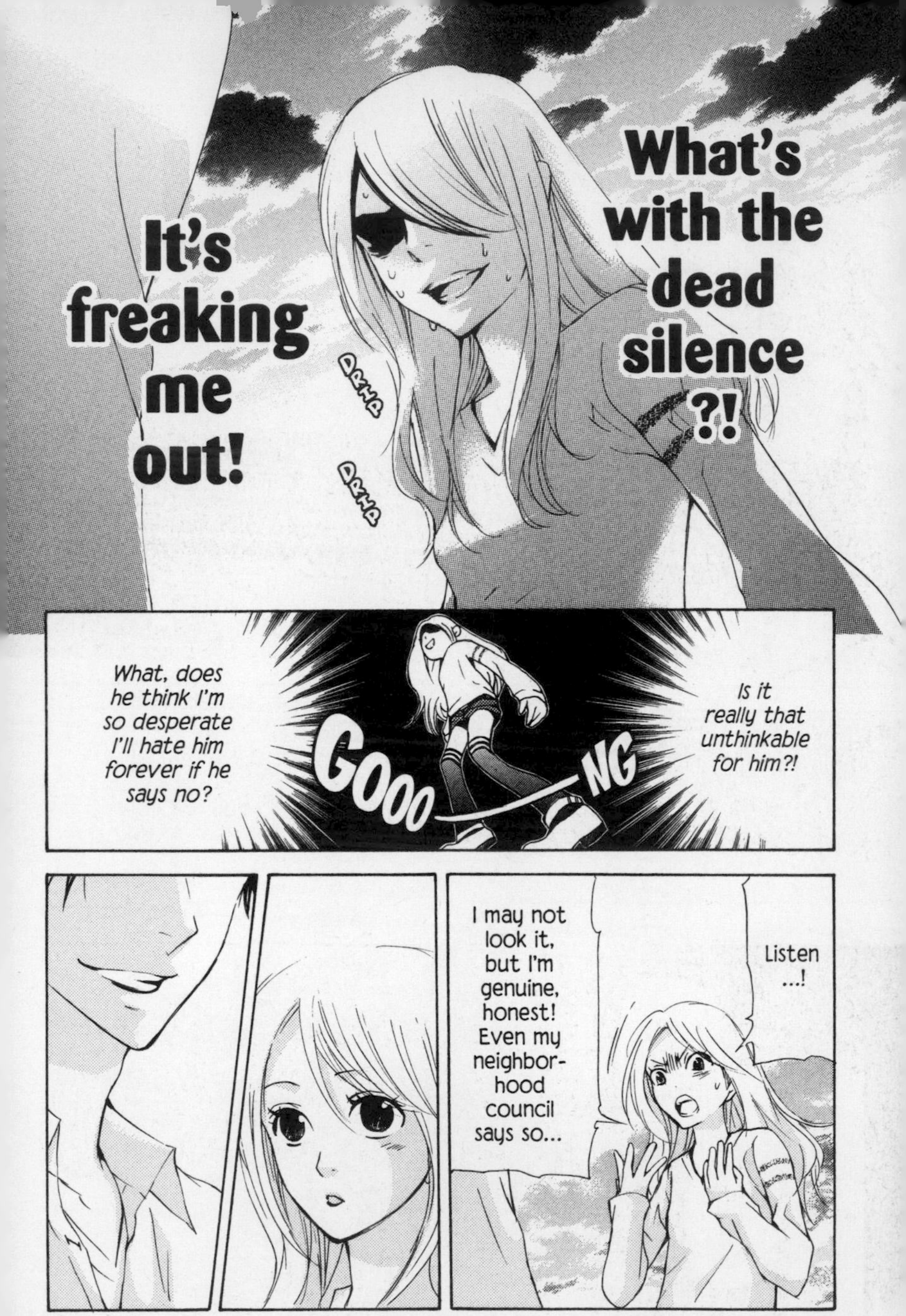
What's with the dead silence?!
It's freaking me out!
DRIP
DRIP
Is it really that unthinkable for him?!
GOOO—NG
What, does he think I'm so desperate I'll hate him forever if he says no?
Listen ...!
I may not look it, but I'm genuine, honest! Even my neighbor-hood council says so...

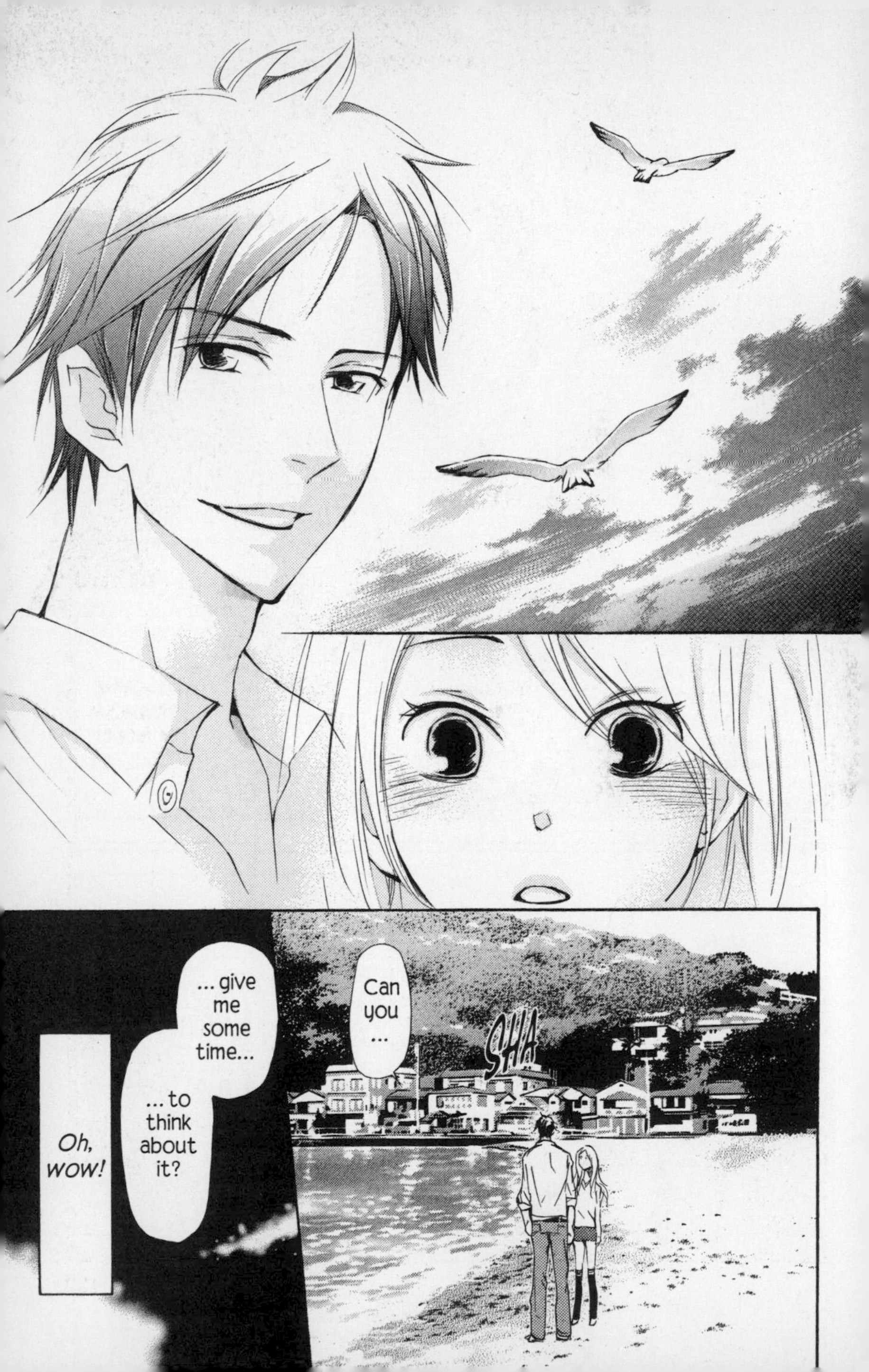
Can you ...
SHA
... give me some time...
... to think about it?
Oh, wow!

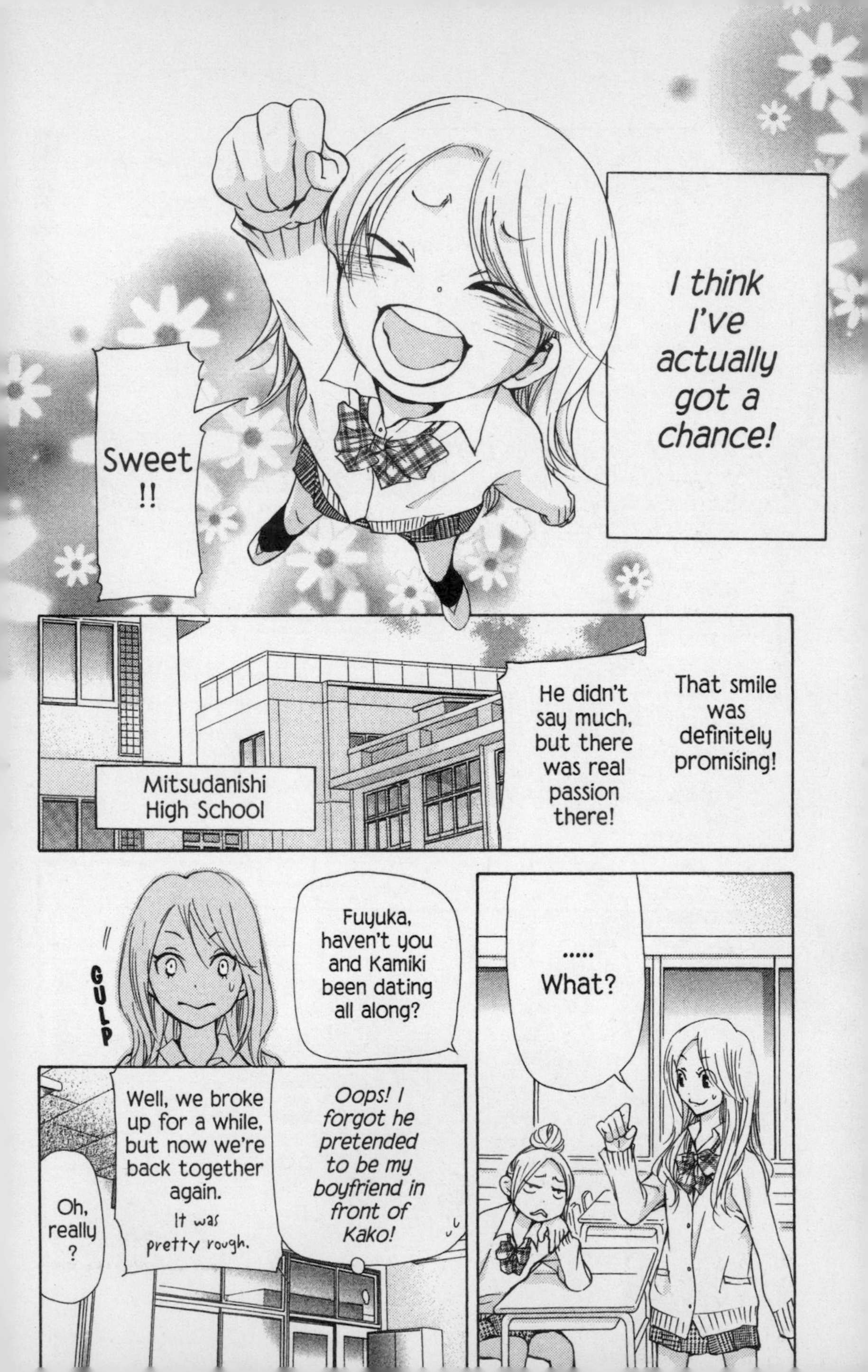

I think I've actually got a chance!
Sweet!!
That smile was definitely promising!
He didn't say much, but there was real passion there!
Mitsudanishi High School
..... What?
Fuyuka, haven't you and Kamiki been dating all along?
GULP
Oops! I forgot he pretended to be my boyfriend in front of Kako!
Well, we broke up for a while, but now we're back together again.
It was pretty rough.
Oh, really?

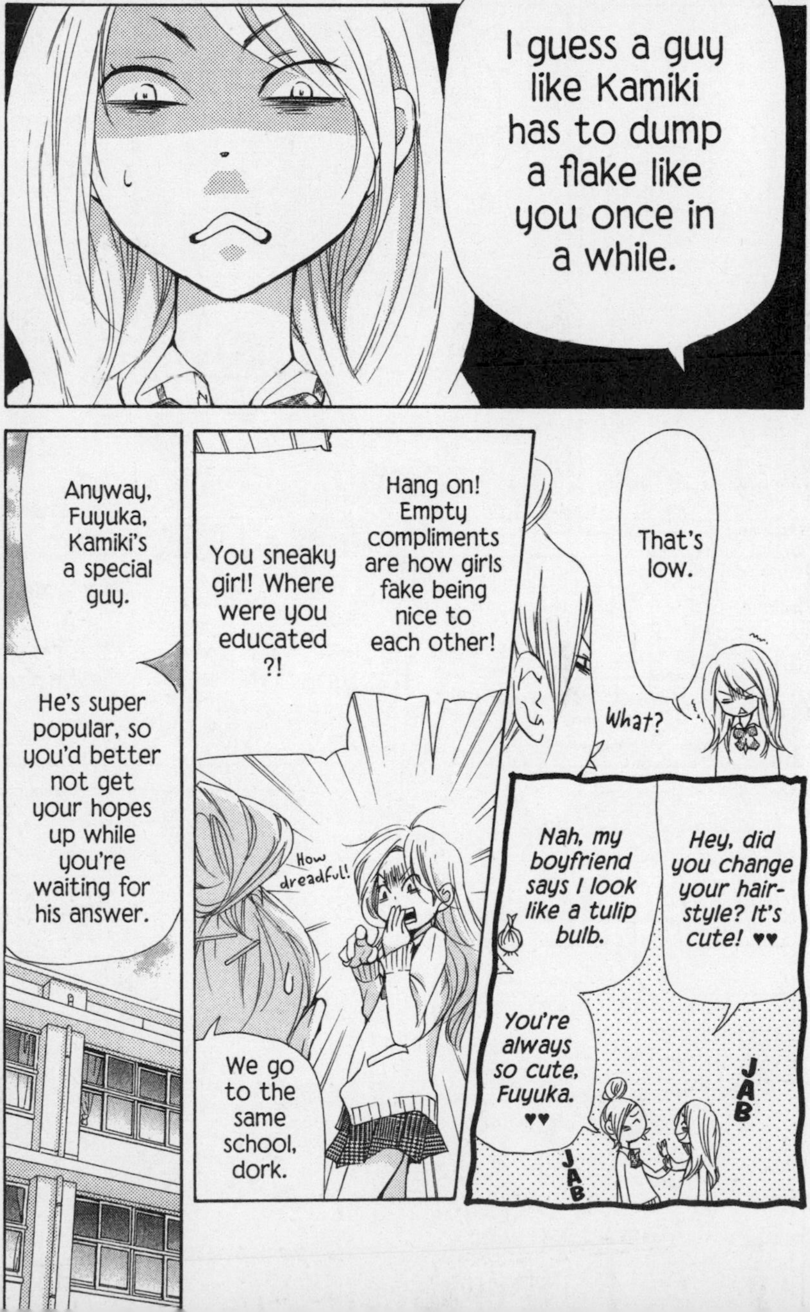
I guess a guy like Kamiki has to dump a flake like you once in a while.
That's low.
What?
Hey, did you change your hair-style? It's cute! ♥♥
Nah, my boyfriend says I look like a tulip bulb.
You're always so cute, Fuyuka. ♥♥
JAB
JAB
Hang on! Empty compliments are how girls fake being nice to each other!
You sneaky girl! Where were you educated ?!
How dreadful!
We go to the same school, dork.
Anyway, Fuyuka, Kamiki's a special guy.
He's super popular, so you'd better not get your hopes up while you're waiting for his answer.

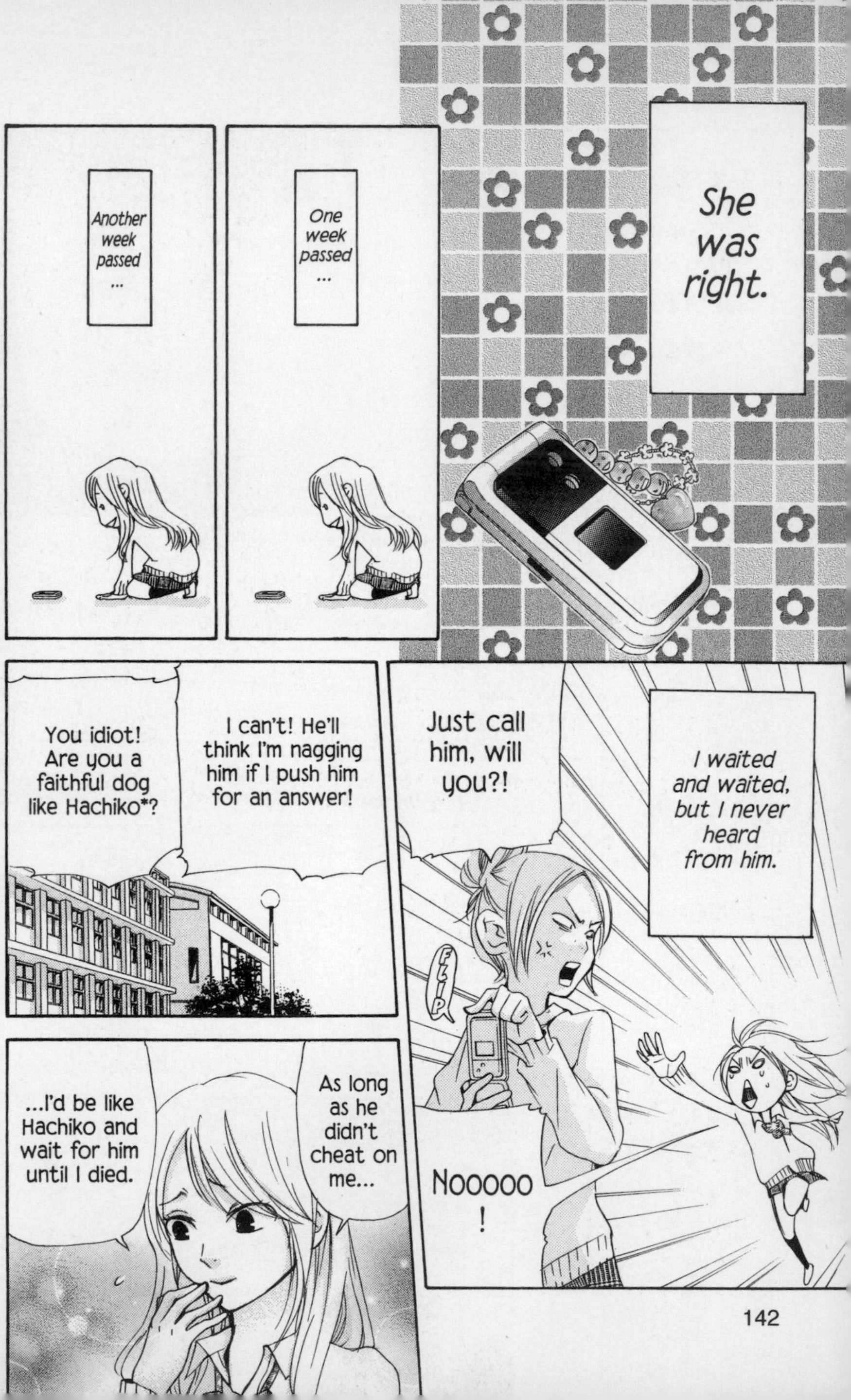
She was right.
One week passed ...
Another week passed ...
I waited and waited, but I never heard from him.
Just call him, will you?!
FLIP
Noooo !
I can't! He'll think I'm nagging him if I push him for an answer!
You idiot! Are you a faithful dog like Hachiko*?
As long as he didn't cheat on me...
...I'd be like Hachiko and wait for him until I died.

*A dog famous for supposedly waiting many years for his master's return

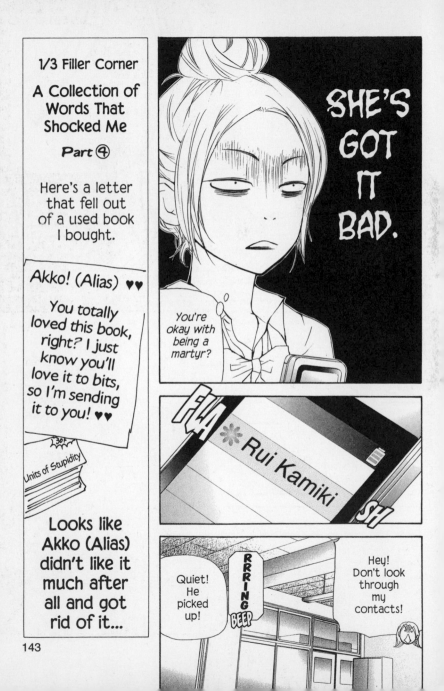

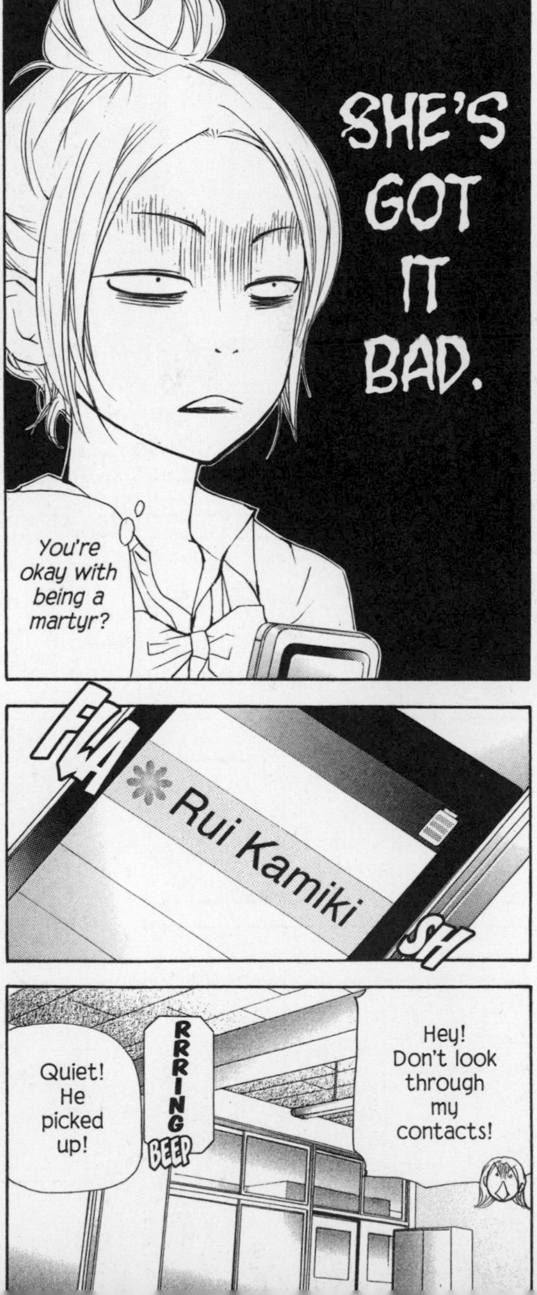
SHE'S GOT IT BAD.
You're okay with being a martyr?
FLA
SH
Rui Kamiki
Hey! Don't look through my contacts!
RRRING
BEEP
Quiet! He picked up!

1/3 Filler Corner

A Collection of Words That Shocked Me

**Part ④**

Here's a letter that fell out of a used book I bought.

*Akko! (Alias) ♥♥*

*You totally loved this book, right? I just know you'll love it to bits, so I'm sending it to you! ♥♥*

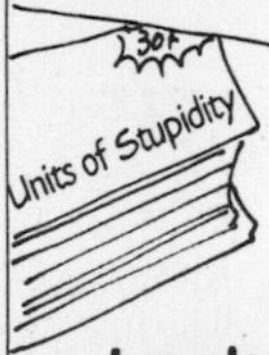
30F
Units of Stupidity

Looks like Akko (Alias) didn't like it much after all and got rid of it...

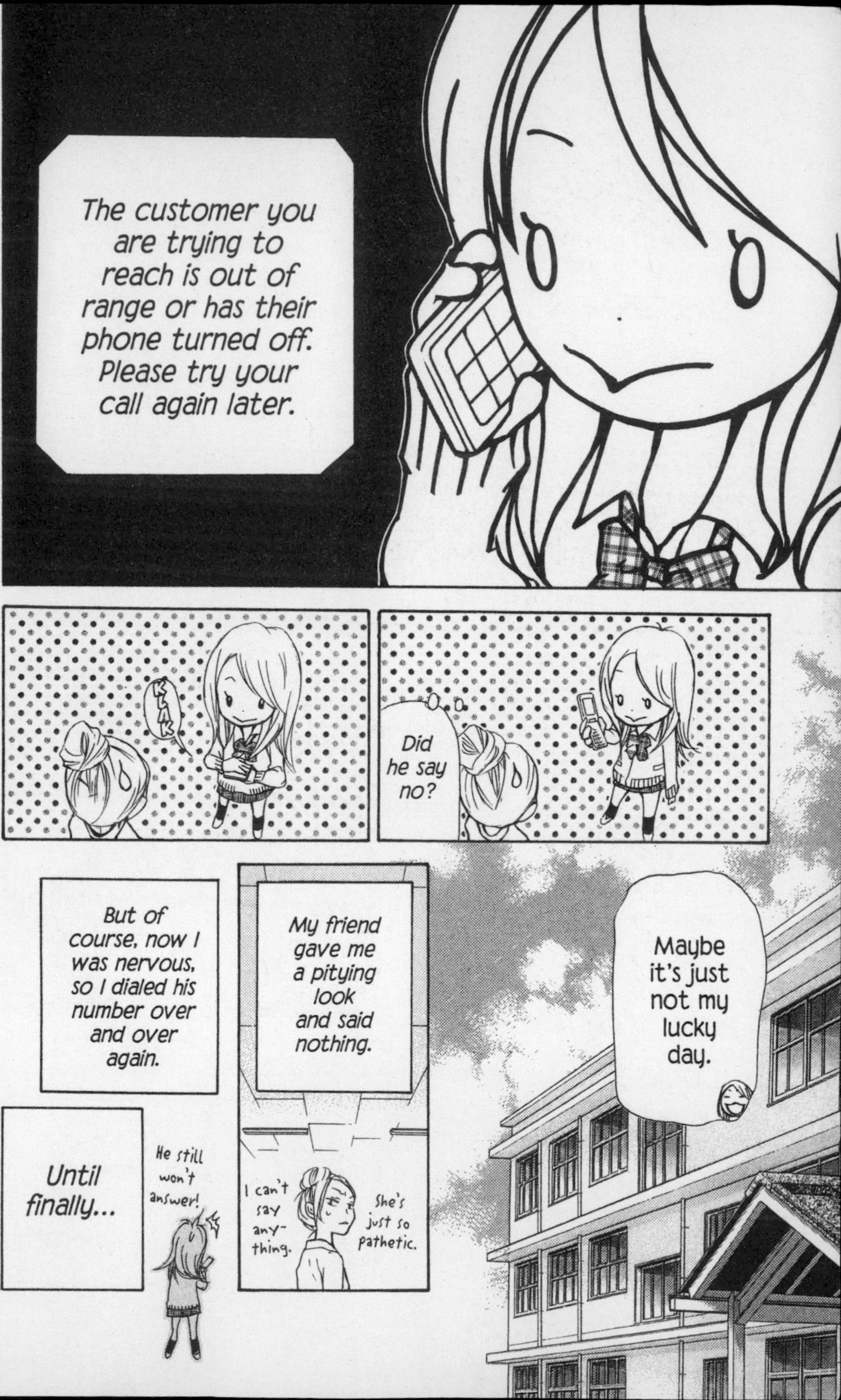
The customer you are trying to reach is out of range or has their phone turned off. Please try your call again later.
Did he say no?
KLAK
Maybe it's just not my lucky day.
My friend gave me a pitying look and said nothing.
She's just so pathetic.
I can't say any-thing.
But of course, now I was nervous, so I dialed his number over and over again.
He still won't answer!
Until finally...

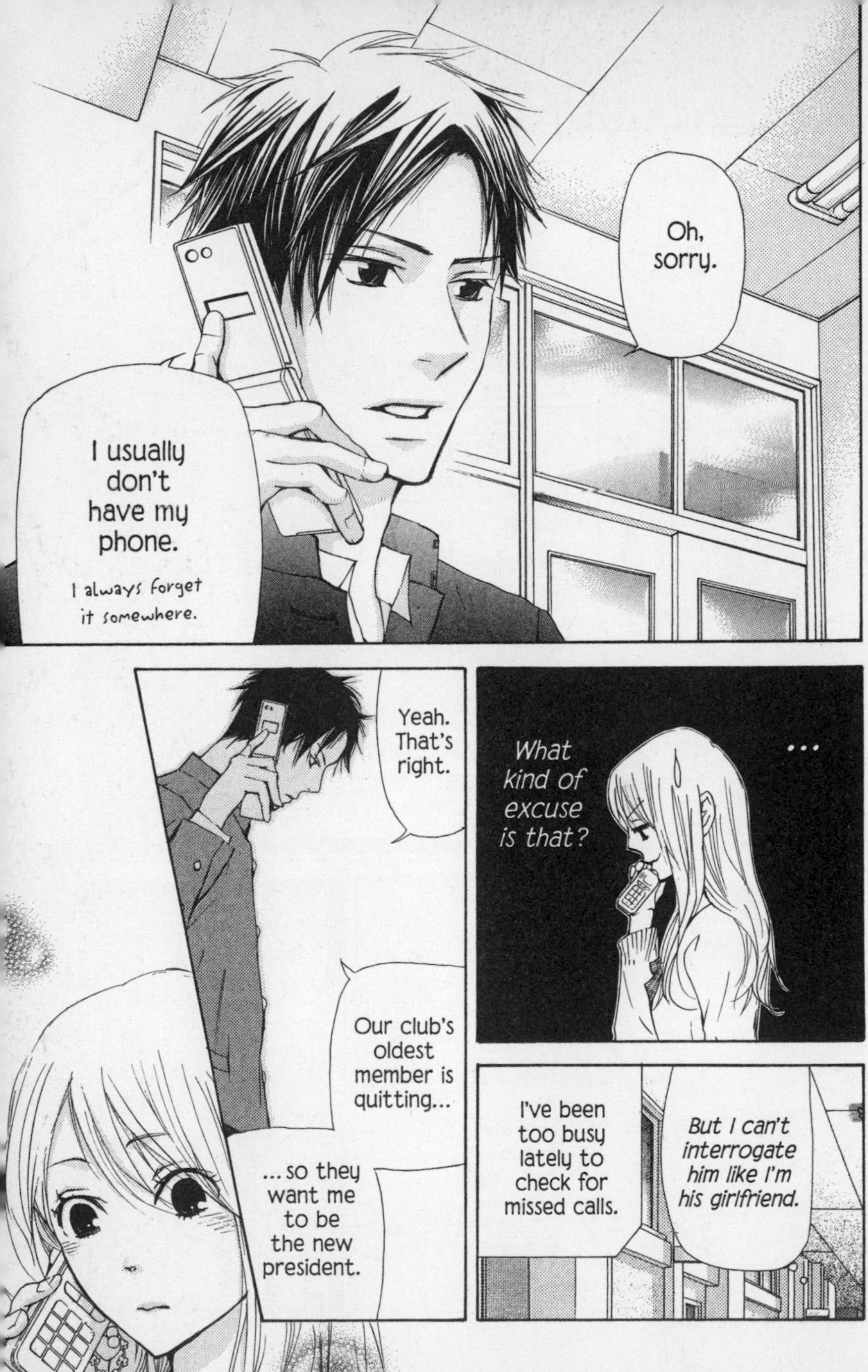
Oh, sorry.
I usually don't have my phone.
I always forget it somewhere.
...
What kind of excuse is that?
But I can't interrogate him like I'm his girlfriend.
I've been too busy lately to check for missed calls.
Yeah. That's right.
Our club's oldest member is quitting...
...so they want me to be the new president.

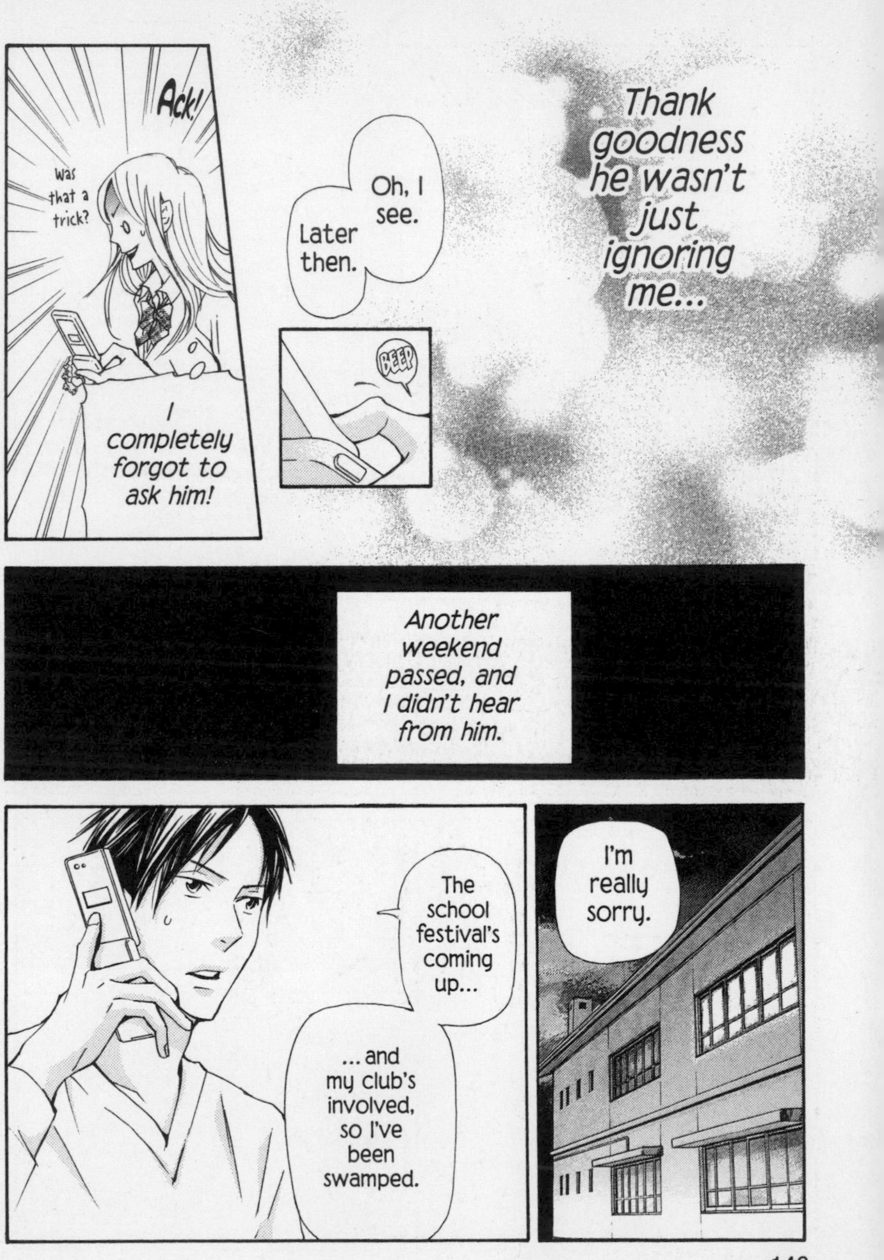
Thank goodness he wasn't just ignoring me...
Oh, I see.
Later then.
BEEP
Ack!
Was that a trick?
I completely forgot to ask him!
Another weekend passed, and I didn't hear from him.
I'm really sorry.
The school festival's coming up...
...and my club's involved, so I've been swamped.

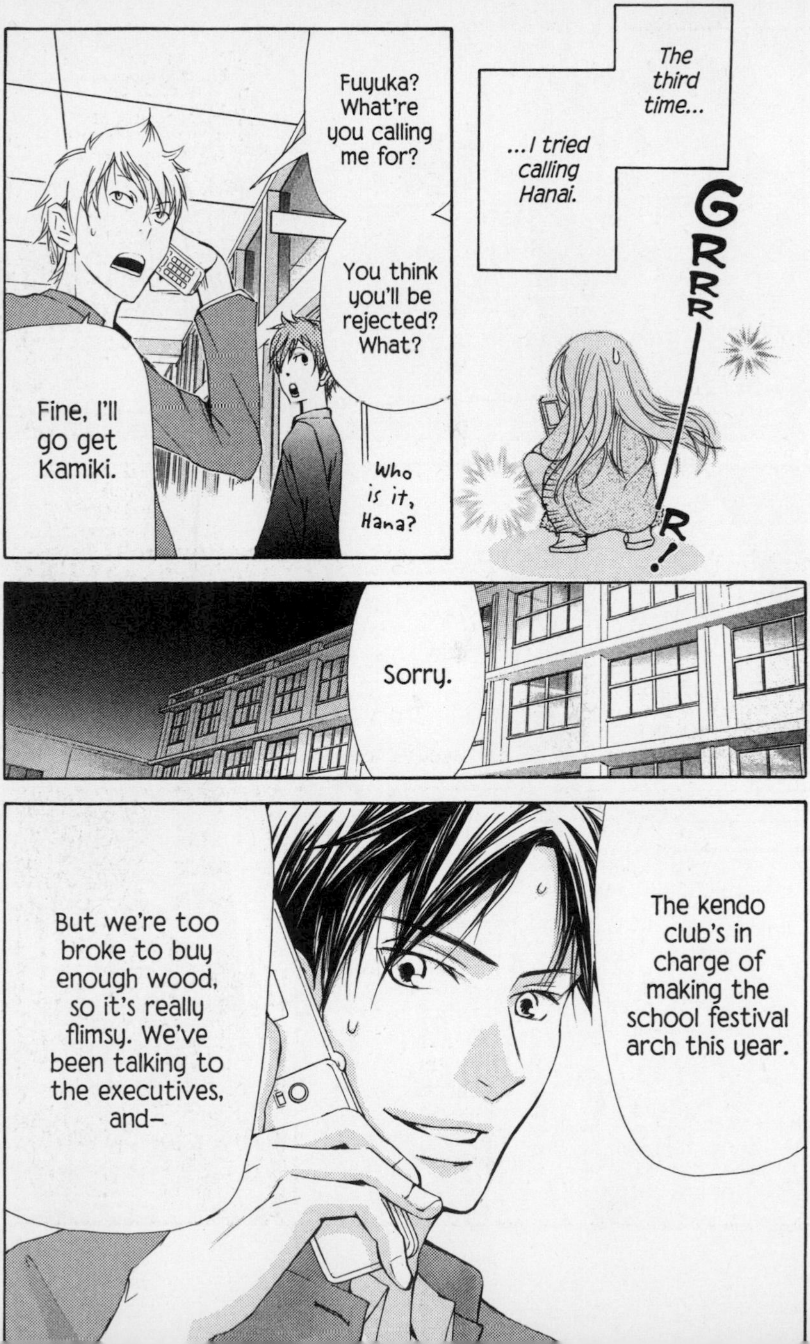
The third time...
...I tried calling Hanai.
GRRRR!
Fuyuka? What're you calling me for?
You think you'll be rejected? What?
Fine, I'll go get Kamiki.
Who is it, Hana?
Sorry.
The kendo club's in charge of making the school festival arch this year.
But we're too broke to buy enough wood, so it's really flimsy. We've been talking to the executives, and–

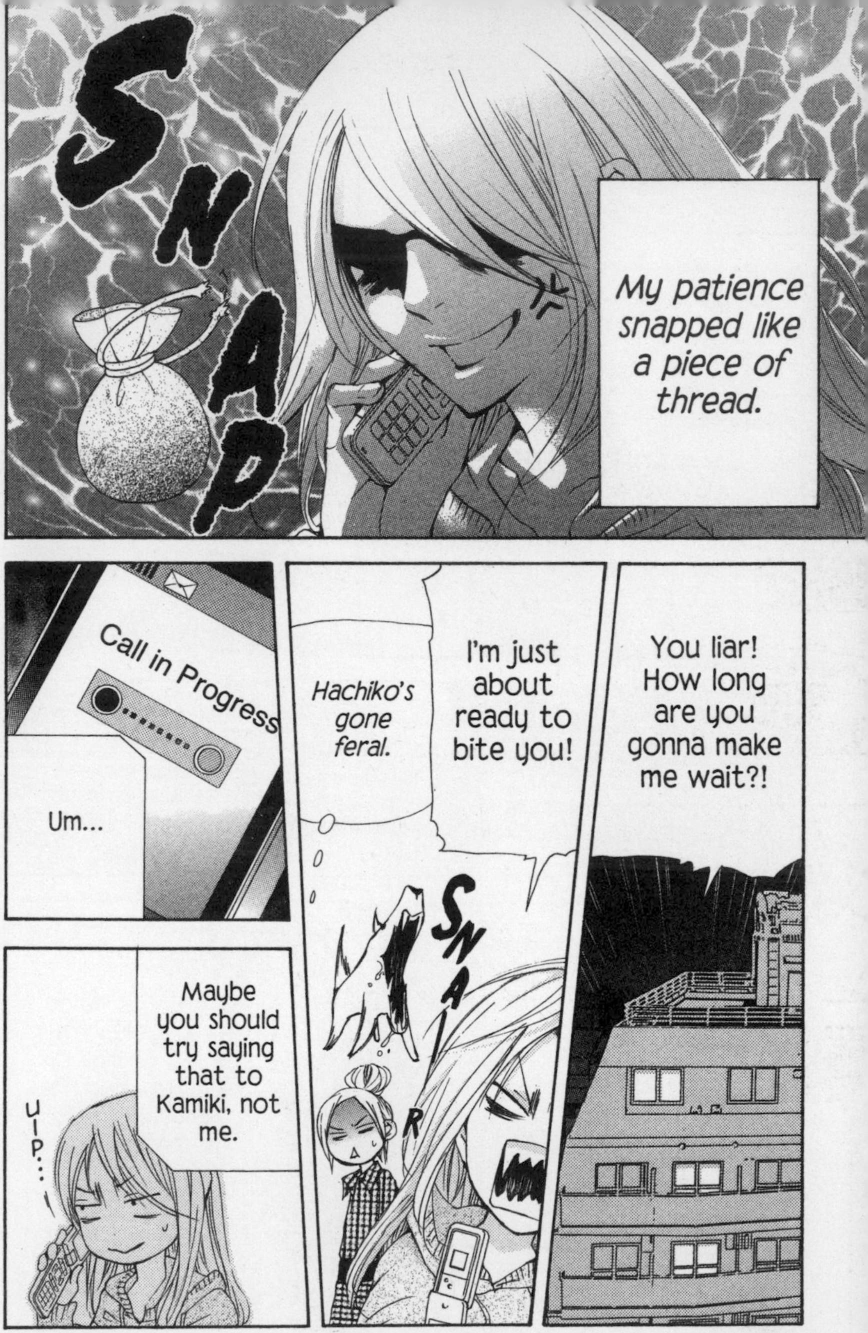
SNAP
My patience snapped like a piece of thread.
You liar! How long are you gonna make me wait?!
I'm just about ready to bite you!
Hachiko's gone feral.
SNARR
Call in Progress
Um...
Maybe you should try saying that to Kamiki, not me.
U-P...

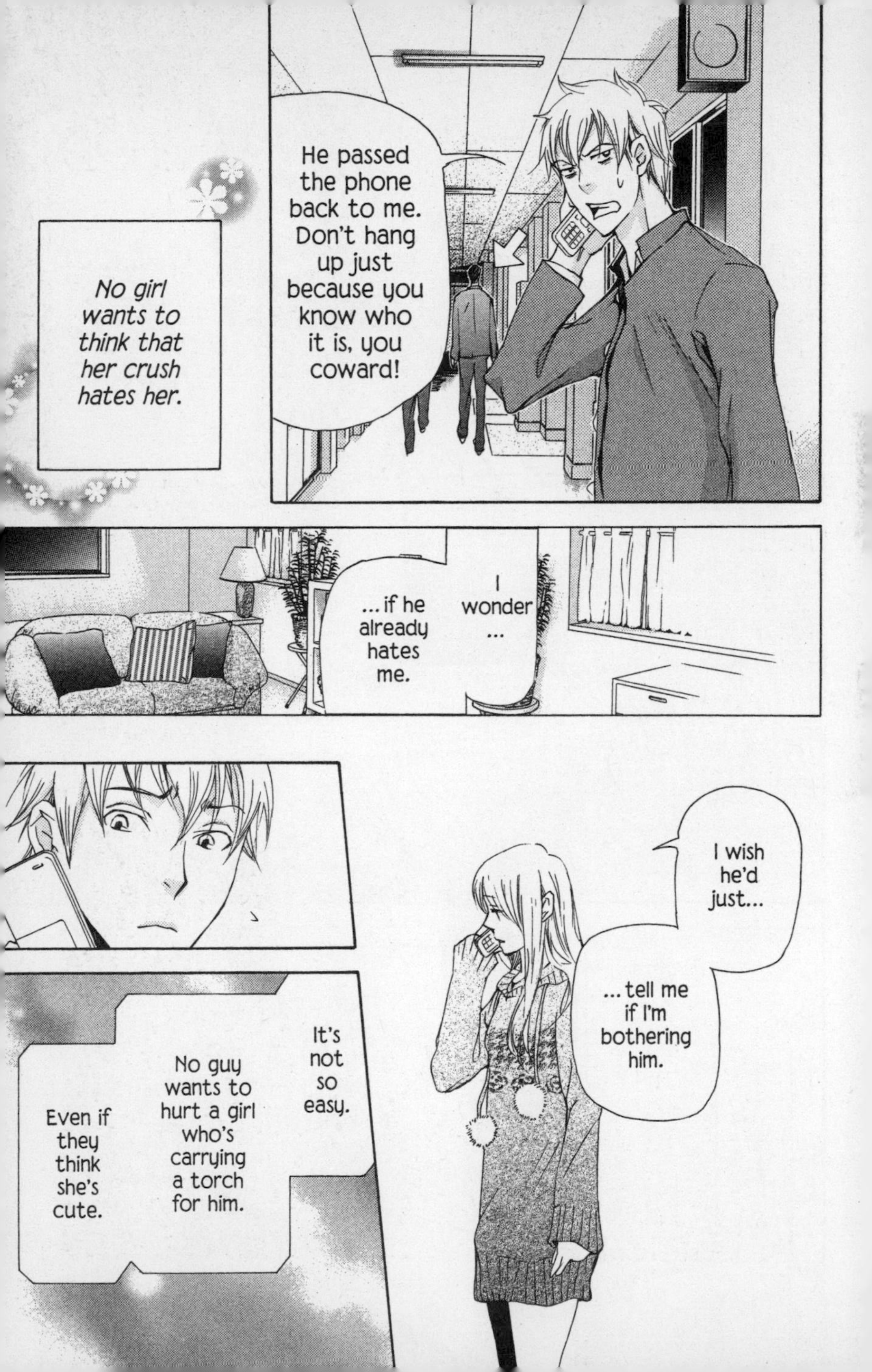
He passed the phone back to me. Don't hang up just because you know who it is, you coward!
No girl wants to think that her crush hates her.
I wonder...
...if he already hates me.
I wish he'd just...
...tell me if I'm bothering him.
It's not so easy.
No guy wants to hurt a girl who's carrying a torch for him.
Even if they think she's cute.

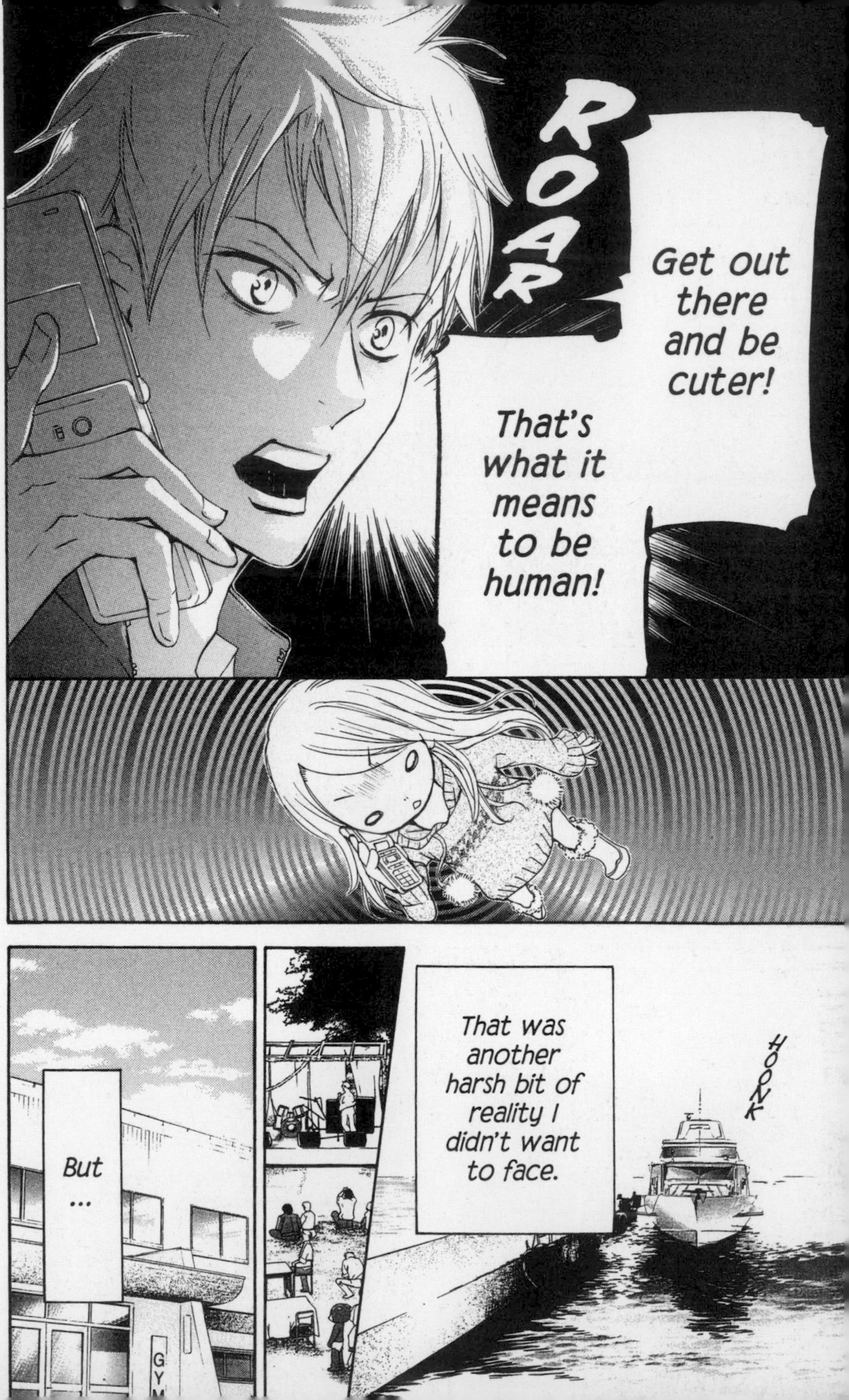
ROAR
Get out there and be cuter!
That's what it means to be human!
HOONK
That was another harsh bit of reality I didn't want to face.
But ...

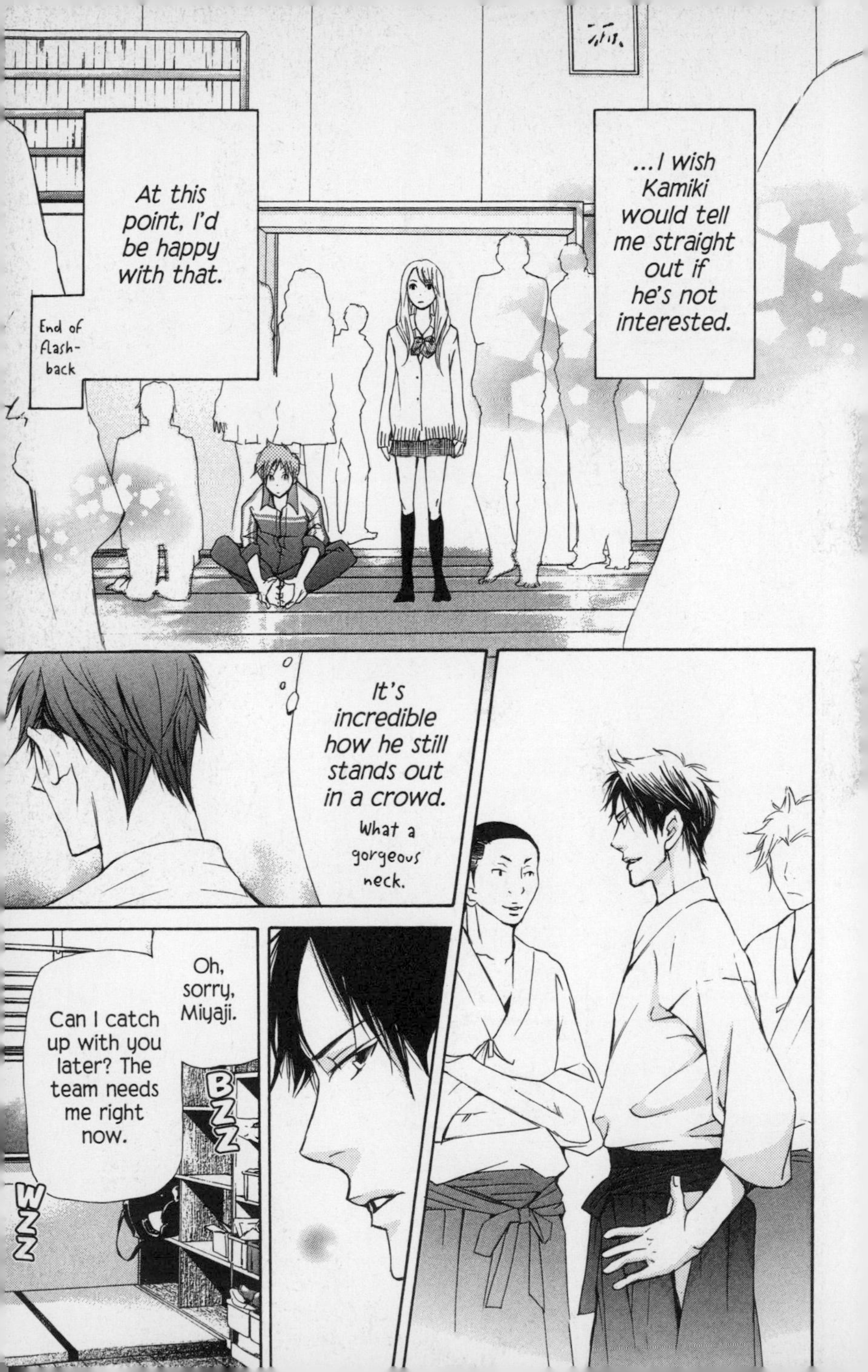
...I wish Kamiki would tell me straight out if he's not interested.
At this point, I'd be happy with that.
End of flash-back
It's incredible how he still stands out in a crowd.
What a gorgeous neck.
BZZ
Oh, sorry, Miyaji.
Can I catch up with you later? The team needs me right now.
WZZ

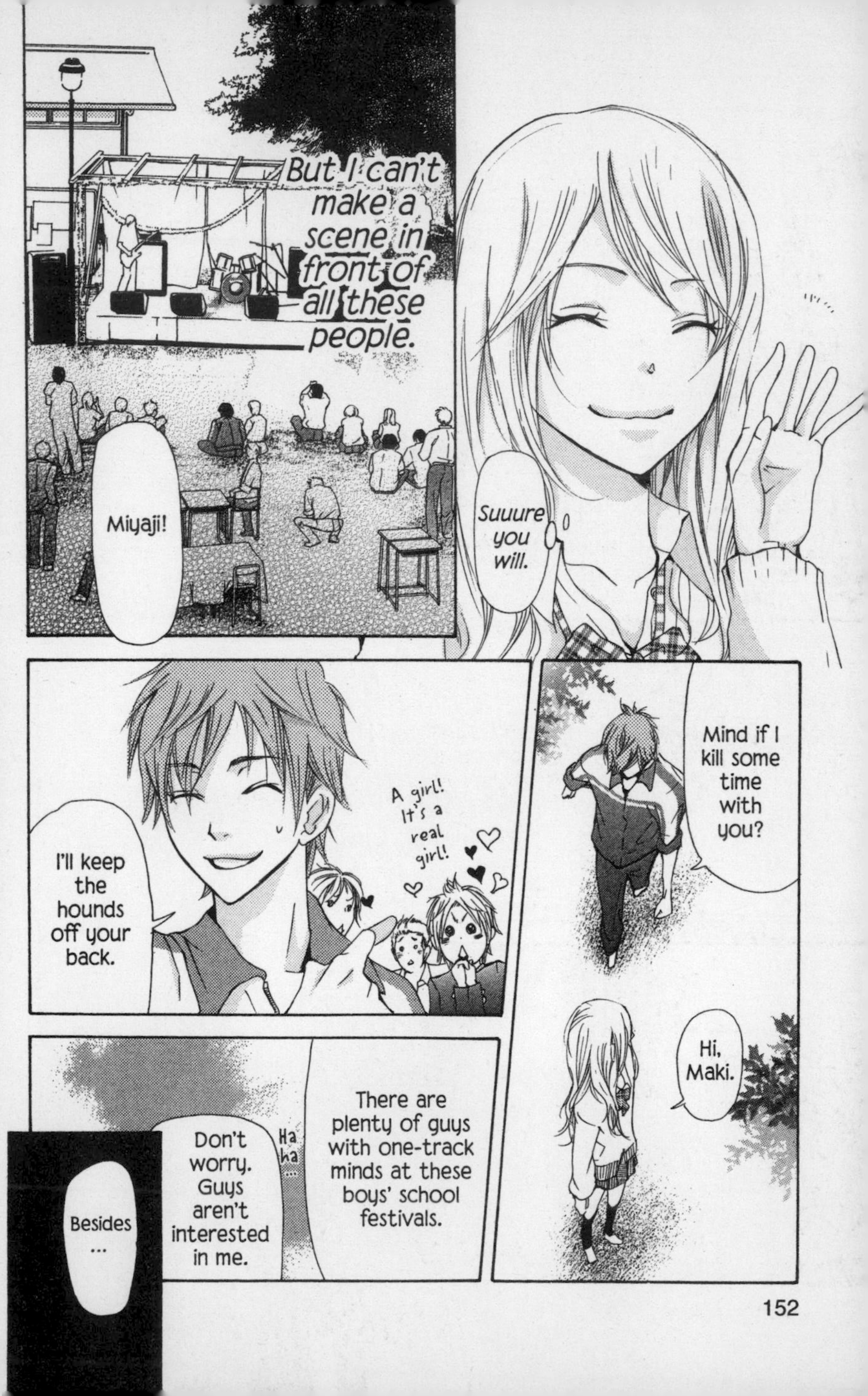
Suuure you will.
But I can't make a scene in front of all these people.
Miyaji!
Mind if I kill some time with you?
Hi, Maki.
A girl! It's a real girl!
I'll keep the hounds off your back.
There are plenty of guys with one-track minds at these boys' school festivals.
Ha ha...
Don't worry. Guys aren't interested in me.
Besides...

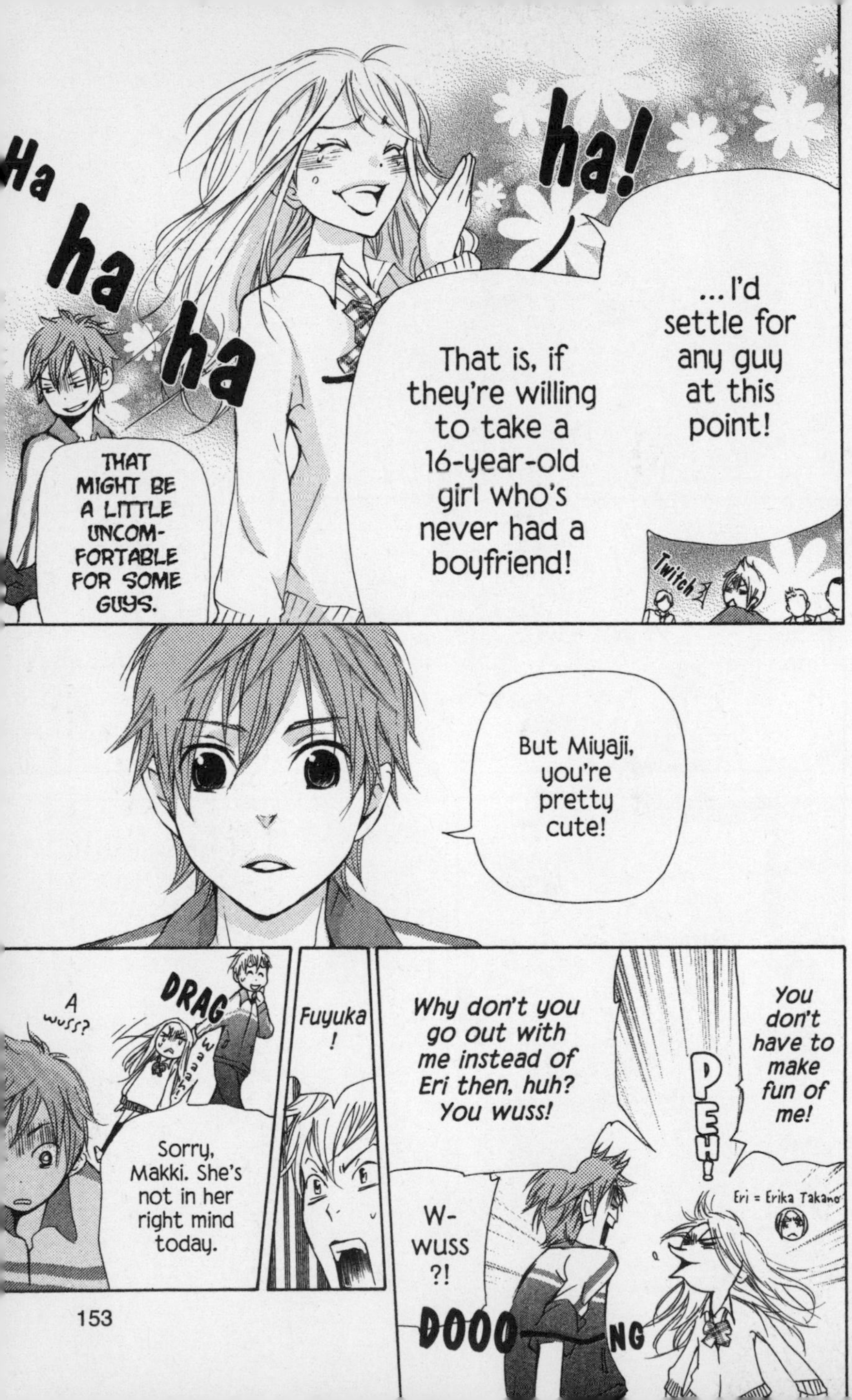

Ha ha ha ha!
...I'd settle for any guy at this point!
That is, if they're willing to take a 16-year-old girl who's never had a boyfriend!
Twitch
THAT MIGHT BE A LITTLE UNCOM-FORTABLE FOR SOME GUYS.
But Miyaji, you're pretty cute!
You don't have to make fun of me!
PEH!
Eri = Erika Takano
Why don't you go out with me instead of Eri then, huh? You wuss!
DOOO-NG
Fuyuka!
W-wuss?!
A wuss?
DRAG
Sorry, Makki. She's not in her right mind today.

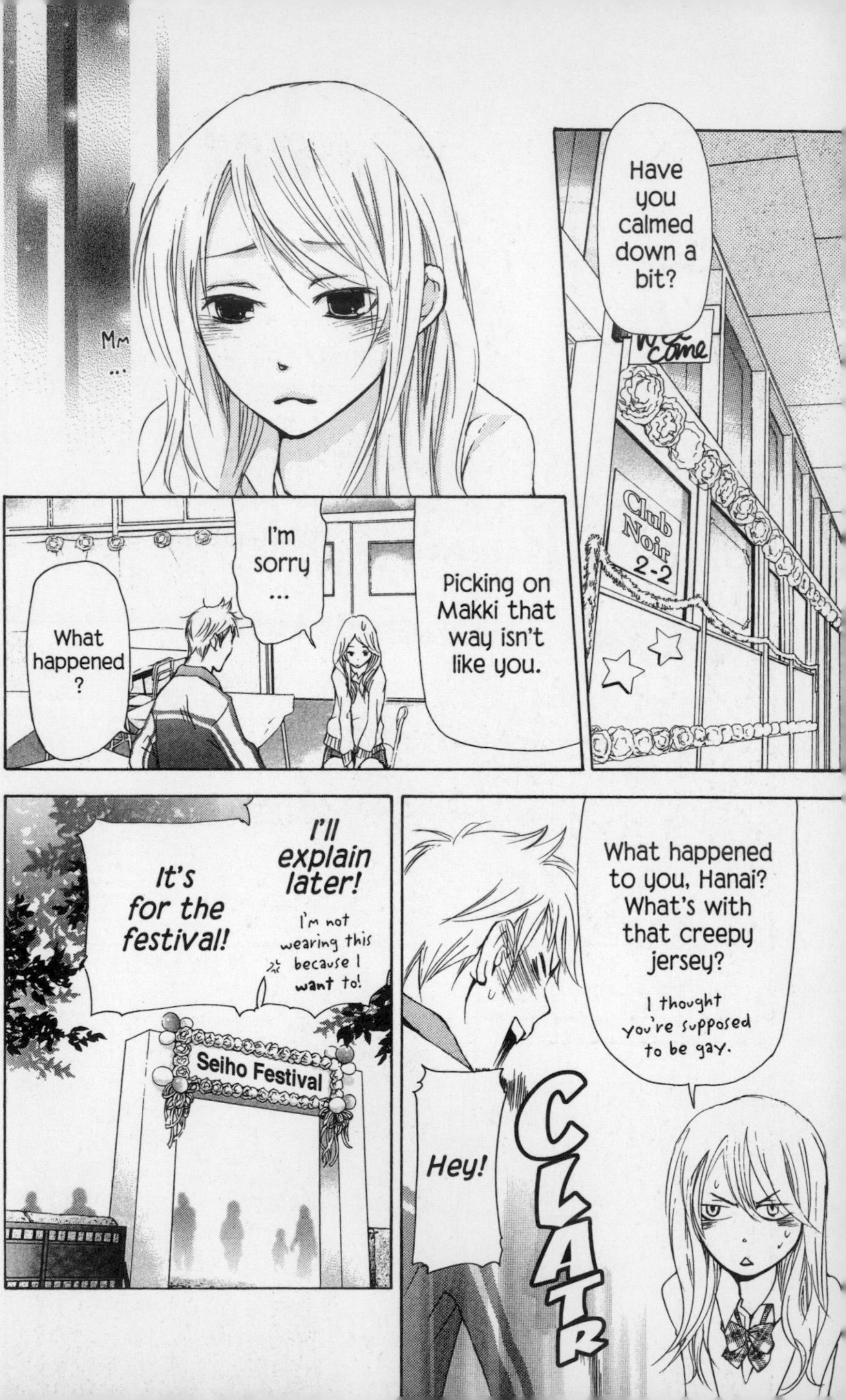
Have you calmed down a bit?
Club Noir 2-2
Mm...
Picking on Makki that way isn't like you.
I'm sorry...
What happened?
What happened to you, Hanai? What's with that creepy jersey?
I thought you're supposed to be gay.
Hey!
CLATR
I'll explain later!
I'm not wearing this because I want to!
It's for the festival!
Seiho Festival

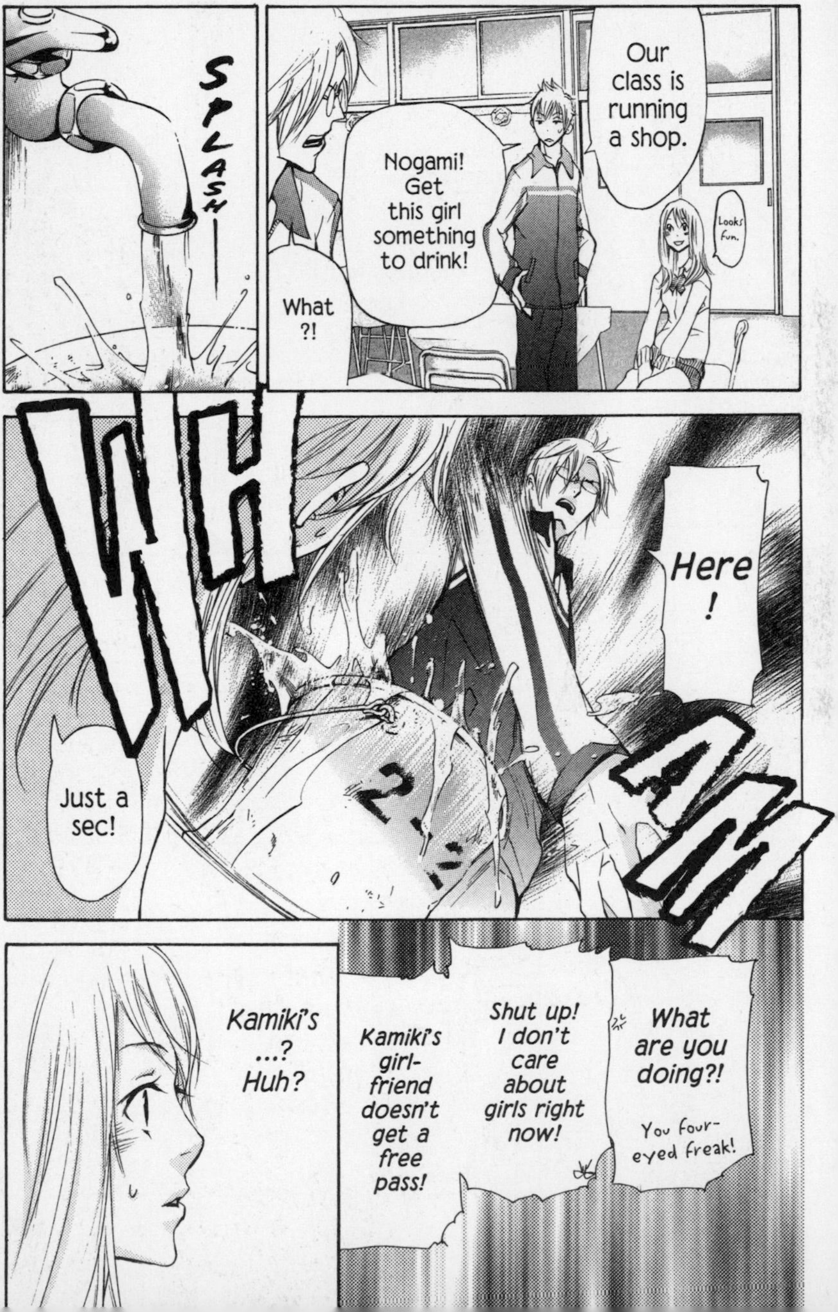
Our class is running a shop.
Looks fun.
Nogami! Get this girl something to drink!
What?!
SPLASH—
Here!
WH
AM
Just a sec!
What are you doing?!
You four-eyed freak!
Shut up! I don't care about girls right now!
Kamiki's girlfriend doesn't get a free pass!
Kamiki's ...? Huh?

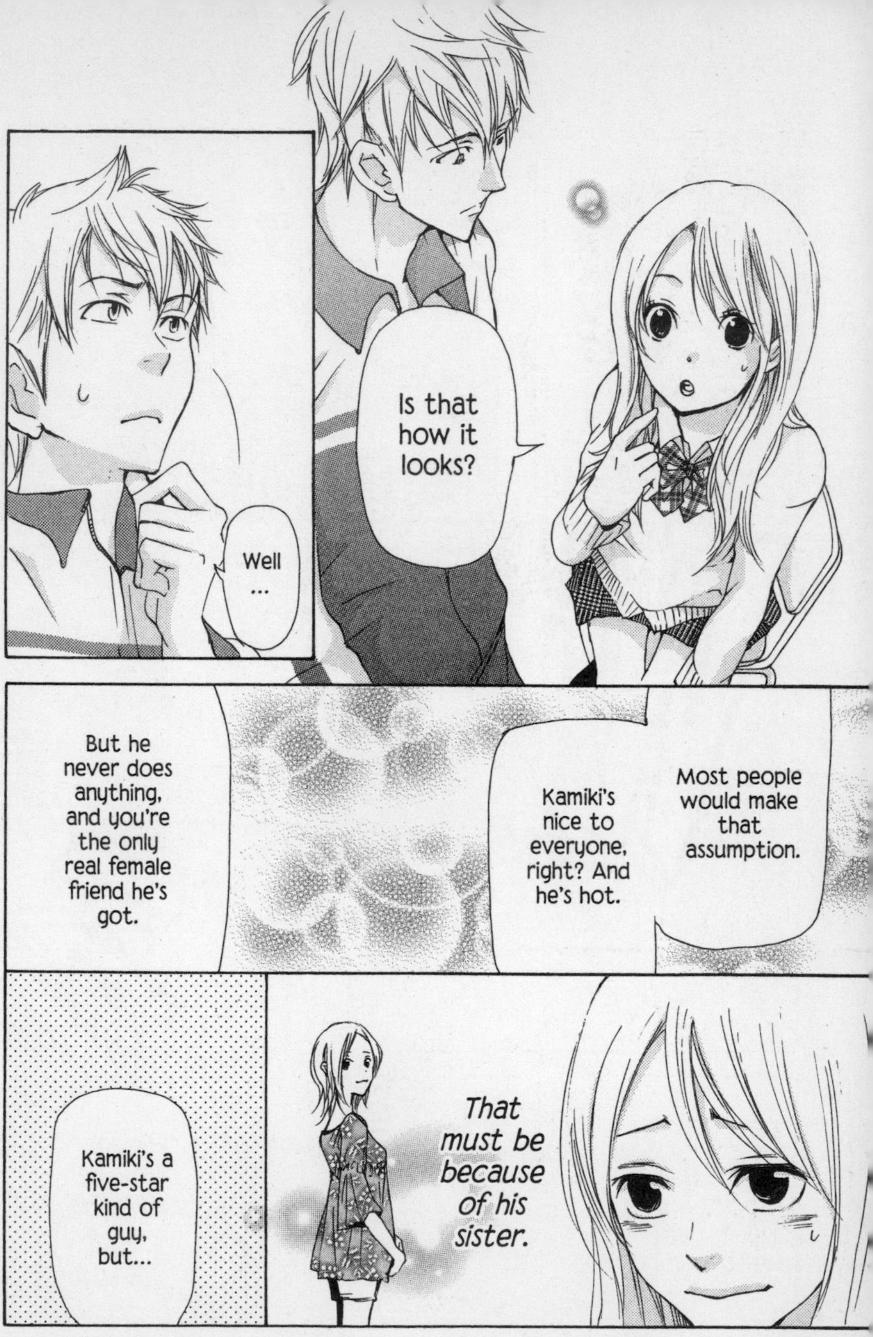
Is that how it looks?
Well ...
Most people would make that assumption.
Kamiki's nice to everyone, right? And he's hot.
But he never does anything, and you're the only real female friend he's got.
That must be because of his sister.
Kamiki's a five-star kind of guy, but...

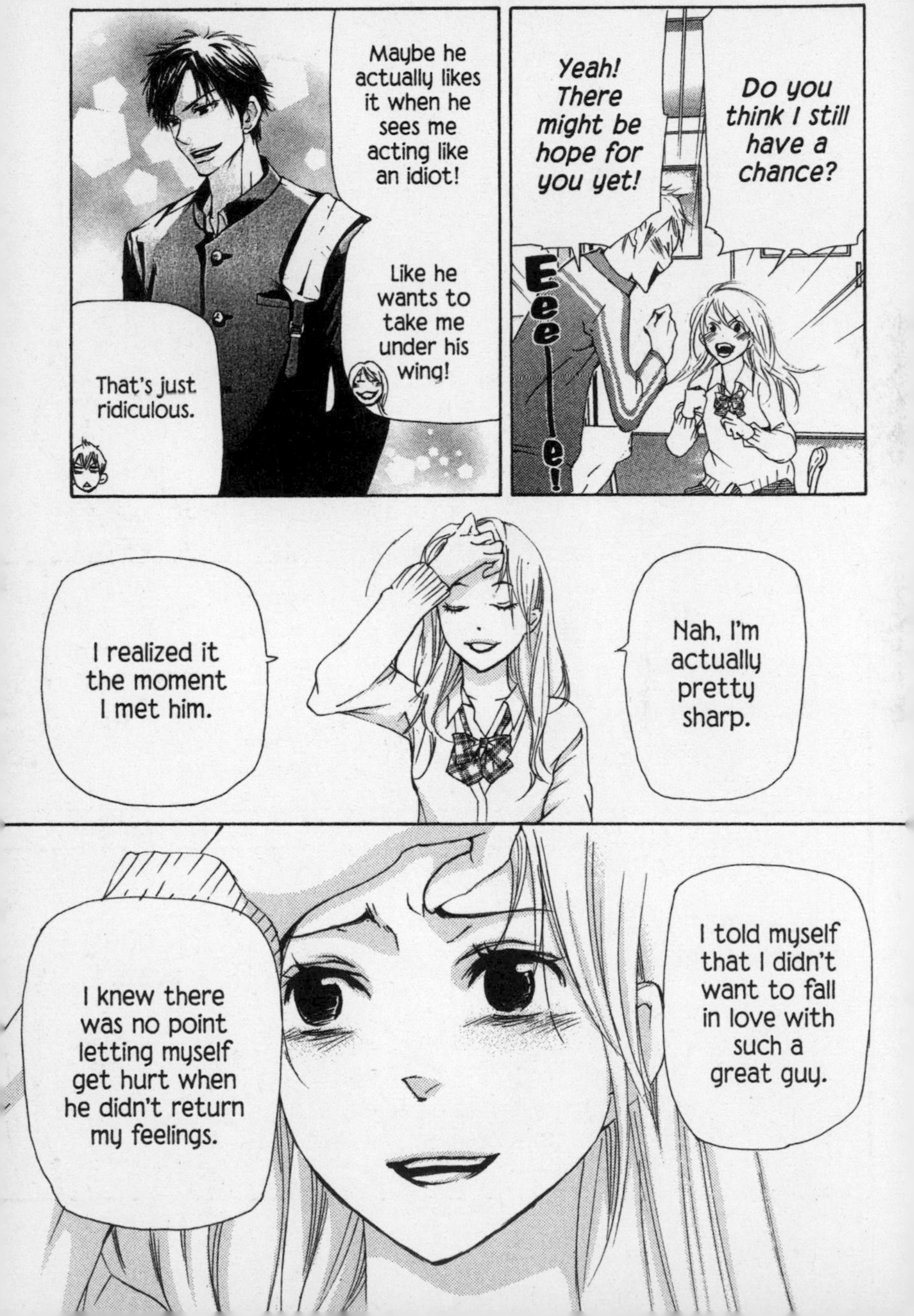
Do you think I still have a chance?
Yeah! There might be hope for you yet!
Eee—e!
Maybe he actually likes it when he sees me acting like an idiot!
Like he wants to take me under his wing!
That's just ridiculous.
Nah, I'm actually pretty sharp.
I realized it the moment I met him.
I told myself that I didn't want to fall in love with such a great guy.
I knew there was no point letting myself get hurt when he didn't return my feelings.

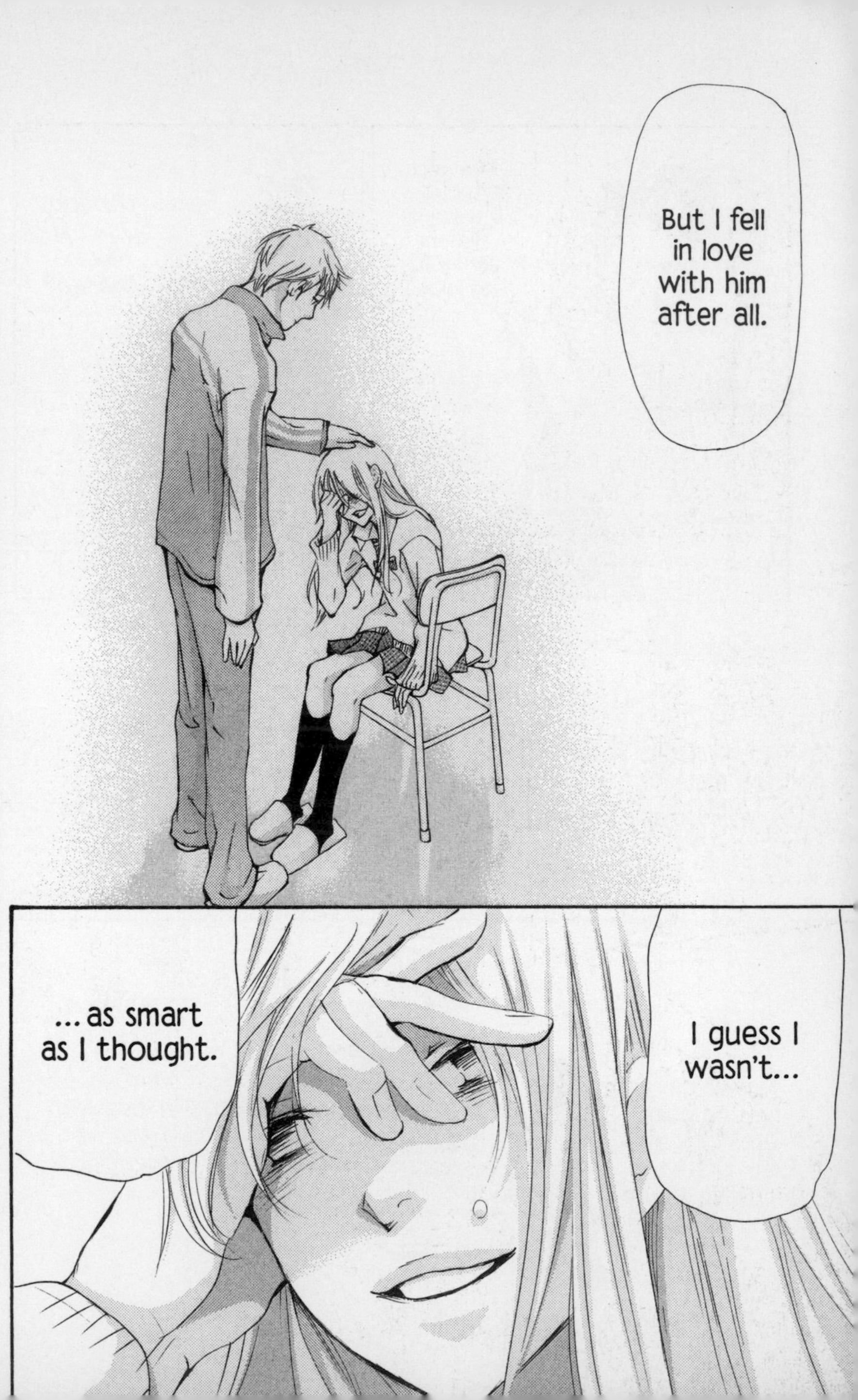
But I fell in love with him after all.
I guess I wasn't...
...as smart as I thought.

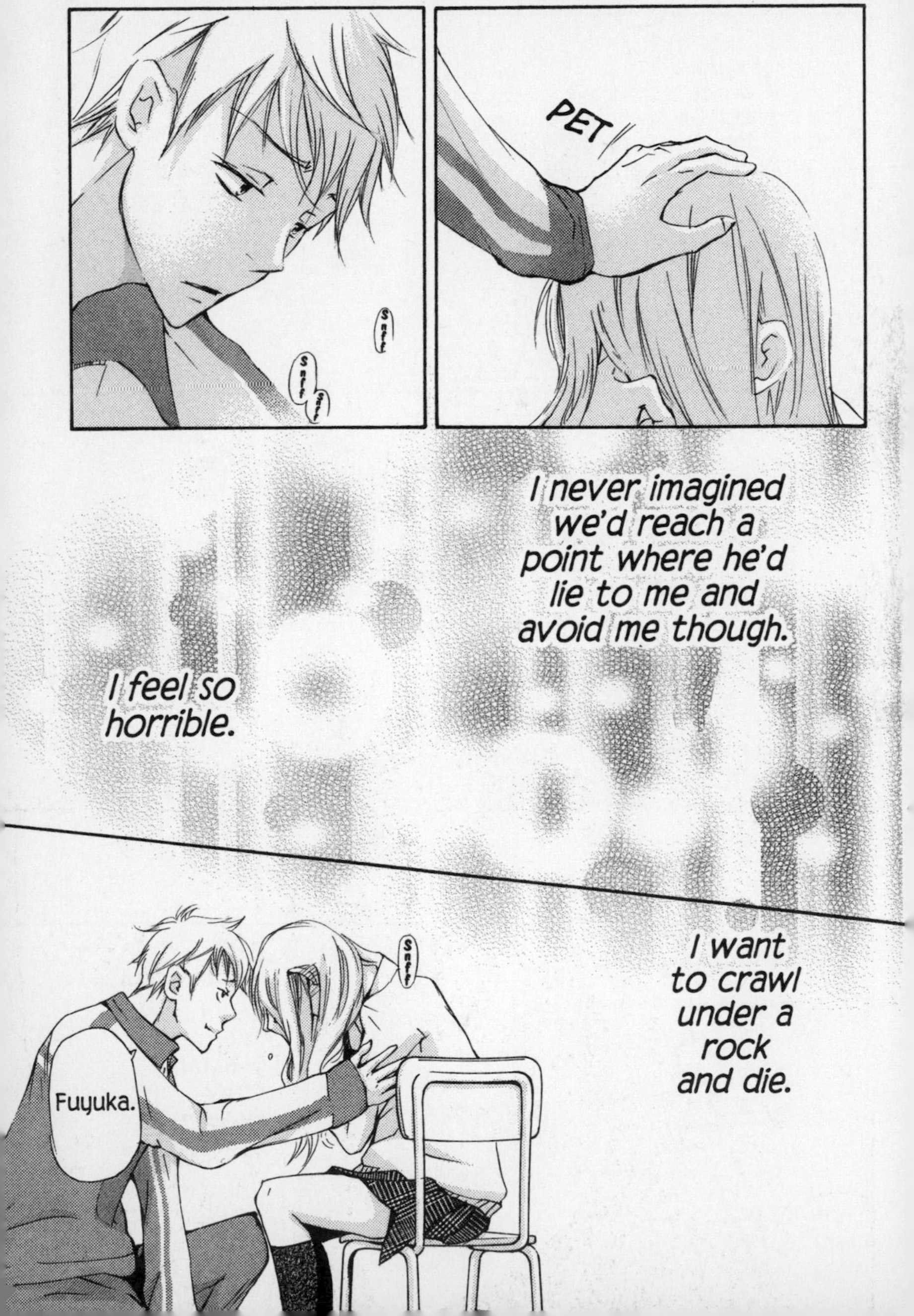
PET
Sniff
Sniff
Sniff
I never imagined we'd reach a point where he'd lie to me and avoid me though.
I feel so horrible.
I want to crawl under a rock and die.
Sniff
Fuyuka.

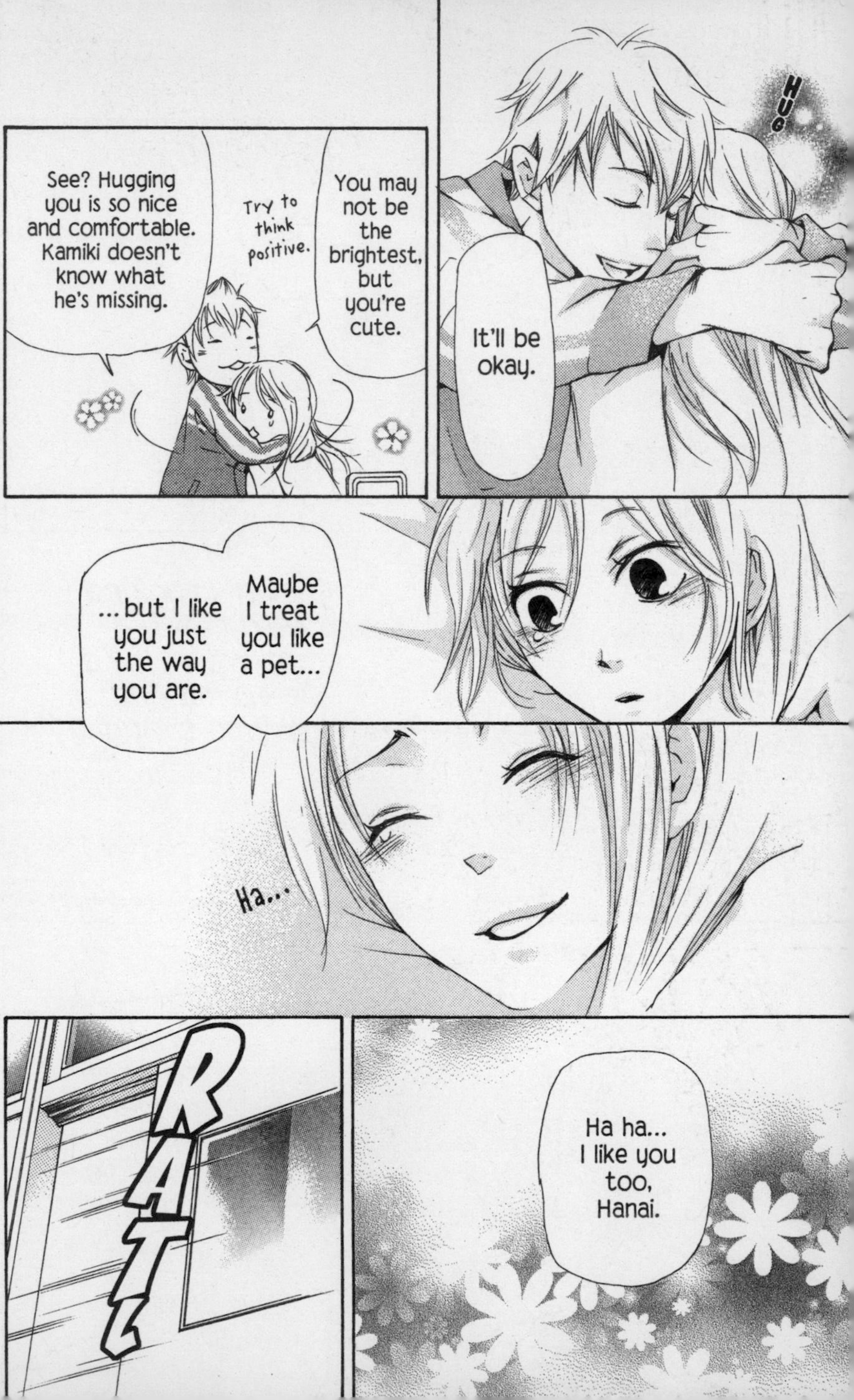
HUG
It'll be okay.
You may not be the brightest, but you're cute.
Try to think positive.
See? Hugging you is so nice and comfortable. Kamiki doesn't know what he's missing.
Maybe I treat you like a pet...
...but I like you just the way you are.
Ha...
Ha ha... I like you too, Hanai.
RATTL

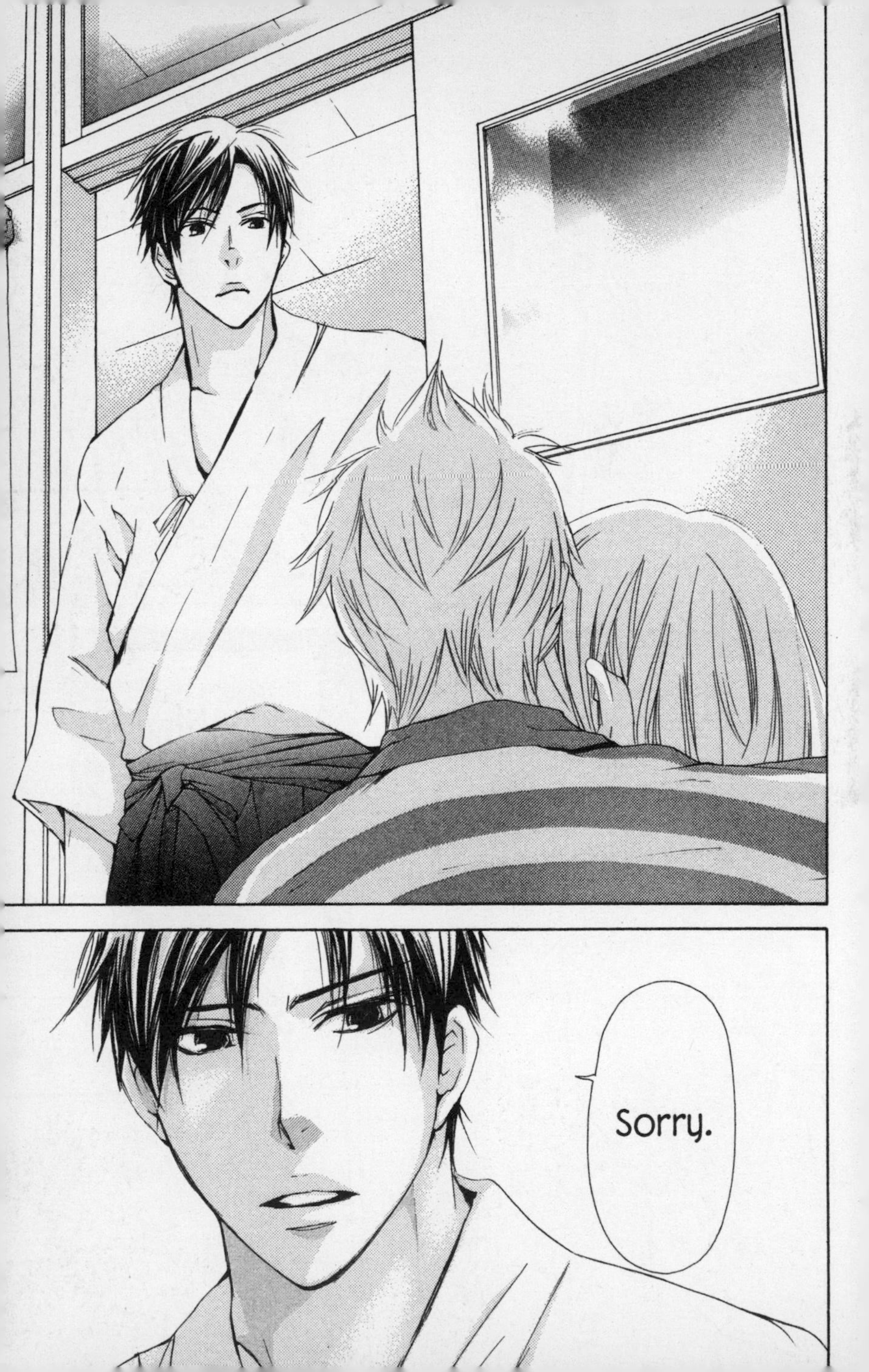
Sorry.

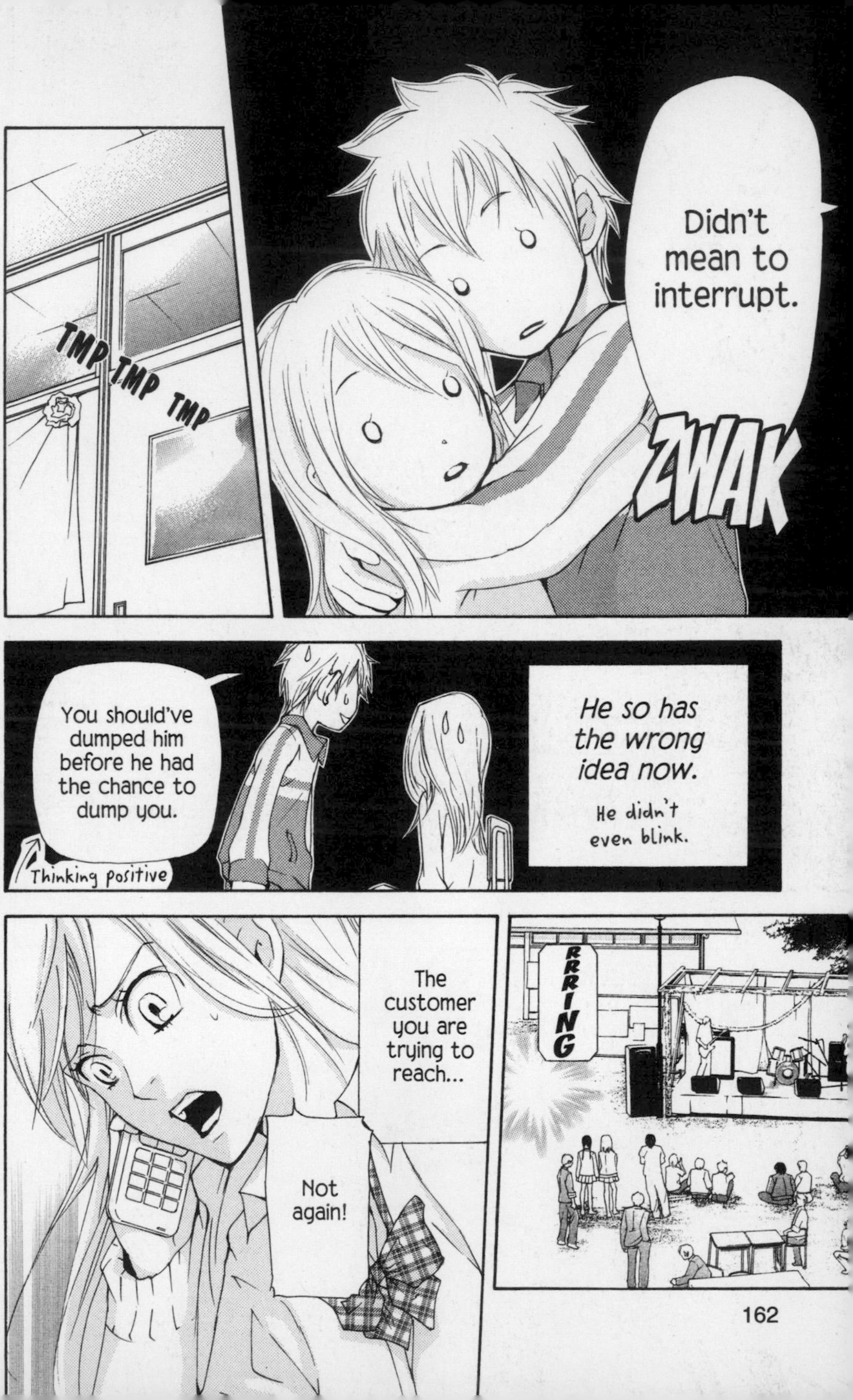
Didn't mean to interrupt.
ZWAK
TMP TMP TMP
He so has the wrong idea now.
He didn't even blink.
You should've dumped him before he had the chance to dump you.
Thinking positive
RRRING
The customer you are trying to reach...
Not again!

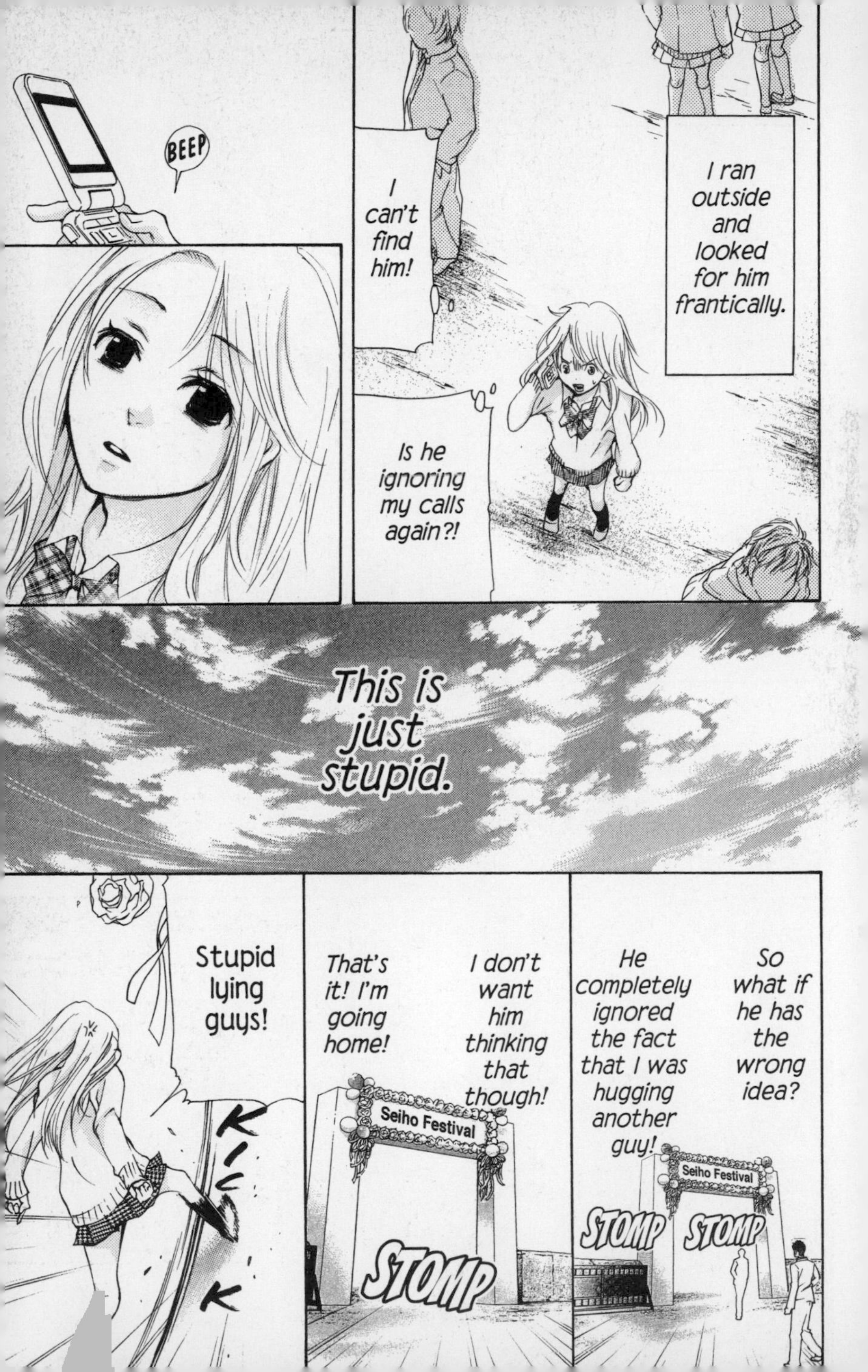
I ran outside and looked for him frantically.
I can't find him!
Is he ignoring my calls again?!
BEEP
This is just stupid.
So what if he has the wrong idea?
He completely ignored the fact that I was hugging another guy!
Seiho Festival
STOMP
STOMP
I don't want him thinking that though!
That's it! I'm going home!
Seiho Festival
STOMP
Stupid lying guys!
KICK

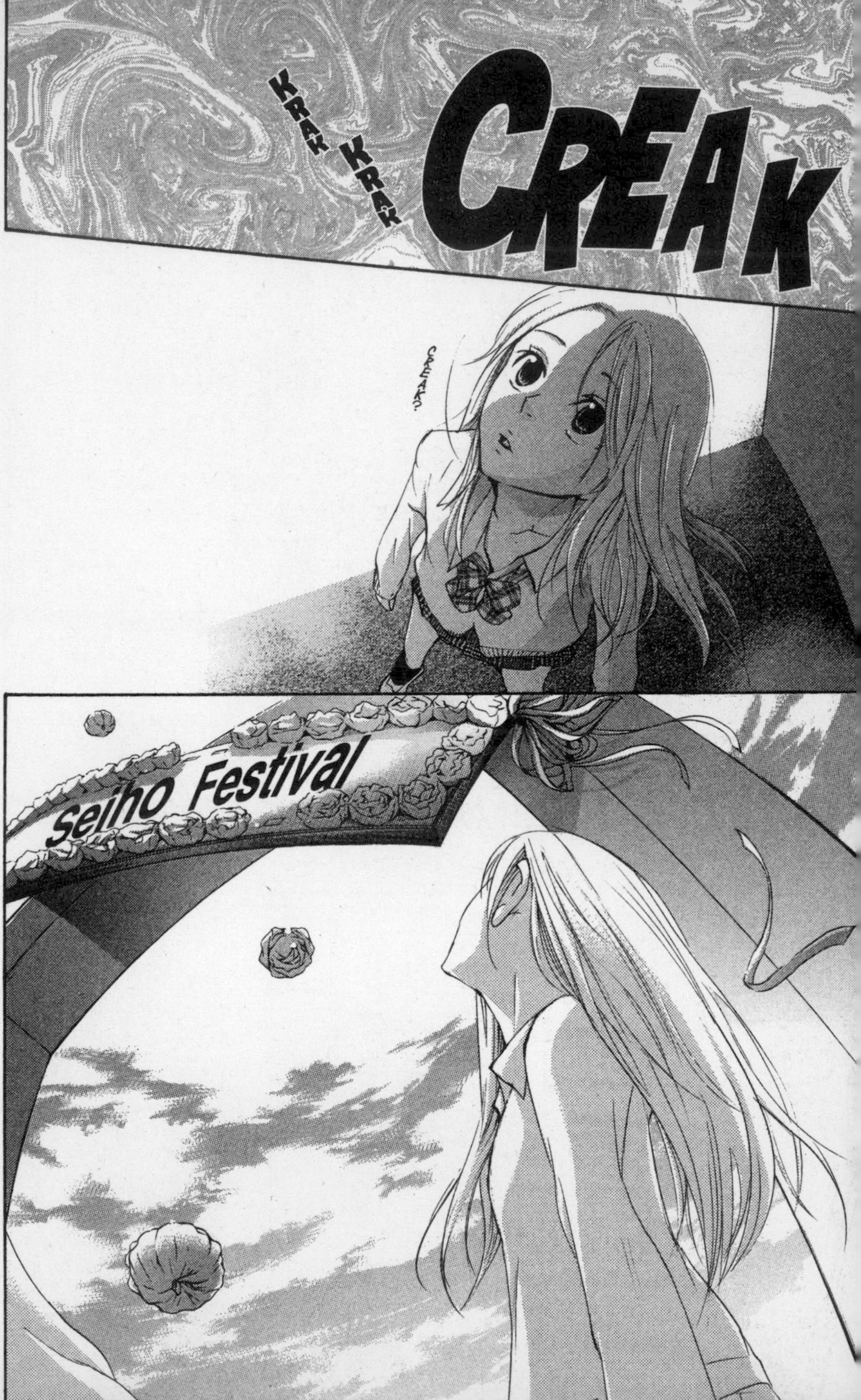
CREAK
KRAK KRAK
CREAK?
Seiho Festival

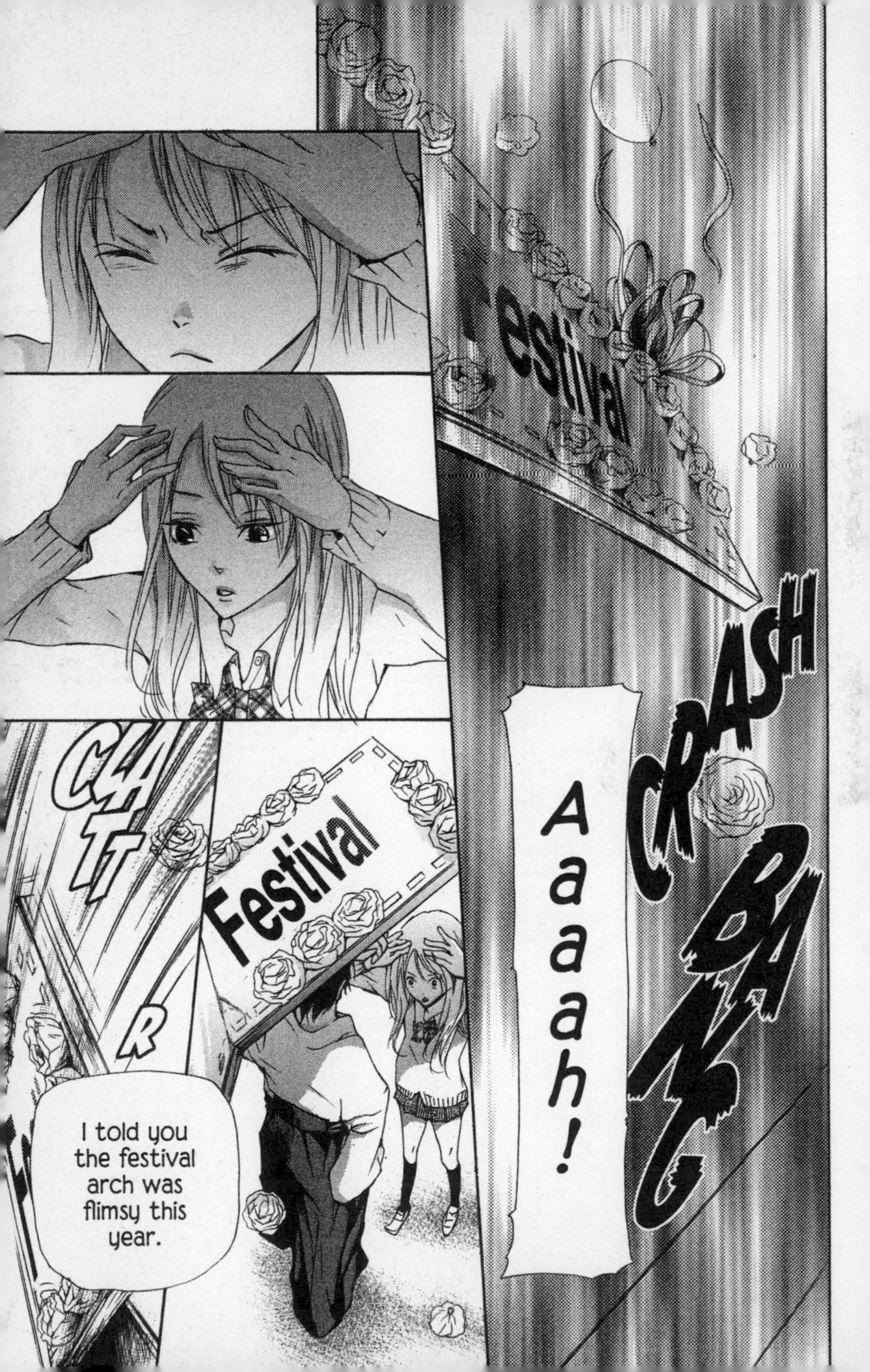
estival
Aaaah!
CRASH
BANG
CHATTR
Festival
I told you the festival arch was flimsy this year.

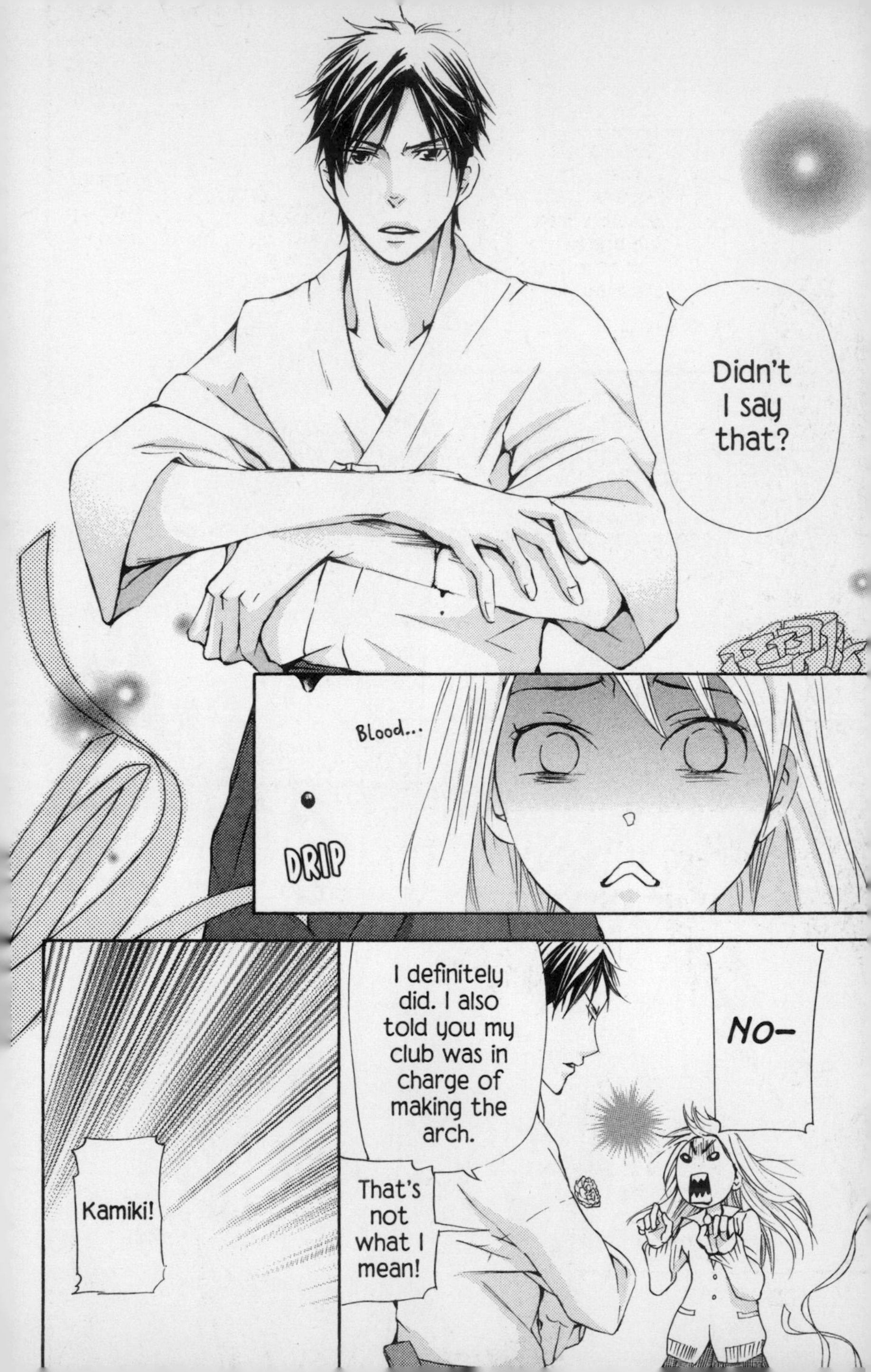
Didn't I say that?
Blood...
DRIP
No-
I definitely did. I also told you my club was in charge of making the arch.
That's not what I mean!
Kamiki!

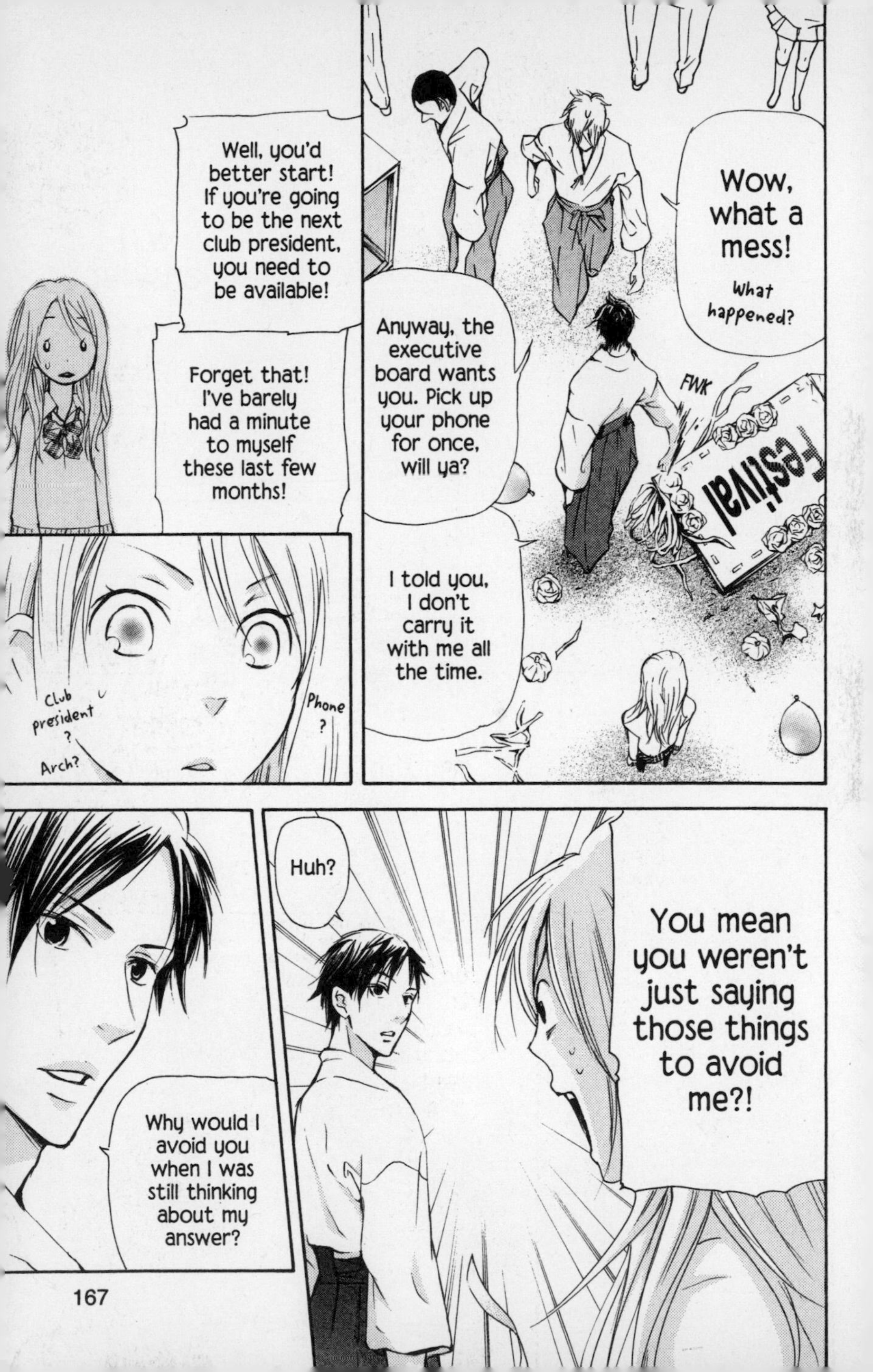
Wow, what a mess!
What happened?
FWK
Anyway, the executive board wants you. Pick up your phone for once, will ya?
I told you, I don't carry it with me all the time.
Well, you'd better start! If you're going to be the next club president, you need to be available!
Forget that! I've barely had a minute to myself these last few months!
Phone?
Club president? Arch?
You mean you weren't just saying those things to avoid me?!
Huh?
Why would I avoid you when I was still thinking about my answer?

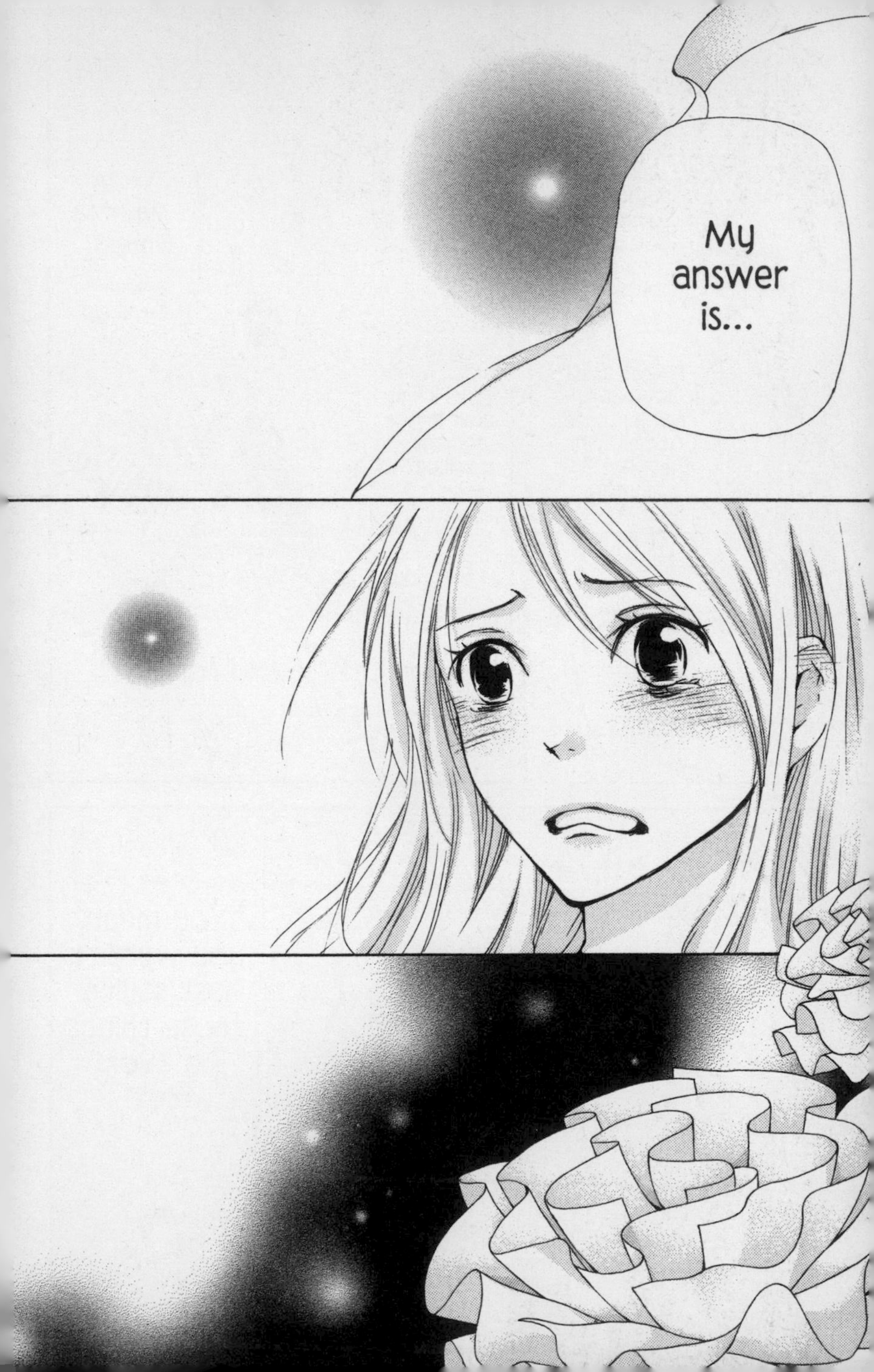
My answer is...

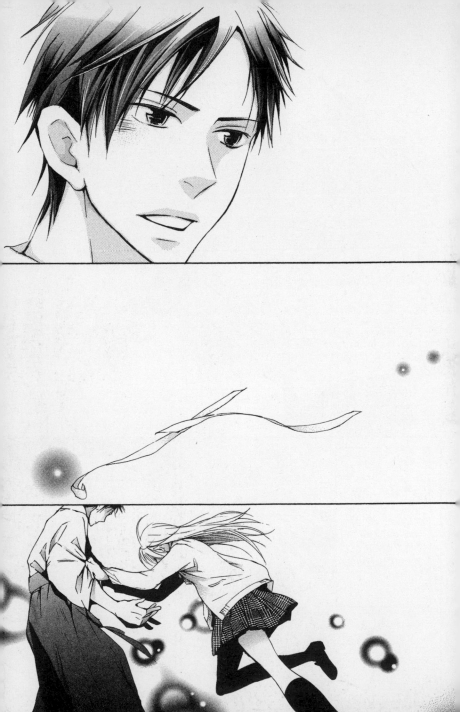

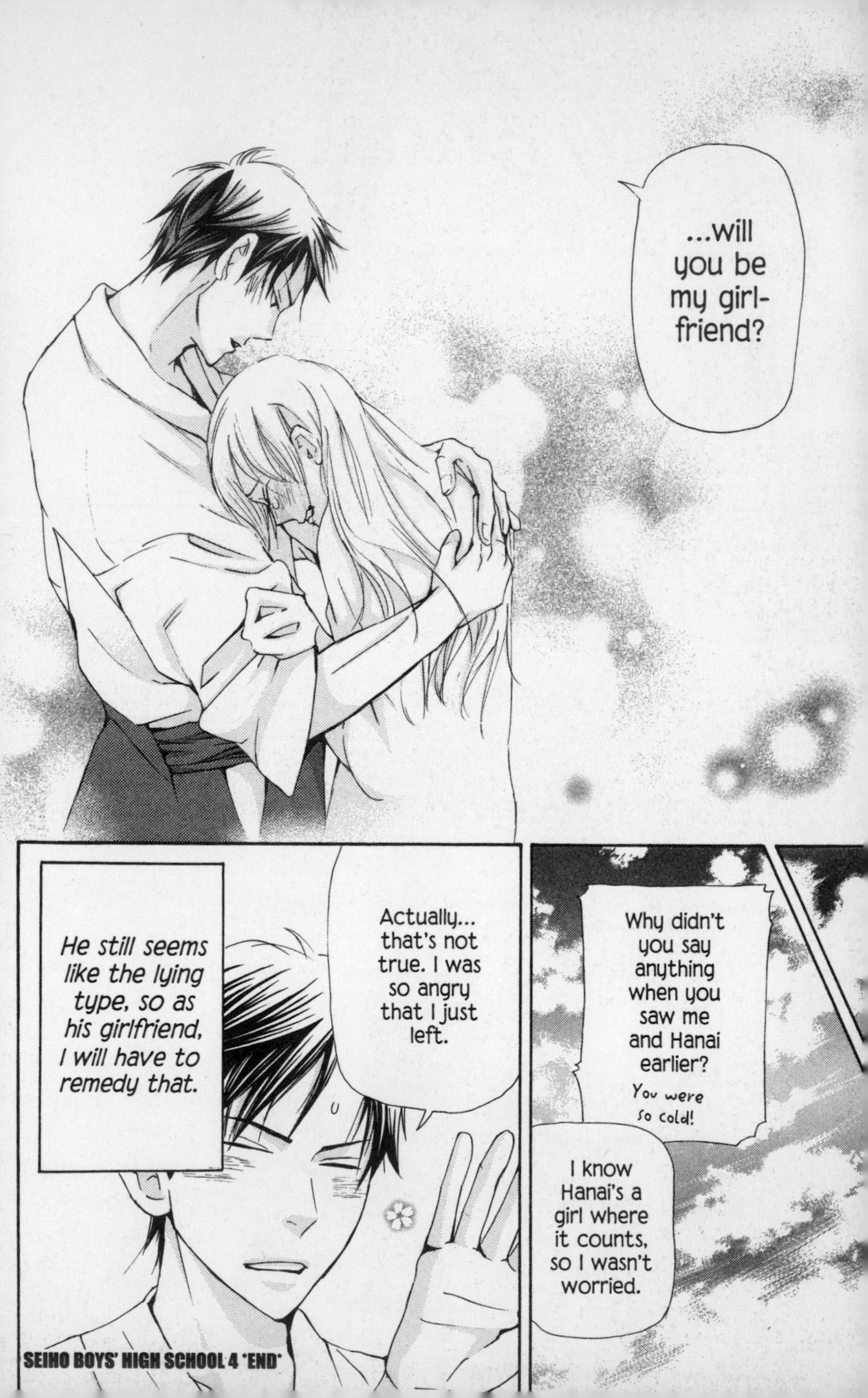
...will you be my girl-friend?
Why didn't you say anything when you saw me and Hanai earlier?
You were so cold!
I know Hanai's a girl where it counts, so I wasn't worried.
Actually... that's not true. I was so angry that I just left.
He still seems like the lying type, so as his girlfriend, I will have to remedy that.

SEIHO BOYS' HIGH SCHOOL 4 *END*

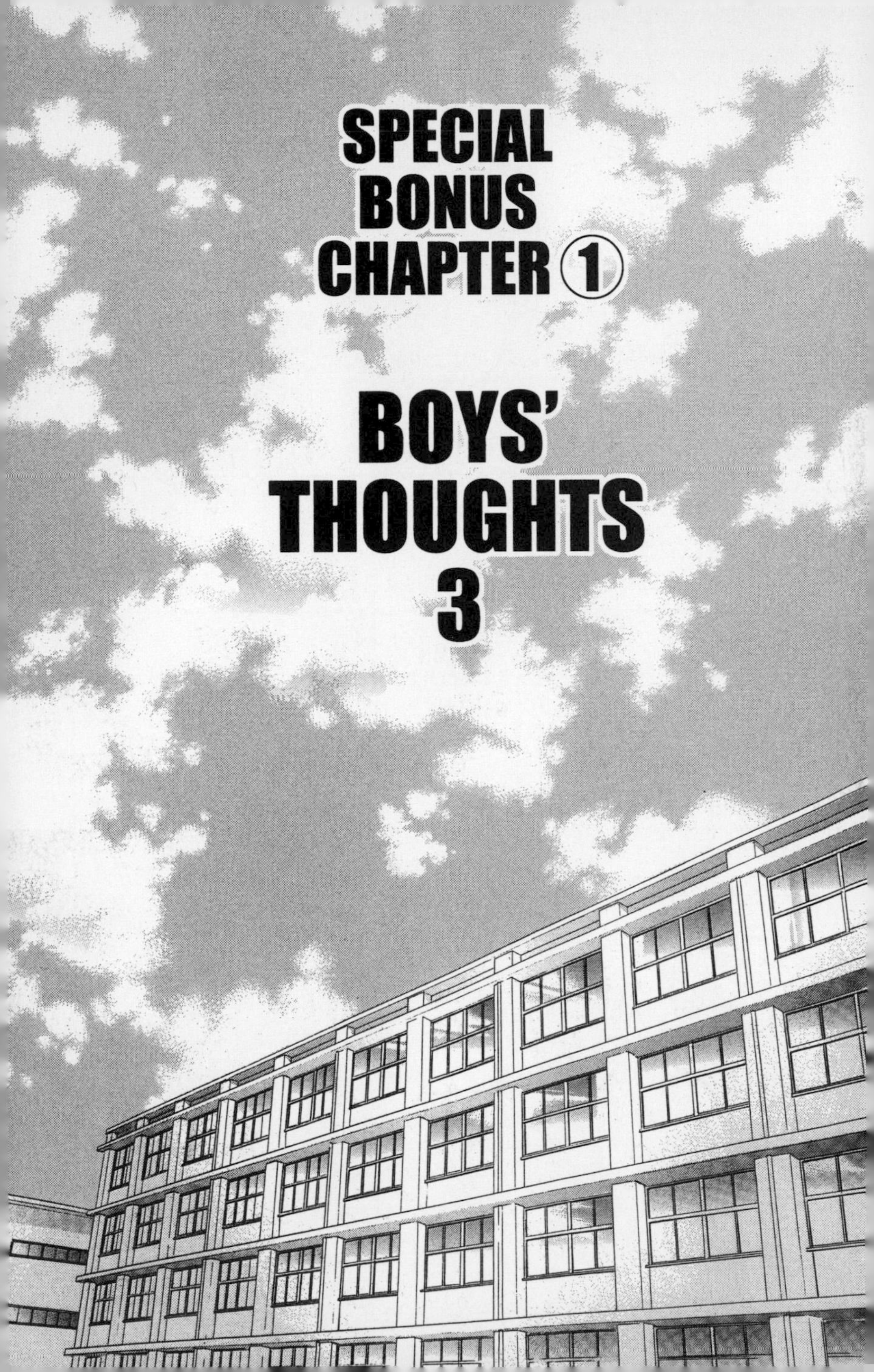
SPECIAL BONUS CHAPTER ①
BOYS' THOUGHTS 3

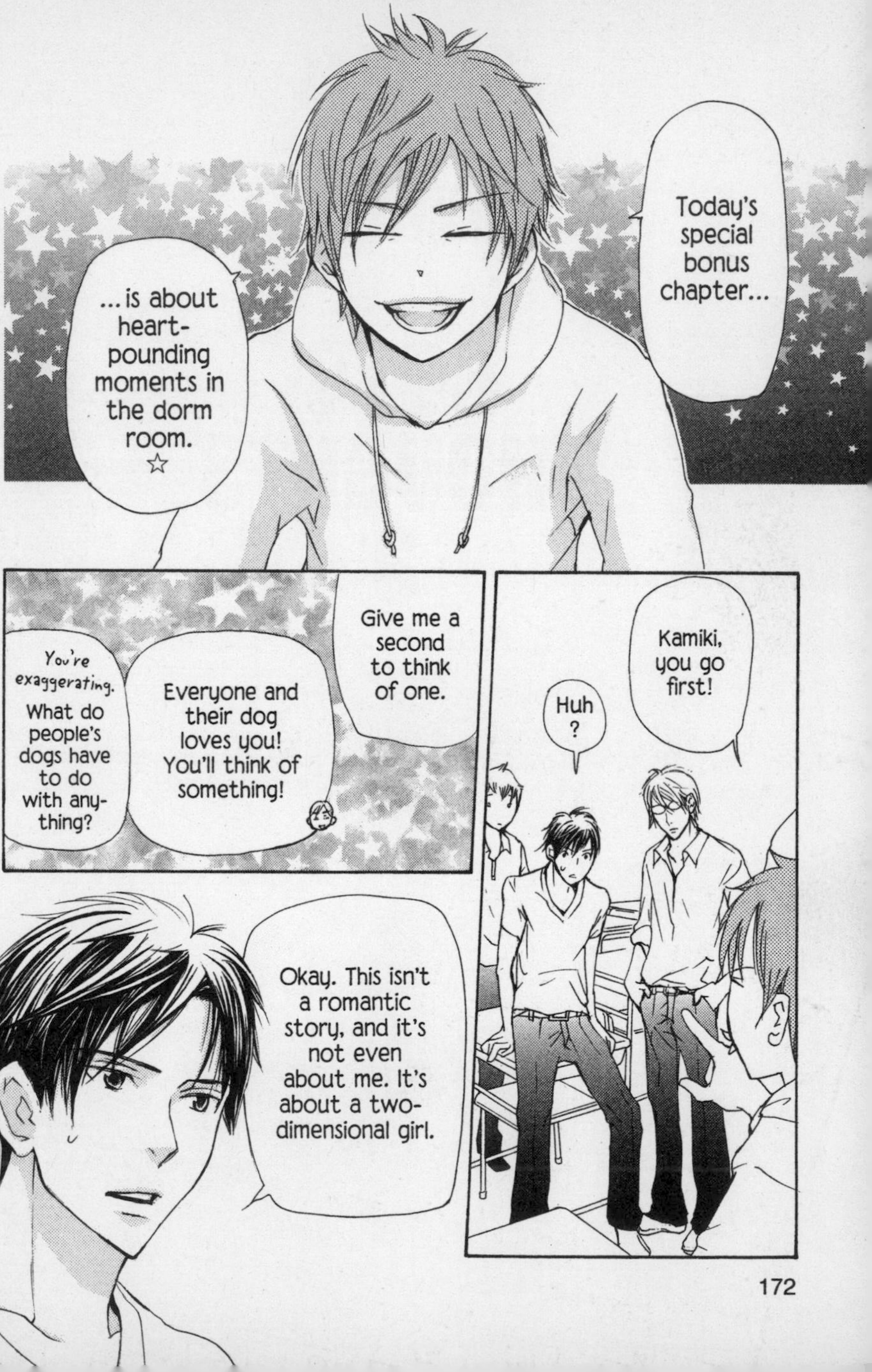
Today's special bonus chapter...
...is about heart-pounding moments in the dorm room. ☆
Kamiki, you go first!
Huh?
Give me a second to think of one.
Everyone and their dog loves you! You'll think of something!
You're exaggerating.
What do people's dogs have to do with anything?
Okay. This isn't a romantic story, and it's not even about me. It's about a two-dimensional girl.

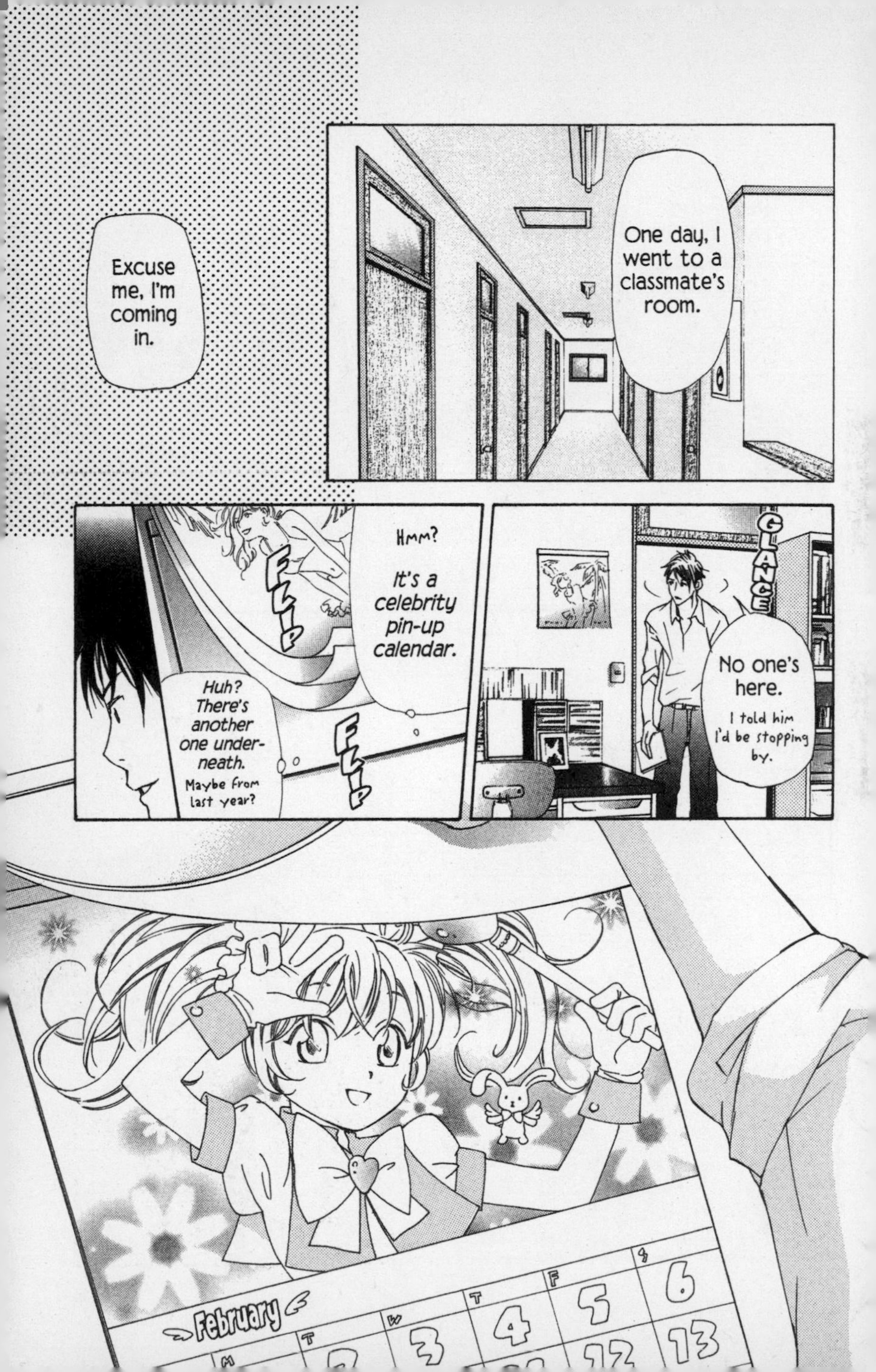
One day, I went to a classmate's room.
Excuse me, I'm coming in.
GLANCE
No one's here.
I told him I'd be stopping by.
FLIP
Hmm?
It's a celebrity pin-up calendar.
FLIP
Huh? There's another one underneath.
Maybe from last year?
February

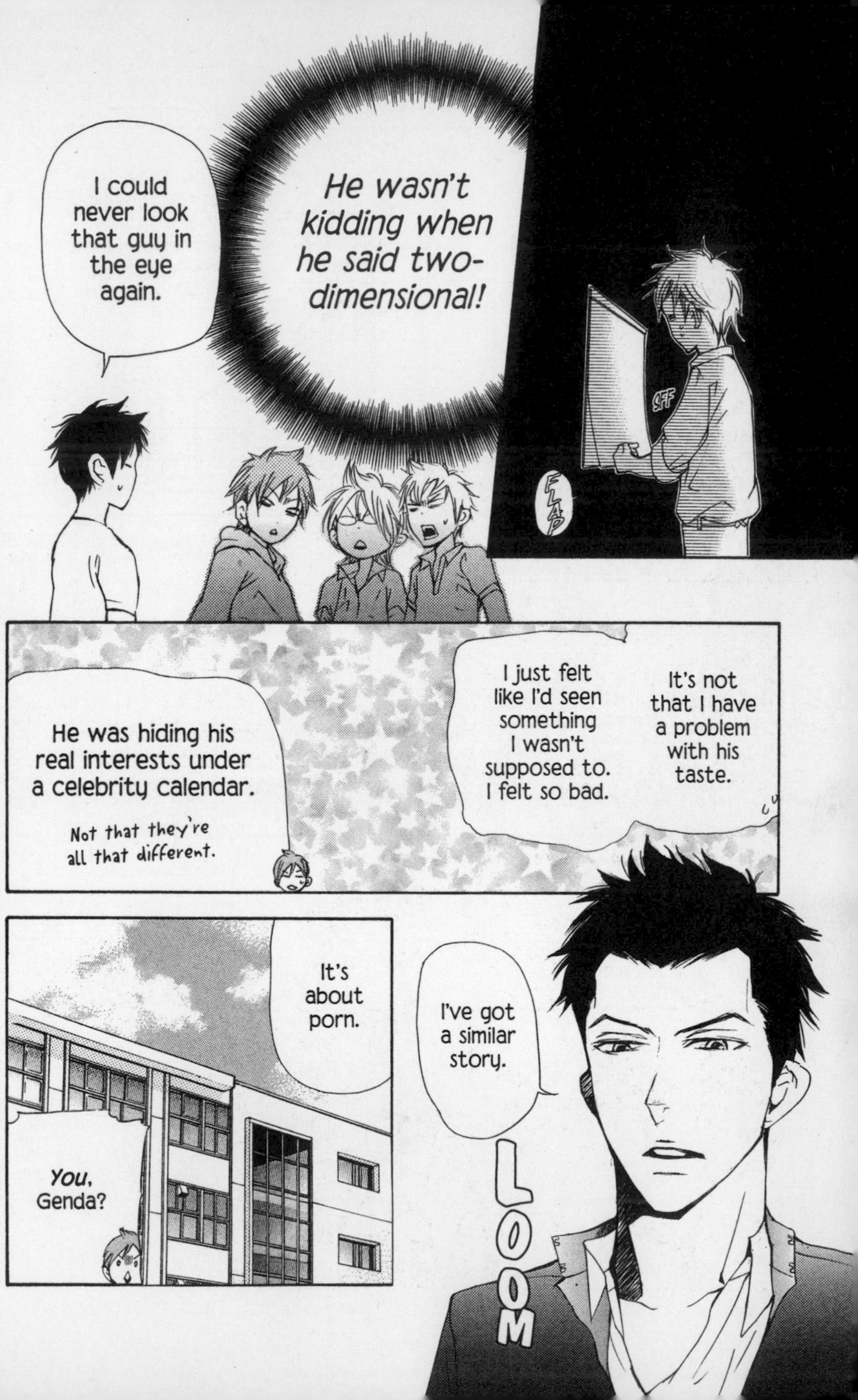
SFF
FLAP
He wasn't kidding when he said two-dimensional!
I could never look that guy in the eye again.
It's not that I have a problem with his taste.
I just felt like I'd seen something I wasn't supposed to. I felt so bad.
He was hiding his real interests under a celebrity calendar.
Not that they're all that different.
I've got a similar story.
LOOM
It's about porn.
You, Genda?

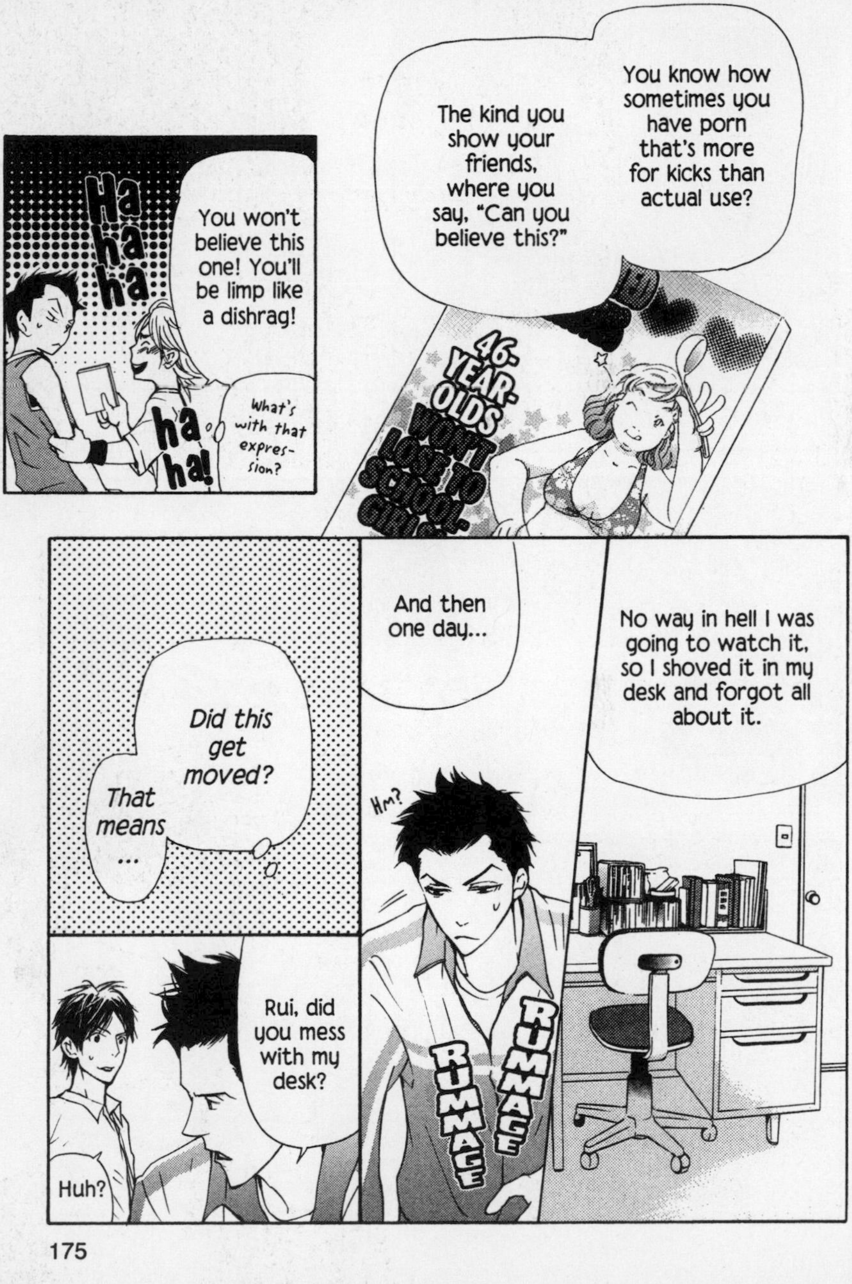
You know how sometimes you have porn that's more for kicks than actual use?
The kind you show your friends, where you say, "Can you believe this?"
46-YEAR-OLDS WON'T LOSE TO SCHOOL-
Ha ha ha
You won't believe this one! You'll be limp like a dishrag!
ha ha!
What's with that expression?
No way in hell I was going to watch it, so I shoved it in my desk and forgot all about it.
And then one day...
Hm?
RUMMAGE
RUMMAGE
Did this get moved?
That means ...
Rui, did you mess with my desk?
Huh?

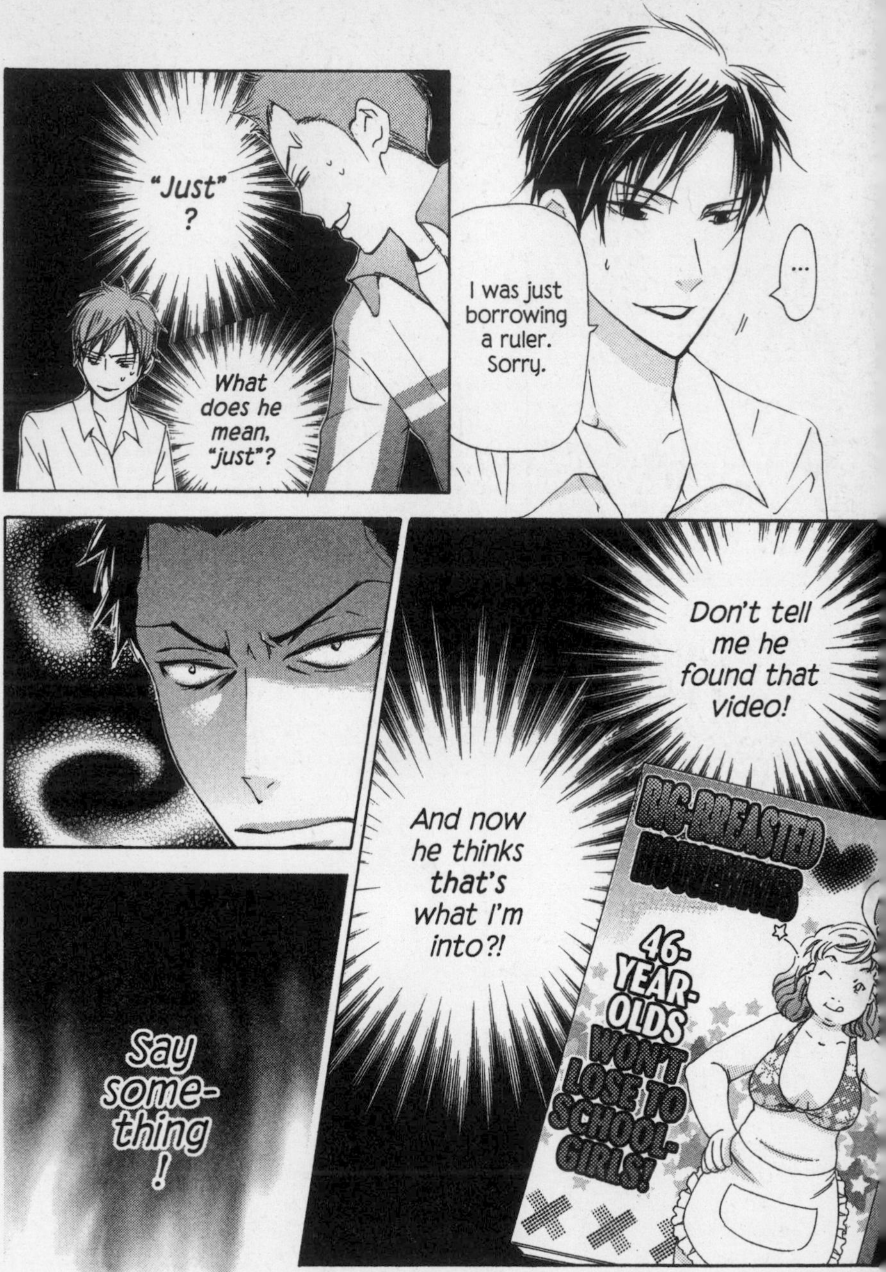
...
I was just borrowing a ruler. Sorry.
"Just" ?
What does he mean, "just"?
Don't tell me he found that video!
And now he thinks that's what I'm into?!
BIG-BREASTED
46-YEAR-OLDS WON'T LOSE TO SCHOOLGIRLS!
Say something!

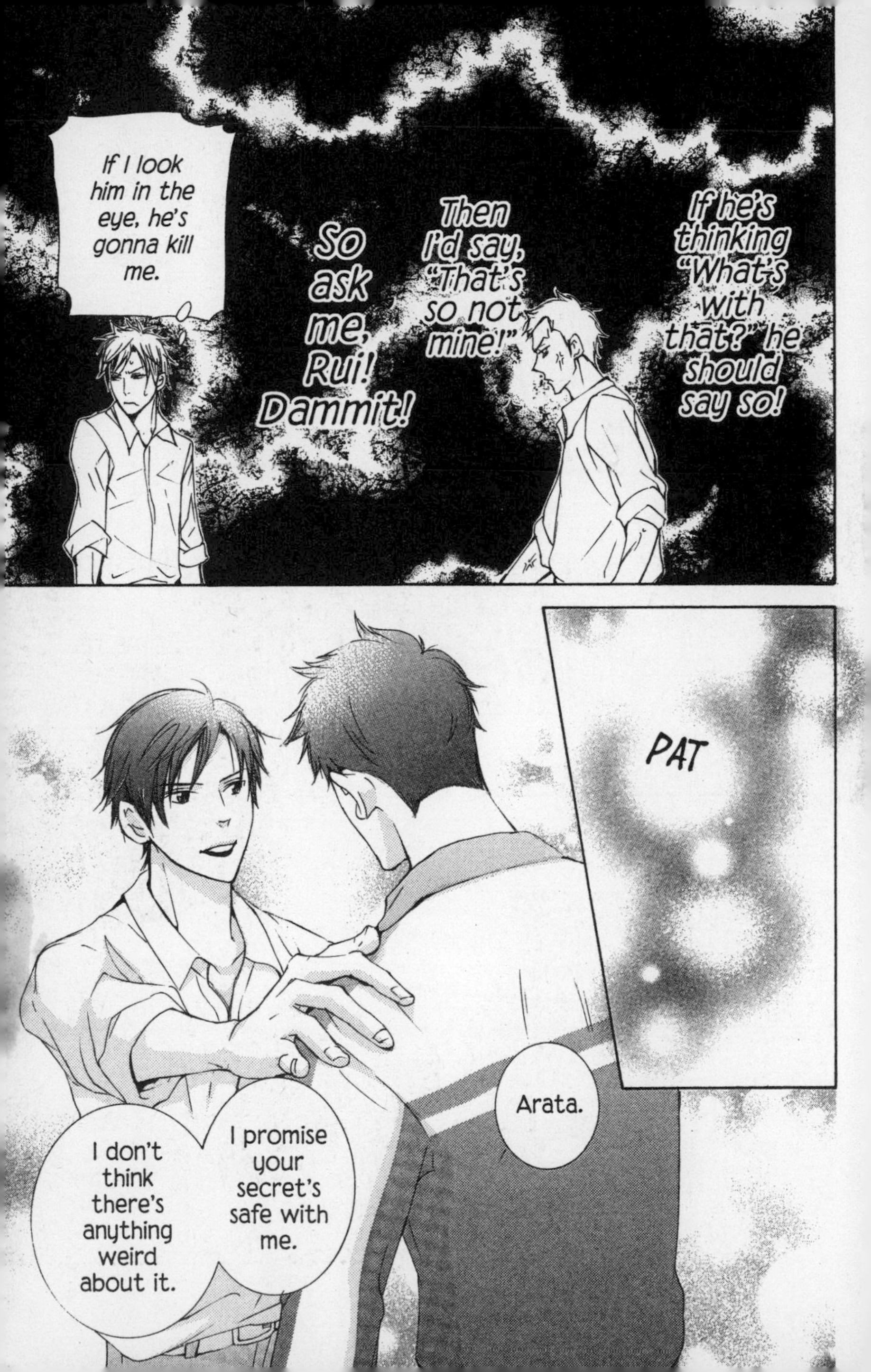
If he's thinking "What's with that?" he should say so!
Then I'd say, "That's so not mine!"
So ask me, Rui! Dammit!
If I look him in the eye, he's gonna kill me.
PAT
Arata.
I promise your secret's safe with me.
I don't think there's anything weird about it.

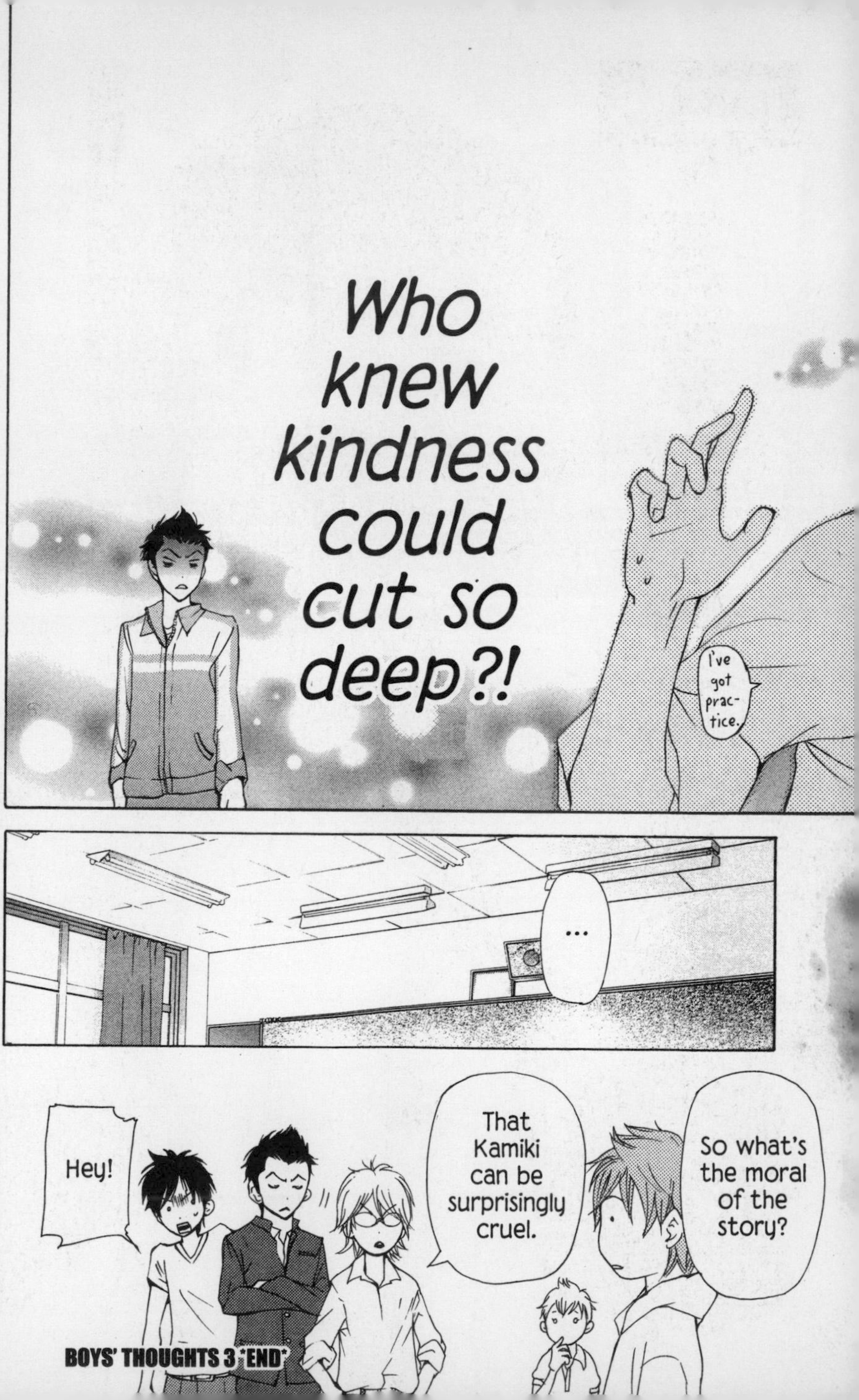
I've got prac-tice.
Who knew kindness could cut so deep?!
...
So what's the moral of the story?
That Kamiki can be surprisingly cruel.
Hey!
BOYS' THOUGHTS 3 *END*

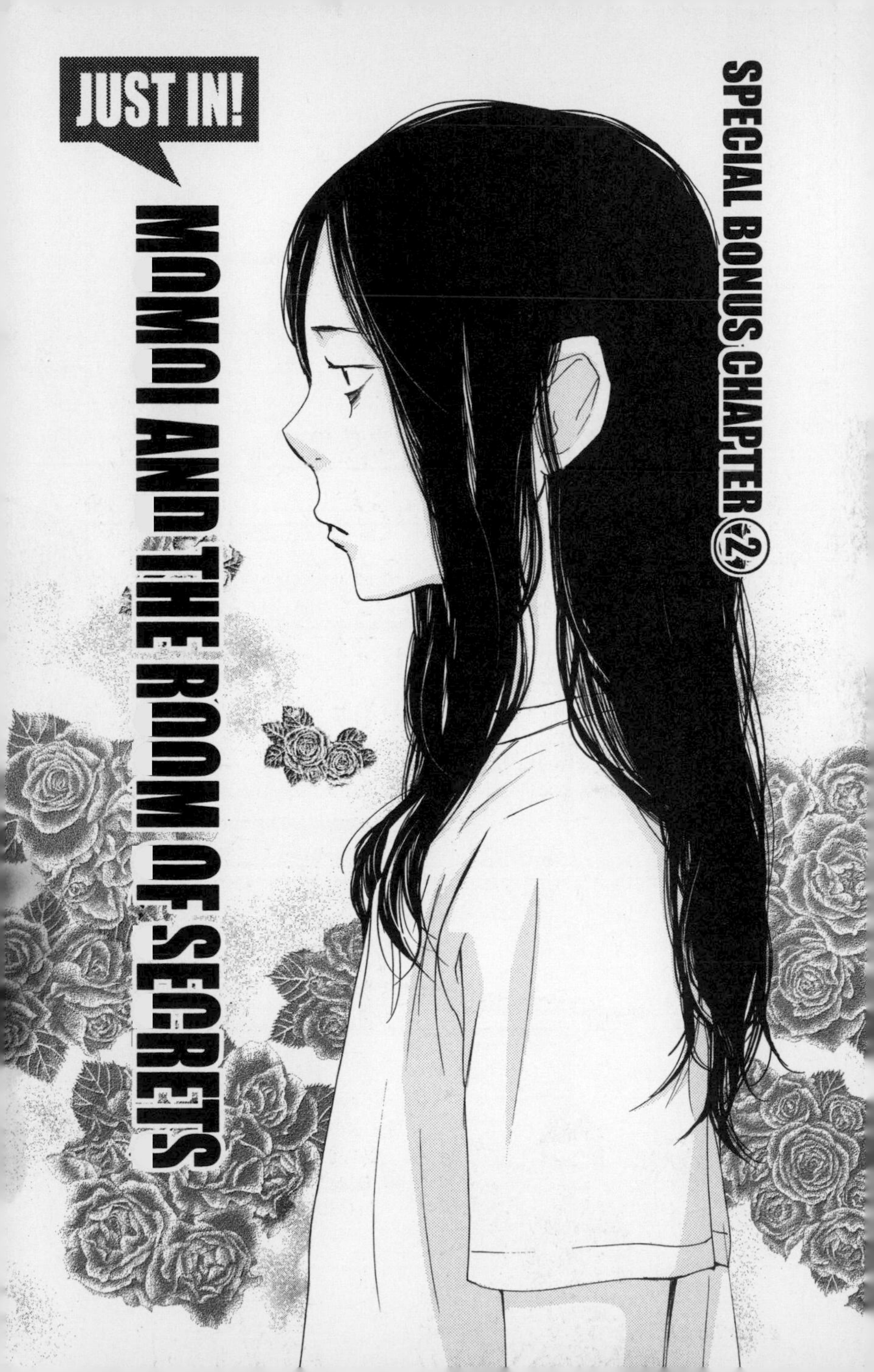
SPECIAL BONUS CHAPTER ②
JUST IN!
MOMOI AND THE ROOM OF SECRETS

Morning
Noon
Night

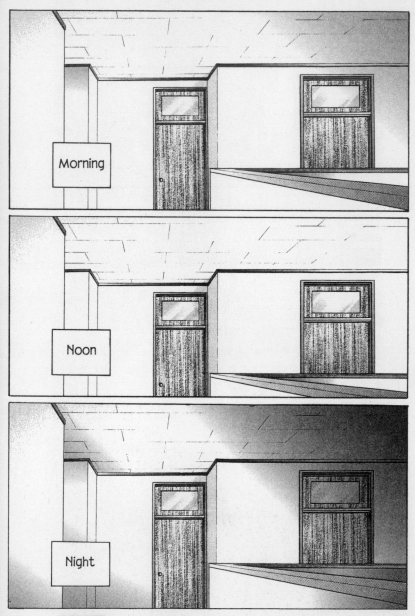

THE END

Even though they're going out, catastrophe strikes!

# IN THE NEXT VOLUME!!

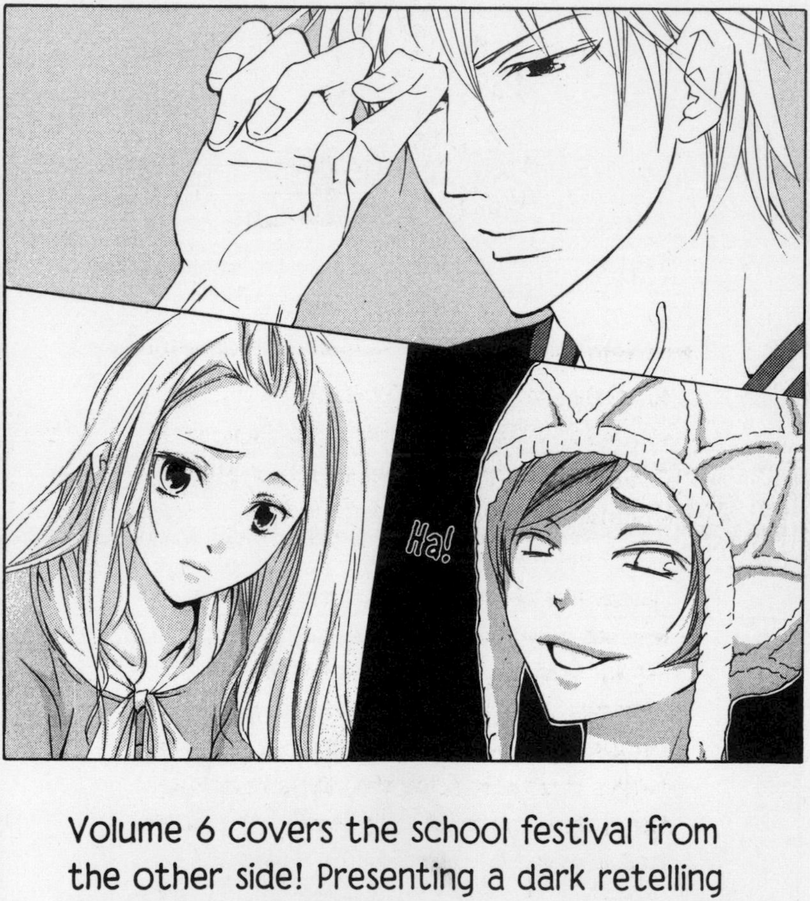
Ha!

Volume 6 covers the school festival from the other side! Presenting a dark retelling from the female perspective, written when the author wondered, "Isn't shojo manga supposed to give you fantasies?"

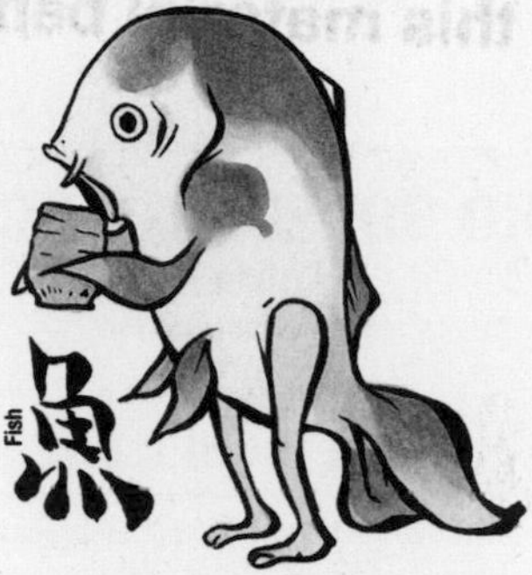
魚
Fish

## Kaneyoshi Izumi

**Every day I think about all the things I want to do, and then I wind up not doing anything. At the very least, I'd like to clean up the room I'm basically nesting in...**

Kaneyoshi Izumi's birthday is April 1, and her blood type is probably type A (but she hasn't actually had it checked yet). Her debut story *Tenshi* (Angel) appeared in the September 1995 issue of *Bessatsu Shojo Comic* and won the 36th Shogakukan Shinjin (newbie) Comics Award. Her hobbies include riding motorcycles, playing the piano and feeding stray cats, and she continues to work as an artist for *Betsucomi*.

# SEIHO BOYS' HIGH SCHOOL
## Volume 5
### Shojo Beat Edition

### STORY AND ART BY
# KANEYOSHI IZUMI

© 2007 Kaneyoshi IZUMI/Shogakukan
All rights reserved.
Original Japanese edition "MEN'S KOU"
published by SHOGAKUKAN Inc.

English Adaptation/Ysabet MacFarlane
Translation/Katherine Schilling
Touch-up Art & Lettering/Maui Girl
Cover Design/Hidemi Sahara
Interior Design/Julie Behn
Editor/Amy Yu

Printed in the U.S.A.

Published by VIZ Media, LLC
P.O. Box 77010
San Francisco, CA 94107

10 9 8 7 6 5 4 3 2 1
First printing, April 2011

www.viz.com

www.shojobeat.com